THE
BOOKSHOP

ALSO BY EVAN FRISS

The Cycling City: Bicycles and Urban America in the 1890s

On Bicycles: A 200-Year History of Cycling in New York City

THE
BOOKSHOP

A HISTORY OF
THE AMERICAN
BOOKSTORE

Evan Friss

VIKING

VIKING
An imprint of Penguin Random House LLC
penguinrandomhouse.com

Grateful acknowledgment is made for permission to reprint an excerpt from
"The Ballad of Bob Wood." Words and music by Woody Guthrie © Woody
Guthrie Publications, Inc. Used by permission.

Image credits may be found on pages 387–88.

LIBRARY OF CONGRESS CONTROL NUMBER: 2023051408
ISBN 9780593299920 (hardcover)
ISBN 9780593299937 (ebook)

Printed in the United States of America
1st Printing

Designed by Alexis Farabaugh

For all the booksellers (especially Amanda)

CONTENTS

THE
BOOKSHOP

INTRODUCTION

Three Lives & Company is a 650-square-foot bookshop on a corner in New York City's West Village. Along the hand-carved shelves and glowing under Jolly Rancher–green lamps, there's fiction and non, frontlist and backlist, picture books and cookbooks, history and travel, queer and poetry, art and architecture, *Granta* and graphic novels, *The Paris Review* and all things New York. The dog treats are behind the counter.

Toby, the owner, sports a soft gray beard and beanie, bodysurfs in the morning Atlantic, walks into Manhattan from his Brooklyn brownstone (no wonder he's so skinny), and drinks a Balzacian amount of coffee. Inside the shop (please don't call it a "store," which the booksellers think sounds too commercial), he's constantly layering, pruning, and rearranging. The colors. The scale. The feeling. No stacks too tall or too short or too crooked. Maybe it's all the coffee. Or maybe it's a family thing. His brother, Madison, is among the world's foremost garden designers.

Over on the lone stool, you'll probably see Abel, one of the regulars. You might also spot Camille, who always remembers to ask about ailing grandmothers or soon-to-be-graduating nephews, and Greg, a writer who could be mistaken for a rugby player. Richie, an unwavering Giants fan, stops by habitually, often with a wedge of Gruyère.

Miriam (hair: brown, face: oval, aura: warm) talks fast, never about herself. Although she has been working at the shop for well over a decade, her eyes still widen when someone walks in. Sometimes they come with a seemingly unsolvable riddle: "I'm looking for a book for my fifty-two-year-old brother. He's going through a divorce, likes cooking and ornithology. Got any good mysteries? And nothing too long. Oh, and it's for his birthday—it was yesterday."

Miriam listens. Two or three beats elapse before she strides over to the long rectangular table in the back. She plucks a paperback from the second row, then presses it into the customer's palm. "He'll love this," she says. The daughter of a Connecticut pediatrician knows exactly what to prescribe.

For the last fifteen plus years, just after Thanksgiving, Toby hosts an annual Top Ten Books of the Year contest. Staff and customers predict which titles will appear on the coveted *New York Times* list. The person with the most correct guesses earns fifty dollars plus (what's now known as) the Miriam Trophy. To this day, Miriam (almost) always wins the Miriam.

Toby, who rarely raises his voice and shies away from the media and from conflict—except when chasing shoplifters—owns the bookshop outright. Yet he doesn't think of it as *his* shop. He says he's merely the custodian. It is the bookshop—not Toby; not Miriam; not Troy the Cookbook Maven; not Joyce, who has been working at Three Lives since before Toby bought it in 2001; and not Ryan, who like Miriam and Toby dabbled in publishing before returning home to bookselling—that has a relationship with the customers. Likewise:

- Abel

- Camille

- Greg

- Richie

- the procrastinating writers and editors

- the dogs and their walkers

- Dr. Gary: the rheumatologist who once diagnosed a bookseller with shingles over by the biographies

- Henry: the Broadway composer who makes melodies from random lines in random books

- Adrienne: who deposits her tickets to the ballet at the shop when she can't make it

- J.: a graphic designer more interested in flirting than in books

- Dean: the octogenarian (sadly, now deceased) who ushered people in off the streets to buy his slapdash self-published memoir, not carried in any other bookstore on earth (Toby avoids conflict)

- and the parade of volunteers who help wrap gifts in December and share popcorn tins and chocolate bars hidden under the counter are all referred to by the same title: "friends of the shop."

They have an attachment to the shop and the shop to them. Sometimes loved ones will phone with news that a longtime customer has died. The bookstore ought to know. When customers send Christmas cards, postcards, letters, and snacks, they address them not to a person.

They are for the shop. Calling them "customers" doesn't even sound right—probably because many of them, some of whom come nearly every day, hardly ever buy anything.

Instead, they stop by to linger, to talk books, and to talk about more than books. Three Lives isn't just another retail outlet. The quintessential "shop around the corner" is part of what makes the Village feel like a village. It has charm, personality, and soul. More than anything, Toby doesn't want to screw it up.

I n many ways, Three Lives is an anomaly. Started by Jill Dunbar, Jenny Feder, and Helene Webb in 1978 and named after a Gertrude Stein book, it has survived Barnes & Noble and Borders, Amazon, the Great Recession, and a pandemic. It doesn't sell puzzles, gift wrap, or mugs with cringeworthy puns. It also doesn't carry many a bestselling title. Among the six thousand books in stock, there's no Danielle Steel. The shop seldom hosts readings. There are no in-house book clubs. There's no wine bar. There's no coffee shop. Three Lives has no presence on Twitter or Facebook or Instagram or TikTok. The booksellers keep track of inventory by hand, jotting down titles sold on yellow notepads.

Conventional wisdom suggests that for bookstores to survive, they need to sell heaps of sidelines (higher-margin nonbook merchandise), host near-daily events, maximize social media, and leverage technology. Yet Three Lives' simplicity is its brilliance. The tiny bookstore is filled with books and books and books and books. The sounds are all muted: quiet conversations, a whisper of Aimee Mann from the speakers, the shuffling of feet, and the hushed symphony of books being set down and pages turned. Staff, who wear no name tags or uniforms, blend with the readers who shop there. Every day they interact. Every day is a community event. And so, while the same books can be bought from Amazon, often at lower prices, Three Lives offers what an internet behemoth cannot: people, conversation, books to be held and happened upon, floors that creak, atmosphere.

Three Lives is what is known as an independent bookstore. There's only one Three Lives. It's owned by one person, a serious reader who can be found in the shop most days. Even among indies, Three Lives stands out. It's located in a neighborhood with unusually affluent and well-educated residents, the sort most likely to buy books.

Nowadays, independents of any type stand out. It wasn't long ago when they were the majority. Back then, they were just called bookstores. In 1958, Americans purchased roughly 72 percent of their books from small, single-store, personal bookshops like Three Lives. Bookstores of all kinds are much rarer than they used to be. As recently as 1993, the US Census Bureau counted 13,499 bookstores (one bookstore for every 19,253 people). That included indies, general bookstores, superstores, specialty shops, and any place with at least 50 percent of revenue derived from books. By 2021, however, there were just 5,591 bookstores left (one bookstore for every 59,283 people). Today, the biggest bookseller isn't even a bookstore. It's Amazon.com. Among brick-and-mortar retailers, the two largest booksellers are Costco and Target. Nobody would call them bookstores, either. Whether independent or corporate, whether in New York or New Mexico, bookstores have been disappearing. If bookstores were animals, they'd be on the list of endangered species.

Bookstores may be endangered spaces, but they are also powerful spaces. The ubiquitous image of the quaint bookshop and the becardiganed bookseller makes us blind to their power. The right book put in the right hands at the right time could change the course of a life or many lives. Readers, writers, and literature are shaped by how and where we buy our books. Pulitzer Prize–winning novelist Michael Cunningham called Three Lives "a sanctuary" and "the most reliable place to go when I need to remember why novels are still worth the trouble they take to write."

Bookstores influence our tastes, our thoughts, and our politics. They also offer serendipity. So much so that Toby keeps a journal of magical moments, like when a customer asks for a book and its author happens to be standing nearby. So did the booksellers at the Borders in Emeryville, California, in 1997. Their spiral notebook recorded tender moments (the little boy with a camera around his neck who asked a helpful bookseller if she'd join his family vacation), irritable customers ("the snob" who demanded *The Little Prince* in its original French, and at once), and the scary ones. ("A Ted Kaczynski type wants to know where the math is. I led him there slowly.")

Bookstores also stimulate our senses. Being surrounded by books matters. Sociologists have found that just growing up in a home full of books—mere proximity—confers a lifetime of intellectual benefits. Books offer warmth, comfort, and refuge. It's no wonder, then, that so many social media accounts deal in what might be called book porn: glimpses of book-stuffed bookstores, libraries, and wood-paneled dens. At the same time, books are imbued with a near-holy spirit. Many of us wince at the idea of throwing one in the trash. That's part of the reason why entering a bookstore can feel like walking into an old church.

The power of the bookstore doesn't just emanate from the books, the architecture, and the staff. Customers also make the space. Neither home nor work, these "third spaces" function as critical sites for intellectual, social, political, and cultural exchange. They nurture existing communities and foster new ones. They are de facto public spaces, gathering spots. They cost nothing to enter. People often just want company. Three Lives has never been more crowded than on the night John Lennon was killed.

More so than bars or coffee shops, they are also places in which to get lost, and, by way of the books, to escape reality. For every chatty customer, there's another who prefers to be left alone. To be by oneself among others. To feel a book's heft. To smell a paperback's perfume. To savor slowed time.

Bookstores are literary playgrounds *and* capitalist enterprises, sometimes more obviously one than the other, sometimes seemingly stuck in the space between. Even booksellers clearly driven by money often have to pretend that they aren't. Low profit margins can be a source of pride. In the 1988 film *Crossing Delancey*, a character toasts to "New York's last real bookstore," bemoaning the forces behind the new, "clean," and "obscenely tall and profitable" stores. Business is cold and calculating; books are warm and invaluable. The whole notion of a book business can seem oxymoronic. In 1821, Thomas Jefferson wrote to James Madison that books are "capital," not products for "mere consumption." A century and a half later, the founders of Three Lives imagined a space that was more of a "living room" than a store.

Books usually find their way to the shelves along the same route. Authors write them and find agents who sell their manuscripts to editors at publishing houses, which edit, design, market, and sell books to retailers, who resell the books to readers. Gatekeepers are everywhere. Authors have to win over agents who have to win over editors who have to win over their colleagues in marketing who have to win over booksellers who have to win over customers.

Even in the age of AI, handselling and word of mouth remain staples. When a trusted bookseller (not just Miriam) tells a customer to buy *this* book, they often do. With more books in print than ever before, books, more than ever before, need to be discovered. Tables and shelves and lighting and booksellers point customers in certain directions. When they walk in with one book in mind, shoppers often leave with another, a phenomenon about twice as common in brick-and-mortar bookstores than on Amazon. While the internet retailer knows who you are, where you live, and which books (and electric toothbrushes) you've bought in the past, the neighborhood bookstore remains an influencer.

That bookstores continue to endure is, in some ways, something of a miracle. Pundits predicted they would be long dead. So did booksellers. One joked that books have "been a dying business for at least five thousand years." That comment was made in 1961, a time that subsequent booksellers would refer to as a golden age. In fact, it seems that everyone remembers a "golden age" around the time they first started in the business.

Nineteenth-century booksellers worried that public libraries would destroy them. In the twentieth century, the bogeyman was the radio, then the movies, then TV, then mass-market paperbacks, and then the superstores. In the twenty-first century, ebooks and Amazon have been the existential threats. The fear that the book business is imperiled—near death, even—has always been an industry staple. In 1887, Henry Holt lamented that "book-stores no longer exist, at least as book-stores. They are toy-shops, and ice-cream saloons" masquerading as bookstores. In 1930, H. L. Mencken asked what could "be done to rescue the poor bookseller," destined to become a bootlegger or, worse, a chiropractor. In 1952, Adolph Kroch, the founder of the eponymous Chicago bookstore, wrote a book called *Bookstores Can Be Saved*. Its first sentence reads: "What is wrong with the bookstores?" His fourteen proposals to save the bookstore didn't come to fruition.

Even so, bookstores *have* survived. And for those who support the quirky, the local, the independent; for those who subscribe to ethical consumerism; for those who crave being blanketed by books and talking to humans about books; and for those who appreciate what's wanting in online transactions, bookstores have never felt more alive.

Just as booksellers have only so many linear feet of shelving, authors tell certain stories at the expense of others. We are all curators. Each of the following chapters is set in a bookshop that represents an important theme in American bookselling history, one that anchors broader discussions and speaks to a larger narrative about the power of bookshops and Americans' changing relationships with them. The bookstore—its design and function—has never been a fixed entity. Bookstores reflect the cultural, intellectual, economic, and political world around them, and they are also actors, institutions that cast their own shadows.

To you, dear reader, who thumbs through the index and finds no mention of your beloved bookstore: I'm sorry. Your disappointment is, in fact, part of this very story. That so many people feel differently about their bookstore than they do about their grocery store or electronics store or any other store is part of the point.

While this book covers a lot of ground, it hardly covers every-thing. Word-count restrictions, ticking clocks, my own blind spots, and the availability of sources imposed limits. Thankfully, I did find troves of letters, diaries, FBI files, catalogs, and receipts in archives across the country. I also visited as many bookstores as I could, talk-ing to people whose lives have shaped them, and been shaped by them.

I spent one morning in the Fifth Avenue office of the man who turned Barnes & Noble into a household name and the same afternoon in the northern nob of Manhattan with a woman who started a small bookstore with no intention of ever making a profit. I interviewed an-other woman who sells books on the sidewalk and still another who serves as CEO of the American Booksellers Association (ABA). I spoke with owners, booksellers, and customers of superindies, such as the Strand and Parnassus and Books & Books, and tiny indies that few people more than a couple of blocks away have ever heard of. Thank-fully, bookstore people like to talk about bookstores.

Some of them I've known for a long time. That Three Lives book-seller who was diagnosed with shingles while putting books on the shelf was my then-pregnant spouse. Amanda worked at the shop for eight years. Over dinner, I heard stories about regulars, sales reps, dogs, celebrity sightings, Swedish tourists, dripping AC units, lost keys, and lost people. I witnessed a slice of it myself at the midnight Murakami releases; when David Mitchell read, signed, and drew funny portraits for sweaty fans; and more so in the quotidian routine. I spent countless hours lingering there. What became obvious was that I was hardly the only one who spent countless hours lingering there.

One time Toby asked if I could help. A few of the booksellers were out sick. And so there I was, working my first and only shift at Three

Lives. I certainly won't ever forget it—in part because when I went down to the basement to fetch something out of storage, I forgot to duck my head. Aside from several minutes spent with an ice pack glued to my forehead, I mostly remember how empowering it felt. People came in and asked *me* what they should read. Such responsibility! Such privilege! Such power!

Why would they trust a total stranger? Although I had never met the customers before, they didn't think of me as a stranger. The reputation, authority, and comfort of Three Lives were for one day vested in me. The shop conveyed a sense of expertise. It suggested that the people working there knew what they were talking about.

When I married one of its booksellers on a Sunday afternoon, Three Lives & Company closed. A little sign on the door announced: "Amanda's getting married!" It was as if Manhattan had turned into a small town. Surely there were readers who came hungry and left disappointed, annoyed even. Other customers surely understood. Some of them were at the wedding.

In 2016, the building that housed Three Lives was sold. Panic set in. What would happen to the beloved corner bookshop? Customers asked how they could help. Toby scouted new locations. His lease was month to month, and the new owners made no secret of their plans to renovate the entire building, like so many in the neighborhood, to make room for luxury apartments upstairs. Then, to many people's surprise, the two parties agreed to a long-term deal. The building owners decided that they wanted to keep the bookshop where it was, a charming anchor for the neighborhood and the palatial residences above.

During the construction and in the midst of the pandemic, Three Lives moved, temporarily, a couple of blocks west. The new spot was next door to a Norwegian coffee shop. Toby discovered that it was a boon to both businesses. Early-morning coffee buyers stopped in for books, and afternoon book buyers stopped in for a third coffee. Personally, for Toby, the coffee shop was too close, too tempting, and made it impossible (with the shop remaining in full view) to take a real break.

When I visited the new Three Lives, I found it mostly the way it had always been. It had its familiar, small-scale charm, though the floors were brighter and less squeaky. The new walls were blue. The basement was less frightening. Joyce, who stayed quarantined in her apartment for most of 2020 and 2021, was back giving hugs. Miriam was still busy ordering books, still asking lots of questions, still refusing to talk about herself. Abel's stool was still there. And so was Abel, still lovably cantankerous. Camille was there, too. Then Greg walked in. He had come to say hello. To the booksellers. To his friends. And to the shop.

The UPS Driver

All new books come out on Tuesdays. Selling them before their publication date is considered unscrupulous, scandalous even. At Three Lives, the books wait for their big day in the basement, over by the teakettle and screwdrivers.

When the packages first arrive, it can feel like Christmas. For many years, Vaughn, the UPS driver, played the part of Santa. He was the one who carried the boxes of books into Three Lives and ferried away the pile of outgoing parcels, discreetly tucked under the front table, the primary display area where all authors dream their books will someday live. Hundreds of pounds of books can arrive at once.

New books mean new work to do. Booksellers open and break down the boxes. They inspect the contents for damage (not uncommon). They check to see if what's in the boxes is what's supposed to be in the boxes.

Years of strenuous labor took its toll on Vaughn. He accumulated a staggering amount of parking tickets—thousands, maybe—as he preferred to leave his big brown truck in an illegal spot rather than try to find a space on the narrow, crooked, and chaotic West Village streets. His back ached. He eventually took a desk job.

Vaughn was neither a Three Lives employee nor a customer, but he was part of the fabric of the place. He always took a moment to chat with the booksellers and they with him. Even the regulars knew him.

During the weeks when he was visiting family in Antigua or the days when he was out sick, there was a temporary Santa—some other perfectly capable UPS person. But when it wasn't Vaughn walking through those red double doors, the joy of seeing boxes of books was tinged with a touch of melancholy.

1.

BENJAMIN FRANKLIN

When we think of a bookstore, we tend to imagine rows of books, neatly arranged titles standing in the window, and quiet browsing. It's fair to say that Benjamin Franklin's bookshop wasn't anything of the sort. Inside his teeming brick building were hulking wood-framed printing presses, fat kegs of ink, cases of type (he used Caslon but preferred Baskerville), reams of paper, pages dangling from the ceiling to dry, and heaps of rags. Philadelphians came to check their mail. Boys carried off stacks of newspapers.

Franklin's shop wasn't called Benjamin Franklin's Bookstore, Ben's Books, or Franklin's Fine Finds. In fact, the word *bookstore* didn't yet exist. The concept of a bookstore—a retail outlet selling primarily books—was still embryonic. Yet Franklin was definitely a bookseller. Teachers bought schoolbooks from him. Ministers picked up religious texts. Almost everyone wanted his famous almanac. He sent Homeric poetry, political tracts, and books and pamphlets on a mind-boggling range of subjects to colonial outposts near and far. His job was never singular—or boring. He was a shopkeeper who sold books (retail and

wholesale), a printer (and sometimes binder), an editor (and sometimes author), a marketer, a publisher, and a postmaster—roles that
blurred.

Charming, industrious, and a writer himself, Franklin was undoubtedly well suited to the job, especially compared with the other
founding fathers: Adams was too prickly, Washington too regal,
Hamilton too antagonistic, Jefferson too profligate, and Madison too
awkward. While Franklin is most famous for his role as a statesman,
diplomat, and inventor, his experience in the book trade was a formative one. For the rest of his life, he self-identified as a printer. He understood that we are what we read. And that what we read is dictated
by what authors choose to write, what publishers choose to publish,
what printers choose to print, and what, where, and how booksellers
choose to sell.

Franklin lived for the better part of the eighteenth century. Over
the course of his life, colonists became more literate, more cultured,
and, ultimately, more American. Books were partly responsible. So
was Benjamin Franklin.

A ll the little money that came into my hands was ever laid out in
books," Franklin wrote of his childhood fondness for reading.
Indeed, young Ben was a bookish boy. He zoomed past his peers in
school, and his father thought he was destined for the ministry. That
was because Josiah didn't know his children very well, especially his
fifteenth. Franklin, born in 1706, was bright, but he was equally unor-
thodox, skeptical, and cheeky. Josiah eventually gave up on his dream
of college for his son, as it was too expensive, and instead turned his
attention to finding him a trade. By the age of ten, Franklin was

working in the family business. He was miserable. He had no interest in a life of making soap.

At twelve, he began working for his older brother James, a printer with an office a few blocks from their modest Boston home. Franklin signed a nine-year indenture, legally binding him to James and forbidding him from marrying, gambling, or haunting alehouses. Not that any of this bothered the boy. He mostly wanted to read. John Bunyan's *The Pilgrim's Progress* and Plutarch's *Lives* were his favorites.

The brothers Franklin operated at the center of the colonial book and printing universe. Founded in 1620, the Boston that Franklin walked was home to just ten thousand people, all living and working near the rocky harbor. Though tiny and provincial by European standards, Boston was the heart of British America.

The first printer in the area set up shop in 1638 in Cambridge, just across the Charles River. Its business was entwined with a two-year-old college, America's first. Harvard's students, faculty, and library made for good customers. (New York, the future capital of publishing, didn't have a single printer until 1694.)

That young Franklin even had access to books was unusual. According to late seventeenth-century probate inventories, 65 percent of colonial households were bookless. The others usually had just a single volume or two, typically the Bible. More robust collections included plays, poetry, and sometimes pornography. Generally, though, the book market was narrow and focused on "godliness and orthodoxy"—just as government and religious leaders wished. Consequently, the earliest printers, James Franklin included, churned out sermons and psalm books, in addition to legislative proceedings, forms, broadsides, and newspapers. Seldom did they print books as we know them.

Most of the books that did circulate came from Europe, imported by the well connected via agents in London. There were a few book-sellers, also clustered in Boston, who bought from the "Old World" to sell in the "New." The first was Hezekiah Usher. His friends called him Hez.

Usher lived above the little shop where he sold books and pam-phlets alongside sugar and wine. Because the market for books was so small, booksellers relied on sidelines such as lottery tickets, musical instruments, and food. Other booksellers followed, congregating around and inside the Towne House, a civic building that functioned as Bos-ton's commercial, social, and political hub. The main attraction was the street-level open-air concourse with a few bookselling stands. The setup resembled that of the Agora in ancient Athens, where vendors congregated by trade—wine here, fish there. The books, made from papyrus scrolls, were sold right in the middle of the market. Those Athenian stalls, which stood some twenty-five hundred years ago, may well be considered the world's first bookstores.

Some of the earliest American bookstores were also essentially pop-ups. John Dunton arrived from England in 1686 with crates of books carefully curated for a Puritan audience. His competitors greeted him, he said, like "sour ale in summer." One offered to buy out his stock entirely and send him back on his way. Dunton pressed on, set-ting up a temporary "warehouse" in Boston and then another in Salem. New Englanders were hungry for books, he reported, but painfully slow to pay for them.

At roughly the same time, another English bookseller landed in Boston. Benjamin Harris was running from the law, a wanted man for having published and sold seditious works. In Boston, he opened a printshop-slash-bookstore-slash-coffeehouse on King Street. At Amer-ica's first bookstore café, colonists sipped on coffee, tea, and hot chocolate; mingled; talked books, politics, and religion; and stepped foot into the burgeoning public sphere. With the café and an emphasis on bestsellers—religious texts, almanacs, and textbooks—Harris's shop was the progenitor of Barnes & Noble.

B y the time James Franklin opened his printshop in 1717, the Boston book market hadn't matured much. A great fire had swept through the city in 1711, burning down the Towne House and many bookselling businesses along with it. Franklin joined James in 1718 and rather enjoyed printing, reading, editing, delivering his brother's fledgling newspaper, and typesetting—a complicated job that involved arranging the letters backward. The real problem was James. He was ill-tempered. Violent, even.

Living in Boston had its delights, namely "access to better books." Franklin was also writing during this time, and he submitted essays to the very newspaper he helped print, *The New-England Courant*. Since James would never knowingly publish anything penned by his little brother, Franklin pseudonymously slipped his pieces under the printshop door, having altered his handwriting and adopted an alter ego, a minister's widow named Silence Dogood. James was impressed and ultimately published fourteen of "her" essays. Even Franklin's fictional self celebrated books. As Dogood wrote, books "enable the Mind to frame great and noble Ideas."

One idea that Franklin read about was vegetarianism. He decided to give it a try, figuring it would save money ("an additional fund for buying books") and time (so he could read more). The diet lasted a while—until that one piece of cod. He couldn't resist fish.

Meanwhile, the meat-eating brother was in serious trouble. In the

June 1722 issue of *The New-England Courant*, James ran an article ridiculing Massachusetts politicos for failing to keep pirates at bay. The colonial leaders were not amused. Since there was no right to freedom of the press, they threw him in jail.

Franklin was forced into the role of publisher. He certainly didn't mind (or miss his brother). He printed one of his own essays (as Dogood), reasoning that there is "no such Thing as publick Liberty, without Freedom of Speech; which is the Right of every Man." Whatever satisfaction the temporary privilege of being publisher afforded wasn't enough. At the age of seventeen and still technically bound to his brother, Franklin fled, ultimately landing in Philadelphia.

He arrived exhausted, ruffled, and famished. On that first day, Franklin scrounged up "three great puffy rolls," found shelter for the night, and soon secured a job with Samuel Keimer, one of two Philadelphia printers. It wasn't long before Franklin developed a reputation as a skilled craftsman. Among the impressed was Pennsylvania's governor, who encouraged him to open a printshop of his own. Backed by the governor and, presumably, with the government as a resourced and reliable customer, Franklin imagined a flourishing business.

For start-up capital, he reluctantly turned to his father. When Josiah refused, the governor himself pledged to fund the venture, advising Franklin to head to London to procure the proper equipment and connections. Franklin arrived on Christmas Eve, 1724. It took only a few days for Franklin to discover that the governor's promise had been a false one: there was no money.

Finding himself on his own, he tried to make the most of it. He took a job with a London printer, a much larger operation than any in the colonies. His colleagues nicknamed him the Water-American because he refused to partake in the ubiquitous beer drinking: a pint before breakfast, with breakfast, after breakfast, with the midday meal, at six, and a last one before bed. (Franklin preferred Madeira.) Franklin also prided himself on healthy habits. Solidly built and standing about five foot nine, he clomped up and down the printshop stairs carrying massive cases of fonts. He swam, sometimes for miles, in the Thames. London certainly had its charms, but after eighteen months, Franklin had absorbed and saved enough (his only luxuries being books and the theater) to come home.

He returned to Philadelphia in the fall of 1726. Shortly thereafter, he organized the Junto, a "club of mutual improvement" where Franklin and friends discussed books and the moral, political, and philosophical questions they raised. In order to have the works on hand, they amassed an impressive collection of poems, plays, and books on history, science, and philosophy, at a time when colonial libraries of any kind were quite rare. (The taxpayer-funded public library model didn't come into being until the mid-nineteenth century.) Their library grew to become the Library Company of Philadelphia, "the mother of all the North American subscription libraries." Franklin briefly served as librarian.

To support himself, Franklin opened and operated a general goods store. He enjoyed selling, but the business foundered when his partner died. Then he met Hugh Meredith. In 1728, Meredith's father, grateful for Franklin's sobering influence on his hard-drinking son, agreed to back a new printing venture, the city's third: Meredith & Franklin.

Franklin was still just twenty-two, and the partners lived and worked together in a three-story brick building on Market Street, a one-hundred-foot-wide thoroughfare lined by taverns, shops, and civic buildings. With the windows open (Franklin believed in the value of fresh air), they could hear the buzz of city life. People walked and talked. Whips cracked. Horses clippety-clopped. Wagons rumbled. Church bells rang.

Within a year, Franklin added another dimension to the business: *The Pennsylvania Gazette*. It's unclear how much he paid for the newspaper, though it was probably not much, considering that it had only ninety subscribers. Meanwhile, the Water-American couldn't stop Meredith from resuming his drinking. In the summer of 1730, they parted ways. Franklin was left with the printing business, the newspaper, and the debt.

He found a superior partner in Deborah Read, his common-law wife. According to his autobiography, they initially noticed each other on that first Philadelphia day. Apparently, neither his tousled appearance nor the fact that he was carrying three rolls in his armpits discouraged the young woman with a round face, generous forehead, and arched brows. After a lengthy and rocky courtship—Deborah married someone else (who turned out to be already married), and Franklin fathered a child with another woman—they informally wed in 1730 and later had two children of their own. The first, Francis "Franky" Folger Franklin, died from smallpox when he was four. Franklin forever regretted not having him inoculated.

Deborah's mother temporarily moved in with the couple and leased a portion of the printshop to carve out her own retail space. She sold pills, lotions for burns, and her "well-known Ointment for the ITCH." The mother-in-law didn't stay long. The creams would be replaced with books.

When Franklin first settled in Philadelphia, he felt something amiss: "There was not a good bookseller's shop." That wasn't just true of Philadelphia. In 1719, a visitor to New York pitied the "but one little Bookseller's Shop." That was one more than Virginia, Maryland, and the Carolinas had.

Franklin, a fixer by nature, was determined to change the landscape. By the early 1730s, he was dealing earnestly in books, starting with the basics: Bibles and prayer books, school texts, dictionaries, and almanacs. He wasn't just selling almanacs; he was writing them. His witty version, *Poor Richard's Almanack*, included a calendar, astrology, proverbs, and predictions. The project came easily to him and delighted readers, selling ten thousand copies a year at a time when most books sold in the hundreds. As *Poor Richard's* author, printer, publisher, marketer, distributor, and retailer, Franklin netted handsome profits, given that fans bought them year after year. Aside from money and an ego boost, the almanac also, he noted, offered valuable "instruction among the common people, who bought scarcely any other books." Improvement—at both the personal and national levels—required character building, which demanded reading.

Franklin's customers included other booksellers, who bought from him wholesale and formed part of a budding network. In 1731, Franklin sent a journeyman to Charleston with orders to establish a new printery-slash-bookshop on Church Street. The initial inventory included one hundred almanacs, twenty-four Aristotles, and other volumes purchased from Franklin. In 1742, he set up a similar venture in New York and later formed a partnership in the Caribbean.

As if Franklin weren't already invested enough, he also jumped into the paper market, offering "ready money" for rags that he resold to papermakers. His ledgers reveal that between 1735 and 1742, he accumulated four tons' worth of rags a year, receiving, in return, thousands of reams of paper that he used for printing and that he sold retail.

Franklin was as much a paper seller as a bookseller and, starting in

1737, also a postmaster. The position gave him advance notice of news from distant places, news that could be republished in his own newspaper. The chief perk of the job was that he now received mail for free. Back then, the receiver, not the sender, had to pay postage.

Juggling the post office, newspaper, and book business became cumbersome. Not inherently organized, he created a schedule. Each morning he woke up at 5:00 a.m. After polishing off some porridge and outlining the day ahead, he'd work from 8:00 to 11:00 a.m. before taking a two-hour break for reading, after which he would return to the shop for another three hours. With the workday finished, he'd eat, reflect on the day, and ruminate over whether he had achieved his daily goal. He also tracked progress toward (and regress from) "moral perfection." He devised a list of virtues—frugality, temperance, silence, order, resolution, industry, sincerity, justice, moderation, cleanliness, tranquility, humility, and chastity (not his strong suit)—on which he judged himself daily, marking infractions on a chart. By 10:00 p.m. he was in bed.

Thrifty Deborah was just as busy and essential to his work. Her husband acknowledged as much: "He that would thrive, must ask his wife." She stitched together pamphlets, bought rags from customers, and tended shop. Since her husband—postmaster, writer, printer, bookseller, heavy reader, and occasional napper—was frequently otherwise engaged, she often ran the business. In fact, their "Shop Book" from the late 1730s is mostly composed of entries in her hand. Perhaps it was she who was most likely to be found in the store.

In 1738, Deborah, Franklin, and the business moved four doors down Market Street to a three-story brick home (between today's Second and Front Streets). Behind was a two-and-a-half-story, twenty-two-foot-wide space that fronted Pewter Platter Alley (now known as

Church Street). A later survey described it as "very plane." Franklin himself boasted of its "simple" furniture. To christen the space, he hung a sign over the door: "The New Printing-Office." The name remained for decades, long after it was new.

With more space, Franklin stocked a broader selection of books: religious works ("Testaments, of large, middling, and small Print"), language guides (French, Greek, and Latin grammars), epic poems (Pope's translation of Homer), philosophy (John Locke), plays (Thomas Otway), and "many other Sorts of Books too tedious to mention." Some of those other volumes were self-help guides, treatises, and other titles he printed himself, at his own financial risk. As with *Poor Richard's*, he was the author, printer, and seller of a panoply of pamphlets and circulars touching on his varied interests, including currency and philosophy. He kept up the sidelines, too, retailing pencils, paper, notebooks, and ink. Occasionally, he even advertised "very good Chocolate." If the price was right, Franklin traded in most anything, whether chocolate, sugar, wine, beer, coffee, scales, or protractors.

In 1739, Franklin got his hands on a hit. George Whitefield, the cross-eyed English preacher with a wig wrapped around his ears like muffs, dazzled colonists during the Great Awakening. At the end of one of his fiery speeches, even skeptical Franklin tossed a couple of coins into the bucket. A deist who had long questioned the church (and who had long stopped attending), Franklin cashed in on the mania for Whitefield. He printed and sold the preacher's journals and sermons, originally via subscription. So many customers reserved copies that Franklin couldn't satisfy the demand, ultimately telling buyers that Whitefield's words would be available to anyone with "Money in their Hands." Over the course of two years, he printed more works by

Whitefield than everything else combined. He even sold engraved pictures of the funny-looking man.

In 1742, Franklin became the first American to print a novel, Samuel Richardson's *Pamela*. Compared with Whitefield's sermons, *Pamela* was long and therefore expensive to produce. Mostly, colonists didn't want to read novels, and it would be decades before another unabridged novel was printed in America.

When titles didn't turn over as expected, Franklin offered them at auction. In the spring of 1744, he sold six hundred books, each marked with the minimum acceptable price. Customers selling books of their own were invited, too, as Franklin also dealt in secondhand books.

Franklin's stock kept expanding. By 1747, he advertised nearly one hundred titles. Beyond the religious, school, and self-help books (including the popular *Every Man His Own Lawyer*—admittedly less frightening than *Every Man His Own Doctor*), he carried John Bunyan, John Milton, and John Locke. Locke's *An Essay Concerning Human Understanding* was a foundational text of the Enlightenment and the Revolution to come.

Meanwhile, the number of bookshops was growing, too. In fact, one opened right next door. It was run by James Read and his mother, Sarah Harwood Read, whose late husband was a cousin of Franklin's mother-in-law (the itch-cream seller), confusingly also named Sarah Read. That two bookdealers—still a rare calling—operated in adjacent shops was certainly unusual. Probably because the Reads were relatives and because they bought from him, Franklin made no effort to crush the competition.

A few bookshops started to appear outside the principal cities. In Bethlehem, fifty miles north of Philadelphia, a local innkeeper began importing and selling books, largely religious, at the behest of the

Moravian Church in 1745. The store eventually adopted the name the Moravian Book Shop. It's still in operation and claims to be the longest-running bookstore in America.

In Philadelphia, Franklin's business had become profitable and steady—steady enough that he turned the day-to-day operations over to a sober partner, David Hall, in 1748. A Scottish printer, Hall had come to Philadelphia to work with Franklin four years earlier. He managed the New Printing-Office until his death in 1772, having sold (literally) tons of books—and wallpaper and eyeglasses, too. Franklin hadn't tired of printing or bookselling. Rather, his wide-ranging interests could hardly be contained. Having "absolutely left off Bookselling," he moved to a "quiet Part of the Town." The forty-two-year-old expected to settle into a relaxed life, with more time for scientific experiments and reading. Of course, he wouldn't find much quiet. He would soon help lead a revolution.

E ven as the colonial population, literacy rates, wealth, and demand for books increased, the book market remained small and privileged. It wasn't until the 1740s that William Parks opened a bookstore in Williamsburg, Virginia, and then another in Annapolis, the first two bookstores in the entire Chesapeake region. Like Franklin, Parks was a bookseller, paper dealer, postmaster, and newspaperman. He sold what might have been the first cookbook printed in the colonies, *The Compleat Housewife*.

The Williamsburg bookstore is particularly noteworthy because its account books have survived. Many of the store's patrons were affiliated with the College of William & Mary, including Thomas Jefferson. In many ways, he was the typical customer; 98 percent of patrons were men of means. This wasn't necessarily a reflection of demand. They were simply the ones who could afford books. Printing required expensive paper and ink. Shipping across the Atlantic was time-consuming and costly, as was distributing goods on horseback and down rivers throughout the colonies. At each stage—printing, importing or exporting, wholesaling, retailing—someone took a profit. Most booksellers priced volumes at 30 to 40 percent above cost. The well-heeled customers who frequented the Williamsburg bookstore usually purchased only a book or two. When Jefferson visited in February of 1764, he left with six books. His selection included a Greek-to-Latin dictionary, which cost him the same amount that a common laborer would have earned for three weeks' worth of work. Jefferson spent four times that on a sumptuous two-volume history of Italy. With that same money, he could have bought fourteen hogs.

Throughout the 1760s, the number of bookstores inched higher. One, a combination apothecary and bookstore, was opened in New Haven near Yale. It was Benedict Arnold's. Philadelphia was by then home to a handful of booksellers, stocking Swift, Voltaire, Chaucer, and Shakespeare. Franklin had started selling Shakespeare back in 1744, as the Bard's work had begun to appear more regularly in the homes of colonial elites. Among the newer crop of Philadelphian booksellers was James Rivington, who had a shop on Front Street, right around the corner from Franklin's. Rivington had been a London bookseller, exporting books to the colonies, and he was known for his generous credit terms and his willingness to take returns. He opened a second bookstore in New York and a third in Boston in 1762. Rivington's expansive catalog included 782 titles. Number 403 was *Mr. Franklin's Very Celebrated Experiments in Electricity.*

It was in 1760 that Rivington announced his "New Book Store" in a *Gazette* advertisement. This was the first known use of the term *bookstore*. Though Rivington was British, *bookstore* developed into a particularly American word. In England, it was called a bookshop.

This is the first known image of an American bookstore, Ebenezer Larkin's bookstore in 1789 Boston. The trade card depicts a well-dressed woman standing in front of the counter inside a shop lined with books. Outside on the fold-down tables sit stationery supplies. Hanging on one side of the doorframe is a slate tablet and on the other a basket of quills.

After Franklin left the book business, he studied electricity (an endeavor that included an ill-advised attempt to electrocute a turkey), founded an academy (later known as the University of Pennsylvania), served as a deputy postmaster for the colonies, and spent a decade and a half in London as an agent of Pennsylvania. He was an early advocate of colonial unity, publishing his famous "Join, or Die" cartoon, a dismembered snake highlighting the then "disunited State of the British Colonies" in a May 1754 issue of his *Gazette*.

Many of his efforts, bookselling included, can be viewed as attempts to unite the colonies through knowledge. Franklin lamented that reading was too uncommon an activity and perceived that libraries and bookstores and printshops were rendering the activity more "fashionable." He later credited the uptick in reading as one of the sources of the Revolution. Historians would have a hard time disagreeing.

Franklin returned from England in 1775. By then, escalating tensions were taking a toll on the book trade. In some ways, print culture had been at the center of the fight. The Stamp Act of 1765, which levied a tax on all printed goods, riled—and united—the colonists like never before. As calls for boycotts of British goods grew louder, colonial booksellers stopped importing books from England altogether. Only after the tax was repealed, and on the day he turned twenty-one, did Henry Knox, future secretary of war, open his Boston bookstore. Despite transatlantic tensions, he called his shop the London Book-Store, advertising an "elegant assortment of the most modern books" and for "as cheap as can be bought at any place in town." The shop attracted politicians of different stripes: emissaries of the Crown, British soldiers, and revolutionary John Adams. Knox's London connections made for uncomfortable negotiations. He apologized to a British wholesaler for not paying an invoice and for not ordering more books, owing to closed ports, boycotts, and the general "unhappy mood of politics" in the wake of the Boston Tea Party. By November 1774, the only new literature he wanted consisted of works "concerning the American dispute." When war broke out in 1775, Knox, who had married one of his customers, left bookselling to take up arms. Enemies ransacked his store.

In January of 1776 came Thomas Paine's pamphlet *Common Sense*. Paine argued forcefully for independence at a time when many were still undecided. It was Benjamin Franklin who urged Paine to move to Philadelphia in 1774 and encouraged him to write the work that would change his life—many lives. It was published anonymously, and many guessed that Franklin was its author. Written in Philadelphia, printed in Philadelphia, sold across the colonies, and read aloud in the streets, coffee shops, churches, and bookstores, *Common Sense* was America's first bestseller. It was probably as popular as any other publication before or after. (Absent copyright laws, printers reprinted subsequent editions. Paine did earn a healthy sum, though, and used a portion of the proceeds to support American soldiers. He bought them mittens.)

Paine's success is best measured not by the number of copies sold but, rather, by how effectively *Common Sense* radicalized colonists, pushing them to support independence, officially declared that summer. His work, and that of other Enlightenment thinkers who promoted republicanism and attacked the monarchy and aristocracy, built an intellectual foundation for the Revolution, an event premised on a new way of thinking spelled out in books, pamphlets, and newspapers. It was part of a flurry of political works that, according to one historian of the Revolution, "has never been equaled in the nation's history." Without the colonial American media infrastructure that Franklin helped establish, the sensation that was *Common Sense*—and perhaps the course of the Revolution itself—would have been different.

With war came all sorts of difficulties: few imports, a paper shortage, widespread economic distress, and fear of violence—especially for Loyalists. Benedict Arnold had given up bookselling along with the idea of independence. An incensed mob in New Jersey hung suspected Loyalist bookseller James Rivington in effigy. Others raided his New York store, smashed his press to bits, and forced him to flee to England. During the British occupation of the city, he returned as the

king's official printer. When the occupation ended and with independence at hand, another mob attacked, thrashing him in the middle of
the street. Did they have the wrong man? Some contemporaries and
later historians claimed that Rivington was not a true Loyalist but,
rather, a spy who used his store as a cover to sell paper inscribed with
secret messages for George Washington. Either way, and as always,
politics and bookselling were intertwined.

I t was Franklin who edited the Declaration of Independence (he
changed Jefferson's "We hold these truths to be sacred and undeni-
able" to "We hold these truths to be self-evident"), negotiated the
peace after the war's end, and then, as an ailing octogenarian, served
as the eldest delegate to the Constitutional Convention. All the while,
he remained invested in books. Ever the inventor and reader, he devised a machine called the Long Arm, a pine stick with a grabber at
one end to retrieve books from high shelves. "Old men," he asserted,
don't belong on ladders. And when in 1788 a group of Philadelphia
booksellers and printers gathered, it was Franklin who insisted on
hosting. He even took the minutes. In attendance was Benjamin
Franklin Bache, his grandson. Grandpa Franklin had set him up in the
business, a profession he believed continued to be an honest way to
make a living, serve the public good, and promote liberty.

Franklin could now look back and see how the various pieces of his
life had coalesced—how printing and bookselling had shaped education, intellectual life, and the means by which colonists consumed
information and developed new ideologies, including revolutionary
ones. Books hold ideas. Ideas hold power.

———

F ranklin died in 1790 at the age of eighty-four. A version of the epitaph he wrote for himself many years earlier is still visible on a plaque near his gravestone, only blocks from his old bookstore:

THE BODY OF

B. FRANKLIN, PRINTER,

LIKE THE COVER OF AN OLD BOOK,

ITS CONTENTS TORN OUT,

AND STRIPT OF ITS LETTERING & GILDING,

LIES HERE, FOOD FOR WORMS.

BUT THE WORK SHALL NOT BE LOST,

FOR IT WILL AS HE BELIEV'D

APPEAR ONCE MORE

IN A NEW AND MORE ELEGANT EDITION

CORRECTED AND IMPROVED

BY THE AUTHOR.

The Smell

Entering any bookstore is a sensory experience. We see, we hear, we feel, we smell. Benjamin Franklin's bookstore was comparatively noisy: all the foot traffic, the regular deliveries, the thundering presses and the groans of men working them. The books looked and felt different, too. But what did the store smell like?

By and large, customers stank. Soap was expensive. The same clothes were worn over and over. Baths were special occasions. Then there was the scent of ink in the barrels, on the pages, and on everyone's hands and aprons. The books had a distinctive aroma as well. Most of the odorants we sense when we smell books are volatile organic compounds, chemicals released over time as the various inks, glues, bindings, and papers decay. Many of today's materials are intended to prolong the lives of books. Doing so introduces new chemicals and new smells.

A lot of people like bibliosmia, the scent of a book. It reminds them of something . . . usually books. It conjures memories of a nose buried in a paperback, the children's section of the local library, or the aisles of a used bookstore. Some say they prefer the smell of a Penguin paperback (and it must be Penguin). Some think old books smell a bit like chocolate. Others find the smell—possibly dusty, musty, mildewy—offensive. Some lose their taste for it. "The sweet smell of decaying paper appeals to me no longer," George Orwell, a onetime secondhand bookseller, wrote. "It is too closely associated in my mind with paranoiac customers and dead bluebottles."

Nonetheless, Powell's, the famed independent Portland bookstore, decided to bottle the aroma. In 2020, it started selling Powell's by Powell's, a unisex fragrance. For $24.99, customers could buy a one-ounce glass bottle that arrived in a neat red box shaped like a book. The fragrance offered notes of wood, violet, and biblichor, invoking "a labyrinth of books; secret libraries; ancient scrolls; and cognac swilled by philosopher-kings." It promised to take "the wearer to a place of wonder, discovery, and magic heretofore only known in literature." Basically, it was supposed to smell like Powell's—to serve as a sensorial reminder of the physical, very real, not-online places where you can still buy books.

The reviews were mixed. A customer named Chris raved about the odor of "old books with a hint of vanilla." But there was one problem. His wife hated it.

Powell's and many other bookstores (just as Hez Usher and Ben Franklin once did) have turned to anything other than books in order to keep selling books. In addition to the bottled bookstore smell, Powell's has ventured into craft beer. In collaboration with a local brewery (microbreweries and bookstores appeal to many of the same folks) and with part of the proceeds going to charity, Powell's introduced a limited-edition hoppy IPA called City of Books. The cans featured the iconic Powell's marquee. Thankfully, the beer was not supposed to taste like bookstore.

2.

THE OLD CORNER

In the building on the corner of Washington and School, editors clutched stacks of manuscripts, printers scurried about in ink-stained clothes, publishers flipped through invoices, and poets browsed shelves of verse. The writers who frequented the Boston bookstore-slash-printshop-slash-publishing-enterprise weren't just the usual aspiring sort. Ralph Waldo Emerson, Oliver Wendell Holmes, and Harriet Beecher Stowe came to talk religion, music, theater, and philosophy. Senator Rufus Choate came to talk books. Nathaniel Hawthorne preferred not to talk at all.

Customers described the scene as a "lounge and resort," a "Literary Exchange," and *the* place to "learn what new books are forthcoming." Henry Wadsworth Longfellow, who regularly made the trip over from Cambridge, relished it all. That the "loiterers" were the "makers of books as well as readers!" only added to the charm: "Such a congregation of authors!" Not everyone was famous. A sea captain, when not aboard ship, essentially lived on a stool in the middle of the shop floor. Anyone could walk in off the street, browse, and strike up a conversation.

The store was a de facto public space, a meeting space, a communal space that wasn't a house or church or political hall. In those cramped quarters, readers, writers, and literature gathered. It was intimate. It was far reaching. It was alive. And it was at the center of a transformation: the birth of the modern American bookstore.

Where Washington Street and School Street crossed was already, in the nineteenth century, known as the Old Corner. In the 1630s, the land was owned by William Hutchinson. His wife, Anne, hosted discussion groups and offered her take on Puritanism. In the process, she upset gender norms and religious-slash-political leaders, who banished her. In 1711, whatever building stood on-site burned along with much of the city. In its place arose a two-story brick structure with a gambrel roof and sandstone quoins. Upstairs was a residence, downstairs a shop for, at various times, merchants, engravers, apothecaries, and milliners. In 1828, it became a bookstore.

At that point, the national book market was still comparatively meager. Few people read for leisure. Few books found a place in colonial homes. Few bookstores lined the streets. Most of the country's readers, books, and bookstores were still concentrated in the Northeast, particularly in the larger cities, like not-yet-terribly-large Boston. Clusters of printers, publishers, and sellers were also emerging in New York and Philadelphia.

Elsewhere, post offices, pharmacies, and general goods stores carried slim selections of popular titles, while individual importers and agents sold books (along with almost anything else) to moneyed buyers. Bookstores remained multifunctional. The words *printer, binder, publisher,* and *bookseller* had capacious, often overlapping meanings.

Most of the stock in most bookstores originated in Europe. The Copyright Act of 1790 protected only American writers, meaning that publishers could reprint European works without fretting about permissions or royalties. Customers could expect to find Boswell, Gibbon, Hume, Locke, and Swift but still rarely novels (despite the Sir Walter Scott fever that began in 1818). Most "American" books were utilitarian: business, legal, academic, medical, scientific, or religious. American literature was in its infancy. The Old Corner Bookstore would help it mature.

The Old Corner was part of a wave of new Boston bookshops. City directories list 137 booksellers between 1821 and 1830. Of those, 73 were on Washington Street, where Henry Knox's bookstore once stood. The mostly small operations rarely remained in one place for long, moving up and down the street, year after year. More than a few disappeared for good. In her study of New York, Kristen Highland found that between 1820 and 1845, most bookstores lasted fewer than five years. Bookselling was precarious—and not terribly lucrative. An 1832 study found that, on average, men in the Boston book trade earned $1.41 a day, boys $0.49, and women, always a minority, $0.45. A typical book retailed for about two long days of women's work.

Nevertheless, a trio of entrepreneurs expected handsome profits when they turned the Old Corner into a bookstore in 1828. Even though they only leased the building, they invested heavily to transform the already 110-year-old space. They converted the upstairs apartment into offices and on the ground floor installed two sets of large (and pricey) bay windows, each with panes about the size of a sheet of paper. They added a second entrance to the bookstore along School Street, so named for the nearby Latin Grammar School, the oldest public school in the United States. Massachusetts's unusual commitment to public education was one of the reasons it boasted relatively high literacy (and book-buying) rates.

The shop's most valuable asset arrived a couple of years later. Thirteen-year-old James T. Fields came by way of New Hampshire and at the recommendation of a family friend who called the young bookstore the best in the city. Like many aspiring booksellers, Fields, who boarded with one of the owners, wrongly assumed that he'd be able to read on the job. Despite living on a junior clerk's salary, he did manage to amass his own library. By the age of twenty, the would-be poet had a collection numbering in the hundreds.

Fields and his fellow clerks certainly found time to enjoy themselves. One favorite game involved guessing which buyers would buy which books. The customers walked in, and the clerks sized them up. What were they wearing? How did they carry themselves? The booksellers made quick guesses. Supposedly, Fields always won, which sparked his reputation as a kind of oracle.

In 1832, William D. Ticknor and two partners (who soon left) bought the store for $24,000. The boy came with the property. Ticknor, who also came to Boston by way of New Hampshire, came to books by way of finance. He was in his early twenties, with thick, curly dark-brown hair and bright blue eyes. He was slight and known to be anxious. In addition to books, he sold toys, pencils, paper, tubes, stethoscopes, and thermometers. He also started a publishing imprint in hopes of developing a specialty in medical books—not that he knew anything about medicine. The domestic book market was still minuscule. There were only 1,553 American-published books in print. (Nowadays, Penguin Random House alone publishes about 15,000 print titles annually, and if you count all formats from all publishers, including self-publishers, there are millions of new titles published each year.)

In 1833, Ticknor published Lydia Maria Child's controversial *An Appeal in Favor of That Class of Americans Called Africans*. While Child expected "ridicule and censure," Ticknor was probably thrilled to issue the book, since Child took the financial risk, paying to have it published herself. When Ticknor put a copy of the book in the shop window, a crowd came and shattered it.

A banking and financial crisis crippled the book trade in 1837, and Ticknor approached bankruptcy. He managed to hold on, and by the early 1840s, the tide turned—in part because of shifting economic winds and in part because of James Fields.

Seven years Ticknor's junior, Fields had unruly dark hair and a thick beard that eventually turned gray, inched toward the floor, and merged with a monstrous mustache, rendering his mouth nearly invisible. He suffered from chronic headaches and grief. His young fiancée had died before they could wed. He would later marry her younger sister, who soon died as well.

Professionally, things went more smoothly. By 1843, he rose to the position of junior partner without having to put up any money. "In consideration of his knowledge" was how the corporate documents described his value. He had already begun tilting the bookstore and its publishing arm toward poetry, fiction, and American writers.

The first to arrive each morning was the "negro porter," who swept the floors. At 7:00 a.m., the clerks appeared. They dusted, packed, unpacked, took inventory, filled the inkwells, and, in the winter, lit the stove. A local poet who wouldn't wait for the store to officially open entertained the boys with verse. Ticknor arrived promptly at

The Old Corner Bookstore, circa 1840.

7:30 and headed straight for his office, a few steps up from the main floor. Stacks of books and papers littered the area around his small desk. Behind him a row of satchels leaned against a bookcase like dominoes. A clock hung on the otherwise bare wall. There was one guest chair, "Hawthorne's chair," where the author spent countless hours sitting quietly as Ticknor worked a few feet away. Ticknor loved his office. He called it "Paradise."

Fields's office was hidden behind a green curtain, to the back and left when customers walked through the main entrance. It held a large desk, a window seat, and several chairs for visitors—and there were always visitors. While Ticknor (and Hawthorne) preferred to work in silence, Fields's nook was "the hub in which every spoke of the radiating wheel of Boston intellect has a socket." His little spot became known as Parnassus Corner, a reference to the Greek mountain mythologized as the sacred home of the Muses. The two offices, both slightly elevated and on opposite sides of the one-thousand-square-foot first floor, represented the two spheres of the business. Fields was in charge of literature; Ticknor was in charge of money.

Between them was a mostly wall-less interior with a row of thin columns. Long counters ran along the edges, with shelves hanging above, all lined with spine-out books. There was a glass case for luxuriously bound editions. Window seats and islands of book-topped tables made for "a coolness, a quiet, a seclusion."

The Old Corner's magnetism was a product of its people (shoppers and sellers) and the space itself. Holmes articulated the allure: "I never can go into that famous 'Corner Bookstore' and look over the new books in the row before me, as I enter the door, without seeing half a dozen which I want to read, or at least to know something about." Browsing, or, as he called it, "Book-*tasting* . . . makes one hungry for more than he needs for the nourishment of his thinking-marrow."

The term *browsing* dates to the fifteenth century, when it was first used to describe how cows and goats and other grazers munch on vegetation. Holmes's description of "book-tasting" perfectly captures the sentiment behind the original and its evolving definition—leisurely poking around in a bookstore. The *Oxford English Dictionary* uses an 1868 quote from poet James Russell Lowell to demonstrate the shifting meaning: "We thus get a glimpse of him browsing—for, like Johnson, Burke, and the full as distinguished from the learned men, he was always a random reader—in his father's library. . . ." Lowell, an Old Corner regular, wrote this in the *North American Review*, the literary magazine that he edited and that was published by Ticknor and Fields.

At the Old Corner, Lowell was able to browse, choosing books from the display tables and pulling them off the shelves, but other stores maintained moats that separated the books from the buyers.

Some of the world's earliest bookstores were entirely unbrowsable. The books sat in enclosed bins and boxes along shelves with their spines standing invisibly against the back wall, or they were piled into horizontal stacks, also with their fore edges, rather than their spines, exposed. Even into the nineteenth century, bookstores kept books in cupboards behind the counter, out of reach to everyone except the clerks. The stock tended to be grouped by publisher, making it easier to keep track of inventory but impossible to browse by genre. How bookstores were organized changed how people thought about books, the way they related to one another, and which books customers discovered.

Some stores seemed to have no organization at all. "There was a certain attempt at arrangement and classification," a confused journalist wrote about a New York basement shop where even the owner didn't know where anything was. By the end of the nineteenth century, arranging books by genre became more common but was hardly universal. The Old Corner was not only unusually browsable among bookstores but also unusually browsable by retail standards in general. Its model of unmediated browsing ("tasting") was what shoppers would ultimately come to expect—and appreciate—in a bookstore.

Browsing led to lingering, which led to conversation, which spilled over to Mrs. Haven's coffee shop next door. In the early afternoon, Fields and friends and editors and book reviewers (whom Fields took pains to keep on his good side) drifted over, where they talked books and snacked on ice cream, coffee, and brandy.

It was Fields to whom everyone wanted to talk, whether at the coffee shop or bookstore. By the summer of 1846, he had inked a deal to publish one of Longfellow's books. Later that year, he published two more Longfellows and an edition of Holmes's poetry. He was a trendsetter.

In 1849, Fields's efforts were rewarded. The firm reorganized as Ticknor, Reed and Fields before soon becoming just Ticknor and Fields. (Reed was a "blank, so far as I am concerned," Hawthorne once wrote.) Its reputation was further enhanced with the publication of Hawthorne's 1850 critical and popular success, *The Scarlet Letter.*

Ticknor and Fields, publisher and bookseller, invested most heavily in poetry, fiction, and essays (in that order). Over the course of the 1840s and '50s, Longfellow was the firm's bestselling author. American writers dominated its top-twenty-five bestseller list. (All but four of the authors were men.) To be sure, reading tastes were evolving nationally, but the Old Corner could buck larger trends. Poetry "never does well" in New York, one writer counseled another, advising that he talk to Fields, who had "such facilities for that peculiar sale." Indeed, the store was full of poetry and poets offering recommendations. Then, as now, word of mouth pushed sales. Those conversations started at the little bookstore on the corner.

As the shop's buyer, Fields had sophisticated taste. He returned books "not in our line" to the publishers; these returns included works that would eventually become part of the canon. Fields said he couldn't convince anyone that *Wuthering Heights* was "a *good* book." He erred more than once. In the spring of 1854, Louisa May Alcott walked the mile from her house to the Old Corner, manuscript in hand, and bounded straight for the green curtain. Fields read the work, delivering the bad news on the spot: "Stick to your teaching, Miss Alcott. You can't write." Alcott didn't listen, of course. The two remained friendly; Fields even loaned her forty dollars. After she published *Little Women*, Alcott returned the money and quipped, "I found writing paid so much better than teaching that I thought I'd stick to my pen." Fields "laughed & owned that he made a mistake," she recorded in her diary. He later published some of her work in *The Atlantic Monthly*, which Ticknor and Fields began publishing in 1859 and which Fields began editing two years later. That the American magazine devoted to literature and politics and graced by the words of New England's finest writers was housed at the Old Corner Bookstore made perfect sense. So did the fact that when a Benjamin Franklin statue was erected in front of City Hall in 1856, it was Fields who wrote the poem to mark the occasion.

B y then, the Old Corner Bookstore was among the most prominent booksellers in the country, and Ticknor and Fields among the most prominent publishers. But the landscape was changing. New York had become the undisputed literary capital. Between 1820 and 1860, the number of bookstores in Gotham increased by an average of 50 percent per decade.

While publishers focused on growing their lists and as more exclusively retail bookstores came of age, Ticknor and Fields remained committed to both. Account books make clear that the firm did not treat them as separate divisions. Both income streams relied on blurred relationships. Fields befriended journalists, editors, and writers, many of whom aspired to be Ticknor and Fields authors and many of whom shopped at the store. Business was personal. When a reviewer panned Longfellow's *The Song of Hiawatha*, Fields fumed, writing a letter to the newspaper that had published the review and promising to stop running advertisements. (Sometimes Fields sent a review copy of a book to an editor along with a suggested review: "No one need know that I wrote it, if you please.")

"Tick" was Hawthorne's friend, bookseller of choice, publisher, and de facto publicist, agent, secretary, and banker. (Hawthorne was very needy.) Ticknor sent him money, took messages for him, and purchased whatever he was asked (even "a lady's watch, good and handsome, but not very expensive"). When Hawthorne wanted a handful of underappreciated American books, he asked Ticknor to send him *Walden*, *Passion-Flowers*, *Up-Country Letters*, *Autobiography of an Actress*, and anything but Whittier. ("I like the man," but his work "is poor stuff.") When Hawthorne wasn't sitting in Ticknor's office, he was writing him, especially when stationed in Liverpool as a US consul. From there, Hawthorne mailed Tick a "big cheese" to share with the "half-starved authors." Hawthorne missed the place, his chair. "I long to see you—or anybody else from the old Corner," he wrote in 1855. He suffered from homesickness and yearned for the two places that "attach me to my native land": his hillside Concord home and that "old 'Corner Store.'"

Combining publishing and retail had its advantages. Ticknor and Fields could observe the kinds of books people picked up and the ones they didn't. Booksellers were on the front lines. Fields had no background in marketing, but he'd been studying consumer behavior since he was thirteen, guessing who would buy what. Now, he insisted on hiring premier tradespeople to produce beautiful books. "We can assure you it is not adapted to 'Boston notions' of good taste," Fields wrote to the binder of a Longfellow collection in 1855. "Our customers take up the book and *then put it down* simply on account of the binding."

Browsing in a bookstore was an experience, one that was changing the very function of the bookstore and one that was altering the trade. The stakes for book and bookstore design were raised. In 1856, Ticknor and Fields published Tennyson's *Poetical Works*, the first title in what became the company's colorful trademark style (soon mimicked by rivals): a slender pocket-size format printed on high-quality paper and covered in deep-blue cloth. The bindings had been brown, and with dust jackets then rare, the bindings were what first attracted customers. The volumes had gilded edges, gold ornamentations stamped on the spine, and the title and author's name also in gold. "I have a greater respect for my own works than ever before—seeing them so finely dressed," Hawthorne wrote of one of his newly issued books. Produced with such quality, books were perceived as decorative objects, deserving of prominent shelf space and worthy of gifting. Indeed, booksellers and publishers promoted the idea that books were ideal gifts. It was a Salem, Massachusetts, bookstore that in 1806 put out the first known American ad for Christmas gifts of any kind. Buyers were encouraged to inscribe a sweet message inside.

Combining publishing with retailing also caused problems. When Fields was traveling through Europe, Ticknor summoned him back to the Old Corner: the store "involves me in more labor than I have the physical strength to perform." They added employees, but the building was only so big. When copies of *The Atlantic Monthly* arrived, they sat on the sidewalks. Come summertime, the pace slowed down considerably. During one hot spell, Fields complained, "The streets are filled with melted horse shoes. . . . Business is no more. Money is *non est* likewise. . . . Boston is a desert." He hated the heat. "At our Corner we gasp for air & find none," he wrote to Longfellow. The underlying problem, Fields concluded, was that he was too fat.

Then there were the awkward negotiations. As publisher, Fields drove down the discounts given to retail booksellers and middlemen— wholesalers or jobbers—who distributed books increasingly quickly by steamboats and westward by rail. Although some publishers sold large lots via auction, Ticknor and Fields usually sold directly to booksellers for two-thirds of the retail price. Prices varied considerably, depending on the number of copies ordered and the type of book. While advance copies meant to test the market could be returned, most books could not. At the same time, keeping wholesale prices too high reduced the booksellers' profits. Publishers increasingly depended on retail bookstores as points of sale. The greater the number of healthy booksellers, the better.

As a bookstore, Ticknor and Fields also had to buy from wholesalers and other publishers. As a buyer, Ticknor and Fields asked for higher discounts than it offered as a seller. It was a delicate balance. When dealing with D. Appleton, a New York publisher-slash-wholesaler-slash-retailer with an elaborate six-thousand-square-foot shop, the two houses exchanged, rather than sold, books to one other. Neither had to put up any cash.

Appleton's bookstore, seen here in 1856, occupied a Greek Revival on Broadway in Manhattan. Here was a place to appreciate books as works of art.

Shipments of European books came slowly and just twice a month, by way of Liverpool. As routine receivers of European cargo, the booksellers were happy to help friends of the store. When Ralph Waldo Emerson ordered a couple of items from overseas, they were added to the crate of books headed for the Old Corner.

Ticknor and Fields's bookstore was constrained by (or maybe benefited from) its modest premises. The same didn't hold for its publishing business, which outsourced much of the production. By 1860, the company had issued 216,536 total copies. Its ninety-four-page catalog highlighted libraries of "Standard Authors"—Charles Dickens and Sir Walter Scott. (Hawthorne bought all the Waverly novels, taking "very great pleasure in arranging them on the shelf.") The firm emphasized American authors, many of them customers: Henry Longfellow (poetry collections for $0.75 and illustrated versions with fancy bindings in assorted colors for $8.00), Nathaniel Hawthorne (*The House of the Seven Gables* for $1.00), James Russell Lowell (*The Complete Poetical Works* in two volumes, cloth at $1.50 and full gilt at $3.00), Julia Ward Howe (*Passion-Flowers* for $0.75), Henry David Thoreau (*Walden* for $1.00), and Charles Sumner (*Orations and Speeches*, two volumes for $2.50).

Sumner was the famous antislavery senator from Massachusetts who in 1856 was beaten with a cane on the Senate floor. Sectionalism affected the book business, too. Ticknor counseled Grace Greenwood that she should delete potentially offensive portions of her book that might "effectively cut off the sale . . . south of 'Mason & Dixon.'" When a Charleston bookseller grumbled about a Ticknor and Fields book that upset his enslaving customers, Ticknor accepted the return without protest. And when a bookstore owner from Jackson, Mississippi, expressed reservations about sending a friend to the Old Corner, he received a reply assuring him (unconvincingly) that they'd be welcome: "Boston is not as much an abolition city as is New York."

In 1860, Ticknor and Fields bought the rights to Harriet Beecher Stowe's *Uncle Tom's Cabin*. Stowe visited the Old Corner and even signed the shop's autograph book. Her novel stirred antislavery sentiment and sold exceptionally well, at least in certain parts of the country. In the South, it was hard to find, as laws in several of the states forbade the importation of antislavery literature. Ticknor and Fields didn't even attempt to sell certain titles in Dixieland. Nonetheless, Southern readers could, and did, manage to get copies of *Uncle Tom's Cabin*. "In Charleston this book cannot be bought," wrote Rosalie Roos in 1853, before describing how she borrowed a copy from someone in the know. Another reader from New Orleans obtained the book directly from New York, after which "it has been going the rounds." Starting in 1851, books weighing less than two pounds (the weight limit soon raised to four pounds) could be sent via regular mail. Before then, bound books were not considered "mailable matter" and had to be shipped by private wholesalers, jobbers, and express companies. The spread of railroads permitted the postal service to accommodate bulkier parcels, books included.

Although *Uncle Tom's Cabin* wasn't the kind of book found in Southern bookstores, the number of bookshops in the region had grown steadily over the first half of the nineteenth century. In 1803, a visiting Frenchman couldn't find one in New Orleans. He surmised that the residents were too obsessed with money and too little interested in literature. That same year, Thomas Jefferson judged that New Orleans was home to a small number of readers, "of whom not more than 200, perhaps, are able to do it well."

New Orleans eventually matured into a Southern literary hub. In the 1810s, Benjamin Levy opened one of its first bookstores. As the Frenchman would have guessed, the shop, which stood across the street from a bank, specialized in business and legal texts. Levy, a twentysomething bookbinder, had come from Long Island to the Crescent City, a place with hardly any other Jews. Levy stocked playing cards, lottery tickets, paper, ink, quills, pencils, and billiard balls. He wore many hats, selling, printing, binding, and publishing books and periodicals, including the *New-Orleans Price-Current and Commercial Intelligencer*, an 1820s and '30s weekly that charted cotton and tobacco prices. He also printed broadsides advertising auctions of enslaved people. Dandridge, a twenty-six-year-old "mulatto," was described as a "first-rate dining-room servant."

Levy knew the business of slavery firsthand. According to the 1830 census, he owned eight enslaved people. It's possible that one or more worked in the bookstore, a node connecting New Orleans enslavers and businessmen with local, regional, national, and international markets and ideologies. In addition to being the only place in all of Louisiana that carried the *North American Review*, Levy's bookstore stocked "scientific" texts that sought to establish the enslaver's identity as a legitimate capitalist, masking slavery's brutality. Unlike the popular Southern magazine *De Bow's Review*, which similarly professionalized the plantation, Levy's bookshop was also a place where statistical tables of cotton prices shared shelf space with memoirs.

In 1842, Levy filed for bankruptcy, the result of real estate deals gone bad. He lost his house and his bookstore. He died in 1860. In his will, he apologized to his grandchildren for not having more to give them. Levy did leave them "my only Legacy," his personal library.

The New Orleans book market soon began to grow. From 1859 to

1860, Ticknor and Fields sold more books to New Orleans bookstores than to retailers in any other Southern city, including Baltimore and Washington, DC. Still, the South remained its weakest market. In the early 1850s, Ticknor and Fields sold two and a half times more Longfellow in similarly sized Cincinnati than in New Orleans. Sales of American-authored books were especially disappointing in Southern outlets. Collections of English authors sold better, indicating the preferred taste of the planter class. Medical books sold well, too, especially those on cholera during a cholera epidemic. In consideration of the dire circumstances, "we are giving you an extra discount," Fields wrote to a New Orleans bookseller.

On the eve of the Civil War, the United States was still a predominately rural nation. Readers in the countryside depended on traveling salesmen, the general store, or the post office. But most decent-sized towns had at least one bookstore, and larger cities had a handful, many more than a generation prior. In 1860, Louisiana was home to forty-three booksellers, with nineteen of them in New Orleans. In Georgia, Savannah had three, Atlanta had four, and Augusta had five. There were five in Nashville and five in Memphis. Charleston had ten. Small-town Harrisonburg, Virginia, managed five. But these were dwarfed by other regions. Maine (population 628,279) had more than twice as many bookstores as Texas (population 604,215) and Louisiana (population 708,002). With fifty, Cincinnati was the bookstore capital of the "West." Boston, including the Old Corner, had ninety-three, for an astounding rate of one bookstore per 1,912 people. There were two hundred and twenty-nine in New York, the largest American city, home to 2.6 percent of the country's population and nearly 11 percent of its booksellers. Nationally, there was one bookseller for every 15,045 people.

In November of 1860, an avid reader from Springfield, Illinois (a town with two booksellers), won a highly polarized presidential election. Abraham Lincoln's name didn't even appear on the ballot in much of the South. Seven states seceded before Inauguration Day. In the spring, war began.

The casualties included more than soldiers. Infrastructure was destroyed and businesses wrecked. In May of 1861, Longfellow visited the "dreary" Old Corner. "Bookselling dead," he rued. By August of 1862, Fields observed that "the Trade is in a state of apathy I never saw approached." The South was cut off from imports, books included. It had always been harder, taken longer, and cost more to stock books in Southern bookstores. Now, it was nearly impossible.

In the spring of 1864, with the Union's prospects improving, Ticknor and Hawthorne set out on a trip. Just before they left, Holmes, the poet and physician, pronounced Ticknor "good for twenty years." A few days later, the bookman died in a hotel bed with Hawthorne holding his hand. Ticknor was fifty-three. A month later, Hawthorne, fifty-nine, died, too.

Ticknor had been at the Old Corner since 1832 and was probably the reason it never moved, even though it had long outgrown the space. He loved the corner and loved his office. With his partner gone, Fields decided in November of 1864 that it was time to move.

The Old Corner building, as it seemed fated to do, remained a bookstore. Regardless of the new businesses' legal names or those of the partners, the booksellers who subsequently occupied the space were forever known by the erstwhile name: the Old Corner. "Old Corner Bookstore" was even emblazoned onto the facade.

The first newcomer was E. P. Dutton & Co. in 1865. On the Washington Street side, a new awning shaded the doorways and windows. While the old shop was sunlit, the new one was dark and cramped. Some of the clerks stayed on. One regular presence was Henry Oscar Houghton, Ticknor and Fields's preferred typesetter and printer. He had since ventured into publishing, and it was across his "tiny old pine desk in the farthest corner" of the shop that he met the young Harvard graduate George Harrison Mifflin. E. P. Dutton & Co. stayed on the corner for just four years, albeit good ones—good enough to encourage the partners to leave for New York.

Then came Alexander Williams, who traded on the prestige associated with the address to become, in 1875, president of a fledgling regional booksellers' organization. The New England Booksellers Association's mission was to implement industry-wide pricing, affording "booksellers a fair living profit." It was modeled on the American Book Trade Association, a short-lived attempt, begun in 1873, to unify booksellers and publishers against discounting, a practice that had increased in the inflationary postwar economy. NEBA members also expressed concern about the growing number of public libraries. In 1876, the American Library Association launched.

Among the officers of NEBA was B. H. Ticknor, William's son. He represented the successor to Ticknor and Fields, James R. Osgood & Co., which later reorganized and eventually merged with Houghton's firm to form Houghton, Mifflin and Company. James Fields was not present at the meeting when NEBA was born, having retired two years earlier (and having celebrated retirement by eating lots of peanuts).

In 1902, the booksellers at the Old Corner changed the name of their firm, officially becoming the Old Corner Bookstore. Just a year later, the Old Corner Bookstore moved from the old corner, leaving the spot without a bookstore for the first time in seventy-five years. Not everyone mourned the loss. *The New York Times* argued that no one should shed "any tears over the removal" and that "the new quarters will be far more pleasant than the old." It was at the new location (also on a corner, Bromfield and Province) where Christopher Morley worked during the Christmas season in 1913, 1914, and 1915. In his quasi-autobiographical novel, *John Mistletoe*, Morley writes that working in a bookstore is the only way to understand "the enormous power exerted by the individual clerk in influencing customers' choices." He put Joseph Conrad in as many hands as he could. He also learned that the new Old Corner wasn't the same as the old Old Corner. The job, so his supervisors made clear, was "to satisfy customers promptly; not to encourage them to loiter and litigate the niceties of belles lettres." The loitering and the litigating had once been the attraction.

Although it fell to less distinguished uses, the building on the corner of Washington and School Streets remained. In 1960, a group of preservationists rallied to save what was the oldest commercial structure in all of Boston. They launched Historic Boston Incorporated, a nonprofit that bought the building and began to restore it, bringing it back (on the exterior, at least) to its 1828 glory, the year it became a bookstore.

Today, the Old Corner Bookstore has a coveted spot on the Freedom Trail and the National Register of Historic Places. It has an architectural significance but more so a social one. It was once a literary jewel, a place where some of the greatest authors congregated, and a regular store—the kind we'd recognize today—where books arrived, were put on the shelf, picked up, tasted, bought, read, and discussed. The Old Corner helped launch American literature and the American bookstore. Now it's a Chipotle.

The Buyer

Considering all the books in print, even the largest bookstores can carry only tiny selections. Almost everything is out of stock. Deciding what to put on the shelf is difficult, sometimes painful. The books that James Fields decided to publish, the books that he put out on the tables, and the books that he talked about with friends over ice cream were given a chance for an enduring life. As the number of books ever increases, these decisions only get harder.

Calibrating and curating are both art and science. Booksellers lean on the advice of publishing representatives who, until recently, visited the stores in person, and the publishers' catalogs, which contain information about the books and the authors, the expected print runs, and planned publicity and marketing campaigns. Store buyers can also be swayed to buy a book (or more copies of said book) by prepublication reviews, sales of the author's previous works, whether someone on staff loved the galley (advance copies are sent to booksellers, reviewers, and media outlets), or just a hunch. Nowadays, booksellers also scour Edelweiss, an online clearinghouse with digital catalogs, electronic galleys, and reviews from booksellers. Booksellers tend to trust other booksellers.

If James Fields was the dean of mid-nineteenth-century bookselling, Paul Yamazaki can make a claim to be today's version. He jokes that he's the only bookseller who "came straight from jail to bookselling." In 1970, he had been protesting the war in Vietnam and was tossed in jail. A judge told him that he could get out if he secured a job. Yamazaki was friends with the poet Francis Oka, who was friends with the poet Lawrence Ferlinghetti, who founded City Lights in 1953. The San Francisco bookstore became famous for its association with beatniks and radicalism. Ferlinghetti, "sympathetic to someone he considered a political prisoner," hired Yamazaki. The rookie bookseller moved onto a houseboat and hitchhiked to the store each day.

By the time Yamazaki arrived, Allen Ginsberg and Jack Kerouac were already historic figures. Yamazaki wanted to branch out. He thought the paperback-only bookstore should stock hardcovers. In the early 1980s, he got the opportunity to act on that opinion when he became the buyer. It was up to him to pick out the thousands of titles for the triangular building with three floors of books and entire rooms given over to poetry and world literature. He refused to stock many bestsellers.

What makes a great buyer? In short, a great buyer is a great reader—and has great patience. "Almost every book needs time," Yamazaki philosophized, ruminating on the role that booksellers play in recognizing talent. Buyers, Yamazaki said, need to reflect on how books will hit their readers. "I think this lack of distinction between the personal and professional contributes to making a great buyer," he added. "It's almost pathological."

Nowadays, Yamazaki recognizes that the future of bookselling rests in the hands of a younger generation. At City Lights, he gives newer booksellers a copy of Alfred H. Barr Jr.'s famous diagram, which once graced the cover of the catalog for the 1936 MOMA exhibition *Cubism and Abstract Art*. Barr was trying to visualize influence, drawing literal lines from Dadaism to surrealism, constructivism to Bauhaus. Yamazaki was trying to do the same, looking back over more than fifty years at City Lights, trying to understand its vast influence and its influences, thinking about the past to imagine different futures. He insists that those futures will be shaped by the books on the shelves—and the books that booksellers choose to put in the customers' hands.

3.

PARNASSUS ON WHEELS

R oger Mifflin wore a red beard and a tweed cap. He was bald, loved to read, and wished he were a writer. Naturally, he became a bookseller—a traveling bookseller.

Around 1908, he visited a secondhand shop in Baltimore. He bought as many books as he could cram into his blue wagon, Parnassus on Wheels. Along both exterior sides, he had installed wooden flaps that, when opened, revealed rows upon rows of books. The inside measured five feet by nine (the size of a Ping-Pong table) and held a small bunk, a small chest of drawers, a small table, a small stove, a small wicker chair, and a small dog. A white horse (not small) named Pegasus drove.

Mifflin spent several summers traveling up and down the East Coast. When his stock thinned, he'd stop at a used bookstore along the way, marking each volume with a series of coded letters that corresponded to numbers (manuscript = 0123456789) to indicate the price paid. Aside from inventory, he didn't have much overhead. There was food for him and the horse and the dog, repairs when needed, and the occasional theft. His expenses ran about four dollars a week. So long as sales were decent, he took Sundays off. Like most booksellers, he said he wasn't in it for the money: "When you sell a man a book, you don't sell him just twelve ounces of paper and ink and glue—you sell him a whole new life." Still, it wasn't easy. "It's hard to make 'em see it," he said, referring to customers he thought too cheap. Even when they wanted to buy, Mifflin sometimes refused. "I didn't think he was up to it yet," he said about one immature reader.

After seven years of traveling around and with revived commitment to finally writing that book of his, he paid a visit to an author who he hoped would buy him out. The writer wasn't home, but his sister, Helen McGill, was. She bought the business on the spot and left a note for her famous brother:

> *Don't be thinking I'm crazy. I've gone off for an adventure. It just came over me that you've had all the adventures while I've been at home baking bread. . . . It's what the magazines call the revolt of womanhood. Warm underwear in the cedar chest in the spare room when you need it.*

> *With love,*
>
> *Helen*

Mifflin repainted the wagon for McGill. Instead of advertising Shakespeare and Lamb, fresh letters spelled out "COOK BOOKS A SPECIALTY."

McGill's entrée into bookselling was sudden and tumultuous. Her brother immediately hunted after her, assuming that at best she'd been duped and at worst she'd been kidnapped. And then there was her budding romance with Mifflin, who initially left McGill on her own but then returned to save her from a band of "hoboes" and ended up copiloting the very wagon he had been trying to ditch. Along the way, they became America's two most famous booksellers—albeit fictional ones.

Mifflin and McGill are the costars of *Parnassus on Wheels*, Christopher Morley's 1917 novel, his first. The book was an instant classic.

For as long as there have been booksellers, there have been traveling booksellers. In 1683, Cotton Mather spoke of "an old Hawker, who will fill this Countrey with devout and useful Books." A 1705 obituary noted the death of a peddler who "used to go up and down the Country selling of Books." While both were likely working for larger bookshops in the city, they were viewed differently from the sellers with permanent locations. People assumed they sold stolen books. People assumed they were trouble. In 1713, the Massachusetts Assembly passed "an Act against Hawkers, Pedlars, and Petty Chapmen," requiring peregrinating merchants to attain permits. Other colonies followed suit.

Peddlers continued to hawk books, especially in the colonies and later in the states with few places to purchase them. They typically sold small, cheap books or pamphlets, often religious works. Parson Weems was the best-known itinerant bookseller. An unconventional salesman with a big head and almost no neck, he later wrote the biography of George Washington that originated the cherry tree myth. Weems worked for Mathew Carey, a renowned Philadelphia publisher with an impressive bookstore not far from Benjamin Franklin's old shop. Carey was eager to sell to the underserved Southern market—and to dump inventory that wasn't selling elsewhere. Weems traveled to small towns, visited meeting rooms and alehouses and churches, talked up books, took names and orders, and returned months later with books in hand. He also grumbled a lot. His commission was too low. He shouldn't have to pay for his own travel expenses. His inventory was mostly junk, not to the taste of local markets. His customers tried to pay him in cotton. And he complained that Carey, his employer, complained too much.

While Weems wasn't toting along anything close to the contents of an entire bookstore, there were bookshops on the move. In 1824, a two-thousand-volume bookstore floated down the Erie Canal, stopping at one waterfront town after the next. By the early twentieth century, the closest thing to the traveling bookstore was the traveling library. In 1905, a Maryland librarian employed a wagon, two horses, and a janitor to drive and deliver hundreds of books, house by house, in rural Washington County until a train rammed into his wain. Other librarians began using bookmobiles to visit children in rural areas and city playgrounds.

Then came Christopher Morley's book. "If there is anything more romantically interesting than selling books, it is selling books from a caravan," *Publishers Weekly* asserted. By the summer of 1920, Bertha Mahony had launched the Caravan Bookshop, the "first bookstore on wheels." Mahony stayed behind while Mary Frank, on leave from the New York Public Library, and Genevieve Washburn, who had worked in a library and, more importantly, had experience driving ambulances, operated a motorized truck with two generous awnings that spread like wings and an interior large enough to accommodate a dozen customers and one thousand books. A group of publishers funded the project in hopes that it would spread the gospel of reading and, no doubt, elicit media attention. The Caravan Bookshop covered much of New England, from Plymouth to Provincetown, Kennebunk-port to Northport, Middlebury to Lake Placid.

Like children hearing the jingle of an ice cream truck, readers learned of the approaching Caravan as Washburn honked her way through downtowns. When it stopped, she put out a set of tables and chairs. "Is Christopher Morley inside?" customers asked, peering through the window before snapping up copies of *Parnassus on Wheels*, the Caravan's bestseller. The booksellers wrote to Morley from the road: "We owe it to you that people are so kindly disposed. Their imaginations have been touched, and they view us thru romantic spec-tacles."

Real life wasn't so glamorous. The days were long, the crowds usu-ally thin. The wear and tear took its toll—on the booksellers, on the vehicle, and on the books. When it rained, sales neared zero. There was also competition with more traditional bookshops. The Acorn Bookshop in Portsmouth welcomed the Caravan and even put out an ad for it, but the shop made sure that locals recognized the importance of the community bookstore:

> THE CARAVAN IS COMING THIS WEEK. BE SURE
> TO VISIT IT. YOU WILL FIND MANY INTERESTING
> BOOKS TO BUY. BUT DON'T FORGET THAT,
> WHEREAS THE CARAVAN IS HERE FOR BUT
> ONE DAY, THE ACORN BOOKSHOP IS ON THE
> SQUARE EVERY DAY OF THE WEEK.

The Caravan targeted vacationers in resort towns, "people who know and love books," not the "natives." In its second year, it returned to the most profitable locations. The caravanners had learned that post offices and hotels were prime spots, especially after mealtimes, and that business was abysmal at the beach: "People do not come prepared to buy."

That same summer, rivals entered the fray. D. Appleton & Co. decided that it would sell directly via truck to consumers who summered on Long Island. And the National Association of Book Publishers lent out a book wagon to aspiring sellers as the American Library Association called for "a book wagon for every county of every state."

Frank Shay had been in the book business for decades, including a stint as manager of Schulte's Book Store on New York's Book Row and later at the Washington Square Bookshop. He left to fight in the Great War, having failed to dodge the draft. "Shooting a gun into another man's face," he wrote, "never settled any argument and never will." Once back in Manhattan, he opened Frank Shay's Bookshop on Christopher Street in 1920.

His shop was small, so small he called it a "stall." He did have actual bookstalls on the sidewalks out front, where lanky Shay smoked cigarettes. Inside, he gave his customers space, let them browse. He wouldn't say anything unless they talked first.

The shop stayed open until 11:00 p.m., midnight when there was a crowd. On the wall was a portrait of Joseph Conrad. The center table was lined with face-out books. Some, including Morley's *Parnassus on Wheels* and Sinclair Lewis's *Main Street*, were encased in a special wrapper: "Frank Shay recommends this book. It is sold with the guarantee that if it does not measure up to our statements, we will exchange it for another book or refund the purchase price." (Only 1 of 237 buyers returned *Main Street*.)

Even if a reflection of Shay's taste, the store was not a specialty shop, a fact applauded by one writer bemoaning bookstores focused on "one kind of rubbish. . . . We escape flapper fiction and vellum editions of the Hoosier poet only to encounter propaganda for one queer cult after another—for anarchism, Bolshevism, Cubism, Egoism, Dadaism, Ferrerism, and so thru the alphabet." He continued: "I find something refreshing in a little book-shop like Frank Shay's where the Great Cause is simply selling books." In truth, Shay did more than sell books; he also published books, magazines, and poetry collections, including from Edna St. Vincent Millay and Eugene O'Neill.

There certainly were typical Frank Shay customers. They tended to be artists, especially writers, some clinging to the notion of Village bohemianism. Christopher Morley was a friend of the store. He and Shay went out for "spaghetti and spumoni ice cream." And for at least one week, Shay turned his front window into a display of works by Morley, "the booksellers' guardian angel." Sinclair Lewis, Sherwood Anderson, William Rose Benét, Floyd Dell, John Dos Passos, Theodore Dreiser, and Upton Sinclair also visited. We know, because they and more than one hundred other writers (plus sixteen booksellers) signed the door that separated Shay's office from the shop floor. (Allegedly, Shay installed the door so that people couldn't see him drinking.) The door became an author's "Magna Carta," with writers wanting to sign it. Customers wanted to see it, and Shay advertised it: "Come in and see our door." (The signed door lives on at the Harry Ransom Center in Austin, Texas.) Novelists and poets, editors and publishers, painters and playwrights, and fellow booksellers came as much for the company as for the books.

In the summer, the "authors' bookshop" lacked something essential: the authors. They fled for Cape Cod, Woods Hole, and other New England destinations. They didn't want to stop reading, though, and Shay figured there was an unmet demand for quality books. He spent a wakeful night thinking about Roger Mifflin. Why not give it a try? "Maps are got out. Catalogues of cars are studied" is how he described the preparations. Within a few weeks, Shay's traveling bookshop was no longer a fantasy. He called it, of course, Parnassus on Wheels.

Shay bought a Ford, removed the seats, and installed eight shelves of classics along the back; four rows for nonfiction, children's books, poetry, and plays along the passenger's side; and five rows of foldable shelves with seventy-two inches of fiction along the driver's side. The stock was chosen for his usual sophisticated and mercurial buyers. "Our customers are very precious objects," he stressed. One set of doors flipped up to form an awning, shielding browsers from rain and sun. Another flipped down to form a counter. Shay slept on a cot, lowered from the ceiling each night. To make the venture sustainable, he figured he needed fifty-one dollars in sales a day, though "one is willing to forego profit."

Frank Shay (center) watches as Christopher Morley
baptizes Shay's traveling bookshop with beer in June of 1922.

Like the Book Caravan, Shay favored stopping near post offices. Going door to door rarely paid off, as only about one in a hundred knocks yielded a sale. On the weekends, he camped out in Provincetown. Not infrequently, he was told to scram. Once, someone demanded to see his peddler's license. He didn't have one and was fined. But the same judge who had already bought from him *The Education of Henry Adams* and three Conrad books for "Her Honor" ruled that the license requirement didn't apply to book peddlers.

The "Parnassuswaggoner" didn't last long. The car stalled. Gas was expensive. Plus, "New England thrift seems to be proof against the thrills even of the greatest books." After just one year, Shay jettisoned his bookmobile.

Traveling bookstores were mostly, but not exclusively, seasonal operations concentrated in New England. A married couple toured Michigan's Upper Peninsula. Frank Collins's bookmobile set off from Carmel, California, to Colorado Springs, stopping at vacation destinations along the way.

Inspired by Helen McGill, many mobile booksellers were women. After the first women-led Book Caravan, Helen Boyd cruised around New York's Hudson Valley, small-town Vermont, New Hampshire, and Maine. Havelock Ellis's *The Dance of Life* was a favorite. So was *Parnassus on Wheels*. Over four New England summers, Marion Dodd of the Hampshire Bookshop sold books from a bookmobile, as did several of her former staff in the 1920s. Lesley Frost (Robert Frost's daughter) drove the Knapsack to children's camps. Elizabeth H. Pitney operated the Bookworm Express out of Morristown, New Jersey. Margery B. McClellan sold books from a boat harnessed atop a Ford

Frank Collins (seated) had been selling newspapers in New York until his
"constitution broke." In search of health, he came to California and launched the
Vagabond Book Shop, made from an REO Speed Wagon. Inside was a writing desk,
a dinner table, a medicine cabinet, and a small bed that pulled down from the wall. He
had space for over one thousand books, ranging from popular novels to rare volumes.

engine, the Frigate Bookshop, in St. Petersburg, Florida. Margaret
Follen and Barbara Nolen Strong, then recent Radcliffe graduates,
drove the Radcliffe Rambler. Madelaine Mendelsohn, a onetime Marshall Field & Company bookseller, also went with the obvious choice:
Parnassus on Wheels.

The year after Shay gave up traveling bookselling, he was already
feeling nostalgic and took the reins of Boyd's traveling shop for a
few days. That was enough. He would, though, spend the rest of his life
with books. Within a few years, he closed his New York bookstore. As
Morley recalled, the shop was of a moment: "It was too personal, too
enchanting, too Bohemian a bookshop to survive indefinitely." Shay's
summer experience in New England was a determinative one. He

found Provincetown's charm alluring and decamped there permanently. For a while, he ran a bookstore, this one without wheels.

Most of the other traveling bookstores came to a halt, too. The 1920s heyday of the roving bookstore, provoked by *Parnassus on Wheels*, faded during the Depression, which reduced traffic at summer resorts and the enthusiasm needed to embark on such an endeavor.

The peripatetic bookstore never disappeared entirely. There was a 1938 "labor" bookmobile that distributed progressive works to miners in West Virginia. A paperback bookseller on wheels motored around 1960s Long Island. And there are still mobile book vans that pull up to Saturday farmers' markets. Like twenty-first-century food trucks, bookmobiles are sometimes springboards to brick-and-mortar operations.

B y the time Morley's sequel to *Parnassus on Wheels*, *The Haunted Bookshop*, begins, McGill and Mifflin have retired from the road. They own a brick-and-mortar bookstore in Brooklyn, Parnassus at Home. Mifflin is still working on that book of his. Despite the successful New York shop, Mifflin's "dearest dreams" are of his vagabond days. In fact, the last we hear of the ambitious little man is a thrilling thought: a fleet of Parnassuses!

The Artist + the Suffragette

⚜

Morley's *Parnassus on Wheels* not only charmed readers and spurred traveling booksellers but also sparked a conversation about the role of women in the book trade. So did Madge Jenison. "I advise every woman in the world to sell books," she cheered. "All the leagues of nations and peace parties and disarmament conferences are nothing compared to the right kind of small bookshops selling important books." The Sunwise Turn, which she and Mary Mowbray-Clarke opened on East Thirty-First Street in Manhattan in 1916, was going to be that kind of bookshop.

It certainly was unusual. They spent more than $500 alone on fabric, covering the sofa in purple and the chairs in orange. The walls were painted a burnt orange. They put out boxes of actual oranges on the center table, the one that featured women-authored books. There were sculptures and paintings, including one over the fireplace of a "Japanese lady throwing her dinner into the river." The place was intended to look like the antithesis of "the denaturalized warehouse rooms in which men do business." Buying was intended to be an experience. Jenison said they "tried to make the shop a cult."

The flourishes were surely the work of Mowbray-Clarke, a bookseller who identified as a "cubist, a futurist, an impressionist, all rolled into one." For her, the bookstore itself was a statement piece, a work of modern art that would move people, move them toward the right kinds of books, the right kinds of art, and the right kinds of conversation.

Jenison did not regard the bookshop as a capitalist enterprise. "In a bookshop you drink democracy," she gushed. "People not selected by your own personality come into a shop—all sorts." Many of those customers were women, who not only bought books but also volunteered to sweep the floor, wrap packages, lend a car to deliver books for Christmas, or assist with whatever else was needed to support a women-owned business. Meanwhile, many male customers dismissed them—and the idea that women could be serious readers. Then there were the landlords. They "treated us as if we were sweet puppies."

In the fall of 1917, Jenison joined twenty thousand others in a Fifth Avenue protest for women's suffrage. She marched with a small battalion of women booksellers. The contingent was small, in part because there weren't many of them and in part because they weren't well connected. Membership in the American Booksellers Association was all male—most with mustaches.

Here was the inspiration for the Women's National Book Association, which held some of its first meetings at the Sunwise Turn. The organization offered bookselling education courses and networks of support for women authors, editors, and booksellers. It's still going strong.

In 1920, the Nineteenth Amendment was ratified, prohibiting states from denying the right to vote "on account of sex." It was also the year that Jenison became a "third vice president" of the ABA. She left the bookstore shortly thereafter. Mowbray-Clarke stayed longer—long enough to grow resentful. "Do we make any money?" she asked. "No, we do not." She called out booksellers as generally badly dressed, "timid, ineffectual, inarticulate people Babbitting about the splendid conditions in the trade." Those who romanticized bookshops were fools, "people like Mr. Morley . . . who write delectable moonshine about dream shops into which the shadow of the credit man never enters." In 1927, the shop closed for good.

4.

MARSHALL FIELD
& COMPANY

I n 1925, Chicago had 164 bookstores. Brentano's on Wabash Avenue. Kroch's on North Michigan. The Radical Book Shop on North Clark Street. An occult bookshop on Ingleside Avenue. And a bookstore we might not think of as a bookstore at all. To get there, buyers found the giant building's Washington Street entrance, walked through a door opened by Charley doffing his cap, rode the elevator to the third floor, and walked along the red carpet past the section of rugs and over by the candy. Here was the Marshall Field & Company book department.

A line of tables stretched down the center aisle, one of many in the gigantic sea of books, each with tidy displays of staples—dictionaries and encyclopedias on the first table, atlases on the second, travel books on the third, nature books on the west half of the fourth, with Shakespeare on the east, and gift books on the fifth. Collectible sets of authors found on English lit syllabi huddled near the back. Poetry, art books, illustrated classics, pocket-size volumes, and all things Louisa May Alcott lined the perimeter. Rare books, fine bindings, and a couple of sofas sat to the right. There were sections for magazines, religious texts, translations, biographies, cookbooks, girls' books, boys' books, and picture books. There was a counter for wrapping, a counter where shoppers could ask questions about fiction, and a counter devoted to any questions at all.

Men (in hats), women (in hats), and children (sometimes in hats) browsed. The salesclerks—mostly women in high-collared dresses—waited on them. They didn't dress nearly as stylishly as the shoppers, didn't wear jewelry, and didn't bob their hair. (The employee manual permitted only a "businesslike arrangement of the hair.") Most importantly, they never wore hats. Hatlessness was how you knew who was working. The male salesclerks basically wore whatever they wanted.

Chicagoans called the store Field's. Many referred to the book section as Marcella Hahner's Bookstore. Marcella Burns Hahner was the buyer, manager, and face of the book department for twenty-seven years, becoming "the most conspicuous single figure in American bookselling." Others called her "the Czarina." Bennett Cerf, cofounder of Random House, called Hahner a "despotic lady" who made "mighty publishers in Manhattan tremble when [she] stamped her little foot (and tore up orders)." He meant it as a compliment.

When the Czarina yelled, she stood on her tiptoes. Even then, she barely reached five feet tall. The Czarina was also known for inviting frustrated staff (to whom she was fiercely loyal) and executives from the ninth floor (to whom she was fiercely territorial) to take a seat in one of the handful of armchairs in her office on the edge of the book section.

Americans still buy a large percentage of books outside traditional bookstores. The same was true a century ago, when readers patronized drugstores, cigar shops, newsstands, gift shops, and department stores. Typically the publishers' largest account, Field's ordered books by the thousands. As an English essayist touring America in 1920 put it, the Marshall Field & Company book department "is to ordinary English bookshops like a liner to a houseboat." The book section was said to be the largest bookstore in the world.

Its size didn't diminish its reputation. It felt like a standalone shop. It dealt in bestsellers and fine bindings and was known more for service than for discounts. Hahner was a bookseller's bookseller, lauded as a tastemaker for her personal touch and her "highly intelligent staff of booklovers."

Marshall Field's represents a critical moment in American bookselling history. For while department stores and their book sections would eventually fall out of favor, the book business—especially the biggest publishers, the biggest booksellers, the biggest authors—kept on biggering. In essence, Field's was the first book superstore.

Generally considered the first American department store, A. T. Stewart's New Store opened in Manhattan in the 1860s. It sold a small number of books. By the end of the decade, so did Macy's, eventually carving out a separate book section. Wanamaker's in Philadelphia soon followed. It wasn't until the 1890s, however—the era of mass industrialization, capitalism, corporatization, and consumerism—that department stores truly came of age. They offered an ever-expanding range of goods, no expectation of haggling, free browsing, and, through elaborate advertising and window displays, ill-begotten fantasies of achieving happiness through consumption.

Chicago's population increased ten times over between 1860 and 1890. Fueled by immigration, railroads, and access to the heartland, Chicago ascended to the role of financial capital of the "West" and became the nation's second-largest city. The first bookstore appeared in 1844. Fifteen years later, a clerk named A. C. McClurg started working there and later bought the firm, transforming it into a leading wholesaler, publisher, and retailer. It was the anchor of a stretch of State Street known as Booksellers' Row, much of it destroyed in the Great Fire of 1871. McClurg's subsequently returned to the Row, a second home for the city's literati. The rare-book section was nicknamed the Saints and Sinners' Corner. Brentano's eventually bought it.

Field's came late to bookselling. In 1903, an assistant advised Marshall Field himself that he ought to get into the business, but Field wasn't interested: "Let Col. McClurg sell the books; we're in the dry-goods business." The department stores selling books were engaged in a price war. Publishers and booksellers largely deplored the practice of discounting, which they feared would lead to endless price cuts. When the publishers threatened to cut off any store engaged in the practice, most backed down. Not Macy's, which filed suit and which many assumed had been losing money on books to drive traffic to other sections with higher margins. With the case hanging in the balance and the store alienated from publishers, Macy's book buyers employed extraordinary means to acquire stock, creating imaginary bookshops as a front. In 1913, the US Supreme Court decided in Macy's favor. The court ruled that even if publishers controlled the copyrights, they couldn't dictate the retail prices.

After Marshall Field died, a new store president, James Simpson, rebooted the idea of a book department. He immediately thought of the clerk from McClurg's, the one with bright blue eyes, Gateway Arch-ish brows, and hair that fell to midear—the one so proficient in selling him fiction.

Marcella Burns (later Hahner) was born in small-town Michigan in

1880, orphaned, and raised by an aunt and uncle in a "house full of *Atlantic Monthly*" (though she preferred Dickens). She worked variously as a librarian, a printer, and a clerk in the book departments of several Midwestern stores before landing at McClurg's. Her first task at Field's was overseeing the build-out of the new book section. It was on the third floor, near a women's waiting room and the candy— regular stops for mothers towing children. Part of Hahner's job "was to take a body of women, potential readers, and lead them by easy steps into the realm of good books." It wasn't just women who were targeted. It was casual readers in general, the kinds of people who might not have gone out of their way to visit a bookstore.

By 1914, Field's had grown from a local business birthed in the mid-nineteenth century to a leading retailer with the largest store in the country. It occupied a thirteen-story granite building that spanned an entire downtown block, just a few blocks south of the Chicago River and a short walk west from Lake Michigan. Whereas Washington, DC, as imagined by Thomas Jefferson, was a manifestation of the country's political character, Marshall Field's was a manifestation of American capitalism. A colorful Tiffany dome with 1.6 million shards of carefully pieced-together glass greeted visitors who gazed skyward in the atrium. (It's as beautiful as ever, but hardly anyone notices it anymore.) The interior was befitting of a Paris store. There were separate sections for jewelry, lace, linens, umbrellas, furniture, pottery, hats, gowns, perfumes, shoes, and glassware. The building had its own post office, ticket counter, reading room, writing room, rocking chair–filled "silence room," 68 elevators, 127,000 feet of pneumatic tubing, thousands of employees, and 700 horses standing by for delivery. In all, the retail square footage measured sixty-seven acres.

For the most part, books were still expensive and associated with the well educated and the upper classes. In their 1920s study of "Middletown" (Muncie, Indiana), sociologists found that 76 percent of working-class families purchased no books apart from those required for school. And when they did, they bought just a book or two, usually a picture book or Christmas gift. Regular book buyers were the ideal department store consumers. Even with smaller margins and even if some lost money on books, department stores attracted a "good class of shoppers." Most of those shoppers were women, who effectively reshaped the landscape of downtown, an area previously deemed off limits to unchaperoned white women of privilege. Downtown was evolving into "a place where respectable women could publicly indulge their desires," argued historian Emily Remus. Field's had ladies-only tearooms, restaurants, and lounges. It soon added a separate store for men across the street with a "Men's Grill," the 1910 version of a man cave.

While other stores desperately tried to win over the "carriage trade," Field's was succeeding. Still, it was a de facto public space where anyone could browse or gaze at the Tiffany dome. Yet not everyone was welcome. In 1916, *The Chicago Defender*, a leading Black newspaper, sent in a pair of women who posed as customers. A clerk encouraged the darker skinned of the two to shop in the basement, where the bargain items were located. *The Defender* alleged that there was an official store policy directing staff to show Black shoppers to the basement or ignore them altogether. Among its own staff, until the 1950s, Field's management expressed reluctance at the idea of adding "Negroes to our retail store." Those workers who were Black had to remain largely out of sight. Field's unofficial tagline was "Give the lady what she wants." The reality was "Give the *white* lady what she wants."

O n the third floor, over on the Wabash Avenue side of the building, carpenters outfitted the book section. It was so big that you could barely see from one end to the other. Hahner watched over their progress, complaining about their lack of craftmanship to anyone who would listen, including the carpenters themselves. The "bunch of loafers," as she called them, walked out in protest.

Hahner was already an experienced bookseller with steadfast design principles. "Books are not just merchandise like shirts and shoestrings," she wrote. She wanted to encourage people to encounter new books, to be able to touch them, which is why she opted for fewer shelves and more tables, which "tempt the transient customer." She figured that the hardcore readers would find whatever they came looking for, so the poetry and technical books could be arranged on shelves. If they couldn't find what they wanted, they could certainly find the information booth, which was stocked with book industry journals and magazines, circulars from publishers, telephones, and a vase of fresh-cut flowers. Hahner loved violets and would slip a few into her belt, likely arranging them as she did her books, "very carefully and very logically."

In some ways, bookstores and department stores had seemingly opposite goals. The former had a reputation for being literary, social, and sometimes stuffy spaces with a muted profit motive. Department stores, however, were all about scale, selling anything and everything under one roof and leveraging buying power to reduce costs and increase margins. Hahner's sales strategy centered on service. "Every man and woman on the staff must know as much about the books we buy as I do," Hahner said, insisting over the objection of executives

The book department of Marshall Field & Company, circa 1920.

that they be allowed to take books home at night. It wasn't enough to say something smart about the book a customer had already chosen. They needed to be able to hand them (even the customer aimlessly wandering over from the furs) three or four additional books, the "plus sale."

Although Hahner usually left the handselling to others ("unless the customer is a good-looking man," one colleague teased), she demonstrated the proper technique when necessary. "I don't believe anyone's taken care of you," she'd say. "May I?" she continued, playing to their ego, complimenting their taste, telling them some personal story about an author, and then putting her arms through theirs while bounding toward the "secret" gems. They'd leave with six books. On rainy days, the salesclerks worked the phones, calling regulars with unsolicited recommendations. The books were sent over immediately—thanks to those seven hundred horses.

The department was an instant success. In 1915, its first full year, it grossed $235,000, or more than ten times what a typical bookshop pulled in. The book world took notice. Hahner blurbed books in national media advertisements. In a 1915 endorsement, she wrote, "Being a woman, I thoroughly enjoyed Mr. Locke's big, lovable 'Jaffery.'" Being a woman, she was very much a minority in a field still dominated by men, but one in which women booksellers were becoming more visible, particularly in department stores, where buyers and sellers skewed female. She called bookselling "the rightful avocation of women."

At the 1916 convention of the American Booksellers Association in Chicago, Hahner and booksellers from across the country dined on canapés, spring lamb, petit pois à la française, and mint sorbet as they listened to industry news and a lecture on the role of women. The speaker professed that bookselling required a perfect cocktail: one part pleasant personality, one part proper psychology, and one part intuition—traits, supposedly, natural to women. It was also well understood that bookselling and motherhood didn't mix. When Marcella Burns married a few years later, becoming Marcella Burns Hahner, the assumption was that she would retire. She did not.

Hahner did leave the job temporarily in 1917, during the First World War, when she shipped out to Paris for an eleven-month tour with the Red Cross. The wounded soldiers appreciated her wit—and that she came bearing doughnuts. What struck her most was how much reading meant to "those boys, wounded, sick, almost helpless, yet contriving to turn the pages of a book of O. Henry stories."

After returning to Chicago, Hahner toured an automobile show at the Coliseum. She looked around and thought, *Books are far more interesting than cars. Why not a book fair?* By this point, ninth-floor executives knew well enough to trust Hahner's instincts. And so they authorized $10,000 for a five-day book festival in October of 1919. The store paid for the advertising and to construct forty-six eight-foot-high publishers' booths that lined the book section. Each had a table, a piano lamp, and fresh flowers. While publishers were traditionally competitors and expressed doubt about such cooperation, antagonism gave way to pragmatism. Doubleday exhibited its fall titles and manuscripts from Kipling. Harper had Mark Twain originals, and Little, Brown and Company curated a *Little Women* display, including Alcott's desk. Publishers brought along authors who signed books and chatted with readers. They quickly realized the value: "Authors were made more human."

By the time the fair ended, *Publishers Weekly* had heralded it as monumental. The next year's iteration drew one hundred thousand visitors and featured a handful of curated home libraries: the ideal collection for a doctor, an engineer, a music lover, a "working man" (mostly classics in order to educate himself), and a fashionable woman ("narrow, elegant booklets bound in bright colors or in soft leather, made for the hands of a lady"). There was also a "model bookshop" erected within the book department, itself a model. Similar fairs sprung up in other cities, including in London at Harrods.

Hahner and her staff loved to put on a show—and to move things around: "It has been an axiom of ours always to think of the books section as completely flexible." Tables were on casters. Stock was refreshed. And the constant shuffling had to seem as if it were being done "without any apparent work to get it so."

In 1922, a "Spirit of Spring" theme highlighted books on sports, flowers, vegetables, birds, and dogs. Except for the sizable pillars and globe lamps hanging down from the white ceiling, the book section resembled an outdoor garden. Along the main aisle, books circled hydrangea centerpieces like mulch. Taxidermy bird mounts stood atop hills of books. The following year, Hahner organized a books-made-into-films showcase. Films weren't just competition; they were an opportunity. The book section was transformed into a massive theater with a giant screen and curtain. Movie posters lined the perimeter. The suit of armor worn by Douglas Fairbanks in *Robin Hood* was on display, as was a papier-mâché sculpture fashioned after the lamppost from *Main Street*, adapted from Sinclair Lewis's novel. A friend of Hahner's, Lewis had sent her a "Christmas-Newyear-Easter-Yomkippur-Knightsofcolumbus card" and named a character in one of his 1919 short stories Marcella in her honor.

In the weeks before Christmas, the crowds on the third floor could hardly be contained. Across the country, December book sales were triple that of the average month. The book section employed one hundred seasonal clerks to handle the extra traffic. Gift wrapping was free—and known for being done fastidiously.

No matter the season, Field's hosted author talks and autograph parties, which Hahner made a bookstore staple. Carl Sandburg signed copies of his first Abraham Lincoln volume on the former president's birthday. Gertrude Stein refused to give a talk but did sign books. Admiral Byrd autographed copies of *Little America*. There were so many people in attendance (twenty-five hundred copies were sold) that Byrd asked if he could return "to the peace and comfort of the South Pole."

Once the authors' books had been signed and the customers ushered out, Hahner invited the litterateurs into her office for an intimate soiree. The special guest sat in the most distinguished chair, surrounded by a local writer or critic and a few of Hahner's choice colleagues. The tearoom sent down pastries. Hahner procured liquor (even during Prohibition), all of which was enjoyed as the cleaning crew put the book department to bed, tucking in tables of books with sheets to keep off the dust. The parties kept going at her Astor Street apartment, about a mile and a half away. Her home was filled with signed first editions (the publishers sent Christmas gifts) and dogs. Lots and lots of dogs.

Hahner's success afforded a great deal of power. She complained that the phonograph section was making a racket. And so the Victrolas went. So did the shoeshine stand when she protested the stink. The store president joked that he gave "the lady what she wants," so long as she was named Marcella Hahner. "The department is like an island," one of the salesclerks observed. "Nobody interferes with us."

At Field's, each section had its own budget, its own profit-and-loss statement, and its own buyer. In some ways, the book department operated like an independent bookstore. Yet it had the advantage of being part of an empire. Most small shops didn't have the space or revenues to attract world-famous writers or to carry such a wide range of titles. At Field's, almost every book had a place. There were ten-cent books and forty-dollar books. There was a library with six thousand titles, each rentable for three cents a day. "Just as many kinds of people live harmoniously together in a city, so many kinds of people can buy from a single store," Hahner averred.

When other bookshops delivered packages, a clerk (not a dedicated delivery team with horses and later motorcars) had to take time away from the floor to do so. And while small shops might have let trusted customers defer payment, Field's had 180,000 customers with charge accounts by the end of the 1920s. It also maintained a 100,000-person-plus mailing list. In 1929, these customers were sent a 105-page catalog targeting a range of readers—boys, girls, housewives, garden lovers, antique collectors, bridge players, musicians, travelers—with nearly every genre—biography, history, fiction, poetry, religion, cookbooks, comedy, classics, military, fine bindings, gift books, art, and design. That was in addition to a separate Christmas catalog and another 73-page one just for children. Boys were supposed to read *The Last of the Mohicans*, girls *Little Women*. Everyone was supposed to read *Cinderella*. Accompanying the catalogs and flyers were prepaid postcards. Customers checked off their desired titles. It was as easy as that.

Field's also employed professional display artists to create elaborate street-level spectacles in the windows (except on Sundays, when the windows were covered) and had an enormous marketing budget, taking out half-page ads in leading newspapers and issuing a free bimonthly magazine, *Fashions of the Hour*. A typical issue featured a piece like "Significant Hats for North and South" and a favorite, regular column on all the "Little Things Noticed on a Walk through the Store." A story about an art exhibition in Indiana was accompanied by a list of books (all available on the third floor) related to the Hoosier State. A plug for Field's travel bureau service was paired with a list of novels set in France, Italy, India, and Egypt. Because of Hahner's connections, famous writers regularly contributed. Emily Post wrote for it, as did Christopher Morley, whose 1926 contribution was a short story called "The Stupid Magician." In return, Hahner blurbed one of Morley's books: it should be "sold to all nice children up to sixty."

Her endorsement was ever more valuable. A 1921 ad in *The New*

York Times boasted that one novel "tremendously pleases Marcella Burns Hahner, the head of Marshall Field's book department and one of the keenest judges of books in the country." Writers desperate for book contracts pleaded for assistance. One claimed that the publishers would go ahead "if and when Mrs. Hahner tells them to." Another asked her to clear up a problem he was having with his publisher, who insisted on a title page he found objectionable. He did recognize that the favor could be read as "presumptuous, but that is the penalty of occupying the position that you do in the book trade."

When she thought a book would sell that didn't yet exist, she saw to it that it be written. She convinced one friend to write travel guides, and in 1928, with the help of an editor, she wrote a book of her own, *100 Riddles and 101 Things to Do*. The next year she wrote *100 Points in Etiquette and 101 Don'ts*.

The book department sometimes acted as publisher. Its works included a short Christopher Morley book, *A Letter to Leonora*, adapted from a 1711 *Spectator* essay in which Joseph Addison judged a woman ("Leonora") by her bookshelf. Printed on handmade English paper, it was an homage to bookstores and booksellers. "Did it ever occur to you how complex the bookseller's task is? . . . He must be able to serve, on demand, not only the cocktail of the moment but also the scarcest of old vintages." Morley urged readers "to be a little more of an explorer. . . . The most important books are shy." If readers did so, they would come to fully appreciate bookstores, "places of magic." For his work, Field's paid him $300. He used it to buy a Ford.

Hahner's power and influence made for an unusual relationship with publishers. In short, they needed her. When Richard L. Simon reminisced about starting Simon & Schuster, he recalled collaborating with Hahner. Simon sold sugar and pianos before venturing into publishing by way of a book of crosswords. It was a risky proposition. While puzzles were popular, there were no puzzle books. Hahner promised to order a thousand. "I wasn't really convinced we had something really big until Marcella gave me that order," Simon recalled. A purchase from her "was something like an award of the Congressional Medal of Honor."

Alfred A. Knopf thought the same. Even after he relegated most of the selling to others, he held on to a few of his choice accounts. He'd arrive in Chicago by way of the Twentieth Century Limited and leave with an order for twenty-five hundred copies of the newest Cather novel. Hahner, he credited, "turned the department at Marshall Field in Chicago, which—and this was rather radical—was not on the ground floor, into one of the great bookstores in the country." Indeed, as *The Successful Bookshop*, a pamphlet of tips for would-be booksellers noted, even serious book buyers didn't like hiking to the upper floors or traipsing through linens, blankets, and fancy goods.

Owners of smaller bookstores grew concerned about Field's power and criticized department stores generally for discounting and marketing books as commodities. At the same time, small shops kept tabs on what Field's was doing. When Hahner ordered one thousand copies of *Joy of Cooking*, she wasn't just guessing the market. She was making one. Which is why, when the annual convention of the American Booksellers Association returned in 1925, Hahner wasn't sitting in the audience spooning sorbet. Attendees registered for an afternoon tea with her and a tour of the most famous book department in the country. The following year, the ABA awarded her an honorary fellowship, recognizing her creation of "one of the great book outlets."

Hahner was proud. She and her staff—like those at other

bookstores—believed that their work had a higher purpose. It was about more than sales. "I guess the truth of it is we feel superior to the other people in the store."

D epartment store book sections were now all over the country. In Chicago alone, a dozen department store buyers, including at Montgomery Ward and Sears, tried to keep pace. By 1930, there were 375 book department sections in the United States among 4,053 book-selling outlets in total. General bookstores that sold books and little else numbered 1,557. Smaller outlets that sold some books but mostly other goods—drugstores and such—stood at 2,496. The National Association of Book Publishers categorized department stores as A-level outlets, alongside the leading stand-alone bookstores.

A-level stores clustered in cities and tended to be larger stores with greater revenues. In 1930, New York was home to about 10 percent of the American population, 14 percent of the country's A-level bookstores, and 31 percent of national book sales. Department stores more than carried their weight, pulling in roughly 29 percent of total sales nationally. Another estimate suggested that by the late 1930s, they accounted for roughly 40 percent of the trade, a figure that climbed until the midcentury.

At the same time, roughly 85 percent of American counties had not a single bookstore. Wyoming, South Dakota, New Mexico, and Idaho had no department store book sections and only twelve general bookstores combined. Bookshops congregated in the Northeast. Vermont, New Hampshire, Connecticut, Rhode Island, Maine, New York, Massachusetts, Delaware, and Montana, which had just two bookstores and scarcely any people, led the list of states with the most bookshops on a per capita basis. At the bottom were Louisiana, Mississippi, Alabama, Kentucky, and Oklahoma.

For rural Americans without a local bookstore, there were increasingly convenient ways to acquire books. A sprawling spring 1922 Sears catalog devoted four pages to book advertisements, classics and new, fiction and non, many affordable. Hawthorne's *The Scarlet Letter* was forty-nine cents, as was *Uncle Tom's Cabin*. Arthur Conan Doyle's *Hound of the Baskervilles* was fifty-eight cents.

More influential was the Book-of-the-Month Club, which began in 1926. The idea was to introduce books—supposedly good books—to the masses, including those who lived out of bookstore range. A panel of esteemed judges, Christopher Morley among them, selected a different title each month. By 1929, it had amassed 110,588 subscribers. Booksellers panicked. Some objected to the mass nature of the enterprise, the idea that a handful of men should determine what was essential reading for every American. They also worried it would put them out of business. Getting books in the mail was convenient. So was having an "expert" pick what you should read. Brentano's derided the book club for its "hand-me-down opinions." Even so, booksellers copied the idea. In 1928, the American Booksellers Association started its own book club, Bookselection. ABA member stores stocked and promoted the selected titles. The effort flopped, and within a year, the ABA moved on, adopting an official "anti-book-club resolution."

Field's also sought to capture the market beyond the urban core. Not only did it send its catalogs far and wide, but over the course of 1928 and 1929, it also opened branch stores in Chicago's suburbs: Lake Forest, Evanston, and Oak Park, Hemingway's hometown. Each spawned its own book sections.

At the home store, the book department continued to flex its muscles. When Hahner believed in a book, she went all in, sometimes even putting up fifteen-foot billboards to advertise it. Throughout the 1930s, she regularly teamed up with publishers, building room-size displays for an imprint. And she continued to rearrange. In 1934, she transformed the department into a dreamlike Paris, lining the aisles with Left Bankish wooden bookstalls.

As the Great Depression endured, the marketing efforts faced headwinds. Publishers experimented with new tactics. In 1936, the National Association of Book Publishers joined with *The New York Times* to sponsor a giant book fair at Rockefeller Center that, like Field's earlier versions, included exhibits, author meet and greets, and a model "modern" bookshop with five thousand titles. Visitors left with a souvenir, *Ex Libris*, a short anthology printed and bound on-site and compiled by Christopher Morley, who included bits and pieces about books and bookselling from Poe, Whitman, Chekhov, Pepys, Voltaire, and a Chicago printer announcing the birth of his daughter: "Good, clean copy. Weighs 7 lbs., 10 oz. First edition, privately issued. In two colors, white and pink."

After a decade of hard times, the publishing and bookselling world began to embrace paperbacks. In 1939, Pocket Books debuted its small, inexpensive editions of popular titles and became a major player in the emerging paperback revolution. Although it still proudly catered to the elite, Field's wasted no time entering the low-end market. The department sold 33,425 paperbacks in 1939 and credited the cheaper books with bringing in "new faces." (Marshall Field III, through Field Enterprises, later bought Simon & Schuster, along with Pocket Books.)

The introduction of paperbacks also marked the beginning of a new era. Hahner retired in February of 1941. She had started as the First World War began and retired as the second one raged. She left a book department doing a million dollars a year in sales. In September, she had a heart attack. The Czarina was dead.

R ose Oller Harbaugh had been Hahner's assistant from the beginning and one of the few choice guests at those after-hours author parties. Now she was the section's second-ever manager. Letters of congratulations poured in from editors, publishers, and authors, including Benjamin Holt Ticknor Jr., then Houghton Mifflin brass and a descendant of Tick from the Old Corner. Dorothy Parker wrote that she was glad the space, so "dear to my heart," remained in good hands. "I hope I'll never feel quite an outsider in it."

Harbaugh kept most practices in place. Put the books you really want to sell on the stand-alone tables and keep everything fresh, flexible, and within easy reach. She did, however, establish a separate bargain book section in the basement. While she was careful to point out that the basement bins would never carry the same stock found upstairs, the move marked part of the shift away from books as a luxury brand. In 1942, as the war strangled the book business—delayed shipments, publication dates pushed back, labor shortages—Harbaugh mailed out two hundred thousand coupons.

One memorable 1944 event was a signing featuring Judy, a three-thousand-pound elephant. Judy was there to celebrate a Rand McNally "slottie," a book that came with cardboard toys, in this case elephant puzzle pieces. The book department turned into a circus as Judy "signed" copies with a stamp dangling from her trunk. She did tricks, too. But when the party ended, she refused to head back down

The Christmas-season rush, circa 1946.

the freight elevator. The commotion proved so amusing that Harbaugh later wrote her own children's book about it. Naturally, she held a book-signing party at Field's. Judy was not invited.

Rose Oller Harbaugh retired in 1952. In her last full year as manager, the department did $1.5 million in business. At her farewell fete, a quintet played rose-themed songs. The emcee was publisher Bennett Cerf, who had signed off on his correspondence to her with "Love and Kisses." Even in a room full of successful booksellers, the subtext was that they were all in the wrong business. "The hell with dough," they teased.

Bob Bangs was the new manager of the department, now approaching its fiftieth year. The next fifty years were much rockier. The paperback section grew considerably and by 1960 occupied a vast chunk of the book department, now stretched across a cheaply tiled floor. Someone decided to wrap the grand columns in plastic. Perhaps the biggest change wasn't what was there but what wasn't: a sizable staff known for its good taste. The paperback section was "self-service."

Field's, like many retailers, began investing more heavily in the suburbs and faced competition from discount chains. Kmart, Target, and Walmart all started in 1962, all focused on the budget consumer. Even Bloomingdale's discounted its books, except for *Franny and Zooey* (J. D. Salinger was a customer).

Meanwhile, bookstore chains multiplied. By 1980, in and around Chicago, B. Dalton had eleven stores, Waldenbooks had twenty-three, and Kroch's & Brentano's had eighteen. The 1990s were the age of the suburban superstore, a concept that evolved from the giant department store book sections. Field's held on longer than most. In 2003, it invited Barbara's Bookstore, a longstanding indie, to open an outlet inside its centerpiece building.

After a dizzying series of corporate restructurings and sales, Marshall Field & Company became Macy's. The third-floor book department was no more.

B arbara's remains as a shop in the basement. When I visited, there was a life-size cutout of Barack Obama standing near the counter. On one wall was a canvas featuring Judy the elephant at her autograph party. The shop is well organized, outfitted with handsome shelves and sections full of new fiction and nonfiction, bestsellers, Chicago favorites, and cookbooks. There's even a kids' nook. But it's missing one thing: the Czarina.

The Architect

For every bookstore where the tables, shelves, and light seem to be arranged in just the right way, there's another where something seems amiss—too dark, too light, too few books, books arranged too perfectly, books arranged not perfectly enough. Even if we can't articulate exactly why, we recognize when a bookstore feels right. Design matters. Yet there's no single blueprint. Beautiful bookstores take many shapes. After all, Marshall Field's once had an enviable aesthetic.

Imagine if the world's greatest architects designed bookstores, not mansions and museums. Well, one of them did. His name was Frank Lloyd Wright.

Browne's Bookstore opened in 1907 on the seventh floor of Chicago's Fine Arts Building, an 1885 gem along Michigan Avenue, five and a half blocks south of Field's. Two glass doors flanked the counter, leading to the main area, which was already long and narrow before Wright chopped it up further into a series of rather dark alcoves, each rimmed with shoulder-height bookshelves and an oak table in the center. Around the rectangular table were incredibly tall (forty-seven inches) and incredibly uncomfortable-looking wooden chairs. The shop's own opening announcement acknowledged the "very unusual" furnishings. (Those Wright-designed pieces now fetch tens of thousands of dollars.) At the far end was a reading space with a brick fireplace and books in fine bindings. Despite afternoon tea and some classic Arts and Crafts details, it didn't look like a place anyone would want to relax (not in those supertall chairs anyway).

Publishers Weekly credited the owner and architect with having the "courage" to build a bookstore "in the air." Booksellers almost always insisted on being on the ground floor. Trade publications warned against it, too (as well as against having too many columns or too few ashtrays). For good reason, it seems. In less than three years, Browne's Bookstore relocated to the ground floor.

In front of the Fine Arts Building, I saw a sign out front for Exile in Bookville. It encouraged visitors to head to the second floor. Up the snaking marble steps was a spectacular light-filled space with a giant orb dangling from the high ceiling. A line of books sat atop the radiator. One of the owners sat behind the counter. I asked him what it was like to have a bookstore on the second floor. He said it was ideal. Confused, I asked him to explain. Since it required a bit of effort to get to, the shop attracted customers who *really* loved books and *really* wanted to be there. The stunning views of the park were a bonus.

5.

THE GOTHAM BOOK MART

F rances Steloff sat at her alcove desk at the back of the shop. Customers coming to look for her—and they always did— might trip over one of the too many tables topped by too many books or one of the cats named after novelists. Even if they made it past furry Thornton (Wilder) and the oversize table up front covered with "little magazines," and then through the maze of rare and first editions sprawling up, down, and across the shelves, and past the exper-imental literature section with towers of books on the floor, walking by paintings, drawings, and photographs of Joyce, Pound, Woolf, and O'Neill that hung crooked on the wall, and past the books on cinema, and the section devoted to theater, and—Steloff's personal favorite— the room stuffed with religion and philosophy, they might still have trouble spotting her, a slight woman with steely blue eyes and wispy gray hair, sitting amid a jungle of notes, files, envelopes, letters, mail-ing lists, paper clips, receipts, bank statements, catalogs, rubber bands, galleys, and cups of cantaloupe. (She loved fruit.) But if they did man-age to find her, she, in turn, would find them just the right book.

Frances Steloff *was* the Gotham Book Mart. The Gotham Book

Mart *was* Frances Steloff. She, along with the writers and readers who congregated there, turned Gotham into a powerhouse. According to the editors of one academic journal without a habit of exaggeration, "No other American bookstore has done more to encourage experimentation in modern literature." Even as the shop became one of the most famous, the Gotham Book Mart remained "one of the last bookstores," Norman Mailer wrote, "where you can pick up literature, not commerce."

It was also a home, literally. Steloff lived in a third-floor apartment above the shop, often slept outside on the balcony, and came bouncing down the stairs with a pencil tucked somewhere in her hair, which she never seemed to fuss over. But it was more than a home and more than a bookshop. It was a museum, art gallery, therapist's couch, disheveled English professor's office, grandmother's living room, and Parisian café, all wrapped in one.

I da Frances Steloff, known as Fanny and, for most of her professional life, as Miss Steloff, was born on the last day of 1887 to Russian-born, Yiddish-speaking parents in Saratoga Springs, New York. Her formal schooling was brief, and as a young girl, she began a career in sales, hawking flowers to wealthy tourists at the area's hotels and racetrack. Her father, Simon, was an unsuccessful peddler, cattleman (once sued for letting his cows run wild through the streets), and lover of books. Simon, though, only read to his boy. He thought the girls unworthy.

Steloff's mother died when she was three, and an ill-tempered stepmother raised her, eventually driving twelve-year-old Frances out of the house. A wealthy couple from Boston offered to take her in, and neither her father nor stepmother seemed to care. At the first family dinner in Massachusetts, her new guardians served bloody roast beef.

Steloff was a vegetarian. Bored, unhappy, tired of doing chores, and unwilling to eat meat, the teenage Steloff soon ran off, this time to New York.

She found work sewing corsets at Loeser's, a sprawling Brooklyn department store. Needing extra help before Christmas, her boss moved her over to the gift books. After the holidays ended, she begged to stay and was offered a concession: the magazine section. She was thrilled until she realized that she was underpaid (seven bucks a week), and when she got an offer from an up-and-coming bookseller named Theodore Schulte, she took it. Schulte was on his way to becoming a giant of Book Row, and Steloff served as his apprentice, immersing herself in the secondhand trade. "From then on," she recalled, "I knew my work would be with books."

Throughout her twenties, she moved from one bookshop to another. In the book department on the third floor of Kann's, a department store based in Washington, DC, she learned the business of selling discounted bestsellers and discovered that she hated being on the third floor and that department stores didn't feel like real bookshops. (This was before Marcella Hahner's book section at Field's.)

She moved again, this time to McDevitt-Wilson's in New York, where she gained experience working in a small shop with big competition. Then she worked for the big competition, Brentano's. At its Fifth Avenue location, Steloff oversaw cookbooks and knew she wanted nothing to do with them. (Gotham would never sell any.) During lunch, she continued her education, hunting for deals at the secondhand shops down on Fourth Avenue.

In December of 1919, Steloff, then thirty-one, spotted an empty, nearly street-level retail space ("three steps down and duck your head") for rent. She couldn't help but dream. Dodging the cars that hadn't yet overwhelmed the chilly street, she hurried over to the Hotel Astor to see her sister, a cashier. Steloff asked if she should open a bookshop of her own. Her sister said no. Then she asked David Moss, one of her Brentano's coworkers. He, too, said no.

The truth was, she didn't need other people's approval. And so, with one hundred dollars of her own money, a one-hundred-dollar Liberty bond, and a small collection of out-of-print books, she figured she was as ready as ever. On New Year's Day, 1920, after a relatively quiet night in the city, as Prohibition was phased in and as Steloff celebrated her birthday, she and some friends piled her books, her furniture, and a typewriter into a wagon. A horse carried it all from her Sixteenth Street apartment to West Forty-Fifth Street, where awaited her very own bookstore.

The Gotham Art and Book Mart was tiny, which turned out to be a good thing, since Steloff had only enough books to fill half of the two bookcases flanking the fireplace on the far wall—and that was with all the books facing out. She added some knickknacks to the mantel and hung some of her own art on the wall. She wanted the place to feel like a home and rented an apartment upstairs. A half block from Broadway, the bookshop initially catered to actors, set designers, makeup artists, and directors. Booksellers tried to warn her that "actors don't read," and after a few months, she was beginning to suspect they were right. Gradually, though, customers appeared, usually in the evenings after the shows, and mostly to socialize. Steloff decided to keep the shop open until midnight. Her *shop* was already a place for creatives to talk about creating. She, too, hated it when people called Gotham a *store*.

As Gotham approached its third year, Steloff's landlord gave notice: she had to vacate. "I was about to give up," she said, but "my love for books kept me going." In 1923, there was good reason to feel optimistic. The economy was robust. Babe Ruth's New York Yankees had just won the World Series. And Steloff found a new location just a couple of blocks away on West Forty-Seventh Street. Plus, there was a vacant apartment above the shop; she wouldn't have it any other way. The new street, lined with small houses that had front lawns, wasn't exactly bustling.

There, Gotham bloomed. The shop officially dropped the word *Art* from its name. Now the Gotham Book Mart, it had a sign out front with its motto: "WISE MEN FISH HERE." Above was an image of three men standing in a boat, reeling in their big catch.

The space was larger and had room for more poetry and experimental fiction, grouped together in a new section dubbed "Modern." Steloff understood that the young avant-garde writers, those who tired of "stodgy bourgeois art, its sexual prudery and smothering patriarchal families, its crass moneymaking and deadly class exploitation" and embraced a new form of literature flourishing overseas and down in Greenwich Village, preferred to be separated.

As most publishers weren't interested in the experimental, Gotham helped fill the void. In the 1920s, it waded into publishing with 1,350 copies of *Anathema!: Litanies of Negation*, a short collection of essays by Benjamin De Casseres. It featured a foreword by Eugene O'Neill, who called De Casseres "too abstract" for the mainstream. Gotham leaned into the abstract.

The real gem of the shop was out back. Knowing that her customers, in an age without air-conditioning, appreciated being outdoors, "where they could open their collars, smoke, chew, and relax"—Steloff never

smoked, chewed, or relaxed—she transformed an empty and dispirit-
ing backyard into a garden oasis with bushes, flowers, and a lilac
tree named Walt Whitman. It also served as an extension of the shop,
with books piled on green bookstalls, like those of the Parisian
bouquinistes.

Steloff had experienced the wonder of French book buying firsthand on her recent honeymoon. In June of 1923, she had married David Moss, her onetime Brentano's colleague. He had since moved to
Gotham, partnering in the bookshop as well. Though Steloff later admitted that she was never in love and never "felt like a Mrs.," she married the Jewish vegetarian anyway. The first place she visited in Paris
was Shakespeare and Company, the famed bookstore run by Sylvia
Beach. A lifelong friendship between two of the most important booksellers in the Atlantic world commenced.

"The real book-hunting season in New York begins when Miss
Steloff opens her garden," wrote Christopher Morley. "There, suddenly, as a poem or an essay opens itself to the mind, the Gotham
Book Mart opens into its backyard cloister of curiosity." Morley
bought books from the shop, wrote catalog copy for Steloff, and composed poems for overdue account notices. ("Oh Bibliophile, if thou
canst not aspire / To pay this overdue account entire / Then break it
into little bits, and send / At least some portion, for my need is dire.")
Morley loved the garden—so much so that he helped make it a main-
stay of New York's literary world. Encouraged by Steloff, he brought
friends, tequila, and cream-cheese-and-jelly sandwiches to the iron
table under the parasol. In May and timed to Morley's birthday, Steloff
threw an annual bash, celebrating the start of Gotham's garden season. The festivities began with the ceremonial "putting of the umbrella."

Browsing the outdoor bookstalls at the Gotham Book Mart.

Whether to the backyard or front room, the shop attracted artsy customers, including Charlie Chaplin, Rudolph Valentino, and Martha Graham. Graham, grateful to Steloff for lending her expensive art books, occasionally worked in the shop, including one unsuccessful stint behind the cash register and many hours wrapping books. (They didn't put books in bags back then.) In 1928, when the dancer wanted to rent out a Broadway theater for her debut, Steloff personally signed off on a $1,000 loan to make it happen.

While business was fine, Steloff was not. Her marriage, which had been doomed from the start, ended in 1930. After all, it was Moss who had advised her not to open her own bookshop. Steloff was miserable and willing to leave it all behind, but when the lawyers finished negotiating, the shop was hers and hers alone.

Even without a husband, she continued to operate in a largely male world. While women read more than men and more commonly worked in libraries and department stores, they were much less likely to own bookstores. Steloff went out of her way to promote women writers, devoting a large portion of the front window to them.

Whether men or women, booksellers faced tremendous hardship as the boom times of the 1920s (with book sales increasing 10 percent a year) crashed to a halt during the Depression. Gotham's bread and butter—expensive art books and first editions—were hit especially hard. By 1935, Steloff had just thirty-six dollars in the bank. Days went by without a single sale.

Writers struggled more than usual. Sometimes they even needed something to eat. In response, Steloff created the Writers' Emergency Fund, allocating money ("no strings attached") to promising young authors. The fund was short lived; it turned out that the number of writers who needed money was far greater than the number of writers who could donate.

One recipient was Henry Miller, a frequent beneficiary of Steloff's generosity. He once asked her to permit "a most enchanting and gracious Greek woman" to come by the shop, grab a few books, and charge it to his already past-due account. On another occasion, he asked Steloff to telephone a woman to tell her that he'd left magazines for her at Gotham—and that he was thinking about her. But, he insisted, "don't leave this message with any one! Her husband, I understand, is very jealous." And when Miller asked Steloff to help him acquire "a couple of thermos bottles and a little cart," adding that he "could also use a hatchet, or a light axe," Steloff put up a notice in the store with a bucket beneath it for donations. Miller was so appreciative that he told Steloff he wanted her to be his daughter's godmother, though he later decided it would only add to her "worries."

Miller also asked Steloff to test the limits of the law. In 1939, in Paris, he offered Steloff twenty first editions of *Tropic of Cancer* and fifteen of *Black Spring*. After he negotiated a sale price of $200 for the whole lot, the transaction ran aground. Since the US government had banned both books on account of their lewd nature (some called them pornographic), Steloff suggested they skirt the censors by employing a French middleman. Instead, Miller sent them directly to Gotham, only to have customs intercept the cargo. Steloff managed to get the books rerouted to Mexico, where friends happened to be vacationing, and had them smuggle the contraband to Gotham.

When a young man came asking for a copy of *Tropic of Cancer*, Steloff asked why he wanted it. The customer said he was writing a term paper on Miller. Satisfied, Steloff took a copy from beneath the counter and gave the college student, as he later put it, "his passport into the underground." Barney Rosset Jr. would go on to start his own publishing house, Grove Press, which would distribute *Tropic of Cancer*, D. H. Lawrence's *Lady Chatterley's Lover*, and other controversial works. At the time, Gotham was one of the few places where anyone could find Miller's works—so long as you gave Steloff a good reason for wanting them.

By then, Gotham was used to trouble. In the summer of 1928, John Sumner of the New York Society for the Suppression of Vice had raided the shop, seizing hundreds of books. He charged Gotham with violating decency laws, highlighting six offending titles, including James Joyce's *Ulysses*. Moss, at the time still Steloff's husband and co-owner, didn't want to fight the charges. They paid the $250 fine.

After Moss left in 1930, Sumner got his hands on a Gotham Book

Mart catalog and brought another case against Steloff, this time centered on two books: *Chin P'ing Mei: The Adventurous History of Hsi Men and His Six Wives* and *From a Turkish Harim*. Steloff refused to plead guilty. In the end, a judge found the books innocent enough. She then set to work on a new booklist, promoting the very works Sumner had wanted to ban. The following year's catalog featured an entire category of works with "sexual inversion."

Sumner wasn't finished. On December 5, 1935, a man bought a copy of André Gide's autobiography, *If It Die . . .*, at Gotham. Two days later, Steloff was arrested and charged with violating section 1141 of the Penal Laws of New York, which forbade the dissemination of any "obscene, lewd, lascivious, filthy, indecent, or disgusting book." Random House, the publisher of the book, came to Steloff's defense and sent over a lawyer. Though the book contained passages related to Gide's homosexuality, which, the judge claimed, were "undoubtedly vulgar and indecent," he ruled that "books, like friends, must be chosen by the readers themselves." Since the book wasn't "dirt for dirt's sake," Steloff was exonerated. (Gide would go on to win the Nobel Prize in Literature.)

Having twice sparred with, and having twice lost to, Steloff, Sumner might have been expected to cease and desist. Instead, he returned in 1945, this time to complain about a window display. It was the work of André Breton and Marcel Duchamp, who had designed the showcase to celebrate Breton's book *Arcane 17*. The display's most prominent piece was a headless mannequin in a slender apron. The figure had a spigot jutting out of her right thigh. To Steloff's surprise, it wasn't the scantily clad faucet girl that bothered Sumner but, rather, the background poster by Roberto Matta that featured a bare breast. Steloff later covered the breast with a bib that read: "CENSORED."

Steloff was willing to stand up to the censors because she believed

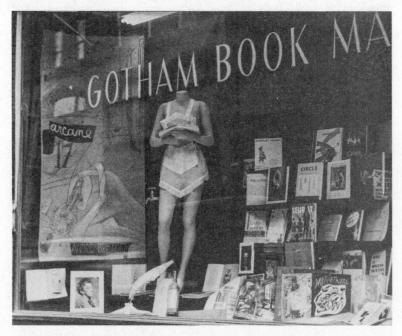

Marcel Duchamp and André Breton's window display at
the Gotham Book Mart in 1945. It was called "Lazy Hardware."

in the profound power of literature, creativity, and freedom of expression. Unlike other booksellers, she never aspired to write the Great American Novel. She was content to remain merely a fan. She thought writers were "the most wonderful people in the world" and vowed to nurture them. When an editor from Viking walked in, Steloff talked up a roster of emerging talent. When Richard L. Simon of Simon & Schuster visited, Steloff sent him home with a manuscript. Writers sought her advice about everything, including cover design (never black, she advised). Gotham was a de facto literary agency and Steloff the powerhouse agent. She wrote to executives telling them what, when, and how to publish. She grumbled to Random House's Bennett Cerf that he was too slow-footed in putting out a reprint of Faulkner's

Absalom, Absalom! "I never could understand why publishers behave the way they do, but you used to be different," she admonished. "I wish I had the time to make up a list of the Sins of publishers." She closed the letter "Love as usual."

Steloff's love for writers wasn't unrequited. They appreciated what she was doing. When Conrad Aiken wanted to fill his Savannah home with Chekhov, Tolstoy, Dostoevsky, Dickens, Kipling, and Trollope, he bought from Gotham. E. E. Cummings ordered a collection of Rilke to be sent to him in Massachusetts. H. L. Mencken bought regularly, even when in Baltimore. (Mencken visited in person when he could, including one time when he and Theodore Dreiser, both looking "as if they had had extra beers," autographed a copy of the Bible and inscribed it "Best wishes from the author.")

Celebrities weren't the only customers ordering books by mail. In fact, mail order comprised a significant—on some days, a majority—portion of Gotham's revenues. The art and theater books, the rare volumes and literary unknowns that Steloff specialized in, were hard to find in New York, let alone in Wichita or Wyoming.

One of Gotham's core authors, whose works couldn't easily be found elsewhere, was the groundbreaking diarist, essayist, and novelist Anaïs Nin. In 1939, she shopped around *Winter of Artifice*. American publishers weren't interested. So Steloff lent Nin one hundred dollars, which she used to print five hundred copies on an antique pedal-powered printing press. Nin sold every last one and used the revenues to purchase paper for her next book, *Under a Glass Bell*. When Edmund Wilson, who cashed checks at the shop register, came by, Steloff handed him a copy and instructed him to read it. Days later, Wilson's review appeared in *The New Yorker*: "The book has been printed by Miss Nin herself and is distributed through the

Gotham Book Mart, 51 West Forty-Seventh Street. It is well worth the trouble of sending for."

Gotham also published and distributed "little magazines" of experimental fiction and poetry. Many were hard to find, cheaply printed, irregularly published, and sold in low volume. By 1940, Gotham had 125 little magazines. Most didn't survive long, and the Dead Little Mags section of the Gotham Book Mart catalog was its most expansive. Ultimately, Gotham stocked tens of thousands of issues of little magazines, amassing a collection probably far greater than any library held.

One of those little magazines was the Parisian journal *transition*, for which Gotham served as the sole American distributor. It featured fragments of Joyce's "Work in Progress," which would later become *Finnegans Wake*. Steloff had long been (illegally) selling copies of *Ulysses*. When *Finnegans Wake* debuted in 1939, Gotham threw an elaborate party—a wake, actually. "You are invited to be a mourner," the invitations read. With food, drink, and Irish pipes, guests formed a processional up to a casket lined with copies of the book.

Joyce's work and the little magazines were essential components of a special twentieth-anniversary Gotham Book Mart catalog called *We Moderns*. (The working title was "Nuts to You but Good Literature to Us," with a cover full of scattered nuts named Stein, Joyce, etc.) In it, modern writers paid homage to fellow moderns, resulting in a ninety-page list of recommended awe-inspiring titles. The catalog was itself a memorable piece of modernist literature. Gertrude Stein wouldn't write about a person, choosing instead an influential "personality": Paris. John Dos Passos introduced E. E. Cummings ("one of the inventors of our time") and a list of three dozen of his works. Ezra Pound provided the bio for T. S. Eliot ("a damn'd good poet"), E. E.

Cummings for Ezra Pound ("let us pull the wool over each other's toes and go to Hell"), and Carl Van Vechten for Gertrude Stein ("Stein rings bells, loves baskets, and wears handsome waistcoats"). The writers had their demands. Cummings agreed only under the condition that no one edit what he wrote—not a letter. They volunteered to write copy for a bookstore catalog because they respected one another. And because they respected Gotham.

Steloff was determined to make the next twenty years just as memorable. Now in her fifties, she showed no signs of slowing down, even if she was exhausted. (Morley addressed his postcards to "Miss Frances Steloff / who ought not to work so hard.") She was exhausted, in part, because she didn't have help—at least not the kind she trusted. Finding good employees was harder than finding a rare first edition, especially during wartime. "I have been to hell and back more than once," she wrote to Henry Miller in 1944. "I find myself running a training school instead of a bookshop." Over the course of just a few months, Steloff complained about the "only half-awake" bookkeeper, the assistant who could not "learn the simplest detail," and the clerk who "squander[ed] plenty of time" and might also have been stealing. She once put an ad in *The New York Times* for an assistant. Twenty-five people applied. She didn't like any of them.

Not everyone liked Steloff, either. Some called her a "taskmaster." One staff member even accused her of hitting another employee with a cane because he was working too slowly. (Perhaps because she felt guilty after striking him, she gave him fresh-squeezed orange juice.) Not all the customers or supposed friends of the store had warm feelings for her. In February of 1935, Steloff became angry with Gertrude Stein for signing books at Brentano's instead of at Gotham. What she apparently didn't know was that ever since they'd first met, Stein had taken "a violent and instant dislike to the nice lady."

Other writers coveted a job at the shop. Tennessee Williams lasted only a few hours. When he showed up late and proved not "very good at wrapping packages," Steloff fired him. Parker Tyler inquired about a position while also grumbling that the shop didn't promote his poetry. Steloff responded bluntly: "I have found it difficult in the past to adjust myself to working with a man. They usually resent criticism." Steloff did hire men but was generally wary of the young, preferring experienced, well-read employees, some of whom would go on to start their own bookshops. After all, the staff needed to be knowledgeable. Customers often asked for suggestions and often about books they could hardly remember anything about.

Though employees came and went, there was always a cat: Thornton (Wilder), Christopher (Morley), and, many years later, Pynchon. Steloff adored animals. That's why she wouldn't eat them. Customers petted, fed, and chatted with the literary kitties who added to the shop's homey atmosphere.

Steloff and her cats weren't the only ones who called Gotham home. "She welcomes the unusual, the uncommercial, the avant-garde. . . . She welcomes those who stand for hours browsing," Anaïs Nin wrote about Steloff. "As a result, everything converges to her store, small magazines, rare books, special, unique people, looking for special books." Young, artistic, and curious shoppers came through the door, many without fat bank accounts. To them, Gotham was a schoolhouse. By subscribing to the catalogs, they learned about modernist literature. They learned who was, and who wasn't, on the list. Even if they didn't buy, they came to browse and to read, spending hours leafing through books and little magazines. Other customers were well read, well educated, and well off, nothing at all like Steloff, who turned the shop lights off every time the sun shone in and saved every rubber band, paper clip, and snippet of string.

When reading had become part of "middlebrow culture" with the rise of the Book-of-the-Month Club and "Great Books" classes, Gotham remained specialized in high art and the avant-garde. Entering the shop could feel daunting, clubbish even. Like someone who doesn't know how to fix a flat sheepishly entering a bike shop, the average reader feared asking the wrong questions. Those looking for bestsellers or self-help guides or cookbooks were turned away—maybe made to feel ashamed. Added to that, browsing wasn't easy. The books were shelved spines out and piled up in the aisles. Steloff seemed to know where each one was, but customers got lost. Occasionally, she'd bark at them. She had a holy reverence for books, and if she saw someone drop one, she'd lose her temper. "I can't bear to see books abused," she said. "Books have feelings."

As the Second World War was ending in 1945, Steloff's landlord declined to renew her lease. She thought about closing for good. Finding another space—moving home and work—daunted the fifty-seven-year-old. Christopher Morley and publisher Mitchell Kennerley wouldn't have it. They found a nearby building owned by Columbia University. It wasn't for sale, but they asked the school to come to the rescue of a small but vital literary institution. In appreciation for Gotham's contribution to the arts, Columbia not only sold its five-story, twenty-foot-wide brownstone to Steloff but also did so at a steep discount, the same price it had paid to acquire the building back in 1913: $65,000.

In 1946, Gotham moved to 41 West Forty-Seventh Street. The new space was triple the size of its predecessor, with the street-facing side of the first two floors almost entirely glassed. The top three floors were set back slightly, allowing for a third-floor patio off Steloff's apartment. Whether at her overcrowded desk in the back of the shop, reading in her rocking chair, or sleeping out on the patio, Steloff was home.

Indeed, there was hardly any separation between residence and store. Steloff had three desks, each straining under the weight of books. One was in the shop downstairs, another in her living room, and a third in her bedroom. Her apartment had so many books—on the table next to the armchair, on the oval sawbuck table, on the six bookcases, and on the floor—that she barely had room for her yoga mat. Downstairs, the new shop carried more little magazines, rare and first editions, secondhand copies of classics, and experimental literature, as well as works on cinema, drama, and religion and philosophy. As a child, Steloff was "starved for books." Now she was surrounded by them. Thousands and thousands of them.

In her trademark apron, Steloff bounced from floor to floor, including the cellar, where books and journals aged like fine wine. When Yale University wanted to curate an exhibition on Gertrude Stein, it turned to none other than the Gotham Book Mart for rare editions of *Three Lives*. Steloff kept everything. Books sat on shelves for "however long it takes for the person who is next destined to read the book to arrive." Successful stores tended to focus on turnover. Whether in the 1930s or the 2020s, the average book in the average bookstore sat on the shelf for about 125 days. The stock turnover rate was (and still is) one of the best indicators of a store's financial success. Steloff didn't care about such metrics.

While the new Gotham had more space, there was no garden. The backyard bookstalls and hours of sitting under the parasol were no more. But the parties continued indoors, and the most storied get-together occurred soon after the move.

In the fall of 1948, Edith Sitwell and her brother Sir Osbert Sitwell, members of "England's most celebrated living literary family," planned a trip to New York. Edith, who called Gotham and Steloff "legends," happily accepted the invitation to a book party. It turned out to be one of the greatest assemblages of twentieth-century poets in a single room—and brought about one of the most famous literary photographs. The writers, many of whom had never met in person, talked shop. Liquor flowed. It was "like a party in a subway train," Elizabeth Bishop described, "with *Life* magazine somehow horning in on it." There was a mad scramble to get into the *Life* photograph, which the magazine insisted feature only poets. But who was and who wasn't a poet? Charles Henri Ford said Gore Vidal shouldn't count. Vidal evidently disagreed and got in the frame anyway, as "poets tripped over trailing wires and jostled each other." As Bishop recalled, "Miss Moore's hat was considered to be too big: she refused to remove it. Auden was one of the few who seemed to be enjoying himself. He got into the picture by climbing on a ladder, where he sat making loud, cheerful comments over our heads." The bookseller who had brought them all together stood just behind the camera in an Indian-print dress.

Gotham continued to host book parties (usually with potato chips and kegs of beer), lectures, and exhibitions on the second floor. It also became home to the James Joyce Society, a group devoted to reading, writing, and talking about all things Joyce. Almost unbelievably, Steloff had never read his work. She preferred Gurdjieff, Gandhi, and

Pictured left, front: William Rose Benét. Behind him: Stephen Spender. Behind him: Horace Gregory and Marya Zaturenska. Behind the Sitwells (seated in the middle) are (left to right) Tennessee Williams, Richard Eberhart, Gore Vidal, and José Garcia Villa. W. H. Auden is atop the ladder. Standing next to the bookcase is Elizabeth Bishop. Sitting in front of her is Marianne Moore. Leaning back against the bookshelves (right) is Randall Jarrell with Delmore Schwartz in front of him. Sitting cross-legged on the floor is Charles Henri Ford. Other writers, including William Saroyan and William Carlos Williams, were present but not in the photograph.

Tagore. Still, she was among Joyce's most ardent champions. And it was her idea, in 1947, to start the association, which grew to include several hundred members and hosted regular lectures, readings, and talks that attracted academics, writers, and even comedian Zero Mostel. Sylvia Beach of Shakespeare and Company was a loyal member, too. Unlike most of the others, she actually paid her three dollars in annual dues.

All the meetings and parties only added to Steloff's grueling workload. The barely five-foot-tall woman developed sciatica. On her worst days, she described working in the shop as "hell." As a matter of routine, she woke up early, headed downstairs, opened the mail, fulfilled orders, wrote letters, cashed checks at Chase National Bank, swept the steps and the sidewalk, shoveled the snow in winter, dusted shelves, helped customers as soon as the doors opened, stocked shelves, worked the register, wrapped books, kept an eye out for shoplifters, and doled out orders to the bookkeeper, the clerk, and the delivery people.

Steloff also waited on many a celebrity. "Thornton Wilder came in sweet and smiling as usual," she recorded in her diary on November 1, 1949. Another time, Richard Wright stopped in to say he wouldn't be around for a while; he was leaving for France. Steloff never missed any of them. In fact, she hardly ever left the shop, not even for lunch. And she hated talking on the phone because "my thoughts are still with the customers." After closing, she'd make some deliveries herself and read galleys and reviews. Then, maybe after a newsreel at the local nickelodeon or a lecture by the swami, she'd head home (Gotham) and get to bed, often well past midnight.

The chores—and the bills—piled up. While she was preparing for the Sitwells' party, she also had to find someone to fix the leaky furnace and come up with the $1,000 to pay for it. Steloff was desperate for help, and by the time she was in her sixties, she had found someone: the wiry, bespectacled Philip Lyman, who became store manager.

Steloff could finally take a vacation. She visited Georgia O'Keeffe, a friend and customer who ordered art books by mail. Even when vacationing in New Mexico, Steloff couldn't help but work. She took a side trip to visit Frieda Lawrence, a writer and the widow of D. H. Lawrence, whose works Gotham carried (even when they were banned) and whose letters Gotham published. On the way, O'Keeffe and Steloff got into a car crash. Steloff broke her right wrist.

Still, she kept going, up and down the stairs, continuing to promote the literary counterculture. Allen Ginsberg, who had briefly worked at the shop, could now see his work on the back wall, featured in the Beat literature section. (Ginsberg sent Steloff Easter cards, even though both grew up Jewish.)

In 1953, poet Lawrence Ferlinghetti opened City Lights Bookstore in San Francisco, the unofficial home of the Beats. Like Gotham, it published works others would not, most famously Ginsberg's *Howl and Other Poems*. Nearly three thousand miles away, City Lights was the closest thing that Gotham had to a rival, but Steloff befriended Ferlinghetti. They traded notes about up-and-coming authors. When Steloff suggested a book of poems, Ferlinghetti argued that the over-priced work (two dollars) wouldn't "sell way out here." Steloff sent a copy of the book anyway, and Ferlinghetti ordered five more. And when Ferlinghetti wanted to publish a City Lights version of one of his favorite books, *Strange Life of Ivan Osokin*, it was to Steloff (also an Ouspensky fan) to whom he wrote seeking advice.

Gotham continued to welcome artistic voices of various kinds. Screenwriter and filmmaker Elia Kazan bought works by D. H. Lawrence, Richard Wright, and Oscar Wilde. There was a book launch for Salvador Dalí in 1962. After a party for Marianne Moore, with Langston Hughes in attendance, Moore phoned—not to express her gratitude but because she was having plumbing problems. Steloff sent a clerk over to her apartment right away.

Gotham had by now become such an illustrious institution that in 1965, a *Chicago Daily News* crossword clue read "Miss Steloff's Gotham." The answer was "bookshop," *not*, it should be noted, "book-store." That same year, Steloff won the Distinguished Service Award from the National Institute of Arts and Letters, which came with a $1,000 prize. She wrote to Djuna Barnes, insisting that Barnes share the prize money with her; it was much better, she reasoned, to support a writer whose books elicited "continual expressions of gratitude" than to use the winnings "to buy clothes or pay bills."

Frances Steloff at the Gotham Book Mart.

Customers continued to value Steloff's personal touch. A woman from Ohio sent a note of appreciation along with a one-hundred-dollar check for the wonderful "services rendered" decades prior. Writer and English professor James Dickey wrote to thank Gotham—not a library, college, or graduate school—for affording him his "literary education." "As long as the Gotham Book Mart exists," he declared, "all is not lost."

Dickey wrote that in 1965. All would not be lost. But it would be different. In 1967, Steloff, seventy-nine-years-old, sold the business.

The new owner was a longtime mail-order customer, Andreas "Andy" Brown, a thirty-four-year-old Californian bibliophile with a helmet of brown hair. Steloff wanted Gotham to outlive her, and in Andy she saw someone with the chops to take over, even if the two weren't alike. Brown was well educated, despite never finishing Stanford Law School. He traveled in erudite circles and was known as an appraiser and aspiring scholar. He was also neater, much neater.

The lawyers prepared the papers. Brown and Steloff spent the better part of a day signing them. Steloff cried. But she was hardly throwing in the towel. She still owned the building and only leased the space to Gotham, which enabled her to keep her apartment. She also continued working at her alcove desk as a kind of bookseller emeritus, albeit a paid one. She could now do so without the responsibility of fretting about the bottom line or negotiating with the fire marshals who never stopped scolding her about having too many books in too many places. "I still feel that it's my child," she said. "But Andy is a wonderful stepfather."

Whether as stepfather or owner or custodian (which was how Steloff conceived of her role), Brown instituted significant changes. He installed air-conditioning. He built a windowless office in the back for himself because he didn't want to be out on the floor. He expanded the staff and tried to clean up. Steloff didn't approve. Whereas Marcella Hahner favored neatly arranged tables to promote discovery, Steloff preferred a jungle of books in which discovery felt serendipitous, rewarding, and lucky, even. The staff concurred, and so did the customers. "The more I straightened things out," Brown recalled, "the more they complained."

Brown, who moved into an apartment on the fifth floor, also transformed the second floor into a full-fledged gallery. One of its early shows was a 1971 Andy Warhol exhibition; Gotham had been distributing his magazines since 1969. In March of 1968, Steloff had attended one of Warhol's famous Factory parties. The eighty-year-old stood out next to Ultra Violet and the other Warhol superstars, mostly young, avant-garde actors, filmmakers, poets, and artists.

Although Gotham was in an area of Midtown now crowded with diamond dealers, the shop forged a connection to the burgeoning downtown punk scene. It promoted poet-slash-artist-slash-musician Patti Smith. Early in her career, Smith had worked at Scribner's Bookstore and would drop in to Gotham on her lunch break, heading straight for the poetry. In 1973, Gotham published her collection *Witt* and in 1977 her chapbook *Ha! Ha! Houdini!* Smith was lodged squarely in Gotham's wheelhouse—up and coming, experimental, and profound.

Brown introduced other changes throughout the 1970s, a decade turned turbulent by a fiscal crisis, a steep reduction in social services, and an increasing sense that the city was crumbling. At Christmastime, he displayed antique ornaments, which sold at a high margin. He also sought to profit from the shop's relationship with Edward Gorey, who would become internationally famous for his often dark and often bizarre illustrated stories, most set in the Victorian or Edwardian era. When Gorey was still an unknown, he'd asked Steloff to stock his work. She'd agreed, but they'd sold modestly. Smitten with the Chicago-born artist, Brown promoted Gorey's books and published a catalog of them. Soon there were calendars and T-shirts with Gorey drawings. It was Brown, Gorey acknowledged, who turned him into a "cottage industry." But toward the end of his life, when Gorey was asked about his heroes, he didn't mention Andy Brown. Instead, he spoke of Frances Steloff.

By the end of the 1970s, Steloff was ready to sell the building, but she wanted to make sure Gotham—and her apartment—remained. She decided she'd offer it to Brown and donate the proceeds (which she figured would be around $1 million) to the American Friends of the Hebrew University. Subsequently, she was persuaded—foolishly, it turned out—to donate the building to the Hebrew University, which would then sell it to Brown. But once the Hebrew University took ownership, it balked and decided to sell to the highest bidder. Incensed, Steloff sued, setting off a decade-long legal battle.

Business kept pace. Steloff, now in her nineties, continued to go to work each day. In came Samuel Beckett, Saul Bellow, J. D. Salinger (when the famous recluse wasn't shopping at Bloomingdale's), John Updike, Woody Allen, and Jacqueline Kennedy Onassis.

When Steloff turned one hundred, the shop hosted an extravagant party. In the gallery was a collection of items highlighting her and Gotham's history, essentially one and the same. Mayor Ed Koch attended. President Reagan sent a note of congratulations, praising Steloff's contributions to American culture. Rarely had booksellers, often stereotyped as having their noses buried in books, earned their dues for helping to shape the world around them.

Forever seeking new revenue streams, Brown acquired the libraries and literary archives of noted writers, including Truman Capote and Tennessee Williams, reselling them piecemeal. He also collected historical postcards. (Steloff thought they were silly.) In 1989, he sold twenty-one shoeboxes' worth to the Getty Institute for roughly $620,000. He needed the money, for by now Steloff and the Hebrew University had settled the lawsuit. Brown could buy the building.

Just after the deal closed, Frances Steloff died at 101 years old in April of 1989. She had been collecting a paycheck until the very end. Gotham shuttered for the day.

Brown persevered through the 1990s, though the never highly profitable business (its most valuable asset was the building) faced escalating challenges. Luckily for Gotham, the shop was never in direct competition with Barnes & Noble. But the internet boom, which ushered in Amazon and, particularly, eBay, created competition for first editions, hard-to-find books, and everything esoteric.

In 2004, Brown sold the building for $7.2 million, more than 110 times what Steloff had paid for it. Brown relocated Gotham once more, this time to East Forty-Sixth Street. The new store was never the same. The truth is, it hadn't been the same since Steloff died.

By 2006, it was all coming to an end. Brown fell behind on rent, and the landlords seized the inventory, inventory that had been carefully stitched together over the previous eighty-seven years. In the spring of 2007, everything went up for auction. Gotham's doors closed for a final time.

The occasion was William Carlos Williams's birthday. It was 1958, and Steloff found herself in a swanky Upper East Side apartment surrounded—as she so often was—by literary giants. Her bold dress was dotted with Chinese characters. Someone asked her what the writing meant. She had no idea and didn't even know it was Chinese. An eavesdropping language professor took the liberty of translating: "If you aspire to something, you will not get it."

Steloff certainly never aspired to be the kind of person who would attend such a party, or who would run one of the world's most revered bookshops, or who would alter the course of American literature and the lives of customers, readers, and writers. Her influence ultimately extended far beyond her own life and the life of her shop. James Joyce has become required reading. Henry Miller is more likely to be thought of as a genius than as a pornographer (though he is sometimes considered to be both). Patti Smith appears on the bestseller list. You can find Anaïs Nin's books at Barnes & Noble. Maybe such literary trajectories would have happened anyway, but maybe Frances Steloff and her Gotham Book Mart played a role. Certainly, she had a knack for putting the right book into the right hands at just the right time.

The Cat

WonTon was a fixture of Chop Suey Books, now known as Shelf Life Books, in Richmond, Virginia. Customers came looking for him. He strutted into Instagram stardom. And when Berkley and Chris Mc-Daniel bought the bookstore from Ward Tefft in 2021, they insisted WonTon be included. WonTon (a.k.a. Wonny) is a cat—mostly black with white feet and a triangle of white fur under his neck. He looks as if he's going to the opera.

WonTon started showing up in 2008. After a few weeks, Tefft adopted him, naming him WonTon. But the cat already had a name: Lloyd. As it turned out, Lloyd lived with a nearby family at night and drifted over to the shop by day. Lloyd-slash-WonTon eventually moved into the bookstore full-time. It wasn't long, Tefft teased, before WonTon "became the mayor."

WonTon's likeness graced the signage out front on West Cary Street, a thoroughfare of artisanal bakeries and coffee shops. College students and considerably older hipsters crowd the sidewalks in the former capital of the Confederacy. Opened in 2002 by Tefft in a space that had been a chop suey restaurant, the bookstore moved, grew, and evolved into its current two-story paradise of new and (many more) used books.

Bookstore cats and bookstore dogs are appealing (and sometimes repellent: allergies, barks, nips) in their own right. Shoppers see cats and dogs just hanging out, and they want to hang out, too. Frances

Steloff always had a cat, and like Gotham, Chop Suey, which was memorialized in Gary Shteyngart's 2018 novel, *Lake Success* (a couple made out in the back of the shop), prided itself on pointing customers past bestsellers. Shelf Life has continued that tradition. When I visited, a University of Richmond professor jumped when she saw her book standing on a dark wooden shelf devoted to local authors.

In July of 2023 and after having earned an impressive number of Employee of the Month awards, WonTon retired from bookshop life. He died four months later. Shelf Life Books still has a cat—cats, in fact. For shortly before Wonny's retirement, the shop welcomed two new feline interns: Page and Mylar.

6.

THE STRAND

New York is famous for its financial district and its theater district. There's a neighborhood for diamonds, another for flowers, and one dotted by art galleries. In the past, there was a vibrant garment district, lighting district, and meatpacking district. Once upon a time, there was also a book district: Book Row.

On Fourth Avenue between Eighth and Fourteenth Streets, Book Row was a stretch of secondhand bookstores, eccentric booksellers, and browsers. Books spilled out onto the sidewalks, stacked into carts that always seemed too small. There were plenty of other bookshops in the city, then, before, and after. But never had so many books, booksellers, and booklovers congregated in one area, not in New York and not anywhere else in the United States. Bookshops were not just part of the neighborhood. They *were* the neighborhood.

While Book Row is now a faded memory, one of its pillars remains. In fact, it is the city's most famous bookstore, with millions of volumes spanning eighteen (once carefully counted) miles, tens of thousands of square feet, and the purview of hundreds of employees. It's larger than all the bygone Fourth Avenue shops put together. Outside are still bargain carts, tucked under the proud red awning of an eleven-story building on the corner of Broadway and East Twelfth Street. It's called the Strand.

Compared with Amazon, the Strand is tiny, but compared with the average bookstore, the Strand is Goliathan. Its size and fame are un-paralleled for an independent (with Powell's in Portland being the only serious contender). Yet for many fans, the store serves as a nos-talgic monument, a museum of resiliency. Most of the books are used and have their own history. Old photographs hang on the walls. Clas-sic red signs adorn the sections. Visitors delight—as have generations of Strand browsers—in getting lost within the maze of book aisles. As that experience becomes rarer, it only feels more precious.

I n 1897, Manhattan was about to swallow Brooklyn and other neigh-bors to form a giant five-borough metropolis. William McKinley was president. New Yorkers zoomed around on madly popular bicy-cles. There were one hundred and eighty booksellers. Of those, forty-nine sold used books. Just three were located on that third-of-a-mile stretch of Fourth Avenue that hooks left (west) as you walk north.

The neighborhood was a literary center in waiting. Just to the south was the Astor Library. The brownstone Cooper Union Building, home to the art and engineering college, bounded the southeast corner of the Row. Across the street, the American Bible Society printed and distributed millions of Bibles ("Scriptures in every language and dia-lect" for sale). New York University was just a short walk away.

Bookshops began to cluster. Peter "the Great" Stammer, a no-nonsense Russian and former typesetter, arrived in 1900. He could usually be found at an overcrowded desk in the middle of his shop.

Over in the corner, oranges simmered on a stove. None of the other stores smelled like fruit.

A handful of booksellers joined Stammer before subway construction—closures, filth, and noise—prompted an exodus uptown. By 1917, they were back, and then some. "Book shops are gregarious, and they grow like mushrooms in groups," a local writer noted as the Row filled out with more than a dozen secondhand bookstores. For the most part, the shopkeepers appreciated the company, as did the customers. Instead of hunting across an entire city or even across an entire state, they found endless variety along just six city blocks. They went from Stammer's to Geffen's to Fliegelman's to Hammond's to Abrahams's to the American Bible Society to the Eureka Book Shop to Gottschalk's for prints to Stone's for magazines to Bender's for books on architecture to Pine's for works in Russian to Wanamaker's book department and, finally, to the then most famous of the bunch, Schulte's.

Ted Schulte was from Buffalo. He wore glasses and had a banana-shaped face. After opening a small store specializing in theology farther uptown in 1899, he settled on Fourth Avenue, just north of Tenth Street, in 1917. His employees included future legends Frank Shay and Frances Steloff. Customers leafed through the bargain carts out front before walking inside, shutting the door on the cacophonous city behind them. Tall stacks of books were scattered across the four-thousand-square-foot main floor, the three-sided balcony above (the Asia and Africa sections), and the basement below (religion). In all, there were more than one hundred thousand books, each arranged as Dewey would have wanted. Browsers wending their way through yanked on pull switches, turning the hanging lamps on and off as they trekked from one section to the next. "If you were coming to New York and just had time to go to one place," a rival bookseller admitted, Schulte's was it. In Christopher Morley's sequel, when Roger and Helen Mifflin relinquish Parnassus on Wheels and open a brick-and-mortar outfit in Brooklyn, their tobacco-filled secondhand shop, Parnassus at Home, is modeled on Schulte's.

Schulte was probably the one who came up with the name Book Row. He certainly recognized its marketing appeal. Early ads billed the shop as the largest secondhand bookstore in the country and listed the address as "Fourth Avenue (Booksellers' Row)." In October of 1917, Schulte and two competitors placed a collective ad in *The New York Times Book Review* heralding Fourth Avenue as "Booksellers' Row."

As the economy boomed in the 1920s, the number of shops on, and off, the Row climbed. Frances Steloff opened her first iteration of the Gotham Book Mart in 1920. Meanwhile, the founder of the Strand was still finding his way around Manhattan.

Benjamin Bass was born in Lithuania in 1901. He arrived at Ellis Island at the age of six and spent most of his childhood in Hartford, Connecticut. When he turned eighteen, having pledged that he was neither an anarchist nor a polygamist, Bass became a naturalized citizen. He headed to New York and tried earning a living in various ways, claiming that he wasn't particularly "good at anything." He might as well work with books, he figured, since he loved reading and regularly frequented the Row. In 1927, he opened the Pelican Book Shop on Eighth Street, just around the corner.

Within a year, he had become a father. Then the bookshop foundered. In 1929, with $300 of his own money and a $300 loan, Bass tried again, this time across from Schulte's on Fourth Avenue. He called it the Strand.

For a decade, the Strand barely survived. The Depression raged. Bass's wife died. Now a widower, a father of two, and a struggling business owner, he put his kids up for adoption. The five-foot-five, 120-pound bookseller with slightly tucked-back ears and a Charlie Chaplin mustache took to sleeping on a cot in the corner of the store each night.

Although the Depression crushed book sales, the secondhand trade fared somewhat better. As H. P. Lovecraft calculated, "I departed from the Schulte Emporium with less in my pocket and more in my hand. But only a dime, remember!" Reduced prices were always an attraction, a deal to be had. There existed a range of shops and a gulf between the antiquarian booksellers selling rare books and the secondhand sellers with more generic stock. Many dealers had some of each. And while general used books were already deeply discounted, shoppers expected to further bargain, though not every proprietor was so willing. When someone asked Stammer to reduce the price of a fifty-cent book, he took the book and tore it into pieces. Curmudgeonly shopkeepers—like the dust—turned off some customers, but they were part of what enchanted others.

Crowds continued to descend on the Row, particularly on Saturdays, when a local bank kept extra hours to dole out cash to book buyers. Judging by surviving photographs, recollections, and journalistic accounts, most customers—like the booksellers—were men, running the gamut from "improper bohemians" to "staid bankers."

The rich and famous shopped there, too. When John D. Rockefeller couldn't locate a copy of a hymnal he remembered from his childhood, his secretary phoned Schulte's with the request—to be

Fourth Avenue bookstalls, 1938.

filled no matter the expense. Schulte found it and billed the wealthiest person on earth for ten whole cents. Across the country, readers, collectors, bibliophiles, and librarians looking for hard-to-find titles called on Fourth Avenue shops. It was their best bet. The hunt was the game. Could you spot a bargain? A rare first edition?

Booksellers prided themselves on knowing what was, and what wasn't, in demand. They also knew the ins and outs of their own collections, down to the book tucked at the bottom of a stack. "There is such a deep-founded relationship between the man and his books and customers," one Fourth Avenue regular wrote, that the bookseller is considered a "co-collector."

The shops needed a constant supply of inventory. The same customers who bought just as often came to sell, toting as many books as they could. Proprietors and clerks examined the offerings, and then the negotiations began. Heaps of ordinary books were bought by the pound. Book Row dealers also frequented auctions where thousands of volumes could be had in one swoop.

If dealers didn't have a wanted book in stock, they were expected to acquire it. They might place an advertisement in one of the several journals aimed at rare-book dealers, but along Fourth Avenue, that was often unnecessary. "If I am short a couple of books," Mrs. Carp of the Green Book Shop explained, "I go through the street with a list in my hand and get what I need." She was entitled to the customary 20 percent booksellers' discount. They were rivals but also friends. At night, they gathered in one of the shops to drink "bathtub booze," commiserate, and argue. Afterward, they'd head out and play billiards, often deep into the night. (Apparently, Benjamin Bass was better at handling books than pool cues.)

They were also sociable with scouts, middlemen who tracked down desired titles or combed through stores looking for books to flip. Some specialized in Judaica, others in witchcraft. The most well-known scout was headquartered a short stroll from Book Row. He'd walk over in a felt hat and with lists of titles in his pocket. Everyone was searching for a mistake, a book priced too low. When one scout discovered a twenty-five-dollar book in Stammer's twenty-cent stand, he unwisely revealed the bargain just after paying for it. "The king of Fourth Avenue" wasn't amused. He tore out the page with the author's inscription—the very page that made the book so valuable. "Now the book's worth what I priced it," he steamed.

Books found their way to the Row by all sorts of means, sometimes illegally. Erudite criminals cased the nation's finest libraries, marking one-of-a-kind works by tipping them forward along the shelf. Less erudite thieves followed, snatching the books and erasing any identifying stamps inside. The notorious Book Row Gang targeted Harvard and other august institutions between Cambridge and Fourth Avenue. Its leader was Charles J. Romm. Known for his expertise in Americana, he operated a Fourth Avenue bookshop of his own. In 1931, a Columbia University librarian visited Romm's shop and spotted several recently stolen books. He was charged with conspiracy, pleaded guilty, and went to jail. He wasn't the only one.

Harry Gold also ran a Fourth Avenue store while working for the Book Row Gang. He used his shop to recruit thieves and as a fence for stolen works. After serving his sentence at Sing Sing, he was welcomed back to Fourth Avenue, where he'd continue to work for decades.

The Strand itself wasn't immune from prosecution. In 1939, Benjamin Bass was arrested for selling 150 copies of a law book that had been stolen. He claimed he was innocent, and a bookseller friend of his, Walter Goldwater, testified on his behalf. In court, Goldwater was asked if someone as seasoned as Bass should have recognized the books as pilfered. Goldwater said no, and the case was dismissed. As the two friends walked out, Bass thanked him and, according to Goldwater, said: "You were just wonderful. After you finished talking, I was almost convinced myself that I hadn't known that those were stolen."

Stolen books weren't the only illicit items floating around the Row. Fourth Avenue was also a favorite destination for erotica. By and large, adult bookshops operating out in the open didn't appear until the 1960s. Before then, and like the Los Angeles smut seller in Raymond Chandler's 1939 *The Big Sleep*, they posed as dealers of "Rare Books and De Luxe Editions." In general, secondhand stores were more likely to stock "a broad spectrum of the most flagitious titles." The customers were well aware.

Biblo & Tannen was a Fourth Avenue bookstore run by Jack Biblo,

a lanky Jew from East New York, and Jack Tannen, a former tie salesman. On a typical Saturday evening, a couple walked in and wasted
no time: "Where is the pornography?" The Jacks didn't have any but
promised to find some. A sale was a sale. They eventually got their
hands on a copy of *Fanny Hill*, a mid-eighteenth-century novel also
known as *Memoirs of a Woman of Pleasure*. So began their dealings in
erotica. Soon they sold "pornographic pamphlets" under the cover of
darkness, operating until 1:00 a.m. and hoping to avoid the watchful eye
of the New York Society for the Suppression of Vice (Steloff's old enemy).
Down the Row, "Fourth Avenue Pirates" copied banned works, often
salacious novels or anthropological texts regarding sexology. For Biblo
and Tannen, who also slept in their store at night, it was the "lucrative
under-the-counter trade" that kept them in business through hard times.

Even though Biblo & Tannen, Schulte's, and the Strand weathered
the Depression, a sense of dread hung over Fourth Avenue. The
fear that their neighborhood of books would disappear was omnipresent. They worried that people would stop reading, as distractions
seemed to be everywhere. Their anxiety wasn't entirely baseless. A
1930 study of one hundred Ford employees and their Detroit families
revealed that they spent just $0.20 on books, compared with $5.55 on
movies and considerably more on radios, phonographs, and pianos.

Booksellers needed profits, of course, but they didn't need much
profit to keep the doors open. "If I wanted to make money, I'd sell
herring," one Fourth Avenue seller claimed. It was a business and a
passion. "You wander into them and neither owner nor salesman pays
attention to you," one customer observed. Failing, or at least not pros-
pering, could even be a source of pride. As the scholar Laura J. Miller

has noted, booksellers "became involved in an elaborate exercise of explaining how their obviously commercial enterprises were not *really* commercial."

Indeed, owners described their businesses as anything but. "I run a clinic, like the Mayos," temper tantrum–afflicted Stammer averred. No matter which Fourth Avenue address they visited, customers could expect to be told that the books they wanted weren't actually the books they wanted. "It's up to us to place something in their hands that might be decisive . . . that might inspire them to great and noble thoughts. . . . A few pennies that we might gain might mean the perdition of lives and souls." Not surprisingly, even in the 1940s, the used and antiquarian booksellers had a disdain for contemporary fiction. "Personally, I think there has not been anything good written since 1915," one seller declared. The customers largely agreed. That's why they were there, in open rebellion "against the trash that is generally today's writing." Going to Book Row was like going back in time.

The proprietors' de-emphasis on the bottom line and fixation with old books and olden times only added to the popular portrait of them as oddballs. "We were all a little peculiar," Biblo admitted. Some worked for themselves because they were unsuited to work for anyone else.

Customers were just as often pegged as slightly deranged. A 1944 *Saturday Evening Post* piece profiled the "literary lunatics." "Book smellers" sniffed at bindings like dogs did to strangers. One antiquarian buyer carried a ruler, purchasing only short books. Others snapped up as many copies as they could of a single title. Bibliomaniacs bought more than they had room for. Bathtubs turned into book bins.

Used books had a distinctive allure: their smell, of course, and also their history, the marginalia, and the feeling that they'd already lived remarkable lives. When George Orwell described the used-book buyers who came into his shop across the Atlantic, he classified them as unbookish: "In a town like London there are always plenty of not quite certifiable lunatics walking the streets, and they tend to gravitate towards bookshops, because a bookshop is one of the few places where you can hang about for a long time without spending any money." Surprisingly, many of the dealers weren't especially big readers, either.

I n 1942, the whole of Book Row was threatened when city officials ordered the removal of the stalls that spilled out onto the Fourth Avenue sidewalk. Although the stalls had been there for decades, the Department of Sanitation now deemed them a nuisance. The bargain book stands were an essential part of the Row, the appetizers for the feasts inside.

Although there was a Booksellers' League of New York and an American Booksellers Association, neither got involved. So Book Row dealers united, forming the Fourth Avenue Booksellers' Association. Members of FABA included Harry Gold (the noted book thief), Schulte, Stammer, Biblo, Tannen, and Bass. They sent Schulte down to City Hall, and whatever he said there worked.

Along with the bookstalls, FABA carried on. Members held regular meetings with food, booze, and conversation, "the bookman's 'three-decker.'" The group issued joint catalogs and advertisements. "FOURTH AVE.—BOOK ROW. A GREAT BOOK CENTER OF THE U.S.A. 22 BOOKSELLERS OFFER FOR SALE THEIR COMBINED STOCKS OF OVER 2 MILLION BOOKS," so a typical 1948 ad cheered in *The New York Times*.

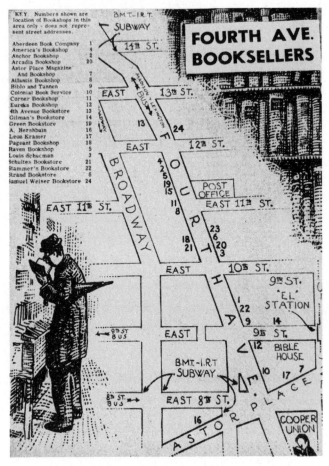

KEY. Numbers shown are location of Bookshops in this area only - does not represent street addresses.

Aberdeen Book Company 1
America's Bookshop 4
Anchor Bookshop 2
Arcadia Bookshop 20
Astor Place Magazine And Bookshop 7
Atlantis Bookshop 8
Biblo and Tannen 9
Colonial Book Service 10
Corner Bookshop 11
Eureka Bookshop 12
4th Avenue Bookstore 13
Gilman's Bookstore 14
Green Bookstore 19
A. Hershbain 16
Leon Kramer 17
Pageant Bookshop 18
Raven Bookshop 5
Louis Schucman 3
Schultes Bookstore 21
Stammer's Bookstore 22
Strand Bookstore 6
Samuel Weiser Bookstore 24

FOURTH AVE. BOOKSELLERS

Commissioned by the Fourth Avenue Booksellers' Association,
this placard highlights the cooperative spirit of twenty-two Book
Row booksellers. The map was displayed inside the stores.

FABA offered a collective voice in the face of ongoing collective
threats, most notably increasing rents. Bookstores were low-margin
enterprises that required lots of space. In the heart of Manhattan, that
was a punishing formula. By the mid-1950s, the situation had grown
particularly precarious. The century-old Bible House, once home to
four bookstores, was demolished. Wanamaker's closed. Other book-

sellers started to flee. Most vowed to stay—or at least to stay together. FABA inquired with the city's commissioner of commerce and public events, Richard C. Patterson Jr., about the possibility of relocating Book Row to a more affordable neighborhood. Patterson was on board: "New York must never go so modern," he pledged, dispatching an underling to meet with the booksellers, one of whom wept.

Patterson devised a plan. Book Row would move to an underground subway concourse between Herald and Times Squares. Going underground wasn't exactly what the booksellers had in mind. They politely declined and, instead, doubled down on their location, printing posters promising that "the Book Row of America Will Remain as Always on Fourth Avenue."

Not everyone was convinced. Although Benjamin Bass had been committed to Fourth Avenue (and had even served as president of FABA), his son, Fred, who returned to his father's care and started working at the Strand at age thirteen, was less so. After a two-year stint in the US Army and with an English degree from Brooklyn College, he was now store manager, and the decision was his. In 1956, their building was set to be demolished. They could've moved a few doors down. Instead, they left the Row.

The new location (Broadway and Twelfth Street) was only a few hundred feet away from Fourth Avenue. But it seemed like another planet. The Book Row booksellers no longer considered the Strand one of their own.

Although the Strand was no longer on the Row and paying much more in rent ($400 a month, up from $110), it was on a corner. It was also much bigger, which was a good thing, as Fred Bass suffered from accumulation. "It's a disease," he confessed. "I simply *must* keep fresh used books flowing over my shelves." By the mid-1960s, the Strand was stocking half a million volumes. On Fourth Avenue, the store had carried mostly history, fiction, and some scholarly works. Customers looking for philosophy tried Arcadia (next door); for poetry, Books 'N Things (a few doors down); and for science and medicine, the Aberdeen Book Company (Harry Gold's place, a few more doors down the block). The new Strand carried just about everything.

Every sign of growth at the Strand was matched by decline on Fourth Avenue. By the 1960s, the legends of Book Row were now actual legends—mostly old men in old buildings reminiscing about the olden days. They questioned the work ethic of younger people. "When our generation dies off, there'll be very, very few secondhand stores," a dealer predicted. One of those next-generation kids, Fred Bass, blamed the elders, the "very interesting, strong, self-centered individuals" who, unlike his father, had failed to pass their "knowledge to the younger generation."

In the late 1960s, twelve bookshops disappeared over the course of four years. Others switched exclusively to mail orders, an increasingly large share of the antiquarian book market. Finding the right edition was often easier—certainly more convenient—by mail, even for New Yorkers. In Helene Hanff's classic *84, Charing Cross Road*, she falls in love with a bookstore she's never visited. Writing from East Ninety-Fifth Street, she admits to the bookseller that she could find what she's looking for "50 cold blocks from where I live" but would rather "ask you first." The "you" was Marks & Co. in London. England was closer than downtown.

In 1969, the barely breathing FABA unsuccessfully petitioned the city to add the name Book Row to the Fourth Avenue street signs. Meanwhile, by 1965, there was at least one TV in 94 percent of American homes. Critics blamed televisions, like radios before and many things after, for sapping attention spans. In 1969, Fred Bass anticipated that books would one day become electronic: "You'll have a telephone with a screen and you'll be able to dial a book."

By the middle of the 1970s, the Strand had 1.5 million books standing on its unfinished wooden shelves. The walls were a sad-looking gray. "Absolutely nothing has been done to beautify (or even to dust) the place," one admirer reported. An army of sixty employees froggered between the aisles and tables and columns and stepladders and browsers and watercooler, a fixture of '70s bookstores. Even with all the help, Bass, approaching fifty, rarely sat still.

The Strand, undated.

A typical day of his in 1977 went something like this: Wake up at 5:00 a.m. Spend the first hour reading David Markson's *Springer's*

Progress. (Decades later, Markson took daily breaks to visit Three Lives & Company, bemoaning his supposed inability to write to the "girl of his dreams" [my spouse]. Markson ultimately bequeathed his entire library to the Strand.) Pack book up. (He had a strict one-in, one-out policy, as his fifteen-hundred-volume home library was already maxed out.) Head out from his Pelham home. Walk into the Strand (usually in a three-piece suit and a pair of half-glasses). At some point, ditch the jacket and roll up sleeves. Scoot from one task to the next. (He never had an office. He never wanted one.) Check inventory. Appraise (in a matter of seconds) books dumped from customers' knapsacks. Mind the rare-book room. Keep an eye out for shoplifters. Tidy bargain bins outside. And manage the "painter-poet-writer-actor-clerks." "They don't feel they are sinning against their art," Bass explained. The workers called him Fred. Benjamin was Mr. Bass.

Those clerks earned $3.83 an hour. And they needed to know books. It was Fred Bass who initiated what would become the famous Strand literary quiz. Applicants matched ten titles with ten authors. But there was a trick: one title and one author had no match. Surely, the guy working in the basement had aced the quiz. After all, he was known as Manhattan's most bookish man.

He went by Burt, Burt Britton. When he was born in 1933, his parents had named him Burton Saperstein. He hated the name. He didn't much like books, either. He grew up in Canarsie, Brooklyn, and claimed to have never finished a book until the age of twenty-three. By 1975, however, he declared himself "the greatest reader alive." "At least in fiction," he qualified.

Britton's relationship with the Strand began in November of 1963. When he learned that John F. Kennedy had been assassinated, Britton wandered around in despair. He walked into the bookstore, "the safest place in the world." He started coming back, so often that the Basses finally suggested he might as well work there. So he did. It was a common path for booksellers—Troy and Toby of Three Lives included—to start as customers.

Britton was regularly seen pacing around the "underground." He was thin, long haired, and sported a beard, less trimmed than Fred's and with a stripe of gray under the chin. He wore tight jeans and a leather vest—the same outfit nearly every day. He managed the review copies, the books publishers sent (free of charge) to newspaper and magazine editors, hoping to land valuable coverage in print. Book review editors sold them to the Strand (at one-quarter of the list price), which then resold them (at one-half of the list price)—a bargain for a newly published book.

The review copies were customer favorites. Friday was the best day for pickings. Some twelve hundred volumes sat spines up. Fran Lebowitz remembered Britton as generous and quick. Watching him work was "like watching a card shark shuffle a deck of cards."

Many copies never made it onto the oversize table with a red sign. Britton sold directly to librarians, often unsolicited, with notes explaining why they should want the books, along with invoices. He also invited herds of librarians to browse in person. When they did, he didn't hesitate to correct their pronunciation of Nabokov's name—or their taste. "It's just as easy to read something good," he would say, replacing the book in their hands with another. He was grumpy *and* charming. When one customer asked him for a book recently published by Farrar, Straus and Giroux, adding, "I don't know the name of it, and it's got a subtitle, but I don't know that either," Britton let him have it: "Jesus Christ! . . . Get outta here!" But as the customer

walked away, Britton told him exactly where to find it. (FSG had published just one book with a subtitle in the previous week.)

Burt Britton (left) and Fred Bass at the Strand, 1977.

Britton lived in an Upper West Side apartment full of ashtrays (he
was addicted) and books (he was addicted). The books (mostly first editions, many inscribed) crowded the shelves, and Britton got fussy
whenever guests started touching them. He lived with a woman named
Korby, whom he married—twice, actually. For a while, they were an
"it" couple. When fashionable Korby Britton appeared in *New York*
magazine next to Julie Belafonte, they were captioned as "Korby Britton (the bookseller's wife) and Julie Belafonte (the singer's)."

Britton seemed to know every writer. He'd take an author—Saul
Bellow, for example—read his entire corpus, and then invite him to

the Strand. Remarkably, Bellow would show up. Then Britton would tell him, as he told everyone, what he ought to read next. And before he left, Britton would tell him to draw a self-portrait. Remarkably, he did that, too.

Britton had been collecting portraits since before his time at the Strand. It all started at a Village jazz club. At the time a maître d' and wannabe actor, Britton was shooing out patrons at 4:00 a.m. on a Tuesday when Norman Mailer refused to leave. Britton said he could stay—so long as he drew a picture of himself.

Britton started amassing a collection of drawings. He didn't think to publish them until a Random House editor told him someone else would inevitably do something similar. He couldn't stand the idea of being called a copycat, so *Self-Portrait: Book People Picture Themselves* appeared in 1976 with 739 drawings, including from Saul Bellow, David Markson, Philip Roth, James Baldwin, Truman Capote (who signed his name backward), Joan Didion (who, instead of drawing, scrawled a few lines of text: "Too thin. Astigmatic. Has no visual sense of self."), Toni Morrison (who sketched wildflowers), and the one who started it all, Norman Mailer (with a cubistic portrait). There were also a few privileged, bookish nonauthors: the Basses, of course, and Frances Steloff, who drew herself as a simple, robot-ish head. Her successor, Andy Brown, also had a portrait. His was of a person in a sailboat christened the *Edward Gorey*. He never could stop promoting.

The Strand launched the book with a memorable party. The store closed early. Workers set up a bar. Britton even put on a suit. Don DeLillo, Ralph Ellison, Ann Beattie, Gay Talese, Kurt Vonnegut, and "some fifteen hundred literary eggs, all in one basket," as *The New Yorker* described it, attended one of the all-time great literary parties—a party held for a guy who worked in the basement.

In the process of turning the Strand into a celebrity haunt, Britton had become a celebrity himself. Long after having given up the dream, he finally became an actor in 1976, playing a version of himself in *The Front*. Woody Allen's character, who masquerades as a writer, wants to bone up on literature. Britton puts Hemingway, Faulkner, Fitzgerald, Anderson, and Dostoevsky in his hands.

In 1978, Britton left his "fiefdom" at the invitation of Jeannette Watson, who was looking for a partner to open a bookstore. She wasn't looking for money; she was the granddaughter of the Watson who founded IBM. She wanted someone who knew books. Publishers and editors all told her the same thing: talk to Britton, the "savviest person in the bookselling business." Watson told him about her plans for a space with "the feeling bookshops used to have." Britton, puffing on a cheroot, didn't seem interested. Later they bumped into each other at the Gotham Book Mart. She again invited him to join her, and this time, Britton said yes. He was bored.

Books & Co. opened on Madison Avenue on the Upper East Side in 1978, the same year Three Lives opened. (One Three Lives founder remembers that only the "millionaire bookstore" got any attention.) Britton desperately wanted the shop to be named Books. He lost that battle, but he did insist on "the Wall," an unavoidable bookshelf of hardcovers authored by the best of the best, according to Britton's rankings. Authors who made it to the Wall of Fame would remain forever. Both Britton and Watson wanted Books & Co. to be more salon, less supermarket.

The booksellers' marriage lasted just one year. Watson said Britton couldn't stop buying books. He was also an egomaniac. In the end, Watson paid him $80,000 to walk out and never come back. He also had to promise not to open a competing bookstore for at least several years. He never did open Books. Apparently, he managed a hamburger joint.

Meanwhile, the Strand basement was at the center of a scandal. The Associated Press had orchestrated a sting operation, intended to expose the editors raking in thousands of dollars from selling review copies. An undercover journalist had taken a job at the Strand. (Maybe Britton, had he still been there, would have sussed out the impostor?) Then the story splashed the papers. Heads rolled. *The Philadelphia Inquirer*'s book review editor was forced to step down for violating an ethics code. He had sold "six crates" of books to the Strand. Even worse, he had used the money to pay for membership to a private club. Board members of the American Library Association also had to explain themselves. In 1978, they sold a whopping thirty-seven thousand review copies. The reporting made clear that the Strand didn't just buy copies that came its way—the beleaguered bookstore actively sought them out.

Although Bass had encouraged editors not to "make waves" about the practice, in truth, the whole operation had occurred out in the open and for years. The store first got into the game when Book-of-the-Month Club judge Clifton Fadiman brought in a haul of review copies. Even before then, in 1937, *The New Yorker* documented the flow of review copies from publishers to editors to Fourth Avenue booksellers. In fact, when Irita Van Doren, the longtime book review editor of the *New York Herald Tribune*, fielded letters from authors and publishers asking her for a review, she often forwarded the books directly to Schulte's.

Just as the scandal brought unwelcome attention to the Strand, the founder, Benjamin (Mr.) Bass died. On Book Row, there were only a handful of bookshops still alive.

C harges of impropriety continued. In 1983, just like his father, Fred Bass was accused of selling stolen books. In another instance, Jill Dunbar, one of the three behind Three Lives & Company, alleged that the Strand was selling books that had been taken from her shop. When she went to get them back, Bass said she'd have to pay for them—presumably with the booksellers' 20 percent discount. Bass claimed he wasn't overly worried about theft, yet he set up a security stand and required customers to check their bags. Visitors found it offputting.

Size was part of the Strand's brand, but the Broadway bookstore wasn't the only one trading on bigness. As Barnes & Noble rolled out superstores, Bass reminded people that the Strand was ahead of the game: "We've been a superstore for ages." Nevertheless, Barnes & Noble posed a threat. To secure the store's long-term survival, Bass wanted his own piece of real estate. Owning the building was one of the ways booksellers managed to stay in business in a city where rents outpaced revenues. And so, in 1996, Bass bought the eleven-story Renaissance Revival that had been the Strand's longtime leased home. He paid $8.2 million. It was a bargain.

I n 1997, the Strand opened an outpost on Fulton Street in Lower Manhattan, replacing what had been a less substantial "annex." The new location, about a third the size of the Broadway hub, hardly resembled its overcrowded ancestor, which was known for the mice. "I keep it a little bit sloppy," Bass said, channeling Frances Steloff.

"When I make it too neat, business goes down." Strand II was different—bright, clean, easy to navigate, and, à la Borders and Barnes & Noble, outfitted with its own music section.

In 2003, the main store tidied up over the course of a series of renovations. Instead of three floors (only one when it first moved in) devoted to books, there were now four. There was an elevator. Air-conditioning replaced fifty fans. It was also much more spick-and-span. But there was still no café. "The Strand will never serve cappuccino!" Bass promised.

With a more polished look, the Strand appeared less like its younger self. Instead of relying on memory and hunches, Bass employed computers and barcodes to appraise books and track inventory. Online sales grew, as did sales of new books and nonbook merchandise. Tourists bought Strand T-shirts, notebooks, hats, and totes. The Strand even opened a satellite shop inside a Club Monaco on Fifth Avenue, sharing space with a swanky coffee shop and 1920s-style haberdashery.

Meanwhile, Fred Bass moved into Trump World Tower. His daughter, Nancy Bass, who had worked at the store as a teen and returned in 1987 with a University of Wisconsin MBA, shouldered much of the responsibility. She didn't inherit the hoarding gene. Her Fifth Avenue apartment had just one room of books. But she knew the business inside and out.

While her father had a habit of buying books by the thousands, she planned to sell them in bulk. She called it "books by the foot." Although once seen as luxury items, books continued to offer evidence (faulty, to be sure) of culture and taste. Ever since the advent of home libraries, people have bought books to flaunt. In the 1920s, a journalist offered best practices regarding "domestic bookaflage":

You can group a few high-brow books at a strategic point
so that as the guest enters his eye will fall upon them at
once and he will whisper to himself: "Ah! At last I am entering the home of a cultivated American!"
You don't have to read them. You are safe. Nobody
any more talks about the books they have read.

Likewise, during the twenty-first-century pandemic, people arranged books in their video backgrounds for maximum visual effect
("shelfies").

At the very least, books served as attractive decor. "Books by the
foot" buyers specified the number of feet of shelf space, the subject
matter, the binding type, and the color scheme. Customers included
Tom Cruise (popular hardbacks), Steven Spielberg (classic books on
film and theater), someone outfitting a yacht (maritime-themed books),
and a family trying to fill a thirty-five-room apartment. The Strand
rented out books for film and TV sets, including Carrie's *Sex and the
City* apartment and Meg Ryan's Shop Around the Corner in *You've
Got Mail* (thirty dollars per foot).

Despite "books by the foot," new books, and some expensive rare
editions, the Strand remained best known for its wide selection of affordable used books. Its customers continued to run the gamut, from
the famous (Michael Jackson and his entourage) to the addicted (one
customer bought eight bags' worth of dollar books every Tuesday for
years on end).

In 2012, the Strand's reputation faced a threat. Workers, first unionized in 1976, battled with management over a contract. The booksellers were in rare company. Only 5.4 percent of all retail employees
belonged to a union. Nonetheless, disputes between bookstore owners

and employees were hardly new. During the Depression, Schulte had lowered his workers' wages. Pickets in hand, the clerks (fifty dollars a week), the salesmen (thirty-five dollars), and the "boy" (eighteen dollars) went on strike in 1933. Schulte didn't understand: "I did everything I could for them, and now they bring in Communists on me and foment trouble." At the Strand, there was a picket line in 1979 and, in 1991, a kerfuffle involving Nancy Bass and an employee. For the most part, the labor struggles didn't spill out into the open.

But now the roughly 150 unionized workers (there were also 30 or so managers who were not part of the union) didn't see a path forward. The contract expired in September of 2011. Nancy Bass Wyden (who had married the United States senator Ron Wyden in 2005) made an offer. The employees demanded higher wages, more days off, and the removal of a proposed two-tiered system of benefits for new hires and existing employees. On May Day of 2012, employees picketed in front of the bookstore, chanting, "Nancy Bass, you're rich, you're rude, we don't like your attitude." They threatened to go on strike. They also lamented to reporters that the Strand had gone corporate—more totes and tchotchkes than ever. Others defended the bookstore. One reminisced about working there: "Being a penniless communist homosexual atheist made me persona non grata to much of American society. Thankfully the Strand was a space willing to use my talents regardless of these exigencies." In June, the union accepted the new contract, a slightly improved offer.

F red Bass died in January of 2018. He was eighty-nine and had worked at the Strand for the better part of seventy-five years. He had been put up for adoption because his father couldn't turn a profit

selling books. Fred had certainly figured the business out. He left his
heirs more than $25 million.

Fred Bass's death, like the death of his father before him, didn't
sound the Strand's death knell. Just as Fred had taken the reins long
before Benjamin died, Nancy Bass Wyden was running the store well
before her father's passing. The Strand was also a much different kind
of place than the personal bookshops dying alongside their owners.
The Bass imprint could always be felt, but the store's image and reputation were never tied to any one person. As the Strand became a powerhouse with hundreds of employees and millions of books, its brand
superseded any individual (even Burt Britton).

The bookstore had become such a jewel that, in 2019, New York's
Landmarks Preservation Commission began the process of landmarking the Strand's building. Bass Wyden was not terribly honored. In
fact, she lobbied against the designation, arguing that landmark status
comes with a "bureaucratic straitjacket." The city was going to "strangle the Strand" to death. She lost the case.

The Strand lost much more when New York became the epicenter
of the emerging COVID-19 crisis in 2020. On March 16, the store
closed. When it reopened months later, it was, by necessity, never
crowded. There were no in-store events. There had been four hundred
a year.

Yet the bookshop built on growth didn't slow down entirely. It
opened two new locations, a stand at the no-longer-hideous LaGuardia Airport and, only a few months behind schedule, a store on the
Upper West Side. They all sold face masks, some with the store's logo.

Then, rather suddenly, in October of 2022, Bass Wyden warned of
potential demise. Revenues had dropped by 70 percent. On social media, she issued a plea to save the Strand. Over the course of a weekend,

twenty-five thousand online orders flooded in. In-store sales surpassed $170,000. One woman bought 197 books. Not everyone agreed the bookshop was worth saving. Critics reminded the press and social media followers about the Strand's checkered history with the union, the fact that the store had laid off many of its employees despite receiving government assistance, and, worst of all, that in the middle of the crisis, Bass Wyden had bought six figures' worth of Amazon stock. (When you're the spouse of a sitting US senator, such transactions can't be hidden.)

With bargain carts parked outside, the Strand is a remnant and reminder of Book Row. As the shops along Fourth Avenue thinned out, megabookstores emerged. The Strand survived as a kind of combination of both, a booklover's paradise with knowledgeable employees and then, also, a must-see tourist attraction.

To celebrate the Strand's ninety-fifth anniversary in the summer of 2022, the Brooklyn Roasting Company opened a kiosk inside the store. It sells pastries and "Strand blend" coffee, cappuccinos, and cortados. Fred wouldn't be happy. But it's not the first time that the shop has evolved. And it surely won't be the last.

The Kids

୦ℰ୭

Kids aspire to be astronauts, not booksellers. (Except for Pam S., who wrote to the ABA's director in 1971, asking how tall she'd have to be to become a bookseller. She already knew, perhaps from personal experience, that booksellers had to "be very polite" when booting unruly children from a shop.) But bookstore kids inevitably consider whether they want to follow in their parents' footsteps. Growing up in a bookstore sounds wondrous. Books aplenty. Encounters with interesting, curious, and sometimes odd people. It could also be maddening and boring and too quiet. Usually, the second generation opts not to follow the first. There are some notable exceptions. Nancy Bass Wyden and Emily Powell are both third-generation booksellers and run the country's two most famous indies.

Then there's Sarah McNally, a philosophy major who gulps green tea and hates traveling. She grew up in Winnipeg, where, in 1981, McNally Robinson started. It evolved into a beloved chain of Canadian independent bookstores. Sarah now runs McNally Jackson, a beloved chain of independent bookstores in New York City. She's heralded as a bookselling whiz, often lauded for her sense of design. (The McNally Jackson branch at South Street Seaport is truly stunning.) Instead of leaning into her bookselling DNA, McNally doesn't share all of her family's merchandising traits. Her mom sold sidelines galore. Other than stationery, McNally doesn't do sidelines. She's a "purist." Her shop, she says with satisfaction, "takes years to learn how to use."

The Kids

The Argosy attracts plenty of Manhattan tourists, people who want to experience a live antiquarian bookstore. Started on Book Row in 1925, it now occupies a six-floor Midtown building, which it owns. Staff sit behind desks mixed in with carts of rare volumes and old maps, all lit by tender green lamps. At first, it feels like you're trespassing. Then it feels like home.

After the Argosy's founder died in 1991, his three daughters took over. They had been working in the shop for fifty years. Now some of their kids are partners. Ben, a third-generation bookseller, returned after eleven years as a Colorado "ski person." He intends to keep the family business going, even if he recognizes omnipresent family drama. The youngest generation wants to modernize. The eldest don't.

In Detroit, Source Booksellers specializes in nonfiction. It's run by a mother (Janet Webster Jones) and daughter (Alyson Jones Turner). The grandmother was a children's book librarian at the Detroit Public Library. She's the one credited with instilling a legacy of a love for books. Janet started selling books in 1989 at pop-up shops and fairs, often with her daughter along for the ride. These days, Janet and Alyson often appear together, with Janet doing most of the talking. She's deservedly proud of what she's built, of the people she's encouraged to become readers—"Three pages a day, every day," she tells folks who claim to be too busy—and of her daughter, who is carrying on the tradition.

Moe was the bagel-eating, music-loving, bad-dancing founder of Moe's Books, a legendary shop with new and used books in Berkeley, California. It first opened in 1959. The bookstore was Berkeley personified: activist, progressive, quirky, intellectual. Doris Moskowitz, Moe's daughter, tries to keep things mostly the same. When faced with difficult decisions, she asks herself, "What would Moe do?" On occasion, she looks over at the bust of the bald bookseller, cigar in mouth. Doris did make some important changes—a new website, for one. But the biggest difference at the bookstore, she said, is attitude. Nowadays, they're "a little nicer."

7.

THE ARYAN BOOK STORE

On December 7, 1941, Japanese pilots bombed Pearl Harbor. The next day, FBI agents stormed the Deutsches Haus in Los Angeles. Through the arched doors of the two-story, turn-of-the-century stucco building was the Aryan Book Store. Agents found a small Adolph Hitler statue on a bookcase, swastikas everywhere, and books, magazines, and pamphlets espousing antisemitism. They also found Hans Diebel, the store's stocky thirty-four-year-old manager, who had a scar on his left hand and a pronounced widow's peak. He wore rimless glasses, baggy clothes, and (for some reason) two belts. He was placed under arrest.

The US government had come to appreciate the subversive potential of bookstores, spaces that could shape Americans' thinking. There certainly were people who walked out of a radical bookstore radicalized. Whether that meant they had simply become educated or something more dangerous depended on perspective. The same held true for defining a radical bookshop. Any colonial outpost selling Thomas Paine's *Common Sense* might have been accused of dealing in radical literature.

In the first half of the twentieth century, radical bookstores took many forms and often served as part of larger, multichannel campaigns. Nazis, as well as Communists and Socialists, organized festivals and parades, dances and concerts, and schools and camps to disseminate critiques of American democracy and American capitalism. Bookstores served as their intellectual hubs, the places where ideologies circulated—and places granted at least a veneer of respectability. Indeed, the Aryan Book Store was much more than a place to buy something. It was the de facto headquarters of American Nazism.

The Aryan Book Store opened in March of 1933, the same month Franklin Delano Roosevelt took presidential office and, across the Atlantic, when an Austrian-born, middle-aged antisemite rose to power. Hitler's message of hate was spun and spread by an elaborate propaganda machine, a machine with its official heart in Germany and limbs stretching across the globe via an army of enablers. The goal was international revolution, a restored German Empire, an earth peopled by an Aryan race. To win over Americans, they focused on Los Angeles, and Hollywood in particular. Although Nazis were more famous for burning books, they also sold them. Destroying books and establishing bookstores were both a tacit acknowledgment of the same truth: books have power.

The bookstore made no secret of its aims. On the ground floor, it was the most visible part of the South Alvarado Street operation that also featured a restaurant, beer garden, and meeting room. The eating, drinking, socializing, and guest lectures, along with the reading, discussing, and browsing, were all intended to recruit Californians to the Nazi cause. As the Depression unfolded, curious passersby, including unemployed wanderers, popped in, looked around, and chatted with booksellers, who gave them easy explanations for the root cause of their suffering. Most of the theories fundamentally boiled down to this: the Jews control everything, and the Jews ruin everything. The store described its specialties as anti-Communism and antisemitism, which it defined as one and the same. One woman remarked that the bookstore "really opened her eyes to the Jewish-Communistic conditions in our country."

On a typical Friday evening, twenty-five people visited, mostly men in their twenties who drove Pontiacs, Buicks, and Studebakers. We know these details, as well as their plate numbers and the exact times at which they arrived and departed, because just around the corner was a spy. Although the authorities downplayed the Nazi threat, American Jews did not. The same year that the Aryan Book Store opened, a Jewish lawyer named Leon Lewis established a team of undercover operatives, men and women, Jews and Gentiles, to expose Nazi plots—plots to take over Hollywood and ultimately America.

The then manager, thirty-one-year-old Paul Themlitz, greeted all his customers. "Take a look at this," he'd say, ushering them over to the latest issue of *Liberation*, a Fascist newspaper. If they appeared receptive, he invited them into one of the private backroom offices. Here was the nerve center of the Friends of New Germany, a group of pro-Hitler German immigrants. In his downtime, Themlitz wrote letters to German-owned businesses warning of Jewish boycotts, an obsession of his. He typed the letters on official stationery embossed with the store insignia, a red oval encircling a large swastika. Themlitz often worked alone but at times employed another bookseller, whom he paid one dollar a week plus room and board. Ideal employees were Americans already familiar with the tenets of Nazism. *Mein Kampf* was required reading.

The newspapers, magazines, pamphlets, and books, some in English and others in German, didn't come by way of traditional means. The store was fed by a combination of niche American publishers who printed or reprinted antisemitic tracts and by German steamships that transported works concealed in burlap. Customs officials at the Port of Los Angeles were not a great obstacle. Themlitz gloated (and probably exaggerated) when he claimed that a bit of cash and a bottle of champagne usually did the trick.

German boats also arrived at Pier 86 in Manhattan, where books found their way to the shelves of the Mittermeier Book Store. A member of the Nazi Party, F. X. Mittermeier had a store on East Eighty-Sixth Street. He sold *Mein Kampf*, *Jews Look at You*, and *The Program of the Party of Hitler*. In preparation for a Madison Square Garden rally of sympathizers, the shop ordered two thousand copies of Nazi Party songbooks. One tune was called "Death to Jews." There were other Nazi bookshops in Chicago and San Francisco.

Business at the Aryan Book Store grew brisk enough to warrant a move to a larger location on Washington Boulevard. On the sidewalk was a sandwich board directing the crowds—mostly men, all in suits—inside. A newsboy hawked copies of the *Silver Ranger*. "Free speech stopped by Jew riot!" he shouted. Above the generous bookstore windows were three signs:

ARYAN BOOK STORE

TRUTH BRINGS LIBERATION

SILVER SHIRT LITERATURE

Inside was a decent-sized counter, desk, and center table. The color scheme was green (for hope) and red (for loyalty). Hitler's speeches played on a phonograph.

A hallway led to a reading room with a generous light well where the regulars gathered. They folded flyers and swapped conspiracy theories. (For example, President Roosevelt was Jewish, and so was the Pope, despite his "Italian name.") Off the reading room was the office of Hermann Schwinn, the leader of the Friends of New Germany and one of America's most notorious Nazis. The bookstore was not separate from political organizing.

As spies infiltrated the shop by posing as friendly customers, others resisted out in the open. On two different occasions in 1934, bricks and rocks crashed through the windows. Themlitz blamed the Communists.

The vandalized Aryan Book Store in 1934. One of the reasons why
Themlitz opted for Washington Street was because "our friends know
where to find us and we have the protection of the boys."

Shortly thereafter, Themlitz was called to testify, albeit not about the vandalism. The McCormack-Dickstein Committee, led by Samuel

Dickstein, a Jewish New York congressman, was one of several 1930s congressional committees charged with investigating "un-American activities." Themlitz didn't deny carrying antisemitic works. He insisted there was nothing disloyal about it; he was merely sharing "the truth about Germany." When showed a photograph of two swastika flags in his bookstore, he asked that the record reflect that there was also an American flag just out of view. And he took grave offense at the charge of engaging in any activity considered "un-American," a term he regarded as being synonymous with Communism. "If you would go down and look over my windows, you would see—I have quite a few anti-Communistic books in my store," he added smugly.

Dickstein also grilled F. X. Mittermeier, the bookseller and a dues-paying member of the Nazi Party. "Have you Shakespeare in there?" the congressman prodded. "Have you got Dickens's works in there?" Mittermeier said no. It wasn't that kind of bookstore.

What was so disquieting about bookstores? To be sure, bookstores disseminated propaganda and functioned as recruitment centers. Yet the government often overestimated the threat, especially in terms of the number and power of Communists in particular. Indeed, while some politicians painted enemies with a broad brush, lumping together a motley crew of political malcontents under the singular umbrella of radicalism, more often, American Nazis (and their bookstores) were not the primary concern. At the congressional hearings on Nazi propaganda, that was explicitly acknowledged: "We are just as interested, if not more so, in anti-Communistic matters." The subsequent and more famous House Un-American Activities Committee hearings focused on Communists.

Congressmen were alarmed at the rising number of Communist bookstores. By the late 1930s, there were probably close to one hundred in the United States, some managed directly by the Communist Party of the USA (CPUSA), which emphasized the importance of reading for "workers to arm themselves with theoretical knowledge as an indispensable weapon in the class struggle." The organization maintained regional "literature squads," with books in English, Russian, German, and Yiddish readily available.

Not far from the Aryan Book Store in Los Angeles was a Workers' Bookshop, one of three Communist shops in the city. Workers' Bookshops were also in Hartford, Pittsburgh, Toledo, Cleveland, Detroit, Philadelphia, Seattle, and Minneapolis. There was a Jugoslav Workers' Bookshop and three others in Chicago (one not far from Marshall Field & Company). In New York in the mid-1930s, there was a Workers' Bookshop in the Bronx, another in Yonkers, two in Brooklyn, and four in Manhattan, including the most prominent of all on the main floor (turn left) of a nine-story building on East Thirteenth Street.

Originally opened in 1927 along Union Square, the Manhattan store had long rows of books spanning theory, "proletarian novels," children's literature, Soviet culture, the arts, unionism, imperialism, and capitalism. If there was such a thing as a radical neighborhood, this was it. It was home to the CPUSA offices, the headquarters of the *New Masses*, and the site of annual May Day parades.

It was also home to Socialists, namely the Rand School Book Store, the most prominent Socialist bookshop in America. The Rand School of Social Science opened in 1906. With appalling income inequality, unsafe working conditions, and no genuine welfare state, Americans were increasingly turning to Socialism. In 1912, Socialist Eugene Debs ran for president, netting more than nine hundred thousand votes. This was before the Great War. Before Socialism became so scary. Before Debs was thrown in jail.

The Rand School was the educational nucleus of the movement, offering courses on the history and theory of Socialism, composition, and public speaking, as well as a Sunday school for kids. Leading thinkers, writers, activists, and authors, Socialists or otherwise, taught classes and gave evening lectures, including W. E. B. Du Bois, William Butler Yeats, Jack London, Charlotte Perkins Gilman, Carl Sandburg, Bertrand Russell, Elizabeth Gurley Flynn, Upton Sinclair, Clarence Darrow, Helen Keller, John Dewey, H. G. Wells, and Diego Rivera.

By 1918, more than five thousand students, mostly workers in their twenties, many of them Jewish immigrants, attended class in the People's House, a handsome building of chunky brownstone and bricks with its name emblazoned in oversize letters on the fifth story. Anyone walking by on East Fifteenth Street between Fifth Avenue and Union Square, just a few turns from Book Row, couldn't miss the archway-framed line of windows. Inside were stacks of books and magazines, newspapers and pamphlets, and bulletin boards tacked with flyers.

Although it sold texts to students, the Rand was more than a school bookstore. It was a hangout with a cooperative restaurant in the same building. While other bookshops struggled to attract laborers ("We never really reached working people," lamented the Sunwise Turn's booksellers), the Rand did—and made money doing so. Over the 1918–1919 academic year, it totaled more than $50,000 in sales, far more than the average bookstore. People ordered by mail from around the country, and customers with no Rand affiliation leafed through the store's selection of alternative newspapers and magazines—*The*

New York Communist, *The Workers' World*, and Margaret Sanger's *Birth Control Review*. There flourished a wide range of pamphlets and books, some published by the store itself, including editions of *The Communist Manifesto*, *Women of the Future*, and *The Salaried Man*.

In June of 1919, state officials launched a raid on New York organizations suspected of plotting to overthrow the government. Fifty officers marching in pairs ransacked the Rand School's bookstore, carting away boxes of books deep into the night. *The New York Times* cheered, labeling the Rand a brainwashing center that fomented "hatred." New York's attorney general promised to shut down the bookstore for good on the grounds of having distributed "the reddest kind of red propaganda" and, worse, radicalizing "the negroes."

The Rand School's attorney, who worked pro bono and self-identified as anti-Socialist, argued that the bookstore sold thousands of titles, including classics that had nothing to do with Socialism. "The New York Public Library and probably every other great public library and book store has on its shelves hundreds of books of the character you condemn," he wrote. "Why not seize their property and blow open their safes?" He charged the state with "frittering away" time and money by "unearthing" books openly displayed in the wide windows, printed in catalogs, and advertised in newspapers.

With factions pulling in opposite directions, the Socialist Party of America splintered in 1919, leading to the formation of the CPUSA. Communism grew as the Socialist Party—and Socialist bookstores— began to fade. By the mid-1930s, the Rand School Book Store, which had once helped fund the school, had only about $8,000 in yearly sales, compared with the more than $50,000 of two decades prior. The small expenses—telephone, towels, stationery, window cleaning— added up. The store was bleeding money.

Two blocks south, the Workers' Bookshop increasingly became a destination. It hosted reading groups, exhibitions on the history of Marxism, and a circulating library where party members borrowed books for fifteen cents a week. Pro-Communist gear was on sale, too. Show your support for the cause, shop staff urged, with an anti-Hearst button or a progressive greeting card. The shop offered periodic sales to workers (available at any Workers' Bookshop nationwide), distributed leaflets, issued a regular newsletter, and sold tickets to balls, dances, and talks by Emma Goldman. It was a physical hub where anyone could read endlessly about Communism and meet real Communists.

The Workers' Bookshop also stocked anti-Nazi works. Among them was *The Brown Book of the Hitler Terror*, which alleged that the Nazi government was responsible for burning down the Reichstag, home of the German Parliament. In 1934, A. B. Campbell found it on the shelf. He was alarmed. It wasn't the content. The price was too low.

Under the National Recovery Administration, the government had finally given publishers and the American Booksellers Association what they had long been lobbying for (and what the Supreme Court had previously denied): legislation forbidding booksellers from discounting. The Roosevelt administration concurred that price-cutting "oppressed small independent booksellers." The new Booksellers' Code required books to be priced, for at least the first six months after publication, at the publishers' list prices. A nine-person National Booksellers' Code Authority was charged with oversight. In reality, the ABA handled most of the complaints. As it turned out, the charge against the Workers' Bookshop derived from a tip from someone at Macy's, the very target of the federal legislation. The *Daily Worker* called the department store "one of the most notorious price-cutters, when it comes to selling publishers' garbage." Ultimately, the case was dropped, and the Booksellers' Code lasted for just over a year. At that point, the Supreme Court struck it down once again, deeming the NRA unconstitutional.

Meanwhile, the Aryan Book Store continued to push anti-Communism at a new Los Angeles location after its previous landlord became wary of the shop's association with Nazism and frustrated by the hostilities (bricks hurled through the windows). In 1936, the bookstore moved into the Deutsches Haus on West Fifteenth Street, sharing a roof with a restaurant serving Munich-style schnitzel. There were swastika candlestick holders along with flyers that warned of Jewish domination and encouraged diners to head to the bookstore after supper. There was a large auditorium used for lectures, film screenings, and Hitler birthday parties. There was also an air-rifle shooting range on the mezzanine. There, Hans Diebel, the new bookstore manager, pretended to hunt down Jews. He pledged that "if the situation got too hot for him personally, he would get himself five Jews before he was stopped."

The bookstore had pine floors, a large glass table, a bench for guests, and a small desk where Diebel wrapped books and recorded sales in his blue spiral notebook. On the bookcase greeting customers as they entered were a few of Diebel's favorite antisemitic cartoons and a copy of *Mein Kampf.*

Diebel expanded the holdings of "the clearing house for Nazi and Fascist propaganda material on the Pacific Coast." Goods came from at least fifteen different German suppliers, some from the New York branch of the German American Bund (the successor of the Friends of New Germany) and from Fascist individuals and publishers around

the country. Among the staples were works from automobile magnate
and antisemite Henry Ford.

Hans Diebel at a firing range, 1940.

Diebel sold newspapers, magazines, pamphlets, copies of Hitler's
speeches, jokebooks, comic books, and picture books. One of his favorite items was a purported Benjamin Franklin speech from the 1787
Constitutional Convention in which Franklin calls Jews "vampires"
who ought to be expelled. The speech was concocted by William
Dudley Pelley, founder of the Silver Shirts, and published in a 1934
edition of *Liberation*. Although the Franklin "Prophecy" was quickly
debunked by historians, and although the Aryan Book Store had, in
its own files, a letter from a Franklin Institute librarian stating that the
piece was fabricated, the myth proved durable. Diebel distributed
thousands of copies and credited it with helping Americans to "see the
light." In the entryway, he put out a seven-inch statue of "one of
America's greatest men." Benjamin Franklin stood next to Adolf Hitler.

H.14   3495

PHOTOSTAT COPY OF OFFICIAL PUBLICATION LIST--GERMAN BUND

Truth brings Liberation.   **Aryan Book Store**
A R Y A N   B O O K   S T O R E .   ESTABLISHED MARCH 1933
H.Diebel   BOOKS, MAGAZINES,
634 W.15.Str. Los Angeles,California. NEWSPAPERS
                                       FOR ENLIGHTENMENT

"The Jewish Question"   by Henry Ford ....$ 1,5o
"Waters Flowing Eastward" by L.Fry. A treatise on Zionism. 1,5o
"Fathers of Lies" by Warren William. Secrets of secret societies. 2,25
"My Battle" by Adolf Hitler. A translation from "Mein Kampf". 2,5o
"All These Things" by A.N.Field. Remarkable expose of World
                     forces in relation to present day chaos...... 2,oo
"The Red Network" by Elizabeth Dilling. Who is who among radicals. 1,oo
"The Roosevelt Red Record and its Background" by Elizabeth Dilling 1,25
"Occult Theocrasy"(2 Vol.) by Lady Queenborough.The most comprehen-
              sive and authoritative work on secret societies. 5,5o
"Republic Reclaimed" by Newton Jenkins. America for Americans. 1,oo
"And so they indicted mo" by Edward Jones.New Deal persecution. 2,oo
"Protocols of the learned Elders of Zion"The devilish plan of
                     Jewry to dominate the World.   -,25
The Hidden Empire" by W.D.Pelley. The truth in a nutshell. -,25
"Dupes of Judah"   A challenge to the American Legion. -,25
"What every Congressman should know" by W.D.Pelley
                     Jews in our Government. .... -,25
"45 Question about the Jews" by Pelley. Be ready to answer. -,25
"Jews say so" by Pelley   There is a Jewish World Plot. -,25
"The Impeachment of Frances Perkins" by W.D.Pelley. .... -,15
"Facing the Facts" by Ernest Sincere. Let America warn in time.-,1o
"The Plan in Action"   "   "   -,1o
"The USA need not surrender" by N.B.White ....   -,1o
"The Patriot"   by Jack Poyton.   -,25
"Hypocrisy" by David Hall jr. Read the Truth about today and
                     tomorrow,and laugh at current history. -,15
"Bombshell against Christianity" by Marcus Ravage,a Hebrew. -,15
"The hidden hand of Judah"   "   "   "   -,15
"Communism's Iron grip on the C.I.O." A Congressional Record. -,15
"Thus speaks the Talmud" The first translation of the Talmud. -,15
"Jews,Jews,Jews"   The Jews are not God's chosen people......... -,15
"What will America do" by A.Warren William Hamilton.If War comes.-,1o
"The Key to the Mystery" This magazine will open your eyes. -,1o
"The Truth about the Protocols"   by Rev.Dr.Winrod   -,25
"The Jewish assault on Christianity"/   "   "   -,25
"The Rulers of Russia"   by Rev.Denis Fahey............... -,2o
"Why are the Jews hated"? by Britons Publ.Society,London,England -,2o
"A Plot for World Conquest"   "   "   "   -,2o
"Zionism"   by The Militant Christian Patriots,London. -,25
"Trotzky"   by a former Russian Commissar............... -,25
"Social Justice"   by Father Coughlin   a weekly paper -,1o
"The Liberation" by W.D.Pelley   a weekly magazine -,1o
"The Free American" by German American Bund. a weekly paper -,05
"Edmondson's Bulletins" by R.Edmondson   Facts in short. -,02
              And many other Publications.
                     Postage extra.
     Publicity is the BEST CURE for all public evil.
 We carry the biggest selection of anti Jewish-Communistic
                 literature in the country.

Aryan Book Store booklist, circa 1939.

Diebel sold the fake Franklin at the bookstore and from temporary booths at fairs, expos, rallies, picnics, festivals, and camps at Hindenburg Park in Los Angeles, in Petaluma, in San Diego, and up and down the West Coast. Dressed in a storm trooper uniform, he would set up a pop-up Aryan Book Store across several folding tables.

He and trusted customers also circulated their own unpublished essays among themselves. One told of a Jewish plot to take over America via coded messages aired on Yiddish radio stations. Written across the top was a warning: "Do not permit a Jew to read this." They also entertained offbeat marketing strategies, such as having a confidant sue the shop for selling *Protocols* to drum up publicity. One strategy Diebel did employ was "snowstorming"—dropping hundreds of leaflets warning of "Jews! Jews! Jews Everywhere!" from the roof of a downtown building.

Diebel lived in Los Angeles, a few miles from the store. He commuted by Chevrolet from his small room in a nondescript boarding-house. He kept it neat and hardly had any visitors. For lunch, he preferred Perry's Cow Butter Store—not because of the food but because of the blond waitress. Diebel had already sworn off marriage, fearing it would distract him from the "job ahead." He had also given up his favorite hobby, stargazing: "Ever since I have been in this movement, I have dropped my interest in everything else."

Like many booksellers, Diebel wasn't in the business to get rich. He was promoting a cause and willing to work for free. An optician by trade, Diebel, in the early years, maintained occasional shifts selling eyewear. He'd open and close the bookstore in the evenings, on weekends, and whenever he found time. Later, he lived off his savings and was among those most likely to be found at the Deutsches Haus. He ran the projector in the auditorium and picked up shifts tending bar at the restaurant. The gig came with free food.

Sales at the bookstore were steady but never terribly robust (though the FBI later questioned its tax returns). As was the case for almost every other bookstore, the fourth quarter was the best quarter. Motivated by mission, Diebel was happy to "give away some literature in order to win friends." And he expected others to chip in. When he wrote to the World Service, an antisemitic international news agency based in Germany, he asked if his "Aryan comrades" would send along free copies of *The Hidden Hand of Judah*. It will "go like hot-cakes," he promised. He requested they be sent with the publisher's name effaced so that it would seem as if they were produced in America. The World Service obliged, even printing an ad for the Aryan Book Store in two of its spring 1939 issues. The bookshop advertised in several other magazines and newsletters, which, along with word of mouth, yielded a geographically diverse customer base. Mail orders came from Tennessee, Michigan, Nebraska, Florida, Illinois, Missouri, and elsewhere. Special orders were common. In April of 1941, Diebel sent a buyer an edition of the New Testament stamped with swastikas. Customers sometimes asked for certain titles in bulk, including someone from Glendale, New York, who wanted one hundred copies of "The Jew Menace."

The Aryan Book Store developed a reputation as *the* leading retailer of antisemitic literature, its influence extending far beyond Los Angeles. People wrote to Diebel asking for information on how Jews got "us into the trouble we have on our hands now?" Students writing term papers about Nazis queried him.

Communist bookstore staff also prioritized purpose over profits, deriding capitalist impulses. Yet they boasted that their sales bettered the "grocery store"–type bookstores. (They also did better than the Nazi bookstores; the Workers' Bookshop in Manhattan was doing about three times the business of the Aryan Book Store.) As manager Walter Garland reported, the customers were seeking not beach reads but, rather, works that resonated with their struggles—and that helped them win arguments with brothers-in-law. In 1940, the top sellers were *The Grapes of Wrath*, *In Place of Splendor: The Autobiography of a Spanish Woman*, and *Native Son*. Less mainstream titles, like *A Textbook of Dialectical Materialism*, did well, too. They also sold sidelines. The Chicago Workers' Book Store advertised fountain pens and Corona typewriters, red ones.

The FBI classified Garland—tall, Black, thin mustache, easy smile—as "most dangerous." Before fighting the ideological war with books, he had served as a lieutenant in the Abraham Lincoln Battalion, a volunteer army that fought against Francisco Franco and Fascism in the Spanish Civil War. In early 1940, he curated a window display tied to "Negro History" week, with works on African American history, titles from Frederick Douglass, and poetry collections. The holiday catalog of the Workers' Bookshop also had an entire section devoted to "Negro People." The CPUSA's advocacy for civil rights was yet another reason why Diebel, and the other Nazis, loathed Communism.

The Workers' Bookshop on Thirteenth Street in Manhattan, 1942.

Communist bookstores also came under attack. In the mid-1930s, a mob raided the Workers' Bookshop in Minneapolis, setting books, magazines, and pamphlets ablaze. The arsonists did leave a note: "Modern Boston tea party—no Communists wanted in Minneapolis." In August of 1940, the police raided the two-year-old Progressive Book Store in Oklahoma City. It had been ransacked by vandals before, and its owner, a civil rights activist named Bob Wood, was once kidnapped, tarred, and feathered by the "White Legion." Now the police arrested Wood, along with his wife and even a carpenter who just happened to be in the store. The police seized ten thousand books, from Engels to Dickens, and tossed them in a prison cell of their own. A group of publishers wrote to the governor in protest, arguing that this was an assault on the freedom of speech. Woody Guthrie, a friend of the movement, wrote a song about the subsequent trial:

Well, the jury they looked at Bob Wood's books
They didn't read 'em but they did agree
Anybody that would read that kind of trash
Ought to be in the penitentiary.

On a hot day that same summer, two bombs exploded in Manhattan. One was at a Nazi consulate, the other at the Workers' Bookshop on East Thirteenth Street. Glass shrapnel sprayed a bust of Joseph Stalin.

By now, German-born Diebel had decided that it was time to become an American. It wasn't a matter of patriotism. The German American Bund needed a new West Coast leader. Under political pressure and wanting to appear less German, the Bund required that members be citizens. Diebel's application met resistance. At his hearing, the neighborhood postman told of customers tapping their heels and saluting Adolf Hitler's likeness. Diebel's character witnesses defended him as a devoted American. One testified that Diebel was merely, and legitimately, concerned about a government "controlled by Jews."

In his own defense, Diebel argued what he thought was obvious: "Jews control most of Hollywood, and Hollywood has been doing a good job of stirring feeling against Germany." He denied being antisemitic while insisting that Jews be barred from holding public office. The judge was appalled. Diebel's petition was rejected. Still, he remained in the United States and at his beloved bookstore.

Shortly thereafter, in 1941, California held its own hearing on "Un-American" activities. Legislators hunted for Communists, Nazis, and Fascists. Key witnesses included Aryan Book Store regulars. One was Franz Ferenz. He operated a Nazi bookstore of his own, also in Los Angeles, on West Seventh Street. The Continental Bookstore sold an array of antisemitic material (not as deep of a stock as the Aryan Book Store), including self-published works. When asked, under oath, if he had hosted a film screening of *Kosher Slaughter*, he cheekily replied: "I have nothing to do with Kosher things."

Overseas, in June of 1941, the Nazis invaded the Soviet Union, breaking a two-year-old nonaggression pact. Although some Americans thought of Hitler and Stalin as equally villainous, the Soviets were now fighting a common enemy. Nazi bookstores were now a graver threat. The FBI started intercepting mail at the Aryan Book Store. Agents shadowed Diebel.

On December 8, the same day that Congress officially declared war after the bombing of Pearl Harbor, FBI agents whisked Diebel away from his bookstore. Counterparts across the country rounded up scores of Nazis, all charged with conspiring to overthrow the government. The evidence consisted mostly of words—words authored, printed, disseminated, gifted, or sold at the bookstore. The indicted included a roster of authors and booksellers.

The "little fuehrer," as newspapers referred to Diebel, bounced from internment camps to jail and then to Ellis Island, where he was held by the Immigration and Naturalization Service. The legal proceedings unfolded slowly—very slowly. The original presiding judge died, prompting a mistrial.

The Great Sedition Trial, as it came to be known, initially attracted much attention. In the end, the charge of violating the Alien Registration Act of 1940 (a.k.a. the Smith Act) by advocating for the overthrow of the government proved difficult to apply to the whole group. After the war ended in 1946, the case was dismissed. Most of the defendants remained in the United States. Diebel pleaded to "start anew" and return to optician work in California, but the attorney general deemed him too "dangerous to the public peace and safety." On July 8, 1948, he left New York on a boat, deported, and lived out the remainder of his life in Germany. A fortune teller had once told Diebel that his life would come to "a peaceful, honorable end abroad or far from the place of birth." She was wrong.

Another more potent Red Scare emerged during the Cold War. The Soviets developed an atomic bomb in 1949, and a hot war in Korea began in 1950, the same year a Wisconsin senator was ready to name names. Communist spies, he alleged, had infiltrated the US government. So began McCarthyism. Loyalty boards hunted for radicals, including among a group of Brooklyn naval officers accused of patronizing the Workers' Bookshop in Manhattan. They were asked about what they saw there and what they bought. Having been to the shop was grounds for dismissal.

Given government pressure, the number of Communists, Communist bookstores, and left-leaning bookstores plummeted. In 1950, the Washington Cooperative Bookshop closed after twelve years of selling Marx and Lenin (and plenty of less controversial titles) in the nation's capital, though it had no formal CPUSA affiliation and Eleanor Roosevelt had even given a talk there once. Nonetheless, the FBI surveilled the store, and Congress seized a list of the roughly twelve hundred cooperative members, mostly government employees. The government added the shop to a list of "subversive organizations." Any federal employee who continued to patronize the bookshop had their loyalties questioned and careers jeopardized. Where people bought their books was, so government officials argued, an indicator of their politics and threat level.

Radical and politically oriented bookstores continued to open, even if the days of prominent Nazi bookstores operating on main streets had passed. In the 1960s and in Southern California alone, there were three dozen right-wing bookstores, many of them started by women and many self-described as "patriotic." In Los Angeles in 1960, Florence Ranuzzi opened the first, Poor Richard's Book Shop, named after Franklin's almanac. An activist who fretted about Communism and "creeping socialism," Ranuzzi supposed that a nonprofit bookshop could stir support. She sold anti-Communist texts, bumper stickers ("Go to College and Learn to Riot," for example), and Cold War survivalist guides on how to build your own nuclear fallout shelter. The Ranuzzis eventually fled for Montana, claiming they were being harassed.

St. Louis's Left Bank Books was founded in 1969 by a group of leftist Washington University students. They focused on anti–Vietnam War and countercultural material. Over time, the bookstore built up an assortment of titles on feminist, gay, lesbian, trans, and women's issues. It sold "Black Lives Matter" yard signs, "Say Perhaps to Drugs" pins, and a Marx-inspired "Birthdays Are for the Bourgeoisie. Get Back to Work" card featuring a print of the big-bearded thinker. In 1975, the John Reed Book Store opened in Portland with Communist staples on offer. Like many of the newer radical shops, it was unsustainable as a business, lasting as long as it did (until 1992) in large part because its workers were volunteers, not paid employees. In 2004, Red Emma's (named after Emma Goldman) opened in Baltimore. The cooperative expanded to a new location in 2022. Along with radical literature, it serves up fair-trade lattes and bagels topped with vegan lox. It's as much a coffeehouse-slash-diner-slash-event-space as it is a bookstore. Radical bookstores of recent vintage are less likely to espouse a singular ideology. Red Emma's website has a lengthy explanation for why it prefers "radical" to "anarchist" or "communist." Basically, it's more welcoming to a wider variety of people and books.

Although radical bookstores are not nearly as numerous or prominent as their ancestors, they continue to be contested spaces. Revolution Books in Berkeley, California, also operated as a nonprofit with a volunteer staff. It promoted pacifism, feminism, and Communism, and it documented the histories of white supremacism and imperialism. In 2018, a man draped in an American flag and wearing a "Make America Great Again" hat threatened to burn the shop down. Others attacked it with twenty-first-century weapons: negative reviews on Yelp.

In 2019, in Washington, DC, a group of white supremacists occupied Politics and Prose, a bookstore that regularly attracts presidents and senators and whose co-owner Bradley Graham keeps a "Make

America Read Again" hat in his office. During an author appearance for *Dying of Whiteness*, protesters chanted, "This land is our land," a nativist twist on the Woody Guthrie song. It also happened to be Independent Bookstore Day, which became a national holiday for, and celebration of, indie bookstores in 2015.

In 2021, also timed to Independent Bookstore Day, a bookseller from Porter Square Books in Cambridge, Massachusetts, published *The Least We Can Do: White Supremacy, Free Speech, and Independent Bookstores*. It called for greater efforts to rid bookstores of harmful books. Conservatives made the same argument, albeit with a different definition of "harmful." School superintendents, teachers, parents, librarians, journalists, state legislators, and booksellers went to war over books, trying to ban certain titles or promote those very books being banned.

For radical bookstores of times past, the physical space was just as important—more important, actually—than the books they sold. In the twenty-first-century digital age, radicals (along with everyone else) have congregated in different ways. There are Facebook groups and 4chan. But where do white supremacists buy their books today? Like the majority of Americans, they don't purchase most of their books at brick-and-mortar Nazi bookstores or local independents. They buy from Amazon, where there's little curation. It sells *Dying of Whiteness* alongside self-published works by neo-Nazis. (The company says it doesn't sell hate speech.) In essence, the new radical bookstore is the "Everything Store," Amazon, which isn't really a store at all.

The Grandmother

Just before the Second World War, a recently widowed Hungarian Jew named Julia insisted that her son finish school. The boy graduated from high school in 1942 and survived the Holocaust. Julia went to a concentration camp. She never returned.

The son came to the US and started his own family. His daughter, Roxanne J. Coady, grew up in a house full of books and with a mother who read to her constantly. In 1990, Coady, leaving behind a partnership in an accounting firm, opened an enchanting bookstore in Madison, Connecticut. She named it after the grandmother she never met: RJ Julia.

The bookstore was intended to be a space "where words mattered, where people would gather, where writer could meet reader." It didn't take long to confirm what she already believed: "Books can change lives." Coady put together a collection to prove it: *The Book That Changed My Life: 71 Remarkable Writers Celebrate the Books That Matter Most to Them*. Billy Collins recalls reading *Lolita*, secretly, while at a Jesuit college. Anne Lamott, whose own book *Bird by Bird* should be on everyone else's list, highlights the Pippi Longstocking series and *Little Women*.

RJ Julia is now one of those famed indie bookstores that has lasted for decades, outliving many of the forces that once threatened to destroy it. Coady credits her success to her father, who credited his success to his mother, who credited success in general to reading. Nowadays, it's Coady's bookstore that could serve as the inspiration for its own collection of reminiscences: *How RJ Julia Changed My Life*.

OSCAR WILDE

C raig Rodwell—twenty-six years old, boyish face, softly swept thick brown hair—sat behind a counter topped with knickknacks. On the back wall were rows of miniature license plates that read "GAY" and a large American flag with stars and "dykes." Over in the corner was Albert, the schnauzer. Above him hung bulletin boards so plastered with flyers for protest marches and gay rights groups that they were nearly illegible. Boxes bulging with files lay scattered across the floor. Books by Oscar Wilde, Gertrude Stein, Willa Cather, Tennessee Williams, and other gay and lesbian authors were displayed face out along the wooden shelves that his mother had helped put up. There were directories to gay bars, gay romance novels, and reference works, including *The Guild Dictionary of Homosexual Terms*, which Rodwell put in the hands of everyone "coming out." There was a small section for newspapers and magazines, including *The Advocate*, a gay newspaper published out of Los Angeles, and *Drum*, described as the "gay version of *Playboy*."

In another corner were rows of albums recorded by gay musicians and several racks of T-shirts and buttons bearing slogans, some funny: "We're Not Just Good Friends," "Heterosexism Can Be Cured," "Think Straight, Be Gay," "More Deviation, Less Population," and the 1968 bestseller, "Ronald Reagan Is a Lesbian." And then there was the phrase, written on a sticker in the front window, that might as well have been the motto for the whole enterprise: "Gay Is Good."

The customers included regulars who came to talk with Rodwell, to post something on the bulletin board, or to browse the latest issues of the magazines. If they stood reading too long, Rodwell barked at them to move along. It was a small shop, not a library. Others nervously stepped through the front door, making their first foray into the gay world—a purposefully visible world with window displays meant to attract curious eyes and with customers in plain view from the street.

Also on the wall behind the register was a black telephone. It functioned as a hotline. People from around the country, some of whom would never have set foot in the Oscar Wilde Memorial Bookshop in New York's Greenwich Village, called with questions like:

"How can I meet people like me?"

"Why do I get picked on?"

"How should I come out to my parents?"

This was no ordinary store.

Oscar Wilde opened during Thanksgiving week of 1967. The first visitors sipped on free coffee and chatted with Foster Gunnison, the cigar-chomping author of *An Introduction to the Homophile Movement*. Anyone wishing to make a purchase was entitled to a 10 percent discount so long as they joined a "homophile organization." That discount, a way to encourage activism, lasted a lifetime.

Anchored by Washington Square Park and home to NYU, Greenwich Village had a long history as an epicenter of literary talent and the avant-garde. The neighborhood of crooked streets was, in fact, defined by counterculture. Bohemians, Bob Dylan's protest music, and Jane Jacobs's anti-car evangelism all belonged to the Village.

Oscar Wilde's Mercer Street neighbors included a yoga studio and a black-light poster room. Down the block was a head shop that sold pipes and gave away feathers to random passersby. There were also gathering spaces for anti-draft activists one night and a "Homophile Discussion Group" the next. Part of the counterculture meant celebrating, or at least tolerating, difference. The Village had become the de facto capital of gay America. That status would become cemented after Stonewall. And, in part, thanks to Rodwell's bookstore.

But back in 1967, even in the Village, the thought of starting a gay bookshop was audacious. Consensual sex between men was still illegal in nearly every state. Novels and plays featuring gay characters and nonfiction works about homosexuality (including plenty of pseudoscience) were not entirely new, but to purchase them, buyers had to order from one of the specialty mail-order book companies cropping up in the 1950s. A few of these businesses eventually opened small storefronts, but they didn't last long. In the late 1950s, the Village Theater Center Bookshop on Christopher Street had a small selection of "literature on homosexual themes." But Rodwell's was the first of its kind—a full-fledged, enduring, highly visible gay bookshop.

Although it was a bookstore, making a profit was secondary to its real mission: to be an information center, a center for the gay community, and a center of the gay rights movement. It succeeded, in large part, because of its owner. The Oscar Wilde Memorial Bookshop was an extension of Craig Rodwell. They were both committed. Unexpected. And bold.

C raig Louis Rodwell was born in the fall of 1940. His parents separated before his first birthday, and by the time he was seven, his mother had shipped him off to Chicago Junior, a boarding school affiliated, like the Rodwells, with the Christian Science Church. He spent the next seven years on the school's one-hundred-acre farm, some forty long miles from his Chicago home.

Like other boys his age, Rodwell played piano and basketball and was a Boy Scout. But Chicago Junior had its own personality. Rodwell woke at five o'clock each morning and, per school rules, ate breakfast in silence. The superintendent was a demanding and looming presence. He insisted that Rodwell learn to "throw like a boy." There was also affection. Housemothers read Rodwell to sleep each night. (His favorite story was Oscar Wilde's "The Happy Prince.") And there was sexual exploration. "I was gay at six, seven, and eight years old and aware of it," Rodwell recalled. He had a middle-school boyfriend. He remembered hand-holding, kissing, masturbating classmates, and oral sex, all of which seemed perfectly "natural." "I thought the whole world was gay Christian Scientist."

As a teenager, Rodwell returned to Chicago and its public schools, where his teachers reprimanded him for being "indifferent." He did excel in drama and ROTC, but he was certainly not on anyone's list of most likely to become a bookseller. In fact, he failed English.

Rodwell soon began frequenting the Clark Theater and the lakeside beach near Oak Street, landmarks of the Windy City's not-so-hidden gay social scene. He also began having sexual relationships with older men. One of these landed his partner in jail for a "crime against nature." Others helped Rodwell make sense of what it meant to be gay in mid-twentieth-century America. It was at a boyfriend's apartment where Rodwell first read the *Mattachine Review* and *One*, the two gay civil rights magazines of the 1950s.

Politics ran strong in the boy. He looked up to the Cubs' Ernie Banks *and* Adlai Stevenson. In junior high, he subscribed to the *Democratic Digest*, the official magazine of the Democratic National Committee. Whether Democrats or Republicans, politicians had no interest in promoting gay rights, an injustice Rodwell couldn't accept. While the media and popular culture (including fiction) portrayed gay men as deviates, perverts, and predators, federal officials attempted to root out gays and lesbians from the government. In city after city, police raided gay and lesbian bars, harassing the clientele and sometimes exposing them by listing the names of those rounded up in newspapers. As a teenager, Rodwell was already unwilling to give the police such satisfaction. He printed out flyers calling for "Homosexuals of the World" to "Tear Off Your Masks" and stuffed them into one Evanston mailbox after another.

To get closer to "[his] people," Rodwell moved to New York, which along with San Francisco was known as a gay mecca. That was relative; it was still a place where many led double lives, where the police raided gay bars, and where gay people were routinely discriminated against.

In 1959, Rodwell arrived at the "mostly gay" digs of a YMCA before bouncing from apartment to apartment, job to job. He worked as a "salad boy" at a well-known gay diner and as a typist at a plastic flower factory. More interesting than this work was politics. The Mattachine Society of New York, a local branch of the national organization founded earlier in the decade, was the obvious hub of the city's "homophile" movement. And so Rodwell—a slight eighteen-year-old at five foot six—headed to the group's office on Broadway near Madison Square Park. But he couldn't join; he was too young. When Rodwell looked around, he saw, instead of young radicals, suit-and-tie conservatives who hid behind pseudonyms and obsessed over the "psychiatric causes of homosexuality." Rodwell did participate in Mattachine-led discussion groups and, when he did, insisted on using his real name. He pushed (some would say annoyed) leadership into adopting broader goals and bolder tactics.

A self-described "instigator," Rodwell enjoyed "wrecking"—"swishing down the street," singing, and holding hands with men to aggravate the "Straights." On Halloween, also his birthday, he dressed in drag. It was the one night when gay men could dress as women without scrutiny. Throughout the year, he cruised in Washington Square Park, prospecting along the "meat rack." One night, a plain-clothes officer whisked him away for allegedly violating park curfew. He knew the real reason why he was being arrested.

Rodwell was arrested again for indecency at Jacob Riis Park, a beach in the Rockaways and a well-known destination for gay men. Officers judged his swimsuit to be too revealing. The police put him in jail. Bored, he taught impromptu ballet classes to his fellow prisoners.

Most nights, cruising didn't land him in jail, and it sometimes yielded long-lasting relationships. In the early 1960s, along Central Park West, Rodwell met Harvey Milk. Years later, Milk would become the unofficial "mayor" of Castro Street in San Francisco and then an official member of the city's Board of Supervisors—the first openly gay man to win elected office in California. In 1978, he was assassinated by a rival. But before all of that, he was Craig Rodwell's boyfriend. And at the time, it was Milk, ten years Rodwell's senior, who was the more cautious. When Rodwell wanted to hold hands in public, Milk refused.

Nonetheless, Rodwell was in love. Harvey was "the first person I thought: Well, maybe I'll spend the rest of my life with [him]." Their breakup, owing to Rodwell's infidelity, was devastating. Rodwell missed their lunches in Central Park and dinners at the Lithuanian restaurant. He didn't want to go on.

Rodwell found a home for his two cats, bought a bottle of Tuinal, and wrote a note for his roommate, whom he didn't expect home until the wee hours of the morning. The note instructed him to call Rodwell's aunt, who was to then call his mother. She was the best person, Rodwell figured, to break the news. He grabbed the pills, stuffed handfuls in his mouth, and crashed to the floor. His roommate found him unconscious and called for an ambulance.

Rodwell survived, and after a dizzying and disturbing recovery in Bellevue's psychiatric ward, he emerged more resolved than ever. Soon after, he led a protest outside the Whitehall Induction Center downtown, demanding that draft boards keep draft statuses secret so that prospective employers couldn't see who had been (or why they had been) declared unfit for duty. Despite his own ROTC credentials and good health, Rodwell was deemed ineligible to serve. The government had labeled him a "sexual deviate."

In the spring of 1966, a year and a half before he opened the bookstore, Rodwell organized a "sip-in." With reporters in tow, Rodwell and three others headed to a Ukrainian bar on St. Marks Place with a noxious sign outside: "If You Are Gay, Please Go Away." The place was closed, so the group marched on. Much to their chagrin, bar after bar served them. That was until they met the becardiganed bartender at Julius's in the West Village. (Three Lives & Company is now across the street.) The bartender initially placed a row of highball glasses on the bar before quickly pulling them back when he suspected what was going on. Although Julius's was a gay bar, its management felt especially vulnerable to a public protest and worried about losing its liquor license.

All the while, Rodwell kept pushing the Mattachine Society. He began writing its newsletters and insisted that the organization become more visible. "I wanted us to be out on the street," he explained. He argued that it needed a storefront, an accessible and prominent place where New Yorkers could learn about the movement and obtain relevant literature. When the Mattachine Society's leadership showed no interest in the idea, Rodwell decided to go it alone. The seeds of Oscar Wilde were sown. Despite knowing "nothing about the book business," Rodwell was about to open one of the world's most remarkable bookshops.

The birth of the Oscar Wilde Memorial Bookshop was announced with a tiny ad on the sixth page of *The Village Voice*. It was swallowed by much larger ads from the nearby Strand on Broadway and Barnes & Noble on Fifth Avenue. The ad made no mention of the kind of store it was or any of the initial twenty-five titles in stock. But its eponymous name, after the famous nineteenth-century writer whom Rodwell described as "the first homosexual in modern times to defend publicly the homosexual way of life," signaled to discerning readers that this was a different kind of bookshop.

News spread quickly—and far. A college professor from Idaho

saw the notice in the paper. In Boise, there was no such kind of store. Had there been one, anyone "who valued his position could not patronize it." The professor ordered a book, requesting that it be sent without a return address and with instructions about how to pay for it. He didn't want his wife to see a check made out to a gay bookshop.

The shop began publishing its own magazine, *The New York Hymnal*, with Rodwell as editor in chief. The lead story of the first issue, February 1968, was about "mafia control" of gay bars, including the Stonewall Inn. Another piece chronicled a matchmaking company. ("There's good news for those hunting a man. A new computerized matching service called Man-to-Man is due soon.") There was a poem and "gaystrology." ("If you know a swishy Sun-in-Aries person, he no doubt has a feminine rising sign and probably a Mars with difficult aspects.") The April edition included a eulogy to the recently assassinated Martin Luther King Jr. Most issues ran ads for local businesses, encouraging consumers to buy gay. There were roundups of gay bars and reviews of gay literature. During election season, the magazine conducted a poll of its readers. They preferred Eugene McCarthy to Robert Kennedy and Kennedy to Nelson Rockefeller and Rockefeller to John Lindsay. The ultimate winner of the '68 election, Richard Nixon, had just 3 percent support. Oscar Wilde was an activist business. It didn't shy away from encouraging customers to vote—or protest.

From the bookshop, Rodwell helped organize "Annual Reminders" in Philadelphia where demonstrators reminded the nation that a country supposedly founded on equality still denied basic rights. Once a year, Rodwell turned his bookstore into a transit station. Chartered buses (five dollars round trip) shuttled protesters from Mercer Street to Independence Hall. "It was like pulling teeth. . . . I had to cajole; I had to convince them, keep stroking them, calming their fears,"

Rodwell said about soliciting picketers. Because participants were already nervous, Rodwell said nothing about the threats of violence.

After a few years, Rodwell grew tired of the Reminders. The self-described "gay militant" was frustrated by activists he thought too slow-footed. After the 1969 Reminder, Fred Sargeant, then Rodwell's boyfriend and an Oscar Wilde employee, wrote to Frank Kameny, co-organizer of the Philadelphia protests, criticizing his old-fashioned ways: "Why did you stop two girls from holding hands by coming up to them and knocking their hands apart? (Such stormtrooper tactics, really!)" Why insist on suits and ties? The Philadelphia protests now seemed lame. That was because, days earlier, something extraordinary had happened. This was the summer of Stonewall.

On the night of June 27, 1969, police raided the Stonewall Inn, a gay bar on Christopher Street and a ten-minute walk from Oscar Wilde. While the raid itself was not altogether unusual, the reaction to it was. Hundreds gathered in the nearby streets, pushing against police barricades. Rodwell heard the commotion and ran over. Before the sun was up, he had drafted a flyer: "Get the Mafia and the Cops Out of Gay Bars." In it, he wrote that Stonewall "will go down in history as the first time that thousands of Homosexual men and women went out into the streets to protest the intolerable situation which has existed in New York City for many years." It bore the signature of the Homophile Youth Movement in Neighborhoods (HYMN), a group largely synonymous with Oscar Wilde. Over the subsequent days of demonstrations, Rodwell distributed five thousand copies.

Oscar Wilde served as the front line of Stonewall activism and a model of what it could inspire: gay-run businesses. Rodwell encouraged "legitimate gay businessmen" to open their own bars, to write the mayor, and to demand that mafia-run places be shuttered.

Fully convinced that the Philadelphia Reminders were not working, Rodwell planned something new. He called it the Christopher Street Liberation Day March, an annual June celebration and protest march that would eventually come to be known as Gay Pride. Solicitations for donations and advertisements for the event, in which tens of thousands marched from Greenwich Village to Central Park for a "gay-in," poured forth from Oscar Wilde. The success of the march depended on Rodwell and his shop: its mailing list, its visibility, its storefront. It was a bookstore that fathered Gay Pride.

When Rodwell filled out the municipal application, he described the parade's purpose as a "celebration and display of unity of gay people." The same could be said for his store. He explicitly advertised counseling for "young Homosexual men and women . . . to help them gain a sense of pride and dignity." Profit could be measured in multiple ways. The shop did about $20,000 in business in 1968, its first full year, but Rodwell was most proud of the fact that Oscar Wilde had offered counseling to more than a thousand people. While much has been written on the importance of gay bars as centers for political activism, the gay bookstore has been overlooked. It was at the center of the transition from the more modest homophile movement to the more open, widespread, and militant gay rights campaign.

Rodwell was a de facto therapist. A fifteen-year-old from Brooklyn who had never met Rodwell wrote, asking how he could find "other homosexuals my own age." He was, he said, "getting increasingly desperate." Two women from a small town in Maine asked for suggestions about adopting a baby. (Rodwell passed along the contact information of a lesbian couple he knew who had gone to Mexico to adopt.) A thirty-one-year-old Torontonian, "harassed by straight punks who beat up on me," requested a photograph of the bookshop. Even if he couldn't make it to New York, seeing an image of the shop from afar provided consolation. Another man wrote from Vietnam in 1969, the year of Stonewall, the moon landing, and Woodstock: "It's so good to know someone is really working to honestly improve the outlook for gay life. . . . I have found life completely meaningless over here—the company I'm in is small and consequently everyone knows everyone else and everyone tries to outdo the other in masculinity." Not wanting to feel alone, he wondered if he could get a job when the war ended.

He wasn't alone. Teenagers from around the country begged to call Oscar Wilde home. An eighteen-year-old from Allentown, Pennsylvania, touted his experience with books (having worked in a library) and customers (having worked at a deli counter). He wished to "help other guys become proud of what they are and—to make them realize that GAY is GOOD!"

The stream of letters and job seekers pleased and surprised Rodwell. When Oscar Wilde opened in 1967, he doubted it would survive long. Instead, it had grown, so much so that in May of 1973, it moved to a larger space, a mid-nineteenth-century brick rowhouse with three front steps and two windows facing Christopher Street. Inside, there was more room for more books, magazines, and T-shirts. The un-painted wooden shelves stretched six rows high. Piles of books sat on the brown carpet, too. The new location was just a few hundred feet from the Stonewall Inn and around the corner from Julius's. The block had become the unofficial queer headquarters. Many years later, it would look out onto the official Stonewall National Monument.

Craig Rodwell at Oscar Wilde in 1971.

Rodwell's success encouraged other gay bookshops. In 1973, Ed Hermance opened Giovanni's Room in Philadelphia, taking the name from a heart-wrenching James Baldwin novel about an American in Paris who struggles through a torrid love affair with an Italian bartender. (The book was always in stock at Oscar Wilde.) Hermance called on Rodwell for advice. On occasion, Rodwell drove to Philadelphia to personally deliver cartons of books.

In 1972, Deacon Maccubbin walked into Oscar Wilde. It changed his life: "I thought to myself that we should have something like this in Washington, DC." Two years later, he opened Lambda Rising. Rodwell's influence extended even beyond the United States. Gay's the Word bookshop launched in London in 1979, a decade after its founder had visited Oscar Wilde and befriended Rodwell.

Rodwell became known as the sage of gay bookselling. The curious reached out to him as they might query a librarian. One request came from a Kentucky monastery, the Abbey of Our Lady of Gethsemani, asking Rodwell to curate a reading list of gay literature in order to educate monks. Others sought recommendations for books to include in a seminar on homophile studies. Rodwell was certainly not an academic; in fact, he doesn't even seem to have been a voracious reader. But by virtue of opening and running a gay bookstore, the activist became the expert.

When a man from Madison, Wisconsin, considered opening a bookshop inside a gay disco, it was Rodwell to whom he wrote. And, in 1977, the owner of the new Stonewall Memorial Bookshop in Chicago asked for guidance on two issues. First, Stonewall was not a household name outside New York. Second, "people assumed a Gay bookshop is a porno bookshop."

This was a problem Rodwell knew all too well. He went out of his way to emphasize the difference between his store and the Times Square joints thriving on "booze, poppers or porn." Even though Rodwell knew there was money to be made from "beefcake" magazines, and even though Oscar Wilde did sometimes sell such magazines, Rodwell wished to cater to the "sophisticated homosexual and lesbian clientele, interested only in good and serious material." Oscar Wilde was not a place for "the 'dirty old men' sort of guys (we call them DOM-s!)," Rodwell insisted. "As a matter of fact, just the other day, a fellow walked in and asked if I have something to offer 'from under the counter.' I sent him to 42nd street." One of the adjectives Rodwell used most often to describe his shop was *legitimate*. Oscar Wilde was not a seedy smut shop, nor was it a gay bar run by the mafia or a sexual playground thinly disguised as a bathhouse. It was both a gay space and a literary space. Literary spaces were generally associated with respectability. While Rodwell didn't want to dress in a suit and tie, wasn't afraid to "swish" down the street, and largely rejected "respectability politics," he also believed that, in some critical ways, image mattered.

Mixed within the admiring notes and requests from job seekers were letters of a different sort: hate mail. "Your store is not gonna be standing when we are done," one threatened. Another promised to "burn and loot that queer Bookshop" run by the "Bastards Queers." It closed with an even more menacing message: "The police might find your queer bodies in the river."

The threats of violence had no end. In the summer of 1977, weeks after the infamous blackout shook a city already reeling from a financial crisis and on edge from the Son of Sam's murder spree, a rock came crashing through one of the windows. A customer was hit and rushed to the hospital. The assailant was quickly arrested—and quickly released before returning for a second round of trouble. Lurking outside, he harassed customers and employees and threatened to shoot. Rodwell replaced the broken window with shatterproof glass and shortened operating hours so that staff could get some relief. He also asked one of the booksellers to adopt a new role: security guard.

Others attacked the store in print. In a 1969 *New York Post* column condemning "Permissive Society," Harriet Van Horne called Oscar Wilde a corrupting influence, right alongside topless dancers and Philip Roth's raunchy novel *Portnoy's Complaint*.

In May of 1970, the New York chapter of the Daughters of Bilitis, a lesbian rights organization, advertised its own forthcoming mail-order book service, claiming that the demand for lesbian literature was unmet by a "certain book store." They didn't need to name names.

Rodwell fumed, but the accusation was reflective of an ongoing tension and truth—the gay rights movement was led by, and focused on, men. Rodwell dismissed rumors of a pending boycott as a "scheme." He also refuted the charges. Women, he noted, accounted for between one-quarter and one-third of all his customers. Roughly a third of his stock was devoted to lesbian literature, and women worked in the shop—for the same wage as men: $2.50 an hour. A woman who had started as a customer—"I began suspecting I was gay ('school-girl' crushes at 21 *are* rare!)"—was then the manager.

Whether geared toward men or women, the titles stocked on the store's already overcrowded shelves swelled as publishers in the 1970s more willingly embraced gay and lesbian themes. In 1973, *Rubyfruit Jungle*—a bildungsroman about a lesbian named Molly—became a shop bestseller. Its author, Rita Mae Brown, was an early Oscar Wilde patron and had been on one of Rodwell's protest buses heading to Philadelphia. In 1976, coinciding with the nation's bicentennial, Jonathan Katz's encyclopedic *Gay American History* debuted. Within a month, Oscar Wilde sold more than a thousand copies. Sporting a walrus-like mustache, Katz signed copies at the shop, as did a fur-coated Tennessee Williams. And in the early '80s, amid bookcases adorned with rainbow flags, Harvey Fierstein cheerily signed copies of *Torch Song Trilogy*.

Besides book signings, the store promoted Lesbian and Gay History Month, curated its own exhibits, and encouraged customers to come out to their parents, inviting the whole family to Christopher Street. Anyone who brought their parents (or a note from Mom or Dad acknowledging that they had a "proud" gay or lesbian child) was entitled to a discount.

Rodwell continued to weigh in on political issues. He lobbied

Mayor Ed Koch to halt the filming of *Cruising* because of its negative portrayal of gay men. He donated money to the production of *The Times of Harvey Milk*, an Oscar-winning documentary about Rodwell's one-time boyfriend. Rodwell also wrote and complained to newspaper and magazine editors. When a Dear Abby column advised parents to encourage a gay son to remain in the closet (claiming that doing otherwise would be "insensitive and inconsiderate"), Rodwell charged the paper with "heterosexism." Even magazines purporting to serve the gay community were not off limits. When they stereotyped gay people, Rodwell told their editors and publishers that they'd never find a spot on Oscar Wilde's shelves. "Any books or T-shirts, or pamphlets or papers" we carry, Rodwell clarified, we do so "because they promote homosexuality in a positive way." Some thought he went too far. One quipped that Oscar Wilde was nothing more than a "gay greeting card store."

As curator of the most famous gay bookstore, Rodwell knew that his decisions carried weight. By selling and making books more available and visible, gay bookstores, in general, changed the landscape of literature. And if Rodwell chose not to carry a certain title, it was possible that a crowd of readers might never hear of it, let alone buy it. Publishers were desperate for his approval and, not uncommonly, displeased when he denied it to them. One remembered Rodwell turning down a story collection that wasn't "gay enough."

Others thought that the country was somehow becoming overly gay. Rodwell kept close tabs on antigay evangelists. In 1983, Jesse Helms reached out to Rodwell (and everyone else on the North Carolina senator's mailing list) to combat "attacks coming from the homosexuals." Anita Bryant, the orange-juice queen and antigay crusader, flooded Rodwell's mailbox, as did Reverend Jerry Falwell, king of the

Moral Majority. "Men kiss men, tongues entwined, openly in public," a disgusted Falwell reported. "I learned the 'homosexual agenda' for America by not only observing their dress and behavior but also the company they keep, the literature they write, the speeches they make, the jokes they tell—and their political goals!" Enclosed in the mailing, Rodwell and the legitimate Falwellians found an envelope marked "FOR ADULTS ONLY!" Inside were fear-stoking photographs personally selected by the reverend and taken by his son. One image showed a man dressed as a nun. Another was of two men kissing. A third depicted a half-naked "gay Jesus Christ." For an additional twenty-five dollars, Falwell offered to send more. (Just keep them away from your children, he warned.)

Rodwell believed that the fight against Falwell, Bryant, and Helms was to be waged not in isolation but as part of a broader campaign for equality. The shop's twentieth-anniversary sticker included the slogan "Glad to Be Gay," alongside the Hebrew word *chai* (meaning "life") and a Black Power fist. And when plans were floated for a Stonewall memorial statue in Sheridan Square, Rodwell objected because the art piece memorialized gay activists through the figures of "four youngish white people." "As Gay people, one of our major problems is our invisibility," he wrote. "For us to turn around and impose the same kind of invisibility and ignorance on our sisters and brothers who are not white is unconscionable."

What strides the 1980s brought in terms of visibility were hampered by a pandemic. AIDS swept the nation, New York City, and Greenwich Village in particular. Customers—fearful of infection by mere proximity—avoided Village restaurants, bars, and shops. A 1987 *Newsday* headline declared Village businesses "Another AIDS

Victim." Rodwell was incensed. He claimed that business at Oscar Wilde remained brisk. The real problem, he said, was the headline. Similarly, when Doubleday sent him an advance copy of *AIDS in the Mind of America*, Rodwell said it mischaracterized gay men as "sex-obsessed," exacerbating "fear and hysteria."

Raising awareness about AIDS and convincing politicians to fund medical research offered another opportunity. Rodwell never seemed to tire of protesting. He marched at the capital. By then, Oscar Wilde had company. A Different Light, which set up shop in Los Angeles in 1979 and later established an outpost in San Francisco, opened a storefront in Greenwich Village in 1983, becoming the neighborhood's second gay bookshop. It would eventually move to a five-thousand-square-foot space in Chelsea.

A Different Light, like Oscar Wilde, had a profound effect on some of its customers and employees. Despite the fact that he earned so little he could afford only a subway ride *or* food, the writer Alexander Chee cited his experience working there, sifting through boxes of books in a storage facility, as transformative: "For me, a young gay writer who wanted to write, well, everything—poetry, fiction, essays—this time in the warehouse was an education I could never replicate." The books were proof of "what the culture allowed and what it did not." Likewise, Dorothy Allison, who went on to write *Bastard Out of Carolina*, a 1992 National Book Award finalist, credited her success to Rodwell's "tiny but wonderful bookstore": "I would never have found my people, my community, never had the encouragement and commentary of other gay and lesbian writers."

But in the early twentieth century, almost all of America's gay bookshops suffered the same fate: they closed.

Craig Rodwell died of stomach cancer in 1993 at the age of fifty-two. *The New York Times* and the *Los Angeles Times* ran obituaries for the gay rights "pioneer." Countless friends of the shop mourned the loss. When he learned he had only a few months left to live, Rodwell sold his beloved bookshop to its then manager, Bill Offenbaker, who in 1996 resold it to Larry Lingle, who in 2003 resold it to Lambda Rising's Deacon Maccubbin, who resold it in 2006 to its final owner and longtime manager, Kim Brinster. Brinster closed the shop for good in 2009 during the Great Recession, which wreaked havoc on American retail. Rodwell had run the bookstore for twenty-six years. Oscar Wilde's last sixteen years saw a new bookselling landscape that proved challenging for neighborhood and specialty bookshops. "It's all Starbucks, the Gap and Barnes & Noble," Brinster lamented in 2003. In fact, Barnes & Noble and other chain bookstores (and then Amazon) carried some of the same stock found at Oscar Wilde. So did Three Lives, right around the corner, which, while never a "gay bookstore," was founded by three lesbians and attracted many openly gay customers. Beyond books, much of what Oscar Wilde had once offered—counseling, a space to organize, somewhere other than a bar to meet gay people—could now be found elsewhere. The bookstore had helped forge a community, a community now more visible and with more supportive institutions. In a way, Oscar Wilde was a victim of its own success.

Once upon a time, it was a bookstore that served as a meeting space for organizing protests, an intellectual space for thinking and learning about sexuality, a safe space for people to ask questions and talk openly—maybe even for the first time—about who they really were. Unlike the mail-order businesses that preceded it and the online stores that succeeded it, the bookshop was not just an outlet for the acquisition of gay literature. It was a space that fomented political change and influenced what people read. It was a space that people visited from around the world and a place where people longed to work. It was a space that changed how its customers, employees, neighbors, writers, and readers thought about homosexuality. It was a place where people met friends and lovers. As one writer, in 1981, put it: "Oscar Wilde Memorial Bookshop is one of the pleasures of being gay."

The Convener

When I asked a number of booksellers whom else I should speak to, the name that cropped up most often was Mitch, Mitchell Kaplan. After chatting with him, I understood why. He's been in the business for more than forty years. He also loves to talk.

Kaplan has always loved books. He was an English major and frequently browsed bookstores. (City Lights, Square Books, Books & Co., and the Gotham Book Mart were among his favorites.) He taught English in Miami's public schools while moonlighting at a B. Dalton (not his favorite). When he opened his first Books & Books in Coral Gables in 1982, Miami was hardly a literary destination. The city, he said, "suffered from an inferiority complex." He intended to change that. He stocked what he thought were the most sophisticated books: those from small, university, and independent presses, as well as art and design books. The customers came, lingered, and bought.

The lingering was his favorite part. While he wasn't consciously building an activist store like Oscar Wilde, he did want to create "a cultural meeting place" where readers could become educated and inspired. He wanted to build a community. He aimed for a homey feel— the kind of home readers wished they lived in, at least. He forwent heavy signage and kept the sections loosely organized.

He was as much a convener as a bookseller. He hosted talks, screened experimental films, and later added a café. He not only created a small chain of Books & Books outlets but also cofounded the

Miami Book Fair. He managed to draw some literary grandees to the first iteration in 1984. James Baldwin gave a talk. Jorge Luis Borges agreed to come, too, but when fair organizers went to the airport to pick him up, he didn't materialize. They called around anxiously only to learn that he was just fine; in fact, he was having a splendid time at the Gotham Book Mart. The blind Argentine was being read to and simply didn't want to leave. Kaplan understood.

The fair helped Miami develop into a reputable "book town." Authors began to make it (and Books & Books in particular) a regular stop on national book tours. Kaplan has an encyclopedia's worth of stories about author visits, including by Joan Didion and her husband, John Gregory Dunne. While Kaplan and Dunne schmoozed, Didion browsed. After they left, Kaplan noticed Dunne's book arranged face out along the shelf—the only book in the entire store with that distinction. Kaplan called it a "beautiful act of love."

When Kaplan became president of the American Booksellers Association, he oversaw the creation, in 2006, of the Winter Institute, which turned into *the* place for booksellers to congregate. Kaplan just enjoys hanging out with writers, editors, and booksellers (preferably over martinis). And so he built a bookstore, a book fair, a conference, and, more recently, a podcast series. His success in bringing people together now means that he's the one oft invited to the party. What our history shows, he said, "is the power of an independent store. We can have a seat at the table in a city rebuilding itself."

9.

DRUM & SPEAR

ey, sister. Hey, brother." That's how booksellers greeted
customers as they entered Drum & Spear on the ground
floor of a nondescript apartment building next to Sam the
barber at the corner of Fourteenth and Fairmont in Northwest DC.
Up front was a table topped with tidy four-story stacks of bestsellers:
The Autobiography of Malcolm X, *The Wretched of the Earth*, and *Look
Out, Whitey! Black Power's Gon' Get Your Mama!* There were con-
tainers of love beads and, seasonally, piles of "Black Christmas"
cards. Under the drop ceiling and fluorescent lights, Makonde statues
gleamed, racks of African dresses stood in the aisles, and newsstands
cradled pamphlets, stapled-together essays, and the Black Panthers'
newspaper. The books were arranged face out and comfortably spaced
along cases leaning gently against the white walls. There were sections for the American Negro, Africa, Third World, and Children.
Posters functioned as a kind of hall of fame. It wasn't the typical lineup
found in social studies classrooms. Huey Newton was here. So was Che
Guevara.

Benjamin Franklin understood that books could be revolutionary, that what colonists read shaped what colonists thought and, in turn, shaped the course of human events. Craig Rodwell understood that, too, as did the people behind Drum & Spear, one of the nation's leading Black bookstores. It had an agenda. It pushed certain titles; it denounced others. It was, as the founders called it, a "movement bookstore."

D rum & Spear opened in the hot summer of 1968. That past February, the Kerner Commission had concluded that the country was "moving toward two societies, one black, one white—separate and unequal." In March, student protesters at Howard University occupied the administration building, demanding that the institution become a truly Black university with a curriculum to match. In April, Martin Luther King Jr. was assassinated in Memphis. Washington, DC, was the heart of the country's emotional reaction. Buildings burned. Armed National Guardsmen ringed the Capitol. Swarms of officers patrolled a population placed under curfew. Thousands of protesters and rioters were arrested. Thirteen people died. Northwest DC experienced the most carnage, much of it centered along U Street and up and down Fourteenth Street, a hub of Black-owned businesses. "Arising from the ashes," as poet Gaston T. Neal put it, was Drum & Spear.

When Judy Richardson arrived, the tear gas smell hadn't fully dissipated. There wasn't much to see: a few empty, freshly stained bookcases and Tony, a skinny guy with a triangular mustache. Tony Gittens had been one of the leaders of the Howard University protests. Richardson, an energetic veteran of the Student Nonviolent Coordinating Committee (SNCC), had left Columbia University with a mattress strapped to the roof of her car. The pair was responsible for getting the store up and running. Neither knew a thing about bookstores.

Neither did twenty-five-year-old Charlie Cobb. Cobb, the one who had tapped Richardson and Gittens to launch the bookshop, was already a seasoned activist, having birthed the SNCC Freedom Schools, an alternative education program for Black kids in Mississippi, just one state where public schools had failed them. Like many of his peers in the 1960s, Cobb had an interest in Black consciousness and Pan-Africanism. He had traveled to Africa and Europe, where he visited the Librairie Présence Africaine, a vibrant Parisian bookstore (still in business). The shop was multidimensional: a place to buy books and the headquarters of a Pan-African publisher and magazine. As Parisian institutions so often are, it was a social and intellectual space. There, in the Latin Quarter, the idea of Drum & Spear was born.

On his return home, Cobb established Afro-American Resources, the parent organization of the bookstore and several other entities, all focused on education. The mission at Drum & Spear was simple: to encourage more Black people to read more about Black people. The booksellers wanted customers to "understand themselves"—their history and, by extension, their future. As Courtland Cox (who, at twenty-seven, was the oldest of the bunch) said, the shop was a kind of archive of "evidence," disproving the massive lie, spread in schools and popular culture, that Black people were not intellectual. When Cobb told the press that Drum & Spear wouldn't "define profit in terms of money," he wasn't exaggerating. The bookstore was a nonprofit. They had sat at lunch counters. They had marched in the streets. Now they would sell books.

They recognized the importance of the name and landed on Drum & Spear, owing to its African iconography. The drum symbolized communication; the spear represented "whatever else might be necessary for the liberation of the people." To stock the store, Richardson and Gittens headed to New York. At Bookazine, the mammoth distributor, Richardson happened upon a Black salesperson who took her around, pointing out every remotely relevant title. Richardson grabbed as much as she could, stuffing books into boxes and boxes into the Drum & Spear minibus.

Meanwhile, Gittens headed to Harlem. He was looking for Lewis Michaux, the owner of the most famous Black bookstore in the country: the National Memorial African Bookstore. Customers called it Michaux's. Michaux called it "the House of Common Sense and the Home of Proper Propaganda." Everyone called Michaux, who had hardly any formal education, the Professor.

The Professor had started selling books out of a wagon and opened a storefront in the 1930s with only a dozen books in stock. Like Bass at the Strand, he slept in the store. Over time, the operation grew— inside and out. The Professor became a fixture on the sidewalk, preaching atop a soapbox or ladder. The Professor was always talking.

When Martin Luther King Jr. came to Harlem in 1958 for a book signing at Blumstein's, a white-owned department store without a book department, Michaux was irate. So were the picketers who lined up outside, demanding to know why King would snub Michaux's, a bookstore with a picture of the civil rights leader on its walls. (At the book signing, a deranged woman stabbed King with a letter opener, nearly killing him.)

Gittens visited in 1968. He found a hunched-over but still animated Professor. Michaux didn't want to talk about Marcus Garvey or Malcolm

X, a friend of the store who once used it as a backdrop for a rally. He wanted to talk about the bookselling business: Never forget to pay your taxes. Don't take on too much debt. And never overstock, he warned, sitting swamped by some two hundred thousand volumes crowding nearly every inch of his small shop and walling off his desk with leaning stacks of books, newspapers, and magazines. The store did have enough room for a dedicated reading spot for customers. The Professor provided the coffee.

The National Memorial African Bookstore, 1970.

Michaux wasn't the first Black bookseller. That was David Ruggles, who in 1834 opened the Anti-Slavery Book Store in Lower Manhattan. With advertisements running in William Lloyd Garrison's abolitionist paper, it served as an overt political space for antislavery activists to gather, learn, and plot. Within a year, an arsonist burned it to the ground. Books and bookstores continued to neglect Black audiences well into the twentieth century; even worse, they often promoted white supremacy.

When Michaux entered the business in the 1930s, there was just one other shop specializing in African, Caribbean, and African American literature. It was down on Book Row and had a Jewish owner. By 1965, there were only about a dozen Black bookstores in the entire country. Drum & Spear opened in 1968, part of a wave of Black bookstores. Harlem was now also home to Una Mulzac's Liberation Bookstore. There, recordings of Malcolm X played on a loop. Mulzac was a former Random House employee and bookstore owner in Guyana until her shop was bombed. She blamed it on the CIA. The nation's capital, with its majority Black population, had been home to a Black bookseller or two, but there had never been a major Black bookstore.

The customers, almost all of whom had never been in a store like this, didn't know where to begin. Drum & Spear's stock was certainly deep: Eldridge Cleaver, Frantz Fanon, Frederick Douglass, Alex Haley, Langston Hughes, W. E. B. Du Bois, Paul Robeson, Richard Wright, Karl Marx, and James Baldwin. Works by academic historians, including Eugene Genovese, James McPherson, and Howard Zinn, were on sale, too. None of those scholars had an asterisk by their name in the thirty-seven-page catalog. Asterisks were reserved for Black authors.

On opening night, a large crowd gathered to celebrate. It included poet LeRoi Jones (later known as Amiri Baraka) and Stokely Carmichael, then the immediate former SNCC chairman and one of the three activists whom FBI director J. Edgar Hoover worried would become the "messiah" of Black nationalism. (The two others were Martin Luther King Jr. and Elijah Muhammad, but it was Carmichael who had the "necessary charisma.") *The Washington Post* ran a piece about the event. FBI agents saw it and within two weeks opened an official investigation into the store. Hoover had already issued a memo regarding the troubling rise of "black extremist bookstores," defined as "propaganda outlets for revolutionary and hate publications." Be on the lookout, he warned, for any "African-type bookstores."

The initial FBI reports described Drum & Spear's founders as "militant black nationalists." Agents scouted for an informant to befriend the four-person staff and subscribe to the mailing list. The FBI sent in three Black agents to pose as customers. They also tracked down everyone who phoned the store. They found a suspected Communist here and a potential agitator there, though the callers were mostly nothing of the sort; rather, they were doctors, teachers, professors, funeral home workers, cellists, authors, editors, distributors, and publishers, including Barney Rosset Jr., the owner of Grove Press and the anti-censorship advocate who had found his taste for the "underground" by way of the Gotham Book Mart. Someone also called from the National Memorial African Bookstore in Harlem. It must have been the Professor.

Agents persisted, even inventing evidence. When one of them was tasked with purchasing a copy of Chairman Mao Tse-tung's *Little Red Book* from Drum & Spear and couldn't find it (they were out of stock), he headed to Brentano's, bought it, and lazily submitted it as evidence of Drum & Spear's Communist-leaning inventory.

Despite a lack of evidence of criminal wrongdoing, the FBI maintained that the shop was "a front for underground or subversive activities." Nothing about the bookstore was "underground." Its doors opened widely at 10:00 a.m. every day. Its aims were printed in bookstore catalogs and manifest at its public events. Gwendolyn Brooks, John Hope Franklin, and Shirley Graham Du Bois came for author talks. There were exhibitions of African art and celebrations of Frederick Douglass Day.

Daily, the staff encouraged patrons to chat, browse, and read. In 1969, the *Washington Afro-American* described the shop as "the hub," a place welcoming of "militants" and "argumentative elders." The usual mix included students and professors from Howard (a fifteen-minute walk away), American University, and the University of Maryland; Black authors, including Toni Morrison; ambassadors and the staff of various African embassies; curious types looking through the window; the folks who lived in the apartments upstairs; neighborhood kids who swept the floor for pocket change; and parents strolling infants.

Parents and kids headed toward what was the most popular section. Although that space wasn't an initial focus, Richardson came to understand the need for "good books about African children." In its regular newsletter, Drum & Spear carved out a section for "black and positive" kids' books. While picture-book characters had become more diverse throughout the 1960s, there was still a long way to go. And some of the books promoted as inclusive didn't pass muster. In 1970, Richardson returned one such title for its "black-boy-panting-after-white-girl" trope.

The shop also sponsored an annual Black Youth Arts Festival. Elementary schoolers submitted drawings, poems, plays, and paintings with African themes. School groups arrived by the busload, touring the shop as if it were a museum. Richardson hosted a weekly radio show, *Saa Ya Watoto* (Children's Hour in Kiswahili). Booksellers read, in character, from African folktales. Richardson reprised her role—fully decked out—on school visits.

Schoolteachers and librarians were among Drum & Spear's best customers. The Library Services and Construction Act (1964) and the Elementary and Secondary Education Act (1965), both part of Lyndon Johnson's "War on Poverty," sent millions of dollars to neighborhood and school libraries in lower-income areas. Drum & Spear's expertise paid off at book fairs catering to public school buyers and caucuses of black librarians.

The focus on children's literature was unique within the small world of Black bookstores. Kids' books attracted parents who wouldn't have otherwise visited. They could then become book buyers, too. Like teary-eyed teachers at graduation, bookstore staff prided themselves on the customers who first came looking for picture books for the kids, then found something for themselves in popular fiction and before long had apartments lined with political and theoretical texts. As one Howard University student remembered, "You could walk into Drum & Spear Bookstore, which many people did from right off the street, and you could read yourself into an international consciousness."

A Drum & Spear bookseller put it concisely: "We were really in the business of education." Half of the bookstore's radio ads were purely educational, without even a plug for the store. And when management discussed who should be eligible for a discount, they agreed the question was "a political one, not financial." The store needed to be "an instrument of our politics . . . to advance our viewpoint."

It wasn't just the customers who got an education. The staff did, too. First-grade teacher Daphne Muse described Drum & Spear as like "walking into graduate school." She began working at the store, reading everything she could, and earned an unofficial degree in diasporic literature. When customers tiptoed in, she handed them a stack of must-reads. For Muse, who got her first Afro haircut next door, bookselling was an awakening. It propelled her into a lifetime of activism.

Whether kids', trade, or scholarly, the titles geared toward Black audiences were still relatively small in number. And so, in 1969, a year after the bookstore opened, Drum & Spear launched its own eponymous press. The venture emerged from a conversation with C. L. R. James, the Marxist historian. His book *A History of Negro Revolt*, originally published in the 1930s, was out of print, despite the fact that the history of Black resistance was as relevant as ever. Reissued as *A History of Pan-African Revolt*, it became Drum & Spear Press's first title.

The publishing arm operated out of a rat-infested brownstone on Belmont Street, not far from the store. Richardson had an office upstairs. Heat was expensive, so in the winter she worked with her coat on, but even then, her teeth chattered. The press's mission was more social than capitalist. And, like the shop, it was keen on targeting parents. Its second publication was *Children of Africa*, a coloring book with images drawn by Jennifer Lawson. (The book quickly sold through its initial print run of ten thousand copies.) Lawson came to DC by way of Mississippi, where she wrote comic books introducing Black voters to local politics.

Working for Drum & Spear Press was a natural evolution. Lawson grew up in Alabama and its segregated libraries. A counterculture shop called Gene Crutcher Books (the "City Lights of Birmingham") served as her "intellectual oasis." There, a teenage Lawson was introduced to James Baldwin, Upton Sinclair, and Lenny Bruce.

The desire to forge an African connection ran so deep that Lawson was part of a team that established a Drum & Spear office in Dar es Salaam, Tanzania. Remarkably, a bookstore with just a few staffers and a small footprint in the nation's capital was now engaged in a transcontinental publishing venture. The ambitiousness of the project didn't faze any of the twentysomethings.

For a small press, Drum & Spear's offerings were unusually diverse. It followed theory-driven history with a coloring book and later put out children's books published in both English and Kiswahili. One of the press's best-known titles was the picture-book *Bubbles*, by Eloise Greenfield. Richardson adored the tale of a Black boy who learns to read and wants to show his mother who, sadly, is too busy to pay attention. The press also published a calendar (*We Are an African People*), books of poetry (including *Enemy of the Sun: Poetry of Palestinian Resistance*), posters designed for schoolrooms, and *The Book of African Names*, meant to help expecting Black parents select baby names "accurately rooted in the ancestral past." One hospital in Wilmington, Delaware, kept the forty-two-page paperback on hand. Black studies programs at Cornell, San Francisco State University, and many in between bought from Drum & Spear in bulk. Roughly five hundred such programs existed by 1971.

Despite heightened interest in Black studies, neither the press nor the store was ever a financial powerhouse. Bank records indicate periods of robust sales, especially in the weeks before Christmas, when the register rang, customers chatted, radiators hissed, and the radio blared (WHUR, Howard University's station). At the beginning of each semester, flocks of college students arrived, many sent by their professors. At other times of the year, bank balances hovered near zero. Funds volleyed back and forth between the parent organization and the bookstore. It wasn't clear which entity was supporting which.

A display of Drum & Spear Press books inside the bookstore, circa 1972.
This image is from Drum & Spear's second location, just around the corner
from the first. It moved to this larger, brighter space in 1970.

Drum & Spear, circa 1972.

Financial instability was hardly the only challenge. A fire in the spring of 1969 destroyed thousands of dollars' worth of books. The fire department found a bottle of flammable liquid on the floor and acknowledged that the three-alarm blaze was suspicious, but it never issued a definitive verdict. Not uncommonly, books were stolen. Moreover, unwelcome customers put staffers on edge. Daphne Muse asked that she not be left alone at night in the store, which stayed open until 10:00 p.m.

Ralph Featherstone made sure she wasn't alone. He was the store manager. His friends called him Feather. He had replaced Gittens, who left to travel through Africa after a year of opening and closing the shop seven days a week. Featherstone was a bright, well-liked former SNCC activist who usually wore a serious face and sometimes overalls. He immersed himself in the bookstore, reading, recommending, and building relationships with publishers. Arthur Wang of Hill & Wang, one of the few seriously invested in African American literature, personally dropped off books. He and Feather would go out for lunch.

In March of 1970, newly married and just hours after locking up at Drum & Spear, Featherstone headed to Bel Air, a Baltimore suburb where one of his friends, former SNCC leader H. Rap Brown (who signed copies of his autobiography at the bookstore), was slated to appear in court. Featherstone never made it. His car exploded. It was a bomb. Feather was dead.

Authorities quickly floated the idea that the bomb was of Featherstone's making, that he had been planning to disrupt Brown's trial and had accidentally detonated the device. Others argued that Feather had been assassinated, perhaps mistakenly, with Brown being the real target.

Area high school students called for a walkout to honor the fallen thirty-year-old. Drum & Spear covered the funeral costs and kept

Feather on the payroll, sending checks to his young widow. On the day of his memorial service, the bookstore remained open; it's what he would have wanted. On the wall, right next to Muhammad Ali and Malcolm X, the staff hung a picture of Feather wearing a polo shirt and lost in thought. The caption read "African Warrior." In response to his death, the booksellers discussed whether they should ban white customers—not that there were many. In fact, staffers assumed that any white person who walked in was FBI.

Meanwhile, the insurance company threatened to cancel the store's policy, fearing that it had become a target. And then, in August, bombs shattered the windows of the Portuguese embassy and the Rhodesian Information Office. The FBI suspected Drum & Spear of being behind the explosions. Someone had reported seeing a Volkswagen minibus, registered to Richardson, near the scene. An exasperated Cox wrote to Cobb, who was in Africa, with the news: "The white folks . . . seem to be after us."

A s if managing one beleaguered shop weren't enough, Richardson and Cox opened an offshoot in September of 1971. Maelezo Bookstore was certainly unique. It operated inside a federal government building. Black employees at the Department of Health, Education, and Welfare (later Health and Human Services) had lobbied for a space of their own. Secretary Elliot Richardson ultimately agreed, leasing them a portion of the ground floor. Critics said he was backing a bookstore that "coddled racist militants" and promoted "hate-whitey" attitudes—and Communism and Socialism to boot.

Richardson wanted an African name for the bookstore, settling on Maelezo. She would come to regret it. Maelezo was hard to remember, hard to find in the phone book, and hard to pronounce. "Politics got in the way of good sense," she conceded.

Name choice notwithstanding, the shop proved popular among Black federal workers, especially during lunch breaks. One bestseller was Iceberg Slim's *Pimp*, a memoir and graphic exploration of his experiences in the sex trade. Richardson wanted nothing to do with the book or the man. Unbeknownst to her, another employee had booked Slim for an autograph session. As she saw him walking in the store, she walked out. "It's the only time ever that I have looked at somebody, looked in his eyes," Richardson remembered, "and saw nothing." Not all books by Black writers had value. Some, she argued, were detrimental. Nevertheless, crowds thronged the store. When Richardson returned, she pointed them toward Langston Hughes.

D rum & Spear's core was now spread thin. Richardson was steering the press and Maelezo. Several of the founders were in Africa, building out the publishing office while organizing the Sixth Pan-African Congress. "I was more concerned with Liberation than the question of business," Cox acknowledged. They were still activists, engaged in projects beyond Drum & Spear.

The press was losing money. It paid too much to printers who printed poorly. And then there was the problem of distribution and demand. The press shut down after only a few years. Sales at the bookstore also slowed. By March of 1974, Drum & Spear was doing about one hundred dollars a day in business, roughly a quarter of what it once pulled in. Cash was short. Taxes were unpaid. Payments to publishers were overdue. Lawsuits for failure to pay necessitated more time, energy, and money to fend off. They tried cutting costs. The watercooler had to go. They reduced salaries. And the store's buyer took a field trip to learn the art, science, and economics of bookselling. It was too late.

What happened to all the customers? By 1974, more than half of the recently established Black studies programs had already vanished. Everyone at the store, from the day-to-day clerks to the founders, sensed a moment passing, a "diminishing fervor and inquisitiveness about Black history." Plus, the bookshop no longer held a monopoly. By 1974, there were eighty bookstores in Washington, DC, including chains, which carried some of the same titles found at Drum & Spear.

Richardson was exhausted. "There's a lot of each of us in the store," she said. It was the spring of 1974, just shy of their sixth year in business. The staff issued a letter to the community. We failed, they wrote. They had kept inventory too high. (Stacks of books sat dormant in the back office.) They had borrowed too heavily. (If only they had listened to the Professor.) They expressed optimism that another Black bookstore would take Drum & Spear's place. But by their own logic, it wasn't clear that another could succeed, at least not if success were measured in terms of financial profit *and* social, cultural, and intellectual profit. Even just in terms of finance, and even among general bookstores, making money was hard. A 1977 report of ABA member stores revealed that just half of them were profitable.

In 2020, Marcus (as in Marcus Garvey) Books was struggling. The Oakland, California, shop with colorful murals on the outside and pictures of Black heroes and African art, scattered plants, and makeshift shelves on the inside opened in 1960 (originally in San Francisco's Fillmore District) and was by 2020 the oldest Black-owned bookstore in the country. Most of the shops opened in the late '60s or early '70s lasted only a few years. The same year that Drum & Spear closed, Michaux's shut down. By the early 1980s, in one journalist's estimation, there were only ten Black bookstores in the entire country.

In the late 1980s and early '90s, the trend reversed. A group of Black booksellers formed a subdivision of the American Booksellers Association. But this boom was also short lived. Like independents of all varieties, they struggled in the era of Borders and Barnes & Noble, and then in the age of Amazon.

When COVID-19 came in the spring of 2020, it sent Marcus Books reeling. Friends donated tens of thousands of dollars to save the store, contributions to keep a for-profit business alive. Just as things seemed bleakest, sales at Marcus and other Black-owned bookstores skyrocketed. In May, a white Minneapolis police officer murdered George Floyd, and interest in books about race and racism soared. Carts and tables with "antiracist" texts were set up at independents across the country. Antiracist syllabi encouraged Americans to educate themselves by reading books like *White Fragility* and *How to Be an Antiracist*, as well as those written by celebrated contemporary Black authors like Ta-Nehisi Coates (whose father owned a Black bookstore in Baltimore) and Colson Whitehead—and to buy them at Black-owned bookstores. Only about 6 percent of indies were owned, or partially owned, by Black people, who constituted 13 percent of the nation's population. Within weeks, Google searches for "Black bookstores" rose one hundred times higher than they had ever been. Those Black-owned bookstores—Marcus Books included—benefited from online sales platforms, set up out of necessity during the pandemic. Revenues at Marcus jumped by 150 percent. Droves of customers from around the world were willing to wait in a digital line hundreds of people deep for the most in-demand books.

Even as the Google searches faded and online sales fell back to baseline levels, the importance of promoting Black booksellers and authors in a predominantly white industry persisted. The ABA launched an antiracism campaign. It promised to diversify its board and to help booksellers address diversity, equity, and inclusion. Some took up the cause on their own. Greenlight Bookstore, a handsome Brooklyn independent started by two white women, Jessica Stockton Bagnulo (a veteran of Three Lives & Company) and Rebecca Fitting, issued a formal apology in July of 2020. They owned the fact that the shop hadn't always been welcoming to Black customers. They developed new hiring practices, antibias training, and staff education programs on local Black history and culture.

Later that year, a former CEO of the ABA, a former CEO of Macmillan, Kwame Spearman, and a group of ten others bought one of the most beloved indies, the Tattered Cover, which has four locations in and around Denver. Because Spearman is Black, the new ownership group called the Tattered Cover "the largest Black-owned store in the U.S." Black booksellers called it "branding." As the manager of Uncle Bobbie's Coffee & Books in Philadelphia said, a true Black bookstore is "about the community that you serve, it is about your mission statement, it is about the books on your shelf, and it is about the way, frankly, that Black people feel about your business—about the way Black people feel safe."

By that definition, Drum & Spear was the quintessential Black bookstore. But "it was more than a bookstore," in the words of those who built it. It was a home. It was a school. And it was a community.

The Guy Who Never Buys Anything

⤷⤶

Ricky lives in Wardensville. That alone makes him unusual. As of last count, the eastern West Virginia town was home to just 258 people. The downtown is basically just a thruway, with trucks thundering past a church, a bank, a gas station, a post office, and a handful of tired-looking homes. The new green building with a black metal roof and string-lit porch looks out of place. It's home to WordPlay, an independent bookstore that opened in 2020, during the COVID-19 pandemic. Marlene and Tom England, the couple who own it, already owned one bookstore in Frederick, Maryland, called the Curious Iguana. They (mostly) knew what they were getting into. Indie bookstores tend to set up shop in urban areas with affluent residents and high foot traffic. Wardensville this is not.

Ricky lives in a small house a short walk from WordPlay. In the summers, he mows lawns. No matter the season, he shows up at the shop at some point during the day, usually en route to 7-Eleven. Ricky never buys anything and doesn't come to talk about books. He does seem to know everything about the local goings-on. He can tell you when the state troopers are out with their radar guns and who is moving in or away. When rumors around town start to fly, Tom and Marlene know not to believe them yet: "Let's wait and hear from Ricky."

Ricky was initially suspicious of WordPlay. That it didn't seem a natural fit was the very reason why Marlene, a West Virginia native, wanted to open it. "Every community should have a bookstore," she said as bookseller Char, an Agatha Christie fanatic, brought us sweating plastic cups of Capon Springs water. The water, she explained, fell as rain seventy years ago and was available at the nearby springs. (Just bring your own jug). She said it was the best-tasting water in America.

Inside the one-thousand-square-foot shop, there's an especially deep stock of Appalachian travel guides and fiction. And there's an entire section devoted to race and social justice. Some of these books, Marlene explained, "may never sell, but I want them on the shelf." She said there's value in people merely seeing them.

Ricky is among those who will never buy *The Black Friend: On Being a Better White Person*. But it's there for him to see. And though Ricky will probably never buy any book, the bookshop is there for him, too.

10.

BARNES & NOBLE

Len Riggio wasn't your typical bookseller. He hadn't read much as a kid, and at NYU, where he never graduated, he studied engineering, not English. Nowadays, he's not your typical retired bookseller, either. A gold-lettered Barnes & Noble sign leads into his Fifth Avenue office, which looks more like an art gallery. I love tall ceilings, he said, reminiscing about the superstores and their supertall ceilings. On his desk was a copy of the latest *New Yorker*, and across the room was a provocative Kerry James Marshall painting of a Black woman and Black Power iconography: an Afro, hair pick, and raised fist. Riggio's a collector. In the library are shelves of art books and two large canvases. Boetti, he said excitedly, describing the artist's technique, nearly touching the canvas. Short and approaching eighty but still powerful looking, Riggio was in jeans, sneakers, and a striped sweater. He walked with purpose over to the scratchboard portrait of Kurt Vonnegut, a style any Barnes & Noble regular would recognize. "I was very close to him," Riggio said. There were some chairs from the early days and a designer piece (Fornasetti), the model for his superstore aesthetic. Design is everything, he said, as if it were a given.

The romanticized version of a bookstore is cozy and creaky, warm and wondrous. Books are everywhere. Old bindings perfume the lamp-lit air. The owner is ever present and seems to have read every book in print. With its aisles of toys, games, and calendars; its coffee, cookies, and cheesecake; its fluorescent lights and tiled ceilings; and sometimes its escalators and shopping carts, Barnes & Noble hardly fit the image. Yet Barnes & Noble was once the face of the American bookstore.

In truth, few bookstores ever met the imagined ideal. Benjamin Franklin sold chocolate. And Riggio always intended Barnes & Noble to be a different kind of bookstore. He wanted his stores to be accessible, unassuming, and inviting. Yet Barnes & Noble was often dismissed as impersonal and overly focused on the bottom line. Independents touted their spirit and individuality, their cultural and social benefits, and their underdoggedness, which stood in marked contrast to the mail-order book clubs, to the paperback-only shops, and—most significantly—to Barnes & Noble, Borders, B. Dalton, Waldenbooks, Crown Books, and other such chains.

Could both types of stores coexist? Not everyone was sure. Some worried that Barnes & Noble would kill the independents and maybe even books themselves. In certain circles, setting foot inside a Barnes & Noble meant risking one's reputation. Nevertheless, Barnes & Noble grew mightily, upending the bookselling model, a model that would itself be upended. But for the latter part of the twentieth century and the beginning of the twenty-first, Barnes & Noble was a powerhouse. It shaped our very notion of what the American bookstore was, and what it might become.

——

I t was the publishers that operated the first bookstore chains. Brentano's began in 1853 as a tiny Lower Manhattan newsstand with an extensive selection of foreign-language books, popular with the sizable immigrant population. Brentano's moved into a storefront—though it was more like a hallway—before uprooting again in 1870 to a stand-alone space along Union Square. A series of fires and opportunities prompted subsequent moves, and by 1902, it had returned to just off Union Square, now with more than a mile of shelves and with branches in Chicago, Paris, and Washington, DC.

Although they were chains, neither Brentano's nor the other publishers-slash-booksellers had to defend themselves from accusations of being cold or overly commercial. To the contrary, writers, intellectuals, and political heavyweights, ranging from Charles Dickens to Ulysses S. Grant, frequented Brentano's. Along Fifth Avenue, publishers' bookshops boasted impressive entrances with doormen standing guard. Inside opulent quarters were bound sets intended for the "gentleman's library" and learned staff. In *This Side of Paradise*, F. Scott Fitzgerald describes a bookish character as "rattling off lists of titles with the facility of a Brentano's clerk."

Chain stores of all types boomed in the prosperous 1920s. By the end of the decade, Americans were familiar with national drugstores, restaurants, hotels, and especially the grocery store giant A&P, which had nearly sixteen thousand locations. In 1929, there were roughly thirty bookselling chains. None were titans—the average had only eleven locations—and none had managed to make the bookstore a fixture of the retail landscape. Six states—Arkansas, Delaware, Nevada, North Dakota, South Dakota, and Wyoming—still had not a

Scribner's moved into a purpose-built ten-story building along Fifth Avenue in 1913. The Beaux-Arts masterpiece was home to both the retail bookstore (seen here) and the publishing offices on the upper floors.

single bookshop. Typically larger and more trafficked than personal bookshops, the chains wielded disproportionate selling power. They accounted for 31.6 percent of all bookstore sales but only 13 percent of the total number of bookstores.

During the Depression, chains suffered, and in the economic bounce following the Second World War, they didn't exactly take off. By 1960, Brentano's had only fourteen outlets; the largest was Double-day, with thirty-three. In all, there were fifty bookselling companies that could reasonably be considered chains, accounting for just 8 percent of the nation's nearly three thousand bookstores. That share would grow larger, fueled by two emerging giants: Waldenbooks and B. Dalton.

Waldenbooks started in the Depression with small lending libraries tucked inside department stores. Although some of the larger department stores, Marshall Field & Company included, operated their own lending libraries, others leased space to third-party operators. At the original Waldenbooks, customers borrowed titles for three pennies apiece. Public libraries loaned books for free, of course, but were often starved for funds and unable to grow their collections.

In 1962, just north of Pittsburgh, Waldenbooks tried something new. It opened the very first mall bookstore, a modest outlet over by the tweed shop. The most distinguishing feature of the mall was its giant moat of parking spaces. The American bookstore had arrived in the American suburb. By 1969, Waldenbooks had fifty-three retail stores plus another seventy-one locations in department stores. The future of bookselling seemed clear.

Waldenbooks' success elicited new competition. Founded in 1966 by a department store operator, B. Dalton was envisioned as the new frontier in mass-market retail. As the company president noted, "We felt that what the book business needed was merchandising know-how, the kind of selling that 'mom-and-pop' stores don't do." He continued: "Naturally, our emphasis was on salesmanship rather than bookmanship." B. Dalton opened its first store in a Minneapolis strip mall. Within four years, there were twelve of them, mostly in the Midwest, each with a trademark parquet floor and about twenty thousand titles—plus some toys, cards, and music.

Throughout the 1970s, a new Waldenbooks opened nearly every week. B. Dalton had 360 locations by 1976, and in 1978, it debuted its twenty-five-thousand-square-foot showpiece on Manhattan's Fifth Avenue. Computers rather than readers calibrated the stock. In 1981, Waldenbooks, with 735 outlets in total, became the first company with at least one bookstore in every state. Nearly a quarter of all bookstore sales came from Waldenbooks or B. Dalton.

Growth begat growth. The organic pace of expansion wasn't enough, so Waldenbooks bought Brentano's. Then, in 1984, all-things-cheap retailer Kmart acquired all 845 Waldenbookses. Two years later, Waldenbooks hit the one-thousand-store mark.

The heyday of the mall bookstore turned out to be ephemeral. The new trend was giant bookstores. They called them superstores.

B arnes & Noble dates to 1874, when Charles Barnes started a wholesale book business out of his home in Wheaton, Illinois. Barnes & Co. developed a specialty in textbooks, and Barnes's son moved to New York, joining forces with a bookselling and publishing firm called Hinds & Noble. After a couple of relocations, Barnes & Noble settled into a retail-friendly space on lower Fifth Avenue in 1932. It would remain the company's flagship store for the next eighty-plus years. Less than a block away, the firm built a "storehouse deluxe." The warehouse doubled as a bare-bones bargain outlet, the Economy Bookstore.

In 1941, Barnes & Noble doubled its Fifth Avenue space and dramatically changed the retail layout. With a focus on efficiency, management dubbed the new model a "book-a-teria." Upon entry, customers took blank charge slips, and as they walked through the smorgasbord of books, they handed their slips to clerks who marked them with the names of desired titles along with prices and ferried their books over to the cashier. At each section—general trade, children's, technical, medical, religious, art, law, language, and rare—shoppers sat on stools, sifting through catalog cards and chatting with section-specific clerks. Midway through the gauntlet were the textbooks. During

A bookstall outside Barnes & Noble in Manhattan, 1933.

The newly remodeled floor of Barnes & Noble in 1941.

peak season—just before and after the semester—shelves, bins, and display tables were folded, moved, and combined to form a 125-foot counter where college students bought and sold textbooks.

In addition to the symphony of registers humming, books thumping to the counter, and telephones ringing (the store was so big that in-store clerks called one another), a loudspeaker played "Music by Muzak," a new background-music platform designed to keep shoppers and workers stimulated. Barnes & Noble was among the first to try it. The regular programming featured upbeat music sprinkled with in-store advertisements and bits of news, such as "World Series scores and war bulletins."

The "book-a-teria" seemed to be working. By 1949, Barnes & Noble had two hundred employees and two million books in stock, and it excelled at getting customers in and out the door. Other bookshops gravitated toward the model. In 1955, Kroch's & Brentano's debuted the "Super Book Mart" in the basement of its Wabash Avenue store. The four-thousand-square-foot space had just five employees. Customers walked around with grocery-style shopping baskets.

The "book-a-teria" display nearest the register was for Pocket Books, mass-market paperbacks. Paperback-only bookstores started appearing in the 1950s, furthering the popularity of softcovers, long dismissed by certain booksellers as an injustice. (Frances Steloff refused to stock them.) Paperbacks challenged the belief that books were items to be treasured and collected, by and for the cultured and well off. Several of the new paperback bookstores evolved into sizable chains. Bookmasters had a half dozen locations in New York, including one on Broadway near Forty-Second Street, next to a pornographic movie house. One of several dozen paperback-only bookstores in the city, it stayed open twenty-four hours a day. (Barnes & Noble later acquired Bookmasters.)

Meanwhile, Barnes & Noble, which had been managed by generations of Barneses and Nobles, began attracting interest from corporate investors. In 1969, a conglomerate named Amtel bought it. Two years later, Amtel sold Barnes & Noble for $1.2 million to a thirty-year-old from Brooklyn.

L en Riggio was working at the NYU bookstore. Classes were boring. The bookstore was not. George, the Polish-born paperback buyer, gave him books to read so long as he didn't scuff them up. He read Hermann Hesse. He read Shakespeare. He read Homer. All were on sale for less than a dollar. There had to be a bigger market. He thought about his Bensonhurst neighbors, mostly working-class folks. Why shouldn't they be bookstore regulars? *If only*, he said to himself, *there were a different type of bookstore.*

When Riggio bought Barnes & Noble, it was hardly a national name. Though the New York store was massive, its reach (except for through mail orders) was limited and its audience predominantly college students. The biggest asset—and the reason he was able to secure a loan to buy the company—was an incredibly inexpensive seventy-year lease for its Fifth Avenue building.

A sign of his ambition and maverick mentality came in 1974, when Barnes & Noble aired the first bookstore commercial on television, a medium that booksellers considered the enemy. The ads depict a quaint bookshop where the varied needs of its customers go unmet. A pigtailed kid wants children's books, and a man, clearly suffering from electric shock, wants a wiring-for-dummies guide. The little book-shop can't help them. Instead, they must go to Barnes & Noble, which has everything. "Of course! Of course!" they say, echoing the company's catchphrase.

After wading into television, Riggio debuted a new pricing strategy, discounting select bestsellers by 40 percent and thereby affording hardly any profit. Rival booksellers were incensed. Riggio kept at it. In 1975, he opened a concept store, a three-story annex across the street from the Fifth Avenue headquarters. Like the Strand, it sold review copies, used books, and remaindered books. Everything was on sale. Customers bought handfuls of books for dollars, plopping them into shopping carts. With its casual seating and tables, the annex planted the seeds for Barnes & Noble's future.

Outside New York, Barnes & Noble opened several annex stores and mall locations, and managed an increasing number of college bookstores. Meanwhile, special-interest stores advertised themselves as niche havens in contrast to the supermarket-ish and paperback stores. By the late 1970s, there were antiquarian bookstores, gay bookstores, Black bookstores, feminist bookstores, children's bookstores, religious bookstores, cinema bookstores, comic bookstores, yoga bookstores, acupuncture bookstores, sci-fi bookstores, wine bookstores, occult bookstores (101 of them), and even an oceanography bookstore.

In 1987, Barnes & Noble made its boldest move yet. With just seventy stores, it acquired B. Dalton, more than eleven times its size, paying $300 million, mostly in borrowed money. Then Riggio bought Doubleday bookstores. Barnes & Noble was no longer a midsize regional player.

/——

The first Barnes & Noble superstore arrived in 1990, with fifteen thousand square feet in a Minneapolis suburb. (Compared with what was to come, the first superstore was only relatively super.) The "information piazza of America" had reading nooks and story-time alcoves. Generous oak tables and captain's chairs beckoned people to stay. Local booksellers expressed concern. They needn't be worried, Barnes & Noble publicists claimed. No, Barnes & Noble wasn't an independent, they admitted, but neither was it a chain, they claimed puzzlingly.

The whole retail landscape was in the midst of transformation. Dollars and traffic flowed away from indoor malls and toward strip malls stitched together by supersize retailers. The big-box stores included Barnes & Noble's main rival. Borders began in Ann Arbor, Michigan, as a small used bookshop in 1971. It had grown tremendously by the time Kmart acquired it in 1992, at which point Kmart already owned Waldenbooks, which already owned Brentano's. Borders-slash-Waldenbooks-slash-Brentano's-slash-Kmart was a powerhouse. For the remaining chains, the best means of survival was to position themselves as acquisition targets.

Barnes & Noble kept growing. Within a few years of its first iteration, the average superstore had doubled in size, becoming roughly six times that of a typical B. Dalton. New locations appeared in big cities and medium-sized suburbs. No two stores were exactly the same; no two stores were all that different. Pictures of famous authors hung on the walls. Columns with wood-paneled bases nodded toward a home library aesthetic and belied the otherwise bright, cavernous atmosphere. The high ceilings were meant to give a sense of "wow."

Although Barnes & Noble defended its employees as serious readers (and plenty of them certainly were), there was no Strand-like literary entrance exam. Nor did customers necessarily care. There were signs everywhere and eventually computers that customers could use to search the inventory themselves.

The largest superstores carried upwards of two hundred thousand titles, many at 20 or 30 percent off list price. The three-tiered newsstand lined with magazines catered to computer geeks and horse enthusiasts and every other kind of enthusiast. The music section could have been its own store. With each passing year came more bric-a-brac. And then there was the café that, unlike a library, encouraged talking, eating, and drinking. In 1993, the same year Barnes & Noble went public, the company struck a deal with Starbucks (named for a character in *Moby-Dick*), aligning two formidable brands.

The publishers, which had also been consolidating into ever larger corporations, understood that if a book was going to take off, it would happen at Borders and Barnes & Noble. Accordingly, they were willing to cede a great deal of power to the chains. Settling on a book's cover design usually involves a delicate negotiation between artist, marketer, editor, and author. Now Barnes & Noble had a seat at the table. If the bookseller didn't approve, it wouldn't be the cover. Co-op advertising, which involved publishers paying to have books placed in the most visible areas, became the norm. Securing a spot on the front table at every Barnes & Noble could cost $10,000 for two weeks. It was a major source of revenue for the bookstore and a major marketing expense for the publisher.

Demanding authors insisted that their books be placed in prime locations. Riggio remembers fielding a call from TV personality Bill O'Reilly, who complained that his book was tucked away in a corner instead of in a giant pile up front. O'Reilly threatened to start a boycott. "I don't give a shit," Riggio fired back.

Wherever the books lived and no matter how tempting the signs, there was never pressure to actually buy anything. Riggio wanted the store to feel like a "second home," a place to just hang out. Wide entrances invited customers in. Bathrooms, seating, and coffee encouraged them to stay. At my local Barnes & Noble in suburban Baltimore in the late 1990s, classmates studied for the SATs for hours, buying, at most, a hot chocolate every once in a while. One friend's parents would go to read (not buy) magazines, cover to cover. Another friend attended a weekly poetry workshop that met there. None of the employees seemed to mind. In fact, executives wanted Barnes & Noble to be permanently inhabited. That was one of the reasons why the superstores hosted so many events, hundreds a year. They also served the company's efforts to silence critics who decried Barnes & Noble as the antithesis of community-centered independents.

Victor Navasky was sold. Although initially skeptical, *The Nation* editor evolved into a Borders and Barnes & Noble superfan: "I try to visit whenever I'm in a town that has one." To him, Barnes & Noble was to 1990s America what the coffeehouse had once been to Europe and what the colonial tavern once was to an emerging American republic. These were institutions where democracy was born; Barnes & Noble was where it was flourishing.

If so, democracy was unspooling across the country. But it came at a great cost: mass casualties of independent bookstores. In 1995, there were roughly seven thousand independent bookstore outlets. Within five years, three thousand of them closed. The dead included Books & Co., arguably the toniest Manhattan shop and the one founded by Jeannette Watson and Burt Britton in 1978. It shuttered in 1997. If any shop was impervious to Barnes & Noble, it would have seemed to be Books & Co., which had an advisory board chaired by Susan Sontag and peopled by Fran Lebowitz, Joan Didion, and Paul Auster. That same year, a Barnes & Noble superstore opened in Park Slope, Brooklyn. (There were already six in Manhattan.) Even before opening day, an independent a block and a half away closed in anticipation. "There was no way we could compete," the dejected owner said.

The ABA, founded in 1900, brought booksellers from across the country together to share best practices, track industry trends, and devise strategies to promote book buying in general. In 1977, it launched *American Bookseller* to keep members abreast of not only opportunities but also threats and what the ABA was doing to combat them. Rarely, though, did unaffiliated booksellers rally together in any concerted manner over a national problem—at least not with much success. Now, the independents faced an existential threat. Booksellers pushed the ABA, which included chains as members and had a board of directors long populated by chain-store executives, to adopt a pro-independent platform. At the 1993 annual ABA meeting, members demanded a pro-independent marketing strategy. In response, the ABA launched Book Sense, an advertising campaign that differentiated the independents from the corporate heavyweights, spotlighting their deep community ties and excellent service. In 1994, the ABA sued a handful of publishers for giving preferential treatment to the chains— namely, for selling them books at deeper discounts.

Despite their efforts, the indies were losing ground. In 1997, Barnes & Noble, with 538 superstores, was opening more than one a week. Together, Borders and Barnes & Noble accounted for 43.3 percent of all bookstore sales. Never had just two companies so dominated the market.

The Goliaths were not just knocking out the Davids. They were destroying one another. In 1998, Barnes & Noble sold more than two hundred million books a year and surpassed, in number of locations, B. Dalton, which had been losing revenue and market share to its partner. The first Barnes & Noble superstore had opened across the street from a B. Dalton. Barnes & Noble was ripping off its left arm with its right.

The battle of the bookstores also played out on-screen. *You've Got Mail* premiered in 1998 (and has been rerun on television ever since). It features Tom Hanks as Joe Fox, heir to the evil empire known as Fox Books (think Barnes & Noble). Meg Ryan's character, Kathleen Kelly, owns the literal and figurative Shop Around the Corner, a cute independent children's bookstore with staff who love books and people. Kelly's boyfriend, before she falls for Fox, is a journalist wary of the chains. His name is Frank Navasky. Like Victor Navasky, the movie comes around to seeing Fox Books as not so terrible after all; rather, it is convenient, accessible, welcoming, and maybe even inevitable.

Throughout the late 1990s, activists intensified their efforts to impede the retail giants, vowing to stand in the way of every new Blockbuster, Borders, and Barnes & Noble that threatened community character. They occasionally managed to amend local ordinances to discourage national chains. Austin, Texas, which led the nation in dollars spent on books per household, was the origin point for a 1998 anti–Barnes & Noble protest known as Bag Day. Participants walked into their local Barnes & Nobles with paper bags over their heads, symbolizing the "faceless entities."

Riggio said none of it got to him. He believed in what he was doing. *You've Got Mail* was "fine." But what wasn't fine was a 1997 *New Yorker* cartoon. Two large, mafia-looking guys walk into a bookstore.

The clerk calls out to the owner: "Emily, a Mr. Barnes and a Mr. Noble would like a word with you." Riggio described it as the "god-awful worst thing ever." Associating him, an Italian American, with the mafia crossed the line.

Accusing Barnes & Noble of being "faceless" was a charge more easily made against BarnesandNoble.com. It launched in 1997, two years after Amazon, with a text-heavy homepage, links all over the place, and a new slogan: "If We Don't Have Your Book, Nobody Does." Although Barnes & Noble maintained a long-standing mail-order business and had worked with IBM and CompuServe to sell books via the internet in the preceding years, the website was a bold step toward what executives envisioned as the future of the book business. Customers would have easy access to every book in stock.

Even as it invested heavily in its online operations, Barnes & Noble continued to expand its brick-and-mortar footprint. By 2007, it had forty thousand booksellers, seven hundred and thirteen superstores, 18.2 million square feet, and $4.65 billion in bookstore sales. Just eighty-five B. Daltons remained (down from nearly eight hundred). The mall-based bookstore era was fading. So were the music sections in many a bookstore as Americans abandoned CDs for digital music.

Another problem was that Americans were reading less. Booksellers of every generation have believed this to be true, but a 2004 National Endowment for the Arts survey offered a "bleak assessment." The percentage of adults who could be considered readers dropped from 56.9 percent in 1982 to 46.7 percent in 2002. Regardless of race, education, and age, adults were reading less, much less. The NEA blamed decreasing attention spans and competing media. The average American home had three televisions, a few radios, VCRs, CD players, and 1.4 video game consoles. In 2007, the NEA issued a follow-up report: *To Read or Not to Read.* The results were even worse. The TV was no longer to blame; it was the internet.

. Technology, so Barnes & Noble leadership believed, could also be the savior. After all, 58 percent of middle and high schoolers reported that they watched TV, instant messaged friends, and peeked to see if any emails had arrived while they read. Don't fight the screen; embrace it. Hence the Nook, introduced in 2009, two years after Amazon's Kindle. Within a year, the Barnes & Noble–branded ebook reader, a small silver device, captured 20 percent of the nascent ebook market. The overall demand for ebooks was still a small fraction of the demand for books in general. But the expectation was that it would soon tilt in the opposite direction.

Barnes & Noble executives and wishful shareholders convinced themselves that ebooks wouldn't cannibalize in-store sales. Customers would still come to browse, they said. They'd still hang out at the cafés, Nook in one hand, Starbucks in the other. Plus, they figured there would be handsome profits from selling the devices. They could make money by selling ebooks and the technological means to read them. With traditional books, they sold bookmarks and book lights. (At rival Borders, there were so many book lights in stock—and so many hours of downtime—that writer Carrie Cogan and her fellow booksellers brainstormed humorous alternative uses, namely "the Itty-Bitty Butt Light™.") But readers don't need equipment. Barnes & Noble booksellers didn't share the executives' enthusiasm. They loved books. They didn't want to steer customers over to a table of electronics.

Excitement about the Nook was short lived. In 2012, it generated $933 million in revenues, which included the original Nook, a Wi-Fi version, a color version, a touchscreen version, a tablet version, and a "GlowLight" version. Despite all the iterations, sales had dropped to

$264 million by 2015. It was losing to Amazon's Kindle. In addition, ebook reader sales and the number of ebooks bought had already peaked. The Nook was on life support. "We weren't a technology-based company; we were retailers," Riggio rued, looking back at what was clearly a wrong turn.

Meanwhile, traditional book sales slowed. US bookstore sales peaked in 2007, the first year of the Great Recession. By measure of the number of stores, Barnes & Noble maxed out in 2009 with 726. It managed to keep revenues relatively steady, and by 2012, its bookstore sales had topped 2008 levels. One reason for the uptick was that rival Borders had gone into bankruptcy in 2011. Then the long downhill slide began. Between 2012 and 2019, in-store revenues fell 28 percent. Barnes & Noble began closing stores.

At the time, it was still generating $3.48 billion in retail sales. (It even sold 10.5 million cookies a year!) But it was a shell of what it once had been. The Nook had failed. BarnesandNoble.com couldn't compete with Amazon. Americans were reading less. What could be done?

What was once a battle between independents and chains evolved into a war between in-person bookstores (Barnes & Noble included) and Amazon. Suburbanites, many of whom had no other bookstores nearby, rallied to save "my Barnes & Noble" as passionately as activists had once protested to keep them out. In Harrisonburg, Virginia, a fifty-thousand-person college town, residents started a petition to save the big-box bookseller when the company announced it would close the local store in 2019. "It's just a part of our lives and we don't want it to go away," a retired English teacher said, underscoring the coffee and newspapers. The shop stayed.

In the summer of 2019, with Barnes & Noble on the brink, a hedge fund swooped in. The investor group, which already controlled Waterstones, Britain's largest bookstore chain, was viewed as a savior (of all things). In charge was James Daunt, a lean, graying, articulate executive with a reputation for being a bookstore whisperer. He had built his own Daunt Books (nine branches, mostly in London, all delightful) and had turned around Waterstones.

Then came the dark spring of 2020. Barnes & Noble shut down its 614 stores. Daunt reckoned that they might as well use the opportunity to repaint and rearrange the furniture. He wanted fewer signs, less clutter, and more serendipity. When in-person bookselling slowly returned, sales rebounded a bit from the shutdown levels, but they remained well below prepandemic norms, numbers already markedly down from the peak.

James Daunt's office is just a few blocks away from Len Riggio's, both near the dizzying Union Square farmers' market. When Daunt walks through, he regularly spots totes from Daunt Books. The nearest branch is thousands of miles away. Mere feet from the market, there's a Barnes & Noble with ample totes in stock. Yet he never sees anyone walking around with one.

When I interviewed him, he remained confident about Barnes & Noble and brick-and-mortar bookstores in general. Today's booksellers are smart, he said. They'll figure it out. Not lost on him was the irony that someone who had started his own indie bookshop now found himself trying to save England's and America's largest bookstore chains. He, too, once saw them as faceless corporations.

His turnaround plan was simple: make Barnes & Noble more like an independent. "We used to be retailers," Daunt explained. "Now we're going to be booksellers." He intended to decentralize the company, empower store managers, and "trust the booksellers." He offered this example: Every Barnes & Noble used to have the same number of bays devoted to the same categories. Shouldn't the Fifth Avenue store manager replace some religious titles with business books? And shouldn't that same manager realize that books sold in Manhattan don't need to be steeply discounted, if at all?

He loathed the idea of a single Barnes & Noble model, though there were some overarching principles: adding more circular tables for better browsing (à la Marcella Hahner); "throwing out a lot of crap," limiting nonbook merchandise to the realm of education or at least to things that pair well with books ("a really attractive square box of chocolates"); having plenty of face-out books arranged on shelves tilted three degrees (he's sensitive to angles); procuring more backlist titles; reducing the rate of returns to publishers (another reason, he argued, to give store managers more oversight, since they have a better sense of their local markets); and moving away from co-op advertising to a more meritocratic system. The supersize concept had clearly fallen out of favor. Some of the more recently opened Barnes & Nobles don't even have cafés—or couches.

Different stores offered different experiences. Bookseller and author Ann Patchett remembered the Mississippi Barnes & Noble near her mother as "a mess," but more recently, she visited one of the chain's stores at a Minneapolis strip mall with her friend Kate DiCamillo, a children's book writer. They browsed and talked literature with a bookseller who seemed to know everything. "We were playing pro tennis with this guy," Patchett said, wowed.

Daunt didn't pass up opportunities to visit other bookstores, either.

Books & Books in Florida and McNally Jackson in New York were some of his favorites. And he also didn't worry about his customers shopping elsewhere. Book buyers "are utterly promiscuous," he said, guessing that somewhere between 99.8 and 99.9 percent of Barnes & Noble shoppers also buy from Amazon. Of course, he'd prefer that they buy from him, or at least from an indie.

The feeling is mutual. "I watch Barnes & Noble as carefully as I watch the independent bookstores," Allison Hill told me. She's the CEO of the ABA, an organization that once labeled Barnes & Noble the enemy. "If something happened to them, it would ripple through the whole industry." Barnes & Noble remains, by far, the nation's largest bookstore chain and the only local bookstore for many Americans. Both Hill and Daunt understand that the bookselling ecosystem needs a critical mass of brick-and-mortar stores to thrive, and both worry about a day when the in-person market becomes so small that publishers orient their entire sales operations around Amazon. The fate of Barnes & Noble is intertwined with the fate of American bookselling and maybe even the fate of reading itself.

The turnaround efforts will take time, Daunt acknowledged. Store managers have to experiment. But there were some hopeful signs. In 2022, he reported that the business was once again profitable. In 2023, the company opened more than thirty new stores. When talking to me, he pulled his cell phone out of his pocket. "That says to me that we're beginning to change," he said, turning the phone in my direction. There was a photograph, which he had taken the day before, of a stylish young woman on the subway, the kind of person, he said, you'd expect to find at Three Lives. On her lap was a Barnes & Noble tote. Daunt grinned.

The Weirdo

Over the course of the twenty-first century, being weird (or nerdy or bookish or all three) has become cool—or at least *cooler*. With the help of an eccentric Austin bookseller, nearly an entire city has embraced weirdness. Indeed, the de facto tagline for the Texas capital is "Keep Austin Weird."

Steve Bercu, co-owner of BookPeople, an indie shop started in 1970 and, eventually, a twenty-four-thousand-square-foot Texas and bookselling landmark, didn't coin the phrase himself, but he was the one who turned it into a rallying cry. In 2002, Borders announced that it was opening a store across the street. Bercu led the protest to stop it. That protest evolved into a citywide campaign to support local, independent, and "weird" businesses. Bercu ordered five thousand bumper stickers printed with "Keep Austin Weird." The bookstore ran out in a week. BookPeople and its allies also commissioned an economic study. The report found that buying books at BookPeople instead of at Borders had three times the impact on the local economy. By 2003, Borders had backed down. The victory turned Bercu into a bookselling hero.

He remained committed to weirdness. He posted advertisements for in-store events in the bathroom. He hired a contortionist for a book party. He once hosted a launch for a book about a murder. The murderer was a former store manager.

Bercu retired in 2018, having distributed hundreds of thousands of "Keep Austin Weird" stickers. By then, visitors could buy T-shirts bearing the slogan at the airport. Borders was long dead.

11.

THE SIDEWALK

Rows of used books lined the folding tables. More sat in plastic crates stacked in cascading hills and some on tattered blankets and chunks of cardboard. Still, the books—near-holy objects—never touched the ground directly. Not even the $1 paperbacks. Here was the sidewalk bookshop.

There were six or seven tables along the south side of Washington Square Park and in the shadow of New York University's out-of-place library, a reddish twelve-story brownstone designed by Philip Johnson. Rick, with thin glasses, a plaid shirt, and a lit cigarette, specialized in all things Timothy Leary. Alan was known to curse and tell his customers to "go to the Strand." "Old Man Al" wore a suit and a beret and always had a cigar in hand. He sold maps. No matter the month, Everett wore shorts, slippers, a fanny pack, and a winter hat. People thought he was homeless; in actuality, he lived in an apartment around the corner on MacDougal Street. Paul wore the uniform of 1990s suburban youth: grunge. Boris was Russian. Tony was from the Czech Republic. Zach was from New Jersey.

They all sold used books, unpacked each morning from Chiquita

banana boxes, gladly offloaded by grocery store managers. The cartons, crates, tables, and tarps spent the night in someone's apartment,
storage unit, or station wagon.

The cluster of sidewalk bookstores below the park was just one of
many in 1980s and '90s New York. On nearby Sixth Avenue, readers
could find Steinbeck and Stein, store catalogs and Dr. Seuss, paleon-
tology and pornography. Like many book dealers before them, sidewalk sellers appreciated the company. Constellations of tables in the
East Village, the Upper West Side, and Midtown invited readers who
could browse many a shop with many a specialty.

Nobody called them bookstores. They were stands, stalls, or tables.
And almost nobody called the people standing behind them booksellers. They were labeled peddlers, hawkers, vendors, pests, nuisances,
sidewalk cloggers, and criminals. Yet they played a vital and oft-
overlooked role in the history of American bookselling. For bargain
hunters, readers who wanted to talk books, and customers who found
more traditional shops off-putting, the sidewalk bookstores were neighborhood institutions. They were a prominent feature of the streetscape,
part of what made the city feel like a city. They also complicated the
notion of what a bookstore was and what it meant to be a bookseller.

In Paris, open-air bookselling dates back to the sixteenth century.
The bouquinistes have been occasionally banned (Louis XV didn't
want them on the walks), but they kept coming back. American expats
from Thomas Jefferson to Ernest Hemingway delighted in browsing
the outdoor stalls, as did the French writers who bought books along
the Seine and wrote books of their own in the cafés. Honoré de Balzac
described the scene in 1845:

How may one walk without looking at those little ob-
long boxes, wide as the stones of the parapet, that all
along the quays stimulate booklovers with posters say-
ing, "Four Sous—Six Sous—Ten Sous—Twelve Sous—
Thirty Sous"? These catacombs of glory have devoured
many hours that belonged to the poets, to the philoso-
phers and to the men of science of Paris. Great is the number of ten-sous pieces spent in the four-sous stalls!

In the United States, many of the earliest bookstores extended their
offerings outdoors by way of shelves, counters, and sidewalk bins. Indeed, Americans have been selling all sorts of goods on the streets for
centuries. In the early nineteenth century, there were scores of urban
markets. In tenement-era New York, the Lower East Side was a sea
of pushcarts. "Shawls, bananas, oilcloth, garlic, trousers, ill-favored
fish, ready-to-wear spectacles" could all be had. The whole place
smelled of barreled pickles. There were books, too. (The books-and-
pickles combination returned to the Lower East Side in 2020 with the
opening of Sweet Pickle Books.)

By 1923, *The New York Times* bemoaned the "thinning ranks of
sidewalk vendors." There were still newsboys, some fruit vendors,
and a buttermilk stand, but "gone [were] the Apple Marys and the
women of the pretzel baskets." The reason was twofold. The first was
bureaucracy—ever-increasing licensing requirements. The second was
the automobile. The motor car had transformed the street into a traffic
thoroughfare. No longer was it a place to buy, sell, or play. Nor was it
a safe place to stroll, making the sidewalks more crowded.

But the appeal of outdoor book browsing endured. The Gotham
Book Mart had garden parties and stalls out back. The sidewalk stands

in front of the Strand were a defining feature. In Boston in the early 1930s, a bookseller fashioned an outdoor bookshop in a corner church-yard. When the weather turned foul (it was Boston), the proprietor covered his wares with rubber curtains. In 1946, a first-of-its-kind pa-perback vending machine, four and a half feet tall, offered pedestrians passing through Manhattan's subway arcade on East Forty-Second Street their choice of fifteen popular titles at 25 cents a pop. In Jack Kerouac's seminal 1957 novel, *On the Road*, a character admits to hav-ing stolen Alain-Fournier's *Le Grand Meaulnes* "from a Hollywood stall." More common were sidewalk newsstands, which sold books, especially during the midcentury paperback boom.

The modern sidewalk-bookstore movement began in 1982. At the time, New York had thousands of sidewalk vendors—90 percent of them sold food, including hot dogs, pretzels, tacos, falafel, souvlaki, and ice cream. There were several hundred others selling jewelry, belts, handbags, crafts, incense, T-shirts, scarves, and art. A few sold books, magazines, and film scripts. They were all required to be li-censed and governed by a municipal code, oft violated, limiting how, when, and where they could sell. In a typical year, vendors received more than one hundred thousand summonses. And yet thousands re-mained on the waiting list to obtain a license.

In the Village, a poet had been selling his handprinted works in Washington Square Park for years. For years, he had been arrested for doing so. He eventually persuaded the ACLU to take his case, and in 1982, it lobbied the New York City Council and Mayor Ed Koch to sign Local Law 33. The bill carved out an exception for the poet with a constitutional rationale: "It is consistent with the principles of free speech and freedom of the press to eliminate as many restrictions on the vending of written matter as is consistent with the public health, safety and welfare." No longer did street booksellers need a license. In fact, the law allowed almost anyone selling written material to do so almost anytime and almost anywhere. Most other American cities, however, kept their prohibitions. And so it was that New York, then home to 482 under-roof bookstores, was to become the capital of the sidewalk bookshop.

New Yorkers jumped at the opportunity. Those who had been on the wait list no longer had to wait—so long as they were willing to deal exclusively in books or other written materials. One newcomer was Khan Saddaiq. He set up in Midtown along with about fifty others who lined ten blocks of Fifth and Madison Avenues. Most sidewalk booksellers sold used books, but Saddaiq specialized in remainders, publishers' unsold copies. He sold them for five dollars.

Even though Saddaiq sold books—and did so in a sport coat and tweed hat, no less—he didn't feel like a real bookseller: "It's not a respectable job." Nor was it easy. There were sudden rains, and cold winds sent his tarp fluttering and customers indoors. Summer brought heat, sweat, and fatigue. Constant street traffic meant constant vehicle exhaust. Nor was the job as independent as it appeared. Like many of his competitors, Saddaiq acquired stock from middlemen who bought remainders from the publishers for cents on the dollar. He was paid on commission. Then why do it? There weren't a lot of other options. He was an Afghan immigrant without a Social Security card.

Kano Anoai-Gillard got started in 1984 somewhat by accident. He had dragged several boxes of used books to the front counter of the Strand, where he was offered just $20 for the lot. Insulted, he packed everything back up, walked outside, and unpacked, book by book, onto the sidewalk. He made $200—and found a job. He settled up-town, near the corner of Broadway and 114th Street, on the edge of Columbia University.

Anoai-Gillard wore a cowboy hat and leather jacket. In the interior pocket, he kept a copy of the administrative code spelling out his right to sell. At night, he stored his books in a white Pontiac. He'd hunt at thrift stores and flea markets, having learned what would sell and to which kind of person. He kept a separate stash of "East Side stuff"—rare, autographed, and first editions—for when he set up by the Met-ropolitan Museum of Art.

A block south of Anoai-Gillard's usual spot was Steve Scipio. He had wanted to write science fiction but settled for selling it, an experi-ence he described as "like science fiction." On a good week, he sold two hundred sci-fi books. He became a fixture of the neighborhood, a kind of public librarian prized for his genre expertise.

Some of the sidewalk sellers had experience in traditional outlets. George Foss started working at the Abbey Book Shop on Book Row in 1967 and eventually bought the store. By 1988, he could no longer afford the rent, at least not if he was also going to pay for his mother's medical bills. "Shopless," he set up four tables across from Grace Church, a Gothic Revival landmark. He had one thousand mostly out-of-print books. Foss was willing to negotiate but drew a line: "This is bookselling, not garbage-selling."

Foss was just a few blocks from Washington Square Park, the heart of Greenwich Village, a neighborhood with a distinguished literary history and, now, folding tables galore. The bestsellers were familiar names: Camus, Heidegger, Rimbaud, Nabokov, Sartre, Angelou, Sal-inger, Kerouac, and Vonnegut. Psychology and philosophy sold well. So did "bad religion."

Rick had started selling when his neighbor tossed out a library. Zachary was a bibliophile who couldn't imagine doing anything else. Peter had collected books and figured it was time to sell some. Jason had too many books and too little money. Others yearned for "freedom." The sidewalks were a genuine social and intellectual hub, much like a café. Sidewalk bookselling usually arose less from quixotic desires and more from places of desperation: "If I could own a store, would I stand out here in the cold?"

Booksellers shared tips about how to bring used books back to life with a bit of tape, alcohol, and Elmer's glue. They watched over one another's tables during bathroom breaks and lunchtime. (The classic Washington Square booksellers' lunch was a chicken sandwich with white sauce.) And they commiserated. "Books are going the way of the opera," one of them said.

Pricing was part science, part art. They penciled in prices on the books themselves, hoping customers would accept them. Experts knew how to maximize value. One ploy involved wrapping two or three books in a plastic sleeve. By virtue of their encased status, they'd sell for four times the normal price. On slow days, Village booksellers might do only fifty dollars in sales. On rainy days, they might sell nothing. Good days meant a couple of hundred. Revenues were also seasonal. Many of the alfresco bookstores shut down in winter. In the offseason, Rick worked as a magician. Peter groomed cats.

To stay afloat, sellers needed to acquire inventory, cheaply and regularly. The best deals were when, like at the Strand, critics, editors, or authors sold or donated review copies. Usually, sidewalk sellers combed through library sales, estate sales, and thrift stores—often outside Manhattan. (New Jersey was "ten-cent book" land.) Customers also came to the sidewalk tables with books to sell. Appraisal was a delicate process. Buyers might feel judged by the books they bought; sellers might feel judged by how much they were offered—if anything at all.

A green car pulled up along Washington Square South with sixty-five books inside. The booksellers huddled around, rifling through tipping stacks. After a quick browse, Paul offered the verdict: it's a "bad batch." But it was up to Zach to break the news to the guy who had remained in his car the entire time. He tried to be gentle: "Just because I'm not buying it, it's not a reflection of your taste or the fact that the books are bad in any way. It's just a reflection of what I think I can sell." The driver rolled his eyes and sped off.

Anyone who walked around the fountain, under the arch, and then west to Sixth Avenue, over by the B. Dalton and on the way to Three Lives and Oscar Wilde, would come upon another row of sidewalk bookstores. Crowds lined the wide walks. Nearby residents tossed troves of treasure into recycling bins. There were tourists and NYU students aplenty. Both made for excellent customers.

The Sixth Avenue booksellers "were fundamentally the same" as us, a Washington Square bookseller said, before explaining that they had a "different style, different method." The Sixth Avenue stock was characterized as less "high end," with more magazines and pornography (though you usually had to ask for it). In truth, the selection was broad. *New York Times* bestsellers went fast, as did everything Charlie Brown.

The biggest difference was that most of the Sixth Avenue sellers were Black. Restaurant owners wouldn't let them use their bathrooms.

The Sidewalk

Some of them slept in churches, shelters, or subway stations. They didn't spend their winters doing card tricks or giving Whiskers a bath.

Hakim Hasan arrived on Sixth Avenue in the early 1990s after being fired from his job as a proofreader at a law firm. Bright, well read, and a regular at Harlem's Liberation Bookstore, he decided it was time to open his own Black bookstore. He assigned books on Black history and culture to passersby. One customer credited Hasan with encouraging him to become a reader. They would talk about everything. He trusted Hasan but not other booksellers. "In the bookstore," he said, the booksellers "have a lot of arrogance." While Hasan had good reason to feel proud, whenever someone he knew from the corporate world saw him, he'd pretend it wasn't his table.

Just up the block was Marvin, a recovering alcoholic with a black straw hat, a black shirt, and black pants. In the wee hours of the morning and with headphones on, a tape player tucked to his hip and a coffee cup in hand, he scavenged through recycling bins and trash cans, calculating future revenues. Then he fetched his crates, banana boxes, and foldout tables from a nearby storage unit, carting them via hand truck to his preferred spot in front of Blockbuster. The busiest times were the mornings, right before lunch, and just after 5:00 p.m. (rush hour). By 10:00 p.m., he called it a night.

Down the line were Ron, Ishmael, and Mudrick. Ron got started when someone gave him a collection of comic books while panhandling. He was an addict with a copy of the Bible always on his table. He said it added energy—and boosted sales. Mudrick was illiterate, homeless, and usually smiling. His competitors taught him the basics, including the art of display (a three-by-five-foot table could hold four hundred books) and pricing: "Two dollars apiece, three for five."

The Sixth Avenue dealers sometimes employed scavengers (middlemen who sold them stock), table watchers (to cover for an hour or sit behind a second or third table, since restrictions limited the amount of space per vendor), and placeholders (who reserved prime spots by putting out tables at 3:00 a.m. and waiting until the bookseller arrived).

Though most of the sidewalk bookstores were in Manhattan, by 1992, Roosevelt Avenue in Queens was home to a row along "Little Colombia." Among the sellers was Cuban-born Ramón Caraballo, who sold Spanish-language books.

No matter the location, sidewalk bookstores attracted friends and enemies. One customer described the "serendipity" of stumbling onto a table of books, the kind of experience associated with smaller bookshops of yesteryear: "I couldn't help contrasting this independent or irregular aura with the supermarket atmosphere of the bookstore chains, where you feel that you're being offered only those books that everyone else is reading." But, the same shopper continued, they also exuded sadness, "as if these books bore some remote resemblance to the people one sometimes sees lying on the pavement." That link—between the people who seemed not to belong on the walks and their tables of books—was at the crux of the emerging war on the sidewalk bookshop.

I n 1987, the city was struggling. So was its mayor, Ed Koch, who had recently suffered a stroke. The stock market crashed. AIDS rampaged. And there were drug epidemics. Koch was eager to restore order. One seemingly easy target was the sidewalk bookseller.

Koch had multiple allies in that effort, including the indoor booksellers. Although they promoted the idea of easy access to information and minimized the importance of profit, they railed against the estimated five hundred to eight hundred sidewalk stores. ABA executives, instead of advocating on their behalf, begged the mayor to address the problem: "Just a few feet away (from a legitimate bookstore), a street vendor gleefully sells with no rent, no taxes, no tickets and often no cost of goods." The implication was that their merchandise was stolen. Sometimes the accusation was more explicit: "We have to suspect, though we have no proof, that [they are] stealing them." The Association of American Publishers even hired a private investigator to determine the provenance of bestsellers sold on Upper West Side sidewalks. Nothing suspicious was found.

When Jill Dunbar perused a Sixth Avenue table and found a book she said had been stolen from Three Lives, she made her case directly to the accused. Hasan walked over and dispensed some advice to the colleague who was confronted: "When a white woman comes here and says something is hers, it's hers." Shoplifting was, in fact, a perpetual problem for bookstores. Even Susan Sontag admitted to pilfering books from Hollywood's Pickwick Book Shop. (She went for Modern Library editions and was once caught red-handed with *Doctor Faustus*.) Three Lives and eleven other bookshops—including Oscar Wilde—jointly issued a flyer opposing sidewalk selling: "Don't Buy Books from Thieves." (Incidentally, it was Sontag, genius and former book thief, who gave the first-ever reading at Three Lives.)

Prompted by the flurry of criticism from "legitimate booksellers," as *Publishers Weekly* called them, the New York State Department of Taxation opened an official investigation into potential tax evasion. Its targets were the mostly poor (some homeless) sidewalk sellers. Although exempt from paying for peddler's licenses, sidewalk booksellers were legally required to pay taxes. That didn't stop Barnes &

Noble from setting up a sidewalk stand outside its Fifth Avenue flagship with a sign reading "No Sales Tax." It was intended to make a
point. One of the only booksellers who, at least publicly, said he didn't
mind them was Fred Bass of the Strand: "They don't harm anyone."

When no evidence of criminality was found, opponents changed
tack. They argued that the sidewalk booksellers were simply unbe-
coming. An ABA executive complained that while traditional bookstores were responsible for shoveling and sweeping the sidewalks,
"these guys come along, unload their boxes, sell books in front of your
store and walk away, leaving you to clean their mess." Carol Greitzer,
a city councilwoman and Village Democrat, proposed rescinding the
peddling booksellers' exemption. She was concurrently waging war
on bike messengers, another group largely populated by financially
insecure nonwhite men. Bike messengers and sidewalk booksellers
seemed like soft targets: vulnerable and visible symbols of nuisance,
blight, and danger.

A few residents maintained that they made the city safer. "You
won't get mugged here," one East Villager promised, pointing to the
vendors. In the West Village, a fifty-one-year-old said he preferred to
park near the tables: "No one's going to break into my car, because the
bookstore is always open." The booksellers understood as much. "I'm
a public character," Hasan said, referring to a concept from Jane Jacobs's most influential book, *The Death and Life of Great American Cities*. A Village resident herself, Jacobs argued that people like Hasan
were what made a neighborhood a neighborhood. A comfortingly
regular sight, they spread neighborhood news, added vitality, and
gained community trust. "People like me are the eyes and ears of this
street," Hasan maintained. Local residents gave booksellers spare sets

of apartment keys. They asked them to watch over double-parked cars and toddlers. Everyone on the block knew them. They were the first people to whom turned-around tourists turned. In fact, the information that Hasan dispensed most often wasn't on literature. It was how to get to Christopher Street.

Nonetheless, the vilification of sidewalk booksellers intensified, culminating in a 1993 bill that was championed, ironically, by the one-time city councilman who had proposed the original version, granting booksellers the freedom to sell without a license in the first place. Now he was a lobbyist. His clients were two Midtown business improvement districts. One of the attorneys described the problem bluntly: "It's mostly about how they look as much as what they're doing."

The New York City Council and the then mayor, David Dinkins, agreed, passing Local Law 45. It affirmed that sidewalk bookstores posed "a threat to the public health, safety and welfare." Owing to their "enormous proliferation," sidewalk booksellers encountered greater restrictions. There were already some limits on where they could set up—not too close to subway stairs, bus stops, crosswalks, or building entrances. Now they were prohibited entirely from certain blocks, including stretches of Fifth Avenue in Midtown, 125th Street in Harlem, and Fulton Street in Brooklyn. But they still didn't need a license.

Rudy Giuliani succeeded Dinkins as mayor and governed on a promise to make the city more livable, cracking down on small-time crime: squeegee men, people jumping subway turnstiles, and noncompliant sidewalk vendors. In the East Village, a lieutenant reported that removing law-breaking peddlers was "a top priority." Any vendor within twenty feet of a building entrance or who did not allow enough room on the sidewalk for passersby would be cleared out. Across the city, the police began spray-painting yellow lines on the curbs to indicate the boundaries of bookselling territory. As the Washington Square South crew pointed out, the police often measured incorrectly.

The West Village booksellers felt further aggrieved by their closest neighbor, NYU. The same year that Local Law 45 passed, the university placed a row of gargantuan planters in front of the library. NYU called it beautification; the booksellers called it a declaration of war. Their preferred spot was now occupied by immovable objects. The booksellers pleaded their case to the local community board. Having never actually received permission to install them, NYU had to unplant the planters. Undeterred, the university sought, and secured, approval to put them back. "We're all for booksellers. We all love books," a university spokesman claimed before adding a clarification: "But we do have a problem sometimes."

Everyone—the university, the cops, the media, even the mailman—seemed to be after them. The "pariahs" fought among themselves. They knew it could be worse. The Sixth Avenue guys were "hit the hardest." The summonses piled up. Hasan got one for having a book dangling over the edge of his allotted space. The police seized everything. And although the summons was later overturned, his books remained in lockup because he refused, on principle, to pay the recovery fee. On another occasion, the police told him he had to move, even though he had carefully measured out his space. Then they came for Mudrick, taking his books because he didn't have a proper tax ID card. A few blocks away, in front of St. Vincent's Hospital, Deborah, in a backward baseball cap, and her partner, Irving "Easy" Rivera, who often sold some nonliterature in addition to books, got used to the routine. Set up shop (quickly). Sell books (quickly). Police come (quickly). Find more books (quickly).

City officials had long been trying to remove vendors from Harlem, particularly along congested 125th Street. There, sellers retailed food, handbags, tapes of Malcolm X speeches, and books. Nearby shop owners (often not Black) complained about them, many of whom were West African immigrants. As part of a 1994 crackdown, the police swarmed. Fights broke out, and twenty-two people were arrested.

Faced with a hostile political and infrastructural atmosphere, many sidewalk booksellers, already beset by a fundamentally challenging business, called it quits before the century turned. Then came 9/11. Tourism and activity on the walks slowed to a halt.

In subsequent years, people bought more books online, gravitated toward ebooks (which had no secondhand market), carried less cash than they used to, and, with eyes fixed on their phones, failed to notice the booksellers right in front of them. Earbuds muted the unsolicited book recommendations. In some ways, the decline of the sidewalk bookstore paralleled the struggles of the independents. But the sidewalk sellers had fewer cheerleaders. The media didn't mourn their loss.

Out in Queens, Ramón Caraballo had moved from the sidewalk to a storefront with two cats in 2003. Barco de Papel sold mostly Spanish-language kids' books. Caraballo missed the excitement of the street, the different kinds of customers. He said that in his neighborhood, "the idea of buying a book in a bookstore is thought of as elite." So he reopened his sidewalk stand, an annex to his brick-and-mortar, a few blocks down.

Some longtime sidewalk sellers managed to hold on. Kirk Davidson got started in 1986 near the West Seventy-Second Street subway entrance. In the three decades since, he had accumulated over two hundred summonses. Certain neighbors loved having him. Others spent their spare time trying to get him booted.

Another holdout was Charlie Mysak. He moved books by way of a duct-taped Honda Civic, which he parked on the street on the Upper West Side, feeding the meter 144 quarters a day. While he was accustomed to summonses, in 2010, the police started seizing his books. "This could very well be the end," he acknowledged with a sigh. The police once confiscated hundreds of books he had left out overnight, covered by a tarp. These were especially valuable, as they had belonged to William Kunstler. Kunstler and Mysak had both been lawyers. Mysak had long since been disbarred, but Kunstler was among the most renowned attorneys in the country, having defended the Chicago Seven, the Attica prison uprisers, and H. Rap Brown, whose trial was interrupted when his friend Feather, a Drum & Spear bookseller, was killed by a bomb. Kunstler was also a friend to sidewalk booksellers. As two Sixth Avenue sellers remembered, he promised the officers who had thrown their books in the garbage that if they did it again, they'd "have to deal with him."

In 2015, Zachary Aptekar was still selling books along Washington Square Park. Usually, he was the only one. Some had switched to selling online. One had opened a traditional bookstore. But most had given up bookselling entirely. Instead of booksellers, the park was now filled with dancers, comedians, jazz trios, and a classical musician who rolled his piano in on wheels. Aptekar's stock hadn't changed much: Mark Twain, Truman Capote, and Jane Jacobs were perennial favorites. His clientele—NYU students, tourists, and some Village residents—remained largely the same, too. But he felt defeated: "It was fun, at one point, with all those wonderful people, the camaraderie, the wonderful books that we'd see on each other's tables, and the whole scene. It's not that anymore." These days, he said, "retail sucks."

A couple of adventurous souls didn't get into the business until after it had already collapsed. Jen Fisher was born in Florida, a fact she seems rather embarrassed about. She arrived in New York in 2012 with $400. She loved books, frequented bookstores, and ran errands for some bookseller friends of hers. Then she decided to set up a sidewalk bookstore of her own.

She settled in the East Village on Avenue A near St. Marks Place. She wouldn't say how she found the spot: "I believe in the mythology of things." She bonded with Tony, who owned the nearby bodega and encouraged her to slide her table down, a bit closer. When anyone gave Fisher a hard time, Tony drifted over.

Her table is typically stocked with art and film books, poetry (she's a poet herself), philosophy, and literary fiction. She has a soft spot for Antonin Artaud and a strong dislike for Paul Auster. ("I won't sell Auster, because then I'll have to talk about him.") Fisher scouts for books across the country, mostly in the winter, that she can flip quickly. But it's not just about economics. She sells only what feels right or what's likely to provoke stimulating conversation. Echoing Sixth Avenue seller Ron and his Bible, she told me that different books produce different energies.

She stows the books in her small Brooklyn apartment and in her large blue Buick. From the trunk to the table and back to the trunk, she moves them with care. The hardcovers are covered in Mylar, and she cleans the books every time they come home. A book that spends a day outside can age a year.

When tired of standing, she takes a seat on the hood of her car. "It's

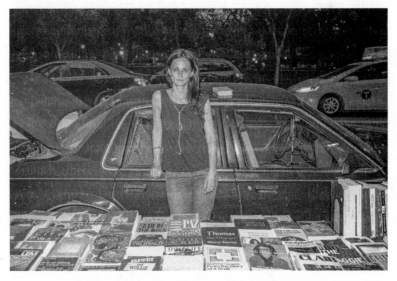

Jen Fisher and her alfresco bookstore, which she calls VorteXity.

exhausting," she said when asked why there aren't more sidewalk booksellers. Plus, the "rent's too high," she joked. Nevertheless, she has embraced being the "rare bird." She wishes there were more stalls, if only so she could browse them.

The police have mostly left her alone. She's received just one ticket. Maybe because there are so few sidewalk booksellers still around, they no longer pose a threat. Or maybe it's because she's a pretty white woman. She does worry that officers could change their stance, or that the community might: "If the neighborhood didn't like me, they could have me out in a second."

She likens her sidewalk bookstore to a barbershop. What she does, mostly, is listen. Some people want to talk about books. Some just want to talk. Most of her buyers don't shop at the indoor bookstores. Some of them are difficult. Sidewalk bookselling is intense, tiring, and far from lucrative. But, she added, it is also "really magical."

The Wall

☙

In 2017, Emma Straub and her husband, Michael Fusco-Straub, opened a bookstore in the Cobble Hill section of Brooklyn. They were both book savvy. Emma knew how to write them; Michael knew how to design them. As it turned out, they also knew how to run a bookstore, especially in the age of social media. It started with the name: Books Are Magic. It was genius. That books (and bookstores) are magic is a given, at least among their core demographic. Buying a Books Are Magic hoodie reflects a love of more than just the eighteen-hundred-square-foot bookstore; it's also a public pronouncement of one's love of reading. So is posting a photograph of a bookstore, a tower of books, or a hardcover, croissant, and mug grouped together in a tempting tableau. On Instagram alone, there have been more than one hundred million posts tagged with #Bookstagram. On TikTok, #BookTok videos have garnered billions of views. While sidewalk bookstores—the most visible variety—have largely disappeared from the public eye, people gawk at screens saturated with books.

Perhaps there's no more fitting #Bookstagram selfie than the one taken standing in front of the original Books Are Magic. (A second location opened in 2022.) Along Butler Street is the windowless Instagram Wall. The background is all black. In large white print, and as if beamed in pink light à la the Bat-Signal, is the store's name: BOOKS ARE MAGIC. It's the perfect scale. When regular-sized adults pose

267

along the wall, the letters arc directly over their heads. They look like reading superheroes.

Inside the just-right-level-of-crowded shop is a mix of wood and brick, a skylight, some industrial lighting, and a few homespun touches. Over in the New York section, I noticed one of my past books. I was smitten. But it wasn't just me. I was browsing with a friend, Marcia, a wise psychologist who carefully moderates her coffee intake. She was similarly charmed by the in-real-life experience, as were tourists, some of whom came for the wall, and regulars, who chatted away with friendly booksellers. A thirtysomething bought what seemed like every book from the New York section (except mine). A couple in the corner giggled as they twirled a rack of cards. "Happy Hanukkah to everyone but Jeff Bezos," one read.

Toward the back was the kids' section. I couldn't resist. I left with two tie-dyed Books Are Magic T-shirts.

12.

AMAZON BOOKS

From the outside, it looked like an ordinary bookstore. Large windows framed a manicured landscape of popular titles. On the inside, the aesthetic was mostly industrial (gray concrete floors, exposed ductwork, dangling lights), part cozy (a carpeted kids' section), and part fortress (enough security cameras to rival a casino). Wooden shelves clutched stacks of face-out books, one, two, or three deep. Planted beneath the books were reviews, written not by the staff but by buyers on Amazon.com. One reader raved about Margalit Fox's *The Confidence Men* ($17.81 for Prime members and $28.00 for everyone else):

> What a great discovery! This history I will NEVER forget, I read of WW's often as they are, of course, source for some of the most interesting stories of any time. The author tells a completely new to me story from WW1.

There may have been no staff picks because there was hardly any staff. There was apparently just one employee at the Amazon Books in

Bethesda, Maryland, a posh Washington, DC, suburb. (On the same Friday afternoon, I counted six employees roving the aisles of Politics and Prose, just a few miles away.) The pale, fortyish employee with an earpiece and a black Amazon polo didn't budge from behind the register. No one was on the floor. No one stood ready to talk books or offer recommendations. But then again, everything in the store already came recommended, sometimes by the thousands.

The Bethesda outlet was not unlike the twenty-three other Amazon Books outlets in 2021, most located in affluent neighborhoods. They had traditional sections—History, Biography, Local, and Fiction—and some unusual ones. One large bay of books was titled "If You Like Nonfiction." (I wondered: *Why not just call it "Nonfiction"?*) Other sections made sense only in the Amazon context: "4.8 Stars & Above," "Page Turners: Books Kindle Readers Finish in Three Days or Less," and the front table full of "Most-Wished-For" titles on Amazon.com.

There were also tables full of Amazon Echos, Rings, tablets, and Alexa-powered devices. When I walked into the Amazon Books at a Manhattan mall, the first thing I encountered was Judge Judy yelling from a jumbo Fire TV. Rarely do bookstores have TVs turned on (or people yelling). Indeed, it was easy to forget that this was a bookstore. A Nintendo Switch sat next to a blender.

After it became clear that the lone Bethesda clerk wasn't going to come talk to me, I met him on his own turf. I asked him about the typical customer. Do they tend to be more interested in George Saunders or waffle makers? Honestly, he said, "they mostly come to return." Customers arrive with mis-sized sweaters and broken forty-watt bulbs bought online. They don't even need to bring a box.

Amazon Books was never intended to be like other bookstores. Nor was Amazon.com intended to be an online bookstore. The goal

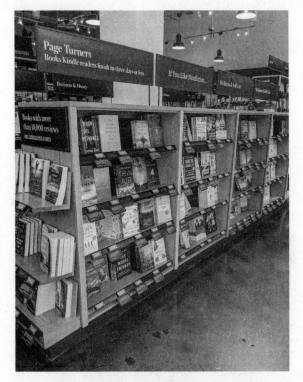

Amazon Books in Bethesda, Maryland.

was to become a titanic retailer, an "everything store." Amazon certainly achieved its goal. In the process, the company transformed the bookstore as we know it.

The first Amazon bookstore opened in 1970 in Minneapolis. But it wasn't *that* Amazon. Actually, it was in many ways the opposite: tiny, not for profit, and feminist. When Julia Morse opened Amazon, she initially sold magazines, buttons, posters, and paperbacks from her porch. She later moved into a storefront that held readings, concerts, and exhibitions. The books were about—and mostly written by—women. Within a few years, the shop had a national reputation. Activists like Gloria Steinem and Rita Mae Brown, a former Oscar Wilde regular, visited.

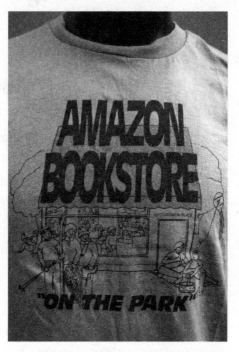

A T-shirt from the original, feminist Amazon bookstore.

The Minneapolis Amazon is often cited as the first (or close second) feminist bookstore in the United States. It certainly was among the first of its kind, a modern bookstore explicitly devoted to women's liberation, even if there were earlier shops promoting feminist causes. In 1916, the Woman's Book Shop opened on Lexington Avenue in New York. It was, according to one scholar, "the first bookstore planned exclusively for women." Elsewhere there were women booksellers who thought of their stores as decidedly different, including at the Sunwise Turn, also launched in 1916.

It wasn't until the 1970s that feminist bookstores began to take off, many inspired by Amazon and its collectivist model. A Woman's Place opened in Oakland in 1970, Womanbooks in New York in 1972, New Words in Cambridge in 1974, the Common Woman Bookstore in Austin in 1975, and the Jane Addams Bookstore in Chicago in 1976. They functioned as political and social centers and sustained an informal network, including a *Feminist Bookstores Newsletter.*

By the early 1990s, the one hundred or so feminist bookstores were pulling in tens of millions of dollars in revenue. Then, like Oscar Wilde and other specialty shops, they struggled to compete with the superstores. When Amazon arrived on the scene, the original Amazon's phones wouldn't stop ringing. People called the two-thousand-square-foot shop with questions and complaints intended for the e-tailer. The staff couldn't take it anymore and, in 1999, sued Amazon.com, claiming it infringed on their trademark, even though the Minneapolis Amazon didn't have a trademark. Internet Amazon argued that no reasonable person would confuse the two. One was a general online bookstore. The other, the lawyers argued, was a brick-and-mortar shop for lesbians. During the depositions of the Minneapolis bookstore's board members, the opposing counsel even asked the question directly: "Are you gay?" The outraged board members refused to answer.

The two Amazons eventually settled. Both could keep using the Amazon name. In 2012, the little feminist bookshop closed for good. By then, almost everything in stock could be found on Amazon.com.

Jeff Bezos was born to a teenage mother who later divorced his biological father and remarried a Cuban immigrant named Miguel Bezos, who adopted the four-year-old. Jeff Bezos was an exceptional child. As his preschool teachers recall, he was often so engrossed in a given activity that they'd have to physically move him, still glued to his chair, over to the next task. In his spare time, he designed, built, and tinkered with things; read voraciously; and watched *Star Trek*. Competitive and relentless, he finished high school in Florida having accumulated nearly every academic recognition imaginable. At Princeton, he graduated summa cum laude with an engineering degree. His success continued on Wall Street. But it wasn't enough. He wanted to build something of his own—a vast online store.

He needed to start small, with just one product. He considered computer software, music, and magazines before settling on books. He loved reading, his wife was an aspiring novelist, and books were small, easy to ship, widely available, and always in demand. Most importantly, there were many more books in print than could ever fit inside even the largest superstores. As Bezos put it, there were no "800-pound gorillas in bookselling." He wanted to be the gorilla.

Bezos wanted a name for the company that began with the letter *A*, and he fancied the idea of the world's largest retailer sharing a name with the world's largest river. He chose Seattle for the location, in part because of its proximity to a major book distribution center. In 1994, Bezos assembled a small team. They met at the local Barnes & Noble.

Bezos didn't know a thing about bookselling. He was, however, an excellent student and signed up for bookselling school, or the closest thing to it: a four-day workshop held in conjunction with the ABA conference in Portland. The instructor was Richard Howorth, then president of the ABA and owner of the legendary Square Books in Oxford, Mississippi. Bezos was one of fifty pupils taking notes on the basics: inventory, marketing, accounting, and customer relations.

Years later, Howorth regretted having taught that one student who kept quiet about his intentions. "If I saw him today," he said, "I'd probably whop him upside the head."

Amazon.com went live in 1995. When a customer ordered a book, the company obtained it from a distributor, repacked it, and shipped it out to the buyer. Even without its own inventory, the company advertised itself as the largest bookstore on earth. (Barnes & Noble sued over the claim.) At the onset, delivery times were slow, a week or longer. Still, sales rose quickly. So did the number of Amazon cheerleaders, including within the book world. Here was an opportunity to sell books across the whole of the United States.

Barnes & Noble's Len Riggio was among the impressed. He thought Bezos "quite genius." He also recognized the threat. In 1996, just a year after Amazon launched, Riggio flew out to Seattle, took Bezos out for a steak dinner, and casually offered to buy the company. Luckily for Amazon, the deal never closed. As Riggio now readily admits, "I would have ruined it."

Amazon quickly expanded, first to music and DVDs, à la Borders and Barnes & Noble. The company also began acquiring its own inventory, cutting shipping times. Still, Bezos prided himself on keeping a lean inventory (informed by algorithms) that necessitated few returns to the publishers. The company dropped prices, especially on bestsellers, as it prioritized growth over profit. Booksellers charged Amazon, as they had department stores, with using books as "loss leaders," discounting so heavily just to get customers in the door (or, in this case, on the website). Then, third-party merchants began to sell via Amazon, too, leading to a vast, chaotic marketplace where used books intermingled with new ones. Someone searching for a title could find all the iterations on the same page (including, later, ebook and audio editions). Then came Amazon Prime, a company membership program. Then came free delivery for Prime members.

From the beginning, Amazon was invested in data. Bezos demanded to know which books his customers—not just a handful of critics—loved, liked, disliked, and loathed. In fact, he wanted everyone to know. He insisted that each book be listed alongside a rating. Publishers and authors worried about the consequences of such public reviews. Amazon also began offering personalized recommendations, the hallmark of indies. The company knew its customers—the books they bought, the reviews they left, the types of books they searched for, their zip codes, et cetera—in ways that brick-and-mortar bookstores never had.

Many of those bookstores were already struggling, losing market share to the chains. Between 1995 and 2000, a staggering 43 percent of independent bookstores went out of business. Then, the once muscular chains started to limp, losing market share to Amazon. By 2006, Amazon's sales had crossed $10 billion.

Then came the Kindle, Amazon's ebook reader. At its fall 2007 debut, Bezos, in khakis and a sport coat (he didn't adopt his younger look until he was older), declared the Kindle the latest development in the evolution of the book. There had been clay tablets, papyrus scrolls, and then the printing press. Now there was a 10.3-ounce device, slimmer than a paperback, capable of holding a home library's worth of books, each just $9.99 and downloadable in less than a minute. The books couldn't be stained by coffee. The font size was adjustable. The Kindle sold out in hours.

Booksellers and publishers panicked. New physical books sold for much more than $9.99. Plus, if ebooks took off—as most people believed they would—then the retail bookstore was on the verge of extinction. Bezos certainly wasn't mourning the potential loss. "Proceed as if your goal," he told a Kindle lieutenant, "is to put everyone selling physical books out of a job."

Publicly, Bezos said that Amazon's success would never spell the end of the local bookstore. "You can be inspired by them," he said, but you can never "duplicate" them. In 2015, as Amazon's yearly revenues topped $100 billion, Bezos decided it was high time to open his own brick-and-mortar bookstore. Like everyone else, he couldn't figure out if bookstores were dead or alive.

Leading the effort was Jennifer Cast, a.k.a. "25," as in Amazon's twenty-fifth employee. She started visiting bookstores, observing customer behavior. She expected to find slow-footed browsers reading long passages. Instead, she noticed that most people poked around for a bit and then bought something. They seemed to want direction.

Cast ordered Amazonians (as they refer to themselves) to raid local Goodwills and shuttle trunkfuls of books to a vast warehouse on the south side of the city that was transformed into a mock bookstore. Amazonians browsed. They offered criticisms. Tweaks were made. The process was repeated, many times over. The most beloved design element was that all the books faced the customer directly, either sitting on tables or out along shelves. "We realized that we felt sorry for the books that were spine out," Cast explained. Every bookseller knows that face-out books sell better, especially the ones at eye level. But most stores don't have nearly enough room to arrange all, or even a majority, of the titles that way. Amazon Books, of all places, decided its stock would be slim and trim. Of course, customers could still order anything they wanted online. In fact, they were encouraged to do so.

Even though the executives behind Amazon Books were avid readers with elite educations (Bezos considered applicants' SAT scores) who started meetings by silently reading to themselves (Bezos banned PowerPoint) and who personally frequented indies (Bezos browsed at the Elliott Bay Book Company), Amazon Books was going to be a different kind of bookstore for a different kind of clientele. They understood that many consumers bought books at Target, Walmart, and Costco. They imagined their bookstores as occupying a middle ground between these retailers and the indies. Amazon Books would be stocked with books that already came recommended by the crowd and in a comfortable enough atmosphere connected to a familiar brand. For those Amazonians who wanted to believe it, they convinced themselves that their stores would be different, different enough not to destroy the remaining indies.

The first Amazon Books opened near its Seattle headquarters in November of 2015 with six thousand titles spread across fifty-five hundred square feet. The most popular new releases were arranged on the wall behind the minimalist checkout. Throughout the store, books were tagged with customer reviews from Amazon.com, the number of stars earned, and the number of people who found said reviews helpful. The staff-favorites section had three picks from Bezos: *The Gift of Fear*, *The 5 Love Languages*, and *Traps*, a novel written by his then wife, MacKenzie. There were a couple of sofas and some Kindles and Fire tablets to play with, but the books were the "hero of the store."

By the end of 2017, when 45 percent of Americans reported buying most or all of their books online, Amazon Books had thirteen locations, including four in California, two in Washington, and two in

New York City. Not everyone was impressed. A *New Republic* head-line read "The Amazon Bookstore Isn't Evil. It's Just Dumb." For *The New Yorker*, Jia Tolentino described the Columbus Circle outlet as "organized like an ill-advised dinner party." What was James Baldwin doing next to David Brooks?

Indie booksellers dismissed the venture. "What we do is very different," the CEO of the American Booksellers Association said in 2017. But no matter what they claimed to the media, booksellers stewed. As soon as the first Amazon location opened, James Daunt hopped on a plane to Seattle. Allison Hill, the veteran bookseller who became CEO of the ABA in 2020, vividly remembered her visit: "I took my stepdaughter with me and said, 'Okay, we're going to go in and run a spy mission. You're going to take pictures. I'm probably going to get a little emotional. It's probably going to upset me.'" As it turned out, she wasn't upset: "That's all you got?" Nancy Bass Wyden of the Strand was the most complimentary of the booksellers I spoke to (all of whom had visited an Amazon Books at least once). She called the stores "efficient." But, she added, they were also "soulless."

At the outset and preparing for the criticism that their company's stock was driven by algorithms, Amazon recruiters tried to poach experienced booksellers, reaching out to the staff at Third Place Books. When critics labeled the bookstore (and the parent company) "faceless," Amazon profiled its "Book Curators"—a.k.a. buyers. Alison was said to have been an English professor. Ian worked in publishing and explored "as many bookstores as possible." Katy read on airplanes. Paige had worked as an editor.

When journalists asked 25 how the company curated its stock, she described the process as "data with heart." Sales metrics and reviews from Amazon.com and Goodreads (also owned by Amazon) fed proprietary algorithms. Although Amazon Books carried well-known titles, the company said the stores were "designed to spur discovery."

B y 2019, Amazon's annual sales had topped $280 billion. Jeff Bezos was the richest person on earth. His company sold roughly half of all new physical books in the United States. Never had there been such a dominant bookseller. Amazon had indeed become the eight-hundred-pound gorilla.

As it gobbled up market share, slaughtered Borders, kneecapped Barnes & Noble, and simultaneously threatened and made clear the value of independents, Amazon continued to push in two opposite directions, promoting ebooks and electronic readers *and* investing in retail book-stores. Meanwhile, journalists, activists, and politicians lambasted the company for not paying its fair share of taxes and for mistreating its employees. They blasted Bezos for being stingy when it came to phi-lanthropy and for obsessing over space travel (*Star Trek* had never left him). The weightiest charge was that Amazon had purposefully de-stroyed brick-and-mortar retail in general and bookstores in particu-lar. Bezos swatted away the assertion: "Amazon isn't happening to the book business. The future is happening to the book business."

Independent booksellers didn't see it as a matter of destiny. Just as they had once defined themselves in opposition to Barnes & Noble, now, with Barnes & Noble as an ally, they defined themselves in op-position to Amazon. Powell's, which had been selling used books via Amazon's marketplace, announced in 2020 (as Amazon's yearly sales reached more than $386 billion) that it would no longer work with the enemy. "It was hard to give up, sort of like smoking," Emily Powell analogized.

When Allison Hill assumed the role of ABA CEO, she prepared for war. She believed that the ABA needed to convince politicians about the existential threat. Legislation or a Federal Trade Commission lawsuit limiting Amazon's market share might be the best hope—the only hope. American booksellers pointed, by way of example, to France, which embraced books and bookstores. In 1981, the French government established fixed prices for books, something many American booksellers have long wished for. Without the ability to discount, larger bookstores couldn't dominate smaller ones—that was the idea, at least. It meant Amazon couldn't sell books for less than any bookstore on rue de Rivoli. Despite equalized pricing, the convenience of free delivery proved tempting, so French lawmakers prohibited Amazon from offering free delivery. In response, Amazon started charging a €0.01 delivery fee. Then the French Parliament set a minimum delivery fee of €3.00. The war will probably never end.

Hill also stressed the need to persuade shoppers, many of whom bought from both indies *and* Amazon, that one was destroying the other. In 2020, the ABA launched a creative campaign called #BoxedOut, timed to Amazon Prime Day. Gesturing toward Amazon's brown cardboard boxes, six indies papered over their storefronts with bold print and provocative text:

Buy books from people who want to sell books, not colonize the moon.

Books curated by real people, not a creepy algorithm.

Don't let indie bookstores become a work of fiction.

Out front were stacks of cardboard boxes and faux books with cheeky titles:

To Kill a Locally Owned Bookstore

*How to Win Friends and Influence People and Then Be
Put Out of Business by a Giant Warehouse Distribution*

*Little Women Who Own Bookstores and Are Getting
Priced Out by Giant Warehouse Retailers*

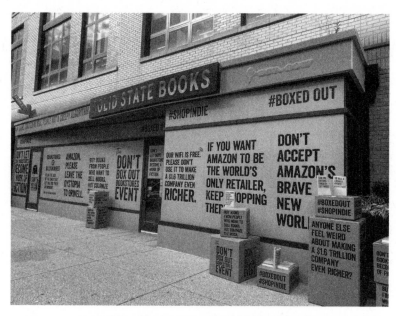

Solid State Books on H Street in Washington, DC.

Meanwhile, the number of Amazon Books outlets kept creeping up, totaling twenty-four by 2021. The company piloted other brick-and-mortar stores, including Amazon 4-star, which sold top-rated books, and Amazon-branded cashierless convenience stores with "Just Walk Out" technology. Whether or not the Amazon Books division was profitable (most everyone assumed it was not), it served a purpose. It was another place to encourage people to join Prime or download the app. It was another place to observe consumer behavior and gather data.

Everyone who knew anything about Amazon understood that the goal was never to have just twenty-four bookstores. Amazon was good at keeping secrets (and they ignored my interview request, though I did speak with one high-level executive off the record). The expectation was that either the model would prove successful and be scaled up or that the whole endeavor would be shut down. Amazon doesn't do small.

I n August of 2021, Amazon Books was still hiring. The company advertised for a retail associate to work in the Bethesda outlet. Except for in the name of the store—Amazon Books—the word *books* or *reading* didn't appear in the job ad. The preferred qualification was a "strong understanding of Amazon devices and Amazon services."

The de-emphasis on employees possessing any particular knowledge of books was part of what ultimately made Amazon Books feel like something that wasn't exactly a bookstore. Whatever Amazon Books was, exactly, executives decided it wasn't working. The presumable lack of profits wasn't enough to justify the gains in consumer data. In March of 2022, seven years after the first one opened, Amazon announced that all Amazon Books outlets would close. Bradley Graham of Politics and Prose wrote an op-ed in *The Washington Post* explaining what had happened: the bookstore business is hard. Even Amazon, or maybe of course Amazon, couldn't figure it out.

In the Boston area, two Amazon Books locations turned into two Barnes & Nobles. The death of the former encouraged the growth of the latter. And across the country, booksellers rejoiced. Amazon was still a grave threat, an existential one even. But they had proven they knew how to do something that the most powerful retailer in the world could not.

The Teacher

Want to open a bookstore? Donna Paz Kaufman is standing by to help. She's trained over one thousand prospective owners since 1992, mostly through seminars held in (not very) grand ballrooms, like the four-day version that Bezos attended.

In 2018, she and her husband, Mark, opened their own bookstore on Amelia Island, a lush barrier island in northern Florida. They started a boot camp in a real live bookstore.

Story & Song Neighborhood Bookstore Bistro, which sells snacks (the "prologue"), soups and salads ("short stories"), sandwiches ("savory plots"), desserts ("sweet characters"), puzzles, games, cards, globes, pens, toffee, beads, photographs, handbags, pottery, and "bird totems," is also home to the Bookstore Training Group. In a classroom with a large screen and a piano in the corner, a dozen wannabe booksellers congregate twice a year to learn about design, lighting, stocking, selling, marketing, merchandising, budgeting, and hiring. They observe the bookstore in action, the daily dance of browsers and booksellers. They toy with the inventory management system. And there's an optional extra half day to study "café operations."

While many alumni have gone on to open bookstores, some attendees come to the realization that bookselling isn't what they had imagined. They walk away from the dream.

The three-day boot camp, with a guidebook and online sessions added in, comes to $1,395; that doesn't include transportation and lodging. Provisional members of the ABA do get a discount.

On their website, the Kaufmans answer a series of FAQs. One asks: "Am I crazy to be thinking about opening a bookstore when all I hear about is how many are closing?" They respond cheerfully but do add an important disclaimer: "A bookstore needs to be more than a place to buy books if it is to survive."

13.

PARNASSUS

There's no single face of independent bookselling. But if there had to be just one, it would be Ann Patchett's. It's a pretty face, lean with plump cheeks. She looks a bit like one of those pale New Englanders who rowed crew at the Olympics while also working full-time as an oncologist. She's actually from Nashville and not terribly athletic, though she did once pass the Los Angeles Police Academy's fitness test. And her writing career could be compared to that of a gold medal–winning decathlete. She's written novels, memoirs, and picture books, as well as essays for *The New Yorker*, *Harper's*, and every other magazine that writers wish they wrote for. Her books are bestsellers *and* critically acclaimed.

Patchett was already a blockbuster author when she cofounded Parnassus Books in 2011. The bookshop leans into her celebrity. There's almost an entire bay of her books. She convinces famous friends to come to the shop and usually puts them up in her own house. Although she tries to avoid what people say about her on the internet (and doesn't watch TV or drink, though she did once do shrooms with a dying friend), she's a media sensation. She's on TV, NPR, podcasts, and, at least once a week, the Parnassus Instagram account, usually in a dress (sometimes a jumpsuit). She recommends books by the stack, each title serving as a character in some larger story. Her dog, Sparky, is often there, too.

Opening a bookshop in 2011 struck many people as crazy. After all, masses of independents had already closed. The future of American bookselling—if there was a future—was Amazon. Yet Parnassus's ultimate success came not despite Amazon but because of it.

A week and a half after JFK died and as Burt Britton moped around the Strand, Ann Patchett was born in Los Angeles. By the age of six, she knew she wanted to be a writer. As an eight-year-old, she was obsessed with flatware; at nine, she got a pig, which she had been begging for since finishing *Charlotte's Web*. When not playing with her pig or polishing soup spoons, the vegetarian was out shooting Coca-Cola cans. After moving to Nashville, she began a long and loving relationship with Mills, the local bookstore she'd walk to after school. Fortuitously, it was next to a pet shop and a soda fountain. "Books, puppies, french fries," Patchett told me, became "inextricably linked."

There were less pleasant memories, too. Her parents divorced, setting in motion remarriages, stepsiblings aplenty, and more than a dozen moves in all. Those experiences, along with her all-girls Catholic school education, provided fodder for several lifetimes' worth of writing. Although she didn't excel in grade school (not even in writing), she studied and wrote short stories and poetry at Sarah Lawrence before graduating to the famed Iowa Writers' Workshop. She published in *The Paris Review*, got an agent, spent a year in Provincetown on a fellowship, and finished a well-regarded first novel.

Success remained far from certain. After graduate school, she found herself unhappily married and then back in Nashville waiting tables. She wrote for *Seventeen* magazine until the age of thirty. Her columns offered advice on such topics as how to ask a guy out: "Try smiling at him (see if you can hold it for three seconds). Sit next to him at lunch (it's a free country)." One piece offered an explanation for why she had remained a virgin for so long: "1. Nobody was asking me to have sex. 2. I was scared to death of the idea."

She moved on to more glamorous magazines—*Elle*, *Vogue*, and *The New York Times Magazine*—along with some less glamorous ones—*Mercedes-Benz Magazine*. Her life of writing books full-time came only after her 2001 novel, *Bel Canto*, her fourth, a story about love, opera, and a South American hostage crisis. It had been a full decade since she finished her first novel, which she drafted in her head while delivering Colossal Cajun Onions to hungry diners at TGI Fridays.

Over the next decade, her acclaim and checking account balance grew. There were no signs, and seemingly no good reasons why, she wouldn't stick to writing. Booksellers dream of becoming writers. Not the other way around.

Then, in 2010, Davis-Kidd closed. Davis-Kidd was a beloved thirty-year-old Nashville bookstore, even if it had been sold off to an out-of-town corporate parent and had come to resemble a superstore with "coffee mugs and scented candles." It was still a bookstore, a community space where shoppers browsed and touched books. And it had some great booksellers. One had worked at Mills when eight-year-old Patchett was a regular, and she still recognized the twenty-something version every time she walked in. Another bookseller was an early Patchett cheerleader, adopting her first novel, *The Patron*

Saint of Liars, for the store's book club. (She would later run Parnassus's book club.)

Then the Nashville Borders closed. The bookselling landscape was more than just bloodied. It was a field of casualties. What remained were just a few Barnes & Nobles and a Books-A-Million. Nashville didn't have any "real" bookstores. At least not what Patchett considered real.

A city without a bookstore wasn't a city worth calling home. Patchett wasn't prepared to move again. She was certain that Nashvillians could support an independent bookstore. After all, Nashville was a city famous for culture. It was the "Athens of the South" and Music City, home to an eclectic mix of high- and lowbrow: Vanderbilt University and a Parthenon replica, the Grand Ole Opry and dive bars, haute cuisine and hot chicken.

As Patchett began plotting, so did Karen Hayes, a Random House sales rep. Born in Alaska, she arrived in Nashville at twelve. She was into science fiction (not flatware). In 1978, she started a career in sales, working the phones for Ingram, the Tennessee-based book distributor. She grew bored of the desk job and spent a year nannying before returning to books as a Ballantine sales rep. Sales reps bridged the gap between publishers and booksellers. Like the booksellers who told customers what books to read, the reps told the booksellers to stock these books. Skilled reps knew how to build trust and sow excitement about forthcoming titles, and they understood the local particularities of retail bookselling: what would sell in which store.

Hayes enjoyed calling on independents, meeting curious people, and visiting mostly charming places. There were certainly some "grumpy old booksellers," too; they knew little about the business, overstocked, and didn't prioritize the customer experience. As the number of bookstores shrank, Hayes's territory expanded. She was assigned to Books-A-Million. "I was miserable," she confessed. "I mean, really miserable." Still, she wasn't about to go and open her own store.

When Davis-Kidd closed, Hayes was devastated. As a sales rep, she knew some long-standing indies that were still doing good business (among her favorites was Carmichael's in Louisville), as well as some successful newcomers. It wasn't impossible. Hayes started drafting a business plan. She drifted toward the idea of starting a cooperative. Then she met Ann Patchett.

Actually, she had met Patchett once before, though only Hayes remembered the encounter. Now they were having lunch at the invitation of a mutual friend. Patchett listened. Patchett looked over Hayes's plan. Patchett thought to herself: *She seems to know what she's doing*.

She went home and talked it over with her husband, Karl. (She had since remarried, this time happily.) Patchett was in. She called her new partner, insisting on one major change. The store would be a for-profit bookstore, not a co-op. Patchett loathed the idea of answering to a board: "Being a novelist means not having a whole lot of esprit de corps." Plus, they didn't need the money. Patchett agreed to invest $300,000. In return for running the day-to-day operations, Hayes would be granted co-ownership. "There's no way in the world I ever would have opened a store without Karen," Patchett acknowledged. And although Hayes might have managed to open a bookstore on her own, it certainly would have been nothing like Parnassus without Patchett. They needed each other. And they still hardly knew each other.

Hayes picked the name Parnassus, having admired Christopher Morley's same-named tale and having long identified with the female bookseller at its heart. Patchett didn't like the name and suggested Independent People or Red Bird Books. Colorful, simple book titles, she noted, were memorable. But since Hayes was the one who would be working at the shop each day, Patchett conceded. (The shop did ultimately adopt the tagline "An Independent Bookstore for Independent People.")

A book-tour veteran, Patchett began paying more attention to the small details of her favorite stores: Malaprop's in Asheville; Powell's in Portland; the Turnrow in Greenwood, Mississippi; and Explore in Aspen. She also thought back to what she loved about Mills, a place that "valued books and readers above muffins." She admired small shops, especially Three Lives & Company. "Maybe it's just that the people who work in tiny stores really do know exactly where every book is located. And they've read them." Booksellers were happy to offer advice. Tuck the children's section near the back, suggested Daniel Goldin of the Boswell Book Company in Milwaukee.

As opening day neared, Patchett maintained that she wasn't interested in running a bookstore, or even owning one. Certainly, "I'm not in this to make money," she clarified. She saw herself as more of a benefactor than a capitalist. It was about protecting an endangered species.

P arnassus opened in the fall of 2011. Comparing the twenty-five-hundred-square-foot shop with superstores ten times the size, Patchett called it "the way bookstores used to be." The immediate vicinity is hardly charming. Unlike Three Lives & Company's red door on the corner of a quaint West Village block, Parnassus is in a shopping center with a cramped and cracked-asphalt parking lot. Across the too-wide and too-trafficked Hillsboro Pike with a too-narrow shoulder is a Walgreen's, an Exxon, and a mall. It's a poster of sprawl—crawling traffic, rows of telephone poles, featureless buildings, placeless places. While some landlords have realized that a bookstore planted beneath a tower of apartment buildings can add value (bookstores, like Starbucks once did, can indicate status), it's doubtful that the Sherwin-Williams next door appreciates the benefits of proximity. And while many a potential bookseller scouts locations based on foot traffic, I didn't see a single pedestrian or cyclist nearby when I visited. The address might be in Nashville, but there is nothing Nashville—or even urban—about the area.

Inside is much closer to heaven—comforting sounds of human conversation and a rolling ladder gently clicking along a wall of honey-colored bookcases. When I walked in, a few booksellers greeted me and then left me to browse, with chalkboard signs cheerily directing the way. In the back I found the children's section, its own retreat. Scattered throughout, lamps hang down from the tall ceiling. I sat on one of the green leather armchairs. There were a couple of plants and a couple of dogs. There's also a piano. It's Nashville after all.

Parnassus Books.

On opening day, three thousand people visited. A nametag-wearing Patchett hopped up on one of the tables. She thanked Hayes (who would never hop up on a table) and promised that Parnassus would always be different. Here were real people and real readers working in a real bookstore. "This is nothing at all like an algorithm," she elaborated, describing the process of matching books to customers. She had a practice of recommending books to family and friends. Now she could advise total strangers. Talking books in this way was, she said, "the greatest joy of my life." Not that it was easy. Every bookseller has met a customer who asks for a book in the vaguest terms: "I don't know the title or the author, but I heard about this book . . ." A good bookshop makes sure they leave happy.

The media was smitten. NPR called. *The New York Times* ran a front-page story. Patchett appeared on *CBS This Morning* and, dressed in a Parnassus Books T-shirt, on the cover of *Publishers Weekly*. She was portrayed as the heroine in a triumphant tale about the life, death, and now revival of independent bookstores.

There were two competing narratives, sometimes spun by the same people, sometimes even in the same sentence. The first could be called the "You've Got Mail" story. Bigger bookstores with bigger stocks and bigger discounts stomped on the indies. Then came Amazon, an even bigger bookstore with an even bigger stock and even bigger discounts. The indies were left for dead. To make matters worse, no one read anymore. The only way to keep independents breathing was by way of charity. Even Patchett likened her bookstore investment to giving to the symphony.

The other narrative was "You've Got Mail (Director's Cut)." The story started the same way, but in this telling, there was an alternate ending. Turns out, the scrappy indies were merely bruised. They proved too valuable, too admired, too beloved to be knocked out. Yes, some badly run bookstores went out of business, but plenty were doing fine—better than fine, actually. Plus, everyone hated Amazon, whose monstrous dominance induced an even greater demand for in-person bookselling and for small, vibrant businesses in general. "You may have heard the news that the independent bookstore is dead, that books are dead, that maybe even reading is dead," Patchett said shortly after opening Parnassus, "to which I say: Pull up a chair, friend. I have a story to tell." Her story, as many a short story, had a compelling pattern. Bookstores grew in size, then ventured online, which in turn "made people long for a little bookstore." The cycle lasted thirteen years, she calculated, the same as for cicadas. One of the world's greatest storytellers, Patchett knew what she was doing: "Say it enough times and it will be true." Indie bookstores were back.

She said it again—"We're not dead, and we're not going anywhere"—to a rousing crowd at the Winter Institute, the annual ABA meeting. Among the crowd of career booksellers and despite having only been in the business for a few months, Patchett had already become the spokeswoman. She appeared on *The Colbert Report*, pitching indies as "a tale of redemption." Then she made *Time*'s list of the "100 Most Influential People." Elizabeth Gilbert wrote Patchett's entry, accompanied by a photo of her standing proudly on a rolling bookcase ladder inside the "sturdy little brick-and-mortar oasis of original thinking." "Can one determined soul really make a dent against the dehumanizing wall of humongous corporate progress?" Gilbert asked before answering the question herself: "Ann Patchett will see to it that the good guys win."

Parnassus was in fact one of a growing number of independent bookstores, a number that had been in free fall for many, many years.

In 1980, Americans bought 40 percent of all trade books from independents. From the vantage point of the 2020s, the 1980s was clearly a
"golden age." But comparatively speaking, it was hardly golden. After
all, back in the 1950s, Americans bought 72 percent of their trade
books at independents. By the early 2000s, that number had dwindled
to 13 percent.

In the 1950s, indies were so numerous that they weren't even referred to as indies. They were just called bookstores or, sometimes,
"personal bookshops." There was the rare reference before then. One
of the earliest uses appeared in *Publishers Weekly* in 1930: "In how
much better position [compared to the chains] the independent bookstore is to develop store spirit, the interest of salespeople, and an attitude of friendly cooperation!" Even then, its identity existed in contrast
to that of the chains. Major newspapers started to use the term, albeit
still rarely, in the 1970s and, just occasionally, through the 1980s. The
label "independent bookstore" didn't take off until the 1990s, the superstore era. The shortened form, "indie," was popularized in the
twenty-first century.

In 2011, the same year that the flagship Borders No. 1 closed in Ann
Arbor, 102 new bookstores joined the ABA. One was Word Up, which
was housed in a tiny donated space in the Washington Heights neighborhood of Manhattan, known as the "Little Dominican Republic."
Purpose-built for the area, Word Up was "a multilingual, general-
interest, nonprofit community bookshop and arts space."

The bookshop was the brainchild of Veronica Santiago Liu, a creative
spirit who once ran a radio station from her apartment and first got
into bookselling while working at Kim's Video, an esoteric video and
music store that also sold books. In its earliest days, Word Up sold
an array of indie press titles, zines, and chapbooks. Or, as Liu put it,

"really odd shit." People began donating books, which Liu offered up for free. The operation moved to a larger and more permanent location on Amsterdam Avenue and 165th Street. Liu filled it with mostly used books; over time, it grew to include more new titles. It also functioned as a gallery, an event space, and a place where kids could do their homework. It hosted summer camps and training sessions on how to be a street-tree steward. There was no reason, Liu believed, why bookstores should limit themselves to book-related events. She merged the roles of community activist and bookseller. In the bookselling world—at ABA conferences and Facebook groups—she felt like an outsider. The problems that booksellers were talking about "were not reflecting my reality." They were worried about ebooks, rising labor costs, and how to serve the community. At Word Up, serving the community was the whole point.

While Liu had worked as an editor at a small press and started an even smaller one of her own, an increasing number of authors, Patchett included, jumped into the bookselling business. They weren't the first. Benjamin Franklin was a printer, bookseller, and writer. In the 1950s, poet Lawrence Ferlinghetti started City Lights Bookstore. In the 1970s, Larry McMurtry—a onetime book scout who later authored *The Last Picture Show*, *Lonesome Dove*, and much else—got into the antiquarian book trade and eventually had five buildings of books in Archer City, Texas, proving that bookstores could thrive outside big cities—until the internet era put him out of business. In the twenty-first century and in a much different bookselling ecosystem, a number of successful authors owned bookstores: Jonathan Lethem's Red Gap Books in Maine; Louise Erdrich's Birchbark Books & Native Arts in Minneapolis; Garrison Keillor's Common Good Books in St. Paul; Jeff Kinney's An Unlikely Story in Plainville, Massachusetts;

Judy Blume's branch of Books & Books in Key West; and Emma Straub's Books Are Magic in Brooklyn.

And then there was author-slash-actor-slash-playwright-slash-hip-hopper Lin-Manuel Miranda. As bookishness trended and as indie bookstores developed a reputation for being quirky, progressive, and fashionable, starting a store, or saving one, was cooler than patronizing one. Fresh off *Hamilton*, Miranda swooped in to rescue the Drama Book Shop. With a couple of Hamiltonian collaborators, he bought the one-hundred-plus-year-old shop, which was struggling and which had once been a haven for young Miranda and his theater pals. The rejuvenated shop reopened in 2021 with a stunning sculpture of books snaking around the store, a small coffee shop, *Hamilton* props aplenty, and the prospect of bumping into the star himself. Tom Hanks, the on-screen Fox Books villain and one of Patchett's many friends, collects typewriters and wrote a novel, so naturally he considered opening a bookstore, too. (Apparently, he's still considering it.) James Patterson, whose popular books could never be found in many highbrow indies, promised $1 million in grants to independent stores back in 2013 (and has given much more since). Parnassus was among the 178 beneficiaries.

Patterson gave to bookstores as he would to charity; some bookstores—8 percent of them—functioned like charities, operating as nonprofits. The legendary Seminary Co-op in Chicago, which hadn't paid out dividends for decades, morphed into a nonprofit in 2019. Its mission was simple: bookselling. In this telling, bookstores were a public good. The benefit was the experience, "the browse."

Even for some for-profit bookstores, there was no expectation of profit. In 2022, a wealthy venture capitalist and former creative writing major opened a bookstore called P&T Knitwear. That the name might be a hindrance to sales was of no matter. It was part charity, part vanity project, and part bookstore.

P arnassus was hardly in need of philanthropy. Its chief problem was keeping books in stock. Hayes would run over to Costco to buy extra copies of fast-moving titles, peel off the stickers, and pop them on Parnassus's shelves, some of which had been salvaged from the recently deceased Borders.

Parnassus was so successful that, in 2016, it doubled in size, knocking down the wall separating it from Pickles & Ice Cream. Parnassus also added a bookmobile, Parnassus on Wheels, which Hayes bought on eBay and stuffed with one thousand books, mostly aimed at kids, an increasingly important demographic for indies with an eye toward the future.

In 2017, Parnassus expanded further, to the Nashville International Airport. The new outlet bore a resemblance (in a cousin kind of way) to the main store—titles written in chalk, stars dangling from the ceiling, and honey-colored shelves. But much of the indie DNA was absent. Rows of T-shirts, mugs, totes, notebooks, glasses, socks, stuffed animals, and pens obstructed the view of books from the vantage point of the concourse. The flooring was obviously-fake marble. There were no shop dogs. No plants. No piano. No impromptu Yo-Yo Ma concerts. The store was a collaboration with the Hudson Group, the retailer best known for its airport newsstands. (The airport shop, originally dubbed Parnassus on Wings, underwent a renovation and reopened in 2023. It's much prettier now.)

In the summer of 2019, Amazon opened an Amazon Books in the mall across the street from Parnassus. It was hard to read the Nashville location (the next-nearest one being in Washington, DC) as having nothing to do with Parnassus. Patchett was dead certain it wasn't a coincidence: "They've come to kill us." Hayes wasn't happy, either. She vowed to stop shopping at Whole Foods, which Amazon acquired in 2017.

Parnassus and other indies increasingly defined themselves in contrast to Amazon. They emphasized the in-person experience: talking with booksellers, joining a book group, tapping on a piano, listening to story time, chatting with an author, and having books signed and personalized. The Tattered Cover in Denver averaged more than one event per day. Parnassus hosted three hundred a year, generating 20 percent of its revenues. Patchett had no trouble luring the biggest names to the Nashville strip mall or, when that was too small, a nearby auditorium. Elizabeth Gilbert, Donna Tartt, Michael Chabon, Michael Pollan, Colson Whitehead, Erik Larson, Patti Smith, Amy Tan, and Stephen King came.

Although author signings had been a staple since Marcella Hahner brought writers to Field's a century earlier, the scope of events broadened. In the twenty-first century, bookstores became a favorite place to pop the question. There were also bookstore weddings and bookstore dog weddings. In 2014, Patchett's own dog, Sparky, was half of the happy couple that got married at Parnassus. The shop dogs also maintained a blog. They posted holiday gift guides and sometimes sad news: a canine colleague had passed.

When Lesley Stahl called Patchett the "patron saint of independent bookstores," the bookseller didn't back down from the description or the responsibility that came with it. "I am," she affirmed. Patchett's fantastic and outsize success at Parnassus was, in part, thanks to her fantastic and outsize success before and beyond the bookstore. She kept writing bestsellers. She hardly fit the image of a typical bookseller, someone who spends all day in the shop and all night worrying about it.

She was well aware. When an aspirant asked for advice—as they often did—about opening a bookshop in some small town, Patchett acknowledged, "It breaks my heart." Parnassus's success was "not easily replicated." It was hard not to be encouraging, though. At a 2017 talk, in response to a question about how to contribute to the local community, Patchett advised: "If you can, open a bookstore." In the audience was Jhoanna Belfer, a Filipina American poet from Long Beach, California, who worked in hospitality. She left inspired. The following year, she opened Bel Canto Books, named after Patchett's breakthrough novel. Bel Canto was one among an increasing number of woman- and POC-owned bookstores. The ABA had recently begun to make diversity, equity, and inclusion a priority, having acknowledged how historically white the profession had been—and still was. Roughly 85 percent of bookstore owners were white.

Loyalty Bookstore began as a seasonal pop-up in Silver Spring, Maryland, in 2018. It was started by Hannah Oliver Depp, a queer Black bookseller who had previously worked at Politics and Prose and was determined to "listen to, and push, our communities outside of their comfort zone." Loyalty grew to include two storefronts. The one in DC, albeit small, carries lots of romance and books on race and ethnicity. When I visited, it was packed with mostly white post-brunchers. A few miles away in the historic H Street Corridor, Solid State Books had also settled into its permanent home. Filled with book posters and anti-Amazon notices, the handsome Black-owned bookstore would soon expand its footprint by way of a second outpost in the nation's capital.

———

M eanwhile, business at Parnassus continued to boom. In its first
eight years, revenues grew, year over year, by double-digit
percentages. The shop sold a remarkable number of books. The 2019
bestseller was Patchett's own *The Dutch House* (thirty-five hundred
copies). Her media appearances included plugs for the store. When she
published in *The New Yorker*, her two-sentence bio mentioned the
shop. So did her author profile, printed in millions of books. One of
her essay collections got a full-page ad in *The New Yorker* that doubled
as a promotion for Parnassus Books ("shipping worldwide").

The bookstore grew mightily and publicly, powering the popular
story of an indie comeback. In early 2020, a Harvard Business School
professor wrote a paper: "The Novel Resurgence of Independent Bookstores." No group was more excited to hear it than the booksellers themselves. The ABA invited the professor to the Winter Institute.

To be sure, there were signs of growth in an industry prematurely
declared dead. In the five years since Parnassus had opened, the number of ABA-member bookstore locations had increased by 27 percent.
Yet the number of ABA stores is not the same as the number of bookstores, not even indie bookstores. Member companies include stores
that no reasonable person would think of as an indie: online-only
stores, college bookstores, toy stores that sell a few books, and even a
restaurant. Then there's the Hudson News in the Albuquerque International Sunport that probably sells more gum than novels. It counted.
So did the two Hudson Newses in the Seattle-Tacoma International
Airport, the two at LaGuardia, and so on.

The US Census offers a clearer picture. Between 2012 and 2021,
the number of bookstores dropped by 34 percent. That figure in-

cluded chains and independents. The number of Americans working in a bookstore fell by 53 percent. Bookstores remained very small businesses, with 50 percent of them having fewer than five employees. Parnassus had thirty full-time employees (with benefits). Going further back in time, the decline is even more legible. Between 1998 and 2021, more than half (54 percent) of all American bookstores disappeared. Even among ABA member stores, the pace of recent growth was much slower than that of the preceding crash. In 1995, there were 5,550 ABA member firms with a total of 7,000 locations. When Parnassus opened in 2011, there were just 1,512 ABA member companies.

Book sales remained relatively low. The average American consumer (the greatest consumer on earth) spent thirty dollars a year on books. The percentage of American readers kept inching lower, too. A 2020 report found that 44.5 percent of adults didn't read a single book outside what might have been assigned for work or school. The eighteen-to-twenty-four-year-old demographic was worse. Meanwhile, 30.4 percent of Americans identified as "Digital/Audio" readers. Even Parnassus's Karen Hayes multitasked, listening to books as she walked in the park. Patchett's husband, Karl, preferred ebooks. (He doesn't buy them from Amazon, though, Patchett underscored.)

As Allison Hill, who took over the role of ABA CEO in early 2020, tells it, the media was drawn to Patchett and the tale of an indie revival but overlooked the structural forces making for an "incredibly challenging industry." "There was definitely a disconnect between the media reporting this renaissance and behind-the-scenes conversations." With prices set by the publisher, booksellers struggled to respond to increasing rents and payrolls. Before coming to the ABA, Hill ran Vroman's in California, where she led the effort to lure in more than just "hardcore book buyers." The shop added a wine bar with literary-themed cocktails and struck a licensing arrangement with an airport outpost. "We were dancing as fast we could."

By 2017, sales of actual books accounted for just 71 percent of all bookstore sales nationwide. Though most sideline sales came from pens, notebooks, journals, calendars, toys, games, and coffee, some indies ventured further afield. Politics and Prose organized literary walking tours and global excursions.

In her inaugural presidential letter, Hill captured the dueling truths: "Although the renaissance of indie bookselling in recent years has been reason to celebrate, bookstores are still struggling and booksellers continue to lose sleep at night, counting the long list of threats—like rising costs, an election year, a pandemic, a looming recession, and Amazon.com—like sheep."

Hill's letter arrived in March of 2020, just after the news broke: COVID-19 was here.

W ithin weeks, bookstores around the country closed. Those with no e-commerce platform had no way to generate sales. Were bookstores essential businesses that state governments should allow to reopen? In most cases, the answer was no. Yet Walmart, Target, and Costco could stay open because they sold groceries, diapers, and dog food. While they were at it, they continued to sell books—mostly popular fiction, children's literature, and self-help guides. As the owner of Browseabout Books in Rehoboth Beach, Delaware, bemoaned about the local Walmart: "Why were they given the green light and opportunity to sell the very same things we can sell in our shop?"

The booksellers at Three Lives, who kept track of inventory on notepads and in their brains, set up Google Forms to receive and process online orders. Even then, they phoned each customer, talking through the purchase and talking books. Parnassus already had a robust online platform, but it was not nearly robust enough. Hayes and Patchett transformed the retail bookstore into a de facto warehouse. Patchett's sister, Heather, was in charge, practically living among the boxes, tape, and shipping labels. She'd work until 4:00 a.m., fulfilling orders for curbside delivery and mail orders from distant customers, many of whom had never been to Tennessee. They just wanted to support the store. The shop's First Edition Club grew to nearly one thousand participants. Each received a signed first edition every month. (The nearly century-old book-of-the-month-club concept had never gone away; in fact, Oprah Winfrey had made it more famous than ever.) Parnassus's online business was so brisk that when the shop was permitted to reopen, it was impossible to do so. They first had to move everything off-site to a "ship shack."

Other bookshops relied on the fortuitously just-launched Book shop.org. When a customer bought from Bookshop.org, 10 percent of the sale was set aside to dispense to a giant pool of indies. If customers desired, they could identify a particular bookstore to support, and that store would then earn 30 percent of the sale. All orders were shipped directly from Ingram. The "chosen" bookstore didn't need to have a website, have the book in stock, or put the book in a mailer. By the summer of 2021, Bookshop.org had eleven hundred participating stores and was doing $54 million in yearly sales.

Buying from Bookshop.org or ParnassusBooks.net was different than buying from Amazon.com, but not that different. The things that booksellers insisted made indies distinct were absent: organic conversations, serendipitous discovery, being "book-wrapt," the sense of community, small talk with the UPS person, shop dogs and cats, et cetera. When bookstores began reopening, much of the in-person charm was lost in a world of social distancing. At the same time that Amazon embraced brick-and-mortar retail, the indies embraced online sales. Distinctions blurred.

Compared with 2019, 2020 bookstore sales dropped 28.3 percent, even as overall book sales climbed. In 2021, a whopping 825.7 million copies were sold. Reading and book buying, both thought to be dead or at least dying, were on the rise. Publishers and authors had never been so thankful for Amazon. Roughly 70 percent of Americans reported buying books from the online Goliath.

Over the first six months of the pandemic, one indie shuttered each week. That was better than anyone expected. Hill described the indies as "bruised" but cited government support and strong overall book sales as helping to stave off destruction. The pandemic only added to indie bookstores' underdog status and their reputation, in James Daunt's words, as "bastions of liberal values." The project was long in the making. Booksellers put out statements when Donald Trump was elected, advertised themselves as "safe spaces," outwardly supported Black Lives Matter, and were among the first retail shops to shun plastic bags.

Every bookstore is, in a way, political. Like publishers, booksellers must make difficult and often public decisions about what crosses the line. Debates about censorship and cancel culture swirled. In 2020, when *Publishers Weekly* asked two dozen booksellers whether they would carry a hypothetical Trump memoir, the co-owner of Solid State Books responded, "There is absolutely no way we would sell a book by Donald J. Trump. That particular Rubicon was crossed long,

long ago." Most (nineteen out of twenty-four) responded that they would stock it but their customers wouldn't buy it, despite the fact that more than seventy-four million Americans voted for him. In Garrett County, Maryland, where nearly everyone is white and where voters preferred Trump to Biden by more than a three-and-a-half-to-one margin, the indie bookstore is truly the liberal oasis. Inside Book Mark'et, the titles skewering Trump sat right up front, near the sign indicating that masks were required, long after the CDC said they didn't need to be. In the local grocery stores and ice cream shops, no one was wearing a mask—or being asked to. Meanwhile, the only place that I can recall ever being asked to show proof of vaccination was at a New York bookstore in the fall of 2021.

For a segment of indie shoppers, buying was an overt political act, signaling a set of values: supporting communities, small businesses, and maybe even the cultures of reading and democracy. Buyers posted on Instagram and Twitter, aligning themselves with indie brands. Others wanted books without a dose of politics. During the 2020 election season, Patchett took to Instagram in a Biden T-shirt to spout "bitchy remarks" (her words) about Trump. A loyal Patchett fan from Pennsylvania wrote to the author to say that she was tired of having her "face rubbed in the fact that we have different political views." Patchett mulled it over. She decided the customer was right. She wrote an apology. The two remain friends, and the customer remains a customer.

Being political is the point at Word Up, a bookstore that reminded its neighbors to fill out their census forms. It's important to be counted, Liu said, noting the historically undercounted and under-resourced neighborhood.

Word Up's mission is visible from the outside. When I stopped by in 2021, sidewalk stands overflowed with books. A laminated sign read "Pague Lo Que Pueda. Pay What You Can." On the ground was a gallon of motor oil: "Gratis! Free!" The shop takes donations of all kinds. Inside, Liu unpacked a Jenga-ish tower of cardboard boxes from Penguin Random House. She wore bright blue shoes and an orange sweater draped around her like a superhero.

Veronica Liu at Word Up.

While other bookstores had built skyscrapers of Amor Towles's latest and bestselling novel, *The Lincoln Highway*, Word Up didn't have a single copy. Its bestsellers were *For Brown Girls with Sharp Edges and Tender Hearts: A Love Letter to Women of Color* and signed copies of *Wild Tongues Can't Be Tamed: 15 Voices from the Latinx Diaspora*. The political books selling everywhere else didn't move at all at Word Up. No one cared about Bob Woodward. Books with "Trump on the cover" collected dust.

Bookseller Renzo greeted Dante—and everyone else walking in—with a warm buenas. Dante, who wore a backward baseball cap and a denim jacket with an ironed-on Bart Simpson, had never been in an independent bookstore before. He was looking for a gift for his niece. Renzo guided Dante around the kids' section, answering questions, offering suggestions, and talking books for what must have been twenty minutes. Dante left with a haul of coloring books, a book on mythological monsters, and a couple of comics for himself.

Then Nobel walked in. He's a regular, and a bookstore veteran, having worked at Labyrinth Books and, for ten years, the Strand. He said he didn't want to talk about his experience there. Two minutes later, though, he opened up: "It was pretty wild, everything from the sublime to the ridiculous." Bookstores are, he concluded, "really sort of weird."

B ookstores *are* weird. They're unlike any other retail store. They are viewed as cultural landmarks, places where financial profit is secondary to social profit. And yet they need to make money to survive. Competing narratives can't decide whether indies are dying or multiplying. The optimistic version has encouraged people to open new stores and has kept publishers invested in brick-and-mortar bookselling. The pessimistic version has utility as well. Customers feel compelled to "save" a species on the edge of extinction. They appreciate the precariousness of a little bookstore's life. It's not enough to offer occasional support, Allison Hill reminds indie shoppers. For the indies to survive, fans need to buy *all* of their books from local bookshops. They have to shut Amazon off completely. They have to go cold turkey.

Though there's been destruction and though the number of bookstores and booksellers, indie and otherwise, has long been dwindling, there's also been a new wave of booksellers who have begun to change the face of American bookselling. Some of them have already enjoyed tremendous success. In 2021, the not-terribly-large Books Are Magic in Brooklyn sold more than two hundred thousand books. Word Up sold a slew of books *and* helped get people vaccinated. These were stories people wanted to hear. So, too, were the stories about indies still going strong, defying their dismal prognosis. Cottonwood-lined Wicker Park in Chicago has changed much more than has Myopic Books—three floors of used books, narrow aisles, and lots of people talking about postcolonialism—or Quimby's—zines, erotica, comics, and photography. The original Toadstool Bookshop has been in tiny Peterborough, New Hampshire, for more than fifty years. Specialty shops, like the funky art bookstore Printed Matter in New York's Chelsea, still carry stapled-together handmade pamphlets and chapbooks that could never be found on Amazon. Books of Wonder and Wild Rumpus remain wondrous lands for children's literature.

As COVID-case counts yo-yoed in 2022, and as Karen Hayes announced that she'd be retiring, Parnassus continued to thrive. Nationwide, the number of ABA member companies (2,178) and total locations (2,593) ticked up. And then, in 2023, the Federal Trade Commission, along with seventeen states, launched an antitrust suit against Amazon. It's what the ABA, Hill, and independent booksellers around the country had been begging for.

Meanwhile, Patchett kept at it. Not just to sell books but to keep telling the story—the one about the little, mighty, and resilient independent bookshop.

The Bookstore Book

୦୧୭

This is a book about bookstores. It's merely one of many. Fans over at Goodreads have compiled a list of 352 of them. Christopher Morley's novels about Roger and Helen Mifflin are there, as is *84, Charing Cross Road* (my personal favorite). Penguin Random House has an entire webpage devoted to "romances set in bookstores." *The Sentence* is a spooky novel set in a bookstore and written by a woman who owns a bookstore.

When I told people that I was writing this book, the most common response (other than "When will you be finished?") was, in one way or another, about *You've Got Mail*. "Have you seen it?" (Yes.) "Are you going to write about it?" (Yes.) "Maybe you can interview Tom Hanks?" (Maybe.) Aside from Tom Hanks and Meg Ryan, Hugh Grant (*Notting Hill*) and Audrey Hepburn (*Funny Face*) both play memorable (and remarkably good-looking) booksellers. Both find love rather than rare first editions.

To be sure, these films are sappy and tropey. And many of the books about bookstores can easily be dismissed as navel-gazing à la Hollywood's propensity to make movies about Hollywood. But there's a reason why screenwriters and book writers love setting their stories in bookstores. They can be romantic spaces, places full of discovery, of chance, of wonder. They can be community spaces, activist spaces, political spaces. And they can be refuges, places to lose and find oneself.

Whether in mysteries or memoirs, travelogues or true-crime tales, romances or rom-coms, horror or history, bookstores can be more than just passive backdrops. Bookstores can be actors. Bookstores, even the little ones, can shape the world around them. They already have.

ACKNOWLEDGMENTS

Everyone on this list really deserves to be here. Thank you:

Jeron Baker (welcome distractor)

Miriam Chotiner-Gardner (brilliant buyer and seller)

Ellen and Les Cohen (unflagging champions)

Courtland Cox (good trouble)

Toby Cox (humble giant)

James Daunt (bookselling wizard)

Joshua Clark Davis (kindhearted source sharer)

Marlene and Tom England (courageous booksellers)

Alexis Farabaugh (deft designer)

Jenny Feder (the founder)

Jen Fisher (sidewalk spirit)

Josh Freeman (idea shaper)

Amanda Friss (everything)

Miles and Quincy Friss (favorite people on earth or elsewhere)

Rose and Mike Friss (loving parents)

Acknowledgments

Tim Gilfoyle (sweet scholar)

Anthony Gittens and Jennifer Lawson (bookselling pioneers)

Bradley Graham (reading evangelist)

Karen Hayes (sage bookseller)

Philip Herrington (consummate coffee shop comrade)

Allison Hill (*the* industry expert)

JMU College of Arts and Letters (dependable supporter)

JMU Department of History (inspiring colleagues)

Mitchell Kaplan (generous bookman)

Rick Kot (superb editor)

Ali Lake (inviting gatekeeper)

Camille LeBlanc (adept book shepherd)

Veronica Liu (bookselling dynamo)

MacDowell (heaven)

Daphne Muse (creative spirit)

David Nasaw (steadfast adviser)

Emma Parry (agent extraordinaire)

Ann Patchett (booksellers' guardian angel)

Judy Richardson (relentless activist)

Leonard Riggio (charismatic creator)

Lauren Morgan Whitticom (preternatural copy editor)

Andrew Witmer (wise friend and reader)

Nancy Bass Wyden (bookseller in chief)

ABBREVIATIONS

BCR	Books & Co. Records, Manuscript and Archives Division, New York Public Library
CCDU	Courtland Cox Papers, David M. Rubenstein Rare Book & Manuscript Library, Duke University
CRC1	Jewish Federation Council of Greater Los Angeles, Community Relations Committee Collection, Part 1, Special Collections & Archives, University Library, California State University, Northridge
CRC2	Jewish Federation Council of Greater Los Angeles, Community Relations Committee Collection, Part 2, Special Collections & Archives, University Library, California State University, Northridge
CRNYPL	Craig Rodwell Papers, New York Public Library
FK	Frank Kameny Papers, Library of Congress
FSC	Frances Steloff Collection, Scribner Library Archives, Skidmore College

GBMNYPL	Gotham Book Mart Records, Henry W. and Albert A. Berg Collection of English and American Literature, New York Public Library
GBMPENN	Gotham Book Mart Records, Rare Books and Manuscripts, Kislak Center for Special Collections, University of Pennsylvania
HRC	Herbert Romerstein Collection, Hoover Institution Library & Archives, Stanford University
HRUT	Harry Ransom Center, University of Texas at Austin
JRC	John F. Russell Collection, Hoover Institution Library & Archives, Stanford University
JRDU	Judy Richardson Papers, David M. Rubenstein Rare Book & Manuscript Library, Duke University
MFCHS	Target Corporation's Records of Marshall Field & Company, Chicago Historical Society
RG60, NA	(Alien Enemy) Litigation Case Files and Enclosures, 1938–1962, Record Group 60, Department of Justice Records, National Archives, College Park, MD
RG131, NA	Seized Records of the Los Angeles Units of the German American Bund, 1928–1942, Record Group 131, Records of the Office of Alien Property, National Archives, College Park, MD
RK	Ron Kolm Papers, Fales Library & Special Collections, New York University
RS	Rand School of Social Science Records, Tamiment Library and Robert F. Wagner Labor Archives, New York University

Abbreviations

SBPU	Sylvia Beach Papers, Princeton University Library
SBSR	Schulte's Book Store Records, 1918–1959, Rare Book and Manuscript Library, Columbia University
SDSUOH	San Diego State University Oral Histories, SDSU Library

AB	Antiquarian Bookman
DW	Daily Worker
LAT	Los Angeles Times
LG	The Louisiana Gazette
MST	Star Tribune *(Minneapolis)*
NYDN	New York Daily News
NYH	The New York Hymnal
NYR	The New Yorker
NYT	The New York Times
PW	Publishers Weekly
RDC	Democrat and Chronicle *(Rochester)*
SEP	The Saturday Evening Post
ST	The Seattle Times
VV	The Village Voice
WP	The Washington Post
WSJ	The Wall Street Journal

NOTES

Introduction

5 **Americans purchased roughly:** John B. Thompson, *Merchants of Culture: The Publishing Business in the Twenty-First Century* (New York: Plume, 2012), 31.

5 **there were just 5,591:** US Census Bureau, *County Business Patterns 1993* (Washington, DC: Government Printing Office, 1995), https://www2.census.gov/programs -surveys/cbp/tables/1993/cbp-9301.pdf; and US Census Bureau, "County Business Patterns: 2021," dataset, US Census Bureau (website), April 27, 2023, updated May 25, 2023, https://www.census.gov/data/datasets/2021/econ/cbp /2021-cbp.html.

6 **Pulitzer Prize–winning novelist:** Michael Cunningham, *The Hours* (New York: Picador, 2000), 227–28.

6 **Their spiral notebook:** Booksellers Notebook, 1997, in the private collection of Carrie Cogan.

6 **Sociologists have found:** Joanna Sikora, M. D. R. Evans, and Jonathan Kelley, "Scholarly Culture: How Books in Adolescence Enhance Adult Literacy, Numeracy, and Technology Skills in 31 Societies," *Social Science Research* 77 (January 2019): 1–15.

6 **Customers also make:** For more on the concept of "third spaces," see Ray Oldenburg, *The Great Good Place: Cafés, Coffee Shops, Community Centers, Beauty Parlors, General Stores, Bars, Hangouts, and How They Get You through the Day* (New York: Marlowe and Co., 1989).

7 **Three Lives has never:** Jenny Feder, interview by the author, November 2022.

7 **To savor slowed time:** Three Lives & Company, "Labor Day Greetings," newsletter email, August 30, 2022; and Lewis Buzbee, *The Yellow-Lighted Bookshop: A Memoir, a History* (St. Paul: Graywolf Press, 2006), 23. The notion that bookstores can make us slow down is a theme oft embraced by booksellers and browsers.

7 **In the 1988 film:** Joan Micklin Silver, dir., *Crossing Delancey* (Burbank, CA: Warner Bros., 1988).

7 **Thomas Jefferson wrote to:** Thomas Jefferson to James Madison, 16 September 1821,

Notes

Founders Online, National Archives, https://founders.archives.gov/documents/Madison/04-02-02-0322.

7 **A century and a half:** Barbara Livingston, "New York's Three Lives & Company," *American Bookseller*, December 1980, 28–29.

8 **When they walk in:** Thompson, *Merchants of Culture*, 258–62; and Jim Milliot, "Acting On Impulse," *PW*, May 23, 2011, https://www.publishersweekly.com/pw/by-topic/industry-news/bookselling/article/47383-acting-on-impulse.html. The data on impulse buys is convincing but not up to date.

8 **One joked that:** John Wilcock, "Book Row," *VV*, February 16, 1961.

8 **Henry Holt lamented:** Henry Holt, "Communications: On the Decline of the Book-Buying Habit," *PW*, July 2, 1887, 18–19.

9 **"be done to rescue":** H. L. Mencken, "Lo, the Poor Bookseller," *American Mercury*, October 1930, 151–55.

9 **Its first sentence:** Adolph Kroch, *Bookstores Can Be Saved: 14 Proposals Answering the Question, "What Is Wrong with the Bookstores?"* (Chicago: Booksellers Catalog Service, 1952), 7.

Chapter 1: Benjamin Franklin

16 **"All the little money":** Benjamin Franklin, *Autobiography of Benjamin Franklin: Edited from His Manuscript, with Notes and an Introduction*, ed. John Bigelow (Philadelphia: J. B. Lippincott, 1868), 91–92.

16 **By the age of ten:** Franklin, *Autobiography of Benjamin Franklin*, 86.

17 **Its business was entwined:** Isaiah Thomas, *The History of Printing in America: With a Biography of Printers & an Account of Newspapers* (New York: B. Franklin, 1864), 13–18; and Henry Walcott Boynton, *Annals of American Bookselling, 1638–1850* (New York: John Wiley & Sons, 1932), 20–24.

17 **the future capital of publishing:** George Emery Littlefield, *Early Boston Booksellers, 1642–1711* (Boston: Club of Odd Volumes, 1900), 27; and Thomas, *History of Printing in America*, 95.

17 **The others usually:** *A History of the Book in America*, ed. Hugh Amory and David D. Hall, vol. 1, *The Colonial Book in the Atlantic World* (Chapel Hill: University of North Carolina Press, 2007), 68.

17 **the book market was narrow:** Amory and Hall, *History of the Book in America*, 1:127–28.

18 **The first was Hezekiah:** Littlefield, *Early Boston Booksellers*, 12, 30, 68–77; and Hellmut Lehmann-Haupt, *The Book in America: A History of the Making and Selling of Books in the United States* (New York: R. R. Bowker Co., 1951), 47.

18 **Because the market:** Amory and Hall, *History of the Book in America*, 1:45, 1:51; Boynton, *Annals of American Bookselling*, 22.

18 **The main attraction:** Hugh Morrison, *Early American Architecture: From the First Colonial Settlements to the National Period* (New York: Oxford University Press, 1952), 88–89; and Hugh Amory, "Under the Exchange: The Unprofitable Business of Michael Perry, a Seventeenth-Century Boston Bookseller," in *Bibliography and*

Notes

the *Book Trades: Studies in the Print Culture of Early New England*, ed. David D. Hall (Philadelphia: University of Pennsylvania Press, 2005).

18 **Those Athenian stalls:** Homer A. Thompson and R. E. Wycherley, *The Agora of Athens: The History, Shape and Uses of an Ancient City Center* (Princeton, NJ: American School of Classical Studies at Athens, 1972), 171; and Lionel Casson, *Libraries in the Ancient World* (New Haven: Yale University Press, 2001), 17–30. See also Henry Curwen, *A History of Booksellers: The Old and the New* (London: Chatto and Windus, 1873).

18 **New Englanders were hungry:** John Dunton, *The Life and Errors of John Dunton, Citizen of London*, vol. 1 (London: J. Nichols, Son, and Bentley, 1818), xii–xiii, 94, 112, 124, 129.

18 **At roughly the same time:** Benjamin Harris, *The Protestant Tutor* (London: Benjamin Harris, 1679).

18 **At America's first:** Worthington Chauncey Ford, *The Boston Book Market, 1679–1700* (Boston: Club of Odd Volumes, 1917), 27–28; Jürgen Habermas, *The Structural Transformation of the Public Sphere: An Inquiry into a Category of Bourgeois Society* (Cambridge, MA: MIT Press, 1989).

19 **The real problem was James:** C. William Miller, *Benjamin Franklin's Philadelphia Printing, 1728–1766: A Descriptive Bibliography* (Philadelphia: American Philosophical Society, 1974), xvii; and Franklin, *Autobiography of Benjamin Franklin*, 104.

19 **"access to better books":** Franklin, *Autobiography of Benjamin Franklin*, 92.

19 **"enable the Mind":** Silence Dogood, letter to the editor, *New-England Courant*, March 26–April 2, 1722.

19 **He couldn't resist fish:** Franklin, *Autobiography of Benjamin Franklin*, 97, 128.

20 **June 1722 issue:** "Foreign Affairs," *New-England Courant*, June 4–11, 1722.

20 **He printed one:** Silence Dogood, letter to the editor, *New-England Courant*, July 2–9, 1722.

20 **Whatever satisfaction the temporary:** H. W. Brands, *The First American: The Life and Times of Benjamin Franklin* (New York: Anchor Books, 2000), 31, 33–34. To make it seem like Franklin was independently publishing *The New-England Courant*, the original indenture agreement was torn up, but Franklin and James secretly signed a new one, meaning that Franklin was still legally bound to his brother.

20 **On that first day:** Franklin, *Autobiography of Benjamin Franklin*, 111–12, 116, 131.

21 **London certainly had:** Franklin, *Autobiography of Benjamin Franklin*, 142, 146–47, 154.

21 **he organized the Junto:** Franklin, *Autobiography of Benjamin Franklin*, 168–71.

21 **The taxpayer-funded:** Edwin Wolf, *"At the Instance of Benjamin Franklin": A Brief History of the Library Company of Philadelphia, 1731–1976* (Philadelphia: Library Company of Philadelphia, 1976). For more on the development of libraries, see Mark R. M. Towsey and Kyle B. Roberts, eds., *Before the Public Library: Reading, Community, and Identity in the Atlantic World, 1650–1850* (Boston: Brill, 2018); and Matthew Battles, *Library: An Unquiet History* (New York: W. W. Norton, 2003).

Notes

21 **Their library grew:** Franklin, *Autobiography of Benjamin Franklin*, 193–95, 207–8.

21 **Franklin was still just:** Hannah Benner Roach, "Benjamin Franklin Slept Here," *Pennsylvania Magazine of History and Biography* 84, no. 2 (April 1960): 139.

22 **neither his tousled appearance:** Franklin, *Autobiography of Benjamin Franklin*, 112.

22 **died from smallpox:** Franklin, *Autobiography of Benjamin Franklin*, 190, 244.

22 **She sold pills:** Advertisement, *Pennsylvania Gazette*, August 19, 1731.

22 **The mother-in-law:** Roach, "Benjamin Franklin Slept Here," 142.

22 **When Franklin first:** Franklin, *Autobiography of Benjamin Franklin*, 206.

22 **visitor to New York pitied:** As quoted in Amory and Hall, *History of the Book in America*, 1:155.

23 **By the early 1730s:** Advertisement, *Pennsylvania Gazette*, October 14, 1731; Advertisement, *Pennsylvania Gazette*, March 13, 1734; Advertisement, *Pennsylvania Gazette*, May 23, 1734; and Advertisement, *Pennsylvania Gazette*, October 31, 1734.

23 **The project came easily:** Amory and Hall, *History of the Book in America*, 1:45, 1:51.

23 **Aside from money:** Franklin, *Autobiography of Benjamin Franklin*, 236.

23 **The initial inventory:** Franklin, *Autobiography of Benjamin Franklin*, 238; and Ralph Frasca, *Benjamin Franklin's Printing Network: Disseminating Virtue in Early America* (Columbia, MO: University of Missouri Press, 2006), 67–76. Franklin's initial Charleston partner died, and so did his replacement, another of Franklin's journeymen, leaving the business in the hands of his widow, who, according to Franklin, was better equipped than her late husband, especially when it came to bookkeeping. (Franklin attributed this to the fact that she was Dutch.)

23 **As if Franklin:** Advertisement, *Pennsylvania Gazette*, April 4, 1734; Advertisement, *Pennsylvania Gazette*, April 11, 1734; and Miller, *Benjamin Franklin's Philadelphia Printing*, xxxix.

23 **His ledgers reveal:** Benjamin Franklin, *Account Books Kept by Benjamin Franklin: Ledger 1728–1729, Journal 1730–1737*, ed. George Simpson Eddy (New York: Columbia University Press, 1928), 30.

24 **He also tracked:** Franklin, *Autobiography of Benjamin Franklin*, 213–16, 221–23.

24 **Her husband acknowledged:** Franklin, *Autobiography of Benjamin Franklin*, 210.

24 **Perhaps it was she:** Amory and Hall, *History of the Book in America*, 1:51; and J. A. Leo Lemay, "Deborah Franklin, Lord Loudoun, and Franklin's Autobiography," *Huntington Library Quarterly* 67, no. 4 (2004): 608.

25 **A later survey:** Roach, "Benjamin Franklin Slept Here," 144–46; *Pennsylvania Gazette*, April 30, 1752; and Franklin, *Autobiography of Benjamin Franklin*, 210. The division between home and workplace across the property is not entirely clear. Typically, the printing office and post office are listed as being "in Market Street," but sometimes they are described as fronting the alley. Since Market Street was the main thoroughfare, it's likely that Franklin used the Market Street address, but the printing office and bookshop were in the building behind the main residence.

25 **With more space:** Advertisement, *Pennsylvania Gazette*, January 18, 1739; and Advertisement, *Pennsylvania Gazette*, October 13, 1737.

Notes

25 **Some of those other:** J. A. Leo Lemay, *The Life of Benjamin Franklin*, vol. 2, *Printer and Publisher, 1730–1747* (Philadelphia: University of Pennsylvania Press, 2013), 378.

25 **"very good Chocolate":** Advertisement, *Pennsylvania Gazette*, January 18, 1739.

25 **If the price was right:** Benjamin Franklin, *Account Books Kept by Benjamin Franklin: Ledger "D" 1739–1747*, ed. George Simpson Eddy (New York: Columbia University Press, 1929), 40, 41, 85, 121; and Advertisement, *Pennsylvania Gazette*, February 24, 1742.

25 **At the end:** Franklin, *Autobiography of Benjamin Franklin*, 254–55.

25 **So many customers:** Notice, *Pennsylvania Gazette*, May 22, 1740; and Lemay, *Life of Benjamin Franklin*, 2:387–88.

26 **He even sold:** Advertisement, *Pennsylvania Gazette*, May 20, 1742; and Walter Isaacson, *Benjamin Franklin: An American Life* (New York: Simon & Schuster, 2004), 111.

26 **colonists didn't want:** Amory and Hall, *History of the Book in America*, 1:230, 1:267–68; and Lemay, *Life of Benjamin Franklin*, 2:389.

26 **In the spring of 1854:** Advertisement, *Pennsylvania Gazette*, March 29, 1744; and Lemay, *Life of Benjamin Franklin*, 2:392.

26 **Probably because the Reads:** J. Bennett Nolan, *Printer Strahan's Book Account: A Colonial Controversy* (Philadelphia: Patterson & White, 1939), 1–5, 19; and *Pennsylvania Gazette*, November 24, 1743.

27 **It's still in operation:** Franklin, *Autobiography of Benjamin Franklin*, 324–25; "About the Moravian Book Shop," Moravian University, accessed February 12, 2021, https://www.moravian.edu/bookshop/about; Andrew Belonsky, "How America's Oldest Bookstore Has Survived Across the Centuries," *Literary Hub*, March 16, 2020, https://lithub.com/how-americas-oldest-bookstore-has-survived-across-the-centuries/; and Gregory Lee Sullivan, "Visiting the Oldest Bookstore in America—And Its Resident Ghost," *Guardian*, February 25, 2016, https://www.theguardian.com/books/2016/feb/25/oldest-bookstore-in-america-and-resident-ghost-moravian-book-shop-pennsylvania. Franklin visited Bethlehem but didn't mention anything about a bookstore. Today, it is the official bookstore of Moravian University.

27 **He managed the New:** Robert D. Harlan, "A Colonial Printer as Bookseller in Eighteenth-Century Philadelphia: The Case of David Hall," in *Studies in Eighteenth-Century Culture*, ed. Ronald C. Rosbottom, vol. 5 (Madison: University of Wisconsin Press, 1976), 355–69; Amory and Hall, *History of the Book in America*, 1:277–78. For more on David Hall's tenure as a bookseller, see Robert D. Harlan, "David Hall's Bookshop and Its British Sources of Supply," in *Books in America's Past: Essays Honoring Rudolph H. Gjelsness*, ed. David Kaser (Charlottesville: University Press of Virginia, 1966).

27 **Having "absolutely left off":** Benjamin Franklin to Cadwallader Colden, 29 September 1748, Founders Online, National Archives, https://founders.archives.gov/documents/Franklin/01-03-02-0133.

27 **He sold what might:** Cynthia Z. Stiverson and Gregory A. Stiverson, "The Colonial Retail Book Trade: Availability and Affordability of Reading Material in

Notes

Mid-Eighteenth-Century Virginia," in *Printing and Society in Early America*, ed. William L. Joyce et al. (Worcester, MA: American Antiquarian Society, 1983), 142, 156.

27 **he was the typical:** February 4, 1764, Virginia Gazette Daybooks, 1750–1766, Tracy W. McGregor Library Accession #467, Special Collections, University of Virginia Library, Charlottesville, VA; and Amory and Hall, *History of the Book in America*, 1:389–90.

28 **The well-heeled customers:** Amory and Hall, *History of the Book in America*, 1:232, 1:389–90.

28 **With that same:** February 4, 1764, Virginia Gazette Daybooks; and Stiverson and Stiverson, "Colonial Retail Book Trade," 132–73.

28 **Franklin had started selling:** Edwin Wolf, *The Book Culture of a Colonial American City: Philadelphia Books, Bookmen, and Booksellers* (Oxford: Oxford University Press, 1988), 164–67.

28 **Number 403 was:** James Rivington and Samuel Brown, *A Catalogue of Books, Sold by Rivington and Brown, Booksellers and Stationers from London, at Their Stores, Over against the Golden Key, in Hanover-Square, New-York: And Over against the London Coffee-House, in Philadelphia* (Philadelphia: Heinrich Miller, 1762); and Thomas, *History of Printing in America*, 307–10.

29 **This was the first known:** *Pennsylvania Gazette*, December 4, 1760; and *OED Online*, s.v. "bookstore," accessed December 2020, https://www.oed.com/view /Entry/21455.

29 **Though Rivington was:** Amory and Hall, *History of the Book in America*, 1:45.

29 **He was an early:** Benjamin Franklin, editorial, *Pennsylvania Gazette*, May 9, 1754.

30 **Franklin lamented that:** Franklin, *Autobiography of Benjamin Franklin*, 207–8.

30 **As calls for boycotts:** Amory and Hall, *History of the Book in America*, 1:291–92.

30 **Despite transatlantic tensions:** Phillip Hamilton, *The Revolutionary War Lives and Letters of Lucy and Henry Knox* (Baltimore: Johns Hopkins University Press, 2017), 4–5.

30 **The shop attracted politicians:** Francis S. Drake, *Life and Correspondence of Henry Knox: Major-General in the American Revolutionary Army* (Boston: Samuel G. Drake, 1873), 14.

30 **By November 1774:** Drake, *Life and Correspondence of Henry Knox*, 13–14.

31 **He bought them mittens:** Thomas Jefferson to Francis Eppes, 19 January 1821, Founders Online, National Archives, https://founders.archives.gov/documents /Jefferson/03-16-02-0454; and Amory and Hall, *History of the Book in America*, 1:295–96.

31 **"has never been equaled":** Gordon Wood, *The Creation of the American Republic, 1776–1787* (Chapel Hill: University of North Carolina Press, 1969), 6.

32 **Some contemporaries and later:** Catherine Snell Crary, "The Tory and the Spy: The Double Life of James Rivington," *The William and Mary Quarterly* 16, no. 1 (1959): 61–72; and Ruma Chopra, *Unnatural Rebellion: Loyalists in New York City during the Revolution* (Charlottesville: University of Virginia Press, 2011), 41–42, 221.

Notes

32 **belong on ladders:** Benjamin Franklin, "Description of an Instrument for Taking Down Books from High Shelves," January 1786, *The Papers of Benjamin Franklin*, Yale University Library, New Haven, CT.

32 **Grandpa Franklin had:** Thomas, *History of Printing in America*, 237–38; Jeffery A. Smith, *Franklin and Bache: Envisioning the Enlightened Republic* (New York: Oxford University Press, 1990), 86, 101; and Benjamin Franklin to Sir Edward Newenham, 2 October 1783, Founders Online, National Archives, https://founders.archives.gov/documents/Franklin/01-41-02-0040.

33 **A version of the epitaph:** Devry Becker Jones, "Benjamin Franklin Epitaph," Historical Marker Database, revised February 2, 2023, https://www.hmdb.org/m.asp?m=212552.

The Smell

34 **Some say they prefer:** Claire Armitstead, "Can You Judge a Book by its Odour," *Guardian*, April 7, 2017, https://www.theguardian.com/books/2017/apr/07/the-smell-of-old-books-science-libraries.

34 **Some think old:** Cecilia Bembibre and Matija Strlič, "Smell of Heritage: A Framework for the Identification, Analysis and Archival of Historic Odours," *Heritage Science* 5 (2017): 2, https://doi.org/10.1186/s40494-016-0114-1.

34 **"The sweet smell":** As cited in Gordon Bowker, "Orwell's Library," Orwell Foundation, accessed December 5, 2023, https://www.orwellfoundation.com/the-orwell-foundation/orwell/articles/gordon-bowker-orwells-library/.

35 **It promised to take:** "Powell's Unisex Fragrance," Powell's, accessed May 1, 2021, http://web.archive.org/web/20201109121550/https://www.powells.com/book/powells-unisex-fragrance-1110000347670.

35 **His wife hated:** "Powell's Unisex Fragrance."

Chapter 2: The Old Corner

37 **Nathaniel Hawthorne preferred:** "The Old Corner Book-Store: The Famous Literary Landmark of Boston, and the Men Who Met There," *New England Magazine* 29 (November 1903): 303–16.

37 **Customers described the scene:** Charles Mackay, *Life and Liberty in America* (London: Smith, Elder and Co., 1859), 66–67.

37 **That the "loiterers":** W. S. Tryon, *Parnassus Corner: A Life of James T. Fields, Publisher to the Victorians* (Boston: Houghton Mifflin, 1963), 220; and *Final Report of the Boston National Historic Sites Commission*, 87th Cong., 1st Sess., H. Doc. No. 107 (Washington, DC: Government Printing Office, 1961), 138–39.

38 **Clusters of printers:** Robert A. Gross, "Introduction: An Extensive Republic," in *A History of the Book in America*, ed. Robert A. Gross and Mary Kelley, vol. 2, *An Extensive Republic: Print, Culture, and Society in the New Nation, 1790–1840* (Chapel Hill: University of North Carolina Press, 2010), 17.

39 **73 were on Washington:** Ronald J. Zboray and Mary Saracino Zboray, "The Boston Book Trades, 1789–1850: A Statistical and Geographical Analysis," in *Entrepreneurs: The Boston Business Community, 1700–1850*, ed. Conrad Edick Wright

Notes

and Katheryn P. Viens (Boston: Massachusetts Historical Society, 1997), 251–52; Dorothea Lawrence Mann, *A Century of Book Selling,1828–1928: The Story of the Old Corner Book Store on the Occasion of Its One Hundredth Birthday* (Boston: Lincoln & Smith Press, 1928), 5–7; and Tryon, *Parnassus Corner*, 50–51. For more on antiquarian booksellers of the period, see Madeleine B. Stern, *Antiquarian Bookselling in the United States: A History from the Origins to the 1940s* (Westport, CT: Greenwood Press, 1985), 3–20.

39 **More than a few:** Kristen Doyle Highland, "At the Bookstore: Literary and Cultural Experience in Antebellum New York City" (PhD diss., New York University, 2015), 24–25, 66.

39 **A typical book retailed:** Zboray and Zboray, "Boston Book Trades," 216–17, 225. For more on prices, see Warren S. Tryon and William Charvat, eds., *The Cost Books of Ticknor and Fields and Their Predecessors, 1832–1858* (New York: Bibliographical Society of America, 1949).

40 **commitment to public education:** Turk Tracey & Larry Architects, *Historic Structures Report for the Old Corner Bookstore Buildings* (Portland, ME: Turk Tracey & Larry Architects, 2000), 12, 20–21; "Old Corner Book-Store," *New England Magazine*, 306; and Henry Walcott Boynton, *Annals of American Bookselling, 1638–1850* (New York: John Wiley & Sons, 1932), 190–92.

40 **Thirteen-year-old James:** Florence Wilson Newsome, "The Publishing and Literary Activities of the Predecessors of Ticknor and Fields, 1829–1849" (master's thesis, Boston University, 1942), 29; and James T. Fields, *Biographical Notes and Personal Sketches with Unpublished Fragments and Tributes from Men and Women of Letters* (Boston: Houghton, Mifflin and Company, 1882), 7.

40 **Like many aspiring:** Fields, *Biographical Notes and Personal Sketches*, 6–9.

40 **By the age of twenty:** Tryon, *Parnassus Corner*, 28–30, 73–74.

40 **Fields always won:** Fields, *Biographical Notes and Personal Sketches*, 8–9.

40 **In 1832, William D. Ticknor:** Michael Winship, *American Literary Publishing in the Mid-Nineteenth Century: The Business of Ticknor and Fields* (Cambridge, UK: Cambridge University Press, 1995), 15.

40 **He also started:** Newsome, "Publishing and Literary Activities of the Predecessors of Ticknor and Fields," 57; and Tryon, *Parnassus Corner*, 60.

40 **There were only 1,553:** Robert A. Gross, "Reading for an Extensive Republic," in Gross and Kelley, *History of the Book in America*, 2:533.

41 **While Child expected:** Lydia Child, *An Appeal in Favor of That Class of Americans Called Africans* (Boston: Allen and Ticknor, 1833), unpaginated preface; and Winship, *American Literary Publishing in the Mid-Nineteenth Century*, 16.

41 **When Ticknor put:** Shaun O'Connell, *Imagining Boston: A Literary Landscape* (Boston: Beacon Press, 1990), 54–55.

41 **A banking and financial:** Tryon and Charvat, *Cost Books of Ticknor and Fields and Their Predecessors*, xvi.

41 **"In consideration of his":** Tryon and Charvat, *Cost Books of Ticknor and Fields and Their Predecessors*, xvii.

Notes

41 **Ticknor arrived promptly:** Caroline Ticknor, *Hawthorne and His Publisher* (Boston: Houghton Mifflin Company, 1913), 22.

42 **He called it "Paradise":** Ticknor, *Hawthorne and His Publisher*, 114; and Hawthorne to Ticknor, October 8, 1853, in Nathaniel Hawthorne, *Letters of Hawthorne to William D. Ticknor, 1851–1864*, vol. 1 (Newark, NJ: Carteret Book Club, 1910), 1:19.

42 **While Ticknor (and Hawthorne):** "Letter About Boston" (New York) *Home Journal*, July 25, 1857.

42 **His little spot:** M. M. Ballou, "Antique Building," *Ballou's Pictorial* 12, no. 8 (February 1857): 113.

43 **Window seats and islands:** Ticknor, *Hawthorne and His Publisher*, 10–11; Mann, *Century of Bookselling*, 17; "Old Corner Book-Store," *New England Magazine*, 303–16; and "The Old Corner Bookstore," *Harvard Register* 2, no. 4 (October 1880): vi.

43 **"I never can go":** Oliver Wendell Holmes, *Over the Teacups* (Boston: Houghton, Mifflin and Company, 1892), 150–51.

43 **"We thus get":** OED Online, s.v. "browse," accessed December 2020, https://www.oed.com/view/Entry/23882; J. R. Lowell, "Dryden," *North American Review* (July 1868): 186–248; and Tryon, *Parnassus Corner*, 219–20.

44 **The books sat:** Henry Petroski, *The Book on the Bookshelf* (New York: Knopf, 1999), chap. 8.

44 **"There was a certain":** William Loring Andrews, *The Old Booksellers of New York and Other Papers* (New York: 1895), 13.

44 **was hardly universal:** A. Growoll, *The Profession of Bookselling: A Handbook of Practical Hints for the Apprentice and Bookseller, Part I* (New York: Office of the Publishers' Weekly, 1893), 25–28; Ronald J. Zboray, *A Fictive People: Antebellum Economic Development and the American Reading Public* (New York: Oxford University Press, 1993), 136–55.

44 **The Old Corner was not:** Leah Price, *What We Talk about When We Talk about Books* (New York: Basic Books, 2019), 27.

44 **In the early afternoon:** William Charvat, "James T. Fields and the Beginnings of Book Promotion, 1840–1855," *Huntington Library Quarterly* 8, no. 1 (November 1944): 75–94.

44 **he published two more:** Tryon and Charvat, *Cost Books of Ticknor and Fields and Their Predecessors*, 92, 94–99.

45 **Reed was a "blank":** Tryon and Charvat, *Cost Books of Ticknor and Fields and Their Predecessors*, xvii.

45 **American writers dominated:** Winship, *American Literary Publishing in the Mid-Nineteenth Century*, 55, 70–71.

45 **Poetry "never does well":** Ticknor, *Hawthorne and His Publisher*, 149.

45 **Fields said he couldn't:** Tryon, *Parnassus Corner*, 164.

45 **Fields read the work:** Joel Myerson and Daniel Shealy, eds., *The Journals of Louisa May Alcott* (Athens, GA: University of Georgia Press, 1997), 109; and Susan Cheever, *Louisa May Alcott* (New York: Simon & Schuster, 2010), 110–12.

Notes

45 **After she published:** Myerson and Shealy, *Journals of Louisa May Alcott*, 111fn3.

46 **Between 1820 and 1860:** Highland, "At the Bookstore," 65.

46 **Account books make:** Zboray and Zboray, "Boston Book Trades," 240; Michael Winship, "'The Tragedy of the Book Industry'? Bookstores and Book Distribution in the United States to 1950," *Studies in Bibliography* 58 (2007/2008): 152; and Winship, *American Literary Publishing in the Mid-Nineteenth Century*, 174.

46 **"No one need":** Charvat, "James T. Fields and the Beginnings of Book Promotion," 81, 89–90.

47 **Ticknor sent him money:** Hawthorne to Ticknor, June 8, 1852, June 13, 1852, July 13, 1852, January 21, 1853, April 1, 1853, June 20, 1853, July 5, 1853, and August 22, 1853, in Hawthorne, *Letters of Hawthorne to William D. Ticknor*, 1:2–4, 1:6, 1:10–11, 1:14–15.

47 **"I like the man":** Hawthorne to Ticknor, September 30, 1854, in Hawthorne, *Letters of Hawthorne to William D. Ticknor*, 1:63–64.

47 **Hawthorne mailed Tick:** James T. Fields, *Yesterdays with Authors* (Boston: Houghton, Mifflin and Company, 1891), 74–75.

47 **Hawthorne missed the place:** Hawthorne to Ticknor, January 6, 1855, in Hawthorne, *Letters of Hawthorne to William D. Ticknor*, 1:72.

47 **He suffered from homesickness:** Hawthorne to Ticknor, March 4, 1859, in Hawthorne, *Hawthorne to William D. Ticknor, 1851–1864*, 2:73–77.

47 **"Our customers take up":** Winship, *American Literary Publishing in the Mid-Nineteenth Century*, 122.

48 **"I have a greater":** Hawthorne to Ticknor, March 15, 1856, in Hawthorne, *Letters of Hawthorne to William D. Ticknor*, 2:5–7; and Tryon and Charvat, *Cost Books of Ticknor and Fields and Their Predecessors*, xx.

48 **Buyers were encouraged:** Jennifer Harlan, "How a Good Book Became the 'Richest' of Holiday Gifts," *NYT*, December 2, 2022.

48 **When Fields was traveling:** Tryon, *Parnassus Corner*, 151; and Fields, *Biographical Notes and Personal Sketches*, 24.

48 **When copies of:** Tryon, *Parnassus Corner*, 280.

48 **"At our Corner":** Tryon, *Parnassus Corner*, 209, 235.

49 **While advance copies:** Winship, *American Literary Publishing in the Mid-Nineteenth Century*, 152–54.

49 **When dealing with D. Appleton:** Winship, *American Literary Publishing in the Mid-Nineteenth Century*, 148–50, 156–58.

50 **When Ralph Waldo Emerson:** Michael Winship, "The International Trade in Books," in *A History of the Book in America*, ed. Scott E. Casper et al., vol. 3, *The Industrial Book, 1840–1880* (Chapel Hill: University of North Carolina Press, 2007), 155; and Highland, "At the Bookstore," 79–81, 91, 108–115, 122.

50 **the company had issued:** Ticknor and Fields, *Popular Books Published by Ticknor and Fields* (Catalog) (Boston: Ticknor and Fields, 1860).

50 **Hawthorne bought all:** Hawthorne to Ticknor, January 30, 1861, in Hawthorne, *Letters of Hawthorne to William D. Ticknor*, 2:112.

Notes

50 **The firm emphasized:** Ticknor and Fields, *Popular Books Published by Ticknor and Fields* (Catalog) (Boston: Ticknor and Fields, 1855, 1860, and 1861).

50 **When a Charleston:** Tryon, *Parnassus Corner*, 250.

50 **And when a bookstore:** Warren S. Tryon, "The Publications of Ticknor and Fields in the South, 1840–1865," *Journal of Southern History* 14, no. 3 (August 1948): 312.

51 **Stowe visited the Old Corner:** Caroline Ticknor, *Glimpses of Authors* (Boston: Houghton Mifflin, 1922), 83.

51 **it was hard to find:** Michael Winship, "Uncle Tom's Cabin: History of the Book in the 19th-Century United States," Uncle Tom's Cabin & American Culture (digital multimedia archive), 2007, http://utc.iath.virginia.edu/interpret/exhibits/winship/winship.html.

51 **Ticknor and Fields didn't even:** Tryon, "Publications of Ticknor and Fields in the South," 325–26.

51 **Another reader from New:** Barbara Hochman, *"Uncle Tom's Cabin" and the Reading Revolution: Race, Literacy, Childhood, and Fiction, 1851–1911* (Amherst: University of Massachusetts Press, 2011), 2, 84–85.

51 **The spread of railroads:** An Act to Reduce and Modify the Rates of Postage in the United States, 31st Cong., Ch. 20, 9 Stat. 587 (1851); and Richard B. Kielbowicz, "A History of Mail Classification and Its Underlying Policies and Purposes," Postal Rate Commission's Mail Reclassification Proceeding, MC95-1, July 17, 1995, 32.

51 **He surmised that:** Roger Philip McCutcheon, "Books and Booksellers in New Orleans, 1730–1830," *Louisiana Historical Quarterly* 20, no. 3 (July 1937): 608.

51 **Thomas Jefferson judged:** McCutcheon, "Books and Booksellers in New Orleans," 606.

52 **Levy stocked playing cards:** "Printers Ink," *LG*, July 25, 1820; "Playing Cards," *LG*, April 20, 1821; Advertisement, *LG*, April 15, 1822; "Mr. Buckingham," *True American* (New Orleans), March 23, 1839; "Washington Monument Lottery," *LG*, January 27, 1817; and "Lottery," *LG*, February 27, 1813.

52 **He wore many hats:** Bertram W. Korn, "Benjamin Levy: New Orleans Printer and Publisher," *Papers of the Bibliographical Society of America* 54 (1960): 232–33.

52 **a twenty-six-year-old "mulatto":** Hewlett & Bright, "Sale of Valuable Slaves," broadside, May 13, 1835, New Orleans, LA.

52 **Levy knew the business:** 1830 U.S. Census, New Orleans, LA, population schedule, NARA microfilm publication M19, Records of the Bureau of the Census, Record Group 29, National Archives, Washington, DC.

52 **only place in all:** Advertisement, *American Monthly Review* 2, no. 8 (August 1832); and "Agents," *North American Review* 20, no. 46 (January 1825), unpaginated, 16.

52 **Levy did leave:** Korn, "Benjamin Levy," 233–35, 239–40.

Notes

53 In consideration of the dire: Tryon, "Publications of Ticknor and Fields in the South," 309, 322–25.

53 every 15,045 people: *American Publishers' Circular* 5, no. 32 (August 1859): 386–87; *American Publishers' Circular* 5, no. 37 (September 1859): 452–54; *American Publishers' Circular* 6, no. 12 (March 1860): 142–45; and *American Publishers' Circular* 6, no. 13 (March 1860): 165–67. These figures represent the numbers of booksellers, not all of whom necessarily operated retail bookstores. Surely, there were other booksellers not counted.

54 By August of 1862: Tryon, *Parnassus Corner*, 252–54.

54 The South was cut: James N. Green, "The Rise of Book Publishing," in Gross and Kelley, *History of the Book in America*, 2:125.

54 the bookman died: Tryon, *Parnassus Corner*, 274; and Brenda Wineapple, *Hawthorne: A Life* (New York: Knopf, 2003), 372.

55 He had since ventured: Ellen B. Ballou, *The Building of the House: Houghton Mifflin's Formative Years* (Boston: Houghton Mifflin Company, 1970), 113, 134–35, 581.

55 "booksellers a fair living profit": "The Boston Meeting," *PW*, September 4, 1875, 406–9.

55 It was modeled on: Scott E. Casper, "Introduction," in Casper et al., *History of the Book in America*, 3:17.

55 NEBA members also: "Boston Meeting," 406.

55 James Fields was not present: Tryon, *Parnassus Corner*, 362.

56 Just a year later: *A History of the Old Corner Bookstore* (Boston: Old Corner Bookstore, 1903).

56 *The New York Times* argued: Stephenson Browne, "Boston Notes," *NYT*, May 23, 1903.

56 "to satisfy customers promptly": Christopher Morley, *John Mistletoe* (New York: Doubleday, 1931), 139–42; Christopher Morley, "Carrier Pigeons," in *Ex Libris Carissimis* (Philadelphia: University of Pennsylvania Press, 1932), 92; and Helen McK. Oakley, *Three Hours for Lunch: The Life and Times of Christopher Morley* (New York: Watermill, 1976), 58.

56 They launched Historic: Turk Tracey & Larry Architects, *Historic Structures Report for the Old Corner Bookstore Buildings*, 6–7, 28.

The Buyer

58 He jokes that: Stephen Sparks, "Passion Tempered with Patience: An Interview with Paul Yamazaki," *Zyzzyva*, October 19, 2020, https://www.zyzzyva.org /2020/10/19/passion-tempered-with-patience-an-interview-with-paul -yamazaki/.

59 The rookie bookseller: Sparks, "Passion Tempered with Patience."

59 Yamazaki wanted to: Sparks, "Passion Tempered with Patience"; The Literary Life, "Paul Yamazaki on Fifty Years of Bookselling at City Lights," *Literary Hub*,

Notes

January 29, 2021, https://lithub.com/paul-yamazaki-on-fifty-years-of-bookselling
-at-city-lights/.

59 **"It's almost pathological":** Sparks, "Passion Tempered with Patience."

Chapter 3: Parnassus on Wheels

61 **A white horse:** Christopher Morley, *Parnassus on Wheels* (New York: Melville House Publishing, 2010), 25–30, 40.

62 **"I didn't think":** Morley, *Parnassus on Wheels*, 42–43.

62 **She bought the business:** Morley, *Parnassus on Wheels*, 33.

62 **Instead of advertising Shakespeare:** Morley, *Parnassus on Wheels*, 63.

63 **A 1705 obituary:** Hellmut Lehmann-Haupt, *The Book in America: History of the Making, the Selling, and the Collecting of Books in the United States* (New York: R. R. Bowker Co., 1951), 52; and *A History of the Book in America*, ed. Hugh Amory and David D. Hall, vol. 1, *The Colonial Book in the Atlantic World* (Chapel Hill: University of North Carolina Press, 2007), 102.

63 **People assumed they sold:** Daniel J. Boorstin, *The Americans: The Colonial Experience* (Bombay: Allied Publishers, 1958), 297.

64 **And he complained that Carey:** James Gilreath, "Mason Weems, Mathew Carey and the Southern Booktrade," *Publishing History* 10 (January 1981): 27–49; James N. Green, "The Rise of Book Publishing," in *A History of the Book in America*, ed. Robert A. Gross and Mary Kelley, vol. 2, *An Extensive Republic: Print, Culture, and Society in the New Nation, 1790–1840* (Chapel Hill: University of North Carolina Press, 2010), 85–88, 95; and Ronald J. Zboray, *A Fictive People: Antebellum Economic Development and the American Reading Public* (New York: Oxford University Press, 1993), chap. 3.

64 **a two-thousand-volume:** Ronald E. Shaw, *Erie Water West: A History of the Erie Canal, 1792–1854* (Lexington: University Press of Kentucky, 1990), 233.

64 **a Maryland librarian:** Katherine Tappert, "The Automobile and the Traveling Library," *Annals of the American Academy of Political and Social Science* 116, no. 1 (November 1924): 66–68.

64 **"If there is anything":** "Can Books Be Sold by Caravan?," *PW*, July 21, 1928, 229.

64 **By the summer of 1920:** "The Parnassus Is Progressing," *PW*, July 24, 1920, 180.

64 **The Caravan Bookshop covered:** "The Caravan Starts," *PW*, June 26, 1920, 1986–87.

65 **Like children hearing:** "The Adventures of the Book Caravan," *PW*, July 31, 1920, 265.

65 **"We owe it":** "Adventures of the Book Caravan," 265.

65 **"THE CARAVAN IS COMING":** "The Book Caravan Covers Maine and New Hampshire," *PW*, August 21, 1920, 402.

65 **The Caravan targeted:** "Adventures of the Book Caravan," 265.

Notes

66 **"People do not"**: "The Caravan's Second Summer," *PW*, February 26, 1921, 620; Ruth Drake and Pauline Langley diary entries, July 30, 1921, in Horn Book, "Book Caravan Diary Transcriptions," Horn Book Inc. (website), January 1, 1999, https://www.hbook.com/?detailStory=book-caravan-diary-transcriptions.

66 **rivals entered the fray:** "An Appleton Caravan," *PW*, July 23, 1921, 187.

66 **And the National Association:** Frank Shay, "The Book Fliver, 1923 Model," *PW*, August 25, 1923, 613–14; and "Will the Parnassus on Wheels Come True?," *PW*, February 7, 1920, 383.

66 **Frank Shay had been:** For an exploration of Frank Shay and his bookshop, see Molly Schwartzburg, "Frank Shay's Greenwich Village: Reconstructing the Bookshop at 4 Christopher Street, 1920–1925," in *The Rise of the Modernist Bookshop: Books and the Commerce of Culture in the Twentieth Century*, ed. Huw Osborne (London: Routledge, 2015).

66 **"Shooting a gun":** "Frank Shay Dies; Wrote About Sea," *NYT*, January 15, 1954.

66 **He wouldn't say anything:** Holland Hudson, "Progressive Bookselling: Guaranteed Bookselling—One Shop and Its Methods," *PW*, February 12, 1921, 421–23; "New York Day by Day," *Lexington Leader*, November 23, 1922; and Madge Jenison, "And Now It Must be Sold," *Bookman* 57, no. 1 (March 1923): 48–52.

66 **Only 1 of 237:** Hudson, "Progressive Bookselling," 423.

67 **"I find something":** Hudson, "Progressive Bookselling," 423.

67 **Shay did more than:** "Frank Shay Dies; Wrote About Sea."

67 **He and Shay went:** Schwartzburg, "Frank Shay's Greenwich Village," 75.

67 **And for at least one:** Frank Shay to Christopher Morley, n.d., HRUT.

67 **Shay installed the door:** Helen McK. Oakley, *Three Hours for Lunch: The Life and Times of Christopher Morley* (New York: Watermill, 1976), 117. For more on the door, see Molly Schwartzburg, "The Greenwich Village Bookshop Door: A Portal to Bohemia, 1920–1925," HRUT, accessed December 6, 2023, https://norman .hrc.utexas.edu/bookshopdoor/home.cfm#1.

67 **The door became:** Christopher Morley, "Wine That Was Split in Haste," in *Ex Libris Carissimis* (Philadelphia: University of Pennsylvania Press, 1932), 110–11.

67 **Customers wanted to see:** Schwartzburg, "Frank Shay's Greenwich Village," 82–84.

67 **lacked something essential:** "Society," *Greenwich Village Quill*, November 1921, 19.

68 **Within a few weeks:** Frank Shay, "Caravaning on Parnassus," *PW*, July 15, 1922, 124–26; and Frank Shay, "Bookselling on the Broad Highroad," *New York Times Book Review*, May 11, 1924.

68 **Shay bought a Ford:** Shay, "Caravaning on Parnassus," 124–25.

68 **To make the venture:** Shay, "Bookselling on the Broad Highroad."

Notes

69 camped out in Provincetown: "Summer with Some Authors," *International Interpreter*, September 23, 1922, 784–85; and Frank Shay, "Selling Books to Fishermen," *PW*, July 29, 1922, 413.

69 But the same judge: Shay, "Bookselling on the Broad Highroad."

69 The "Parnassuswaggoner" didn't last: "Mr. Quill's Guide," *Greenwich Village Quill*, October 1924, 31.

69 "New England thrift": Shay, "Book Fliver," 613–14; and Shay, "Selling Books to Fishermen," 413.

69 Frank Collins's bookmobile: "Vagabond Book Shop Moves to San Clemente," *Santa Ana Register*, January 20, 1929; "Car Solves Problem of Sick Man," *LAT*, June 17, 1928; and "'Vagabond' Shop Supplies Isolated Summer Resorts with New Books," *Modern Mechanics and Inventions*, July 1929, 94. Confusingly, some of the news stories refer to the bookseller as Frank Collins, and others refer to him as Eric Collin.

69 So was *Parnassus*: Shay, "Book Fliver," 613–14.

69 Over four New England: "Can Books Be Sold by Caravan?," 229–33.

70 That was enough: Shay, "Book Fliver," 613–14.

70 "It was too personal": Morley, "Wine That Was Split in Haste," 108–9.

71 this one without wheels: "Frank Shay Dies; Wrote About Sea."

71 There was a 1938: "To Tour Mine Area with Films and Books," *DW*, June 12, 1938; and Charles Goodwin, "Paperback Bookseller on Wheels," *PW*, October 23, 1961, 26.

71 the last we hear: Christopher Morley, *The Haunted Bookshop* (New York: Grosset & Dunlap, 1919), 285.

The Artist + the Suffragette

72 "All the leagues": Madge Jenison, *Sunwise Turn: A Human Comedy of Bookselling* (New York: E. P. Dutton & Company, 1923), 153.

72 There were sculptures: Jenison, *Sunwise Turn*, 22.

72 Buying was intended: Jenison, *Sunwise Turn*, 17, 43.

72 The flourishes were: As quoted in Ted Bishop's excellent chapter, "The Sunwise Turn and the Social Space of the Bookshop," in Osborne, *Rise of the Modernist Bookshop*, 48.

73 "People not selected": Jenison, *Sunwise Turn*, 113.

73 They "treated us": Jenison, *Sunwise Turn*, 15.

73 Membership in the American: "Women in Business: The Making of Books," *Woman Citizen*, June 15, 1918, 53.

73 In 1920, the Nineteenth Amendment: U.S. Const. amend. XIX.

73 "Do we make any money?": Bishop, "Sunwise Turn and the Social Space of the Bookshop," 51.

74 "people like Mr. Morley": Bishop, "Sunwise Turn and the Social Space of the Bookshop," 52.

Notes

Chapter 4: Marshall Field & Company

76 **The male salesclerks:** Book Section Training Division Instructions, 1 August 1938, Folder 38, Box 2, MFCHS; Emily Kimbrough, *Through Charley's Door* (New York: Harper, 1952), 48–49, 59–60; Lloyd Wendt, *Give the Lady What She Wants!: The Story of Marshall Field & Company* (Chicago: Rand McNally, 1952), 197; and Leslie Goddard, *Remembering Marshall Field's* (Charleston: Arcadia Publishing, 2011), 45, 50. The men were advised to "avoid unusual color combinations" and "loud flashy apparel."

76 **Many referred to the book:** "Marcella Hahner Has a March Sale," *PW*, April 6, 1935, 1417–19.

76 **Marcella Burns Hahner was:** Madge Jenison, *Sunwise Turn: A Human Comedy of Bookselling* (New York: E. P. Dutton & Company, 1923), 153.

76 **Others called her "the Czarina":** "Miss Marcella Burns," *PW*, October 25, 1919, 1058.

76 **cofounder of Random House:** Bennett Cerf, "Trade Winds," *Saturday Review*, January 5, 1952, 4–6.

77 **As an English essayist:** "Art in Chicago," *Times* (London), September 24, 1920.

77 **The book section was said:** William Leach, *Land of Desire: Merchants, Power, and the Rise of a New American Culture* (New York: Vintage, 1993), 23.

77 **Hahner was a bookseller's:** Robert Cortes Holliday, *Men and Books and Cities* (New York: George H. Doran Company, 1921), 197; and "A Gossip on Chicago Bookshops," *PW*, June 28, 1924, 2010.

77 **They offered an ever-expanding:** For a history of department stores, see Leach, *Land of Desire*; Susan Porter Benson, *Counter Cultures: Saleswomen, Managers, and Customers in American Department Stores, 1890–1940* (Urbana: University of Illinois Press, 1986); Richard Longstreth, *The American Department Store Transformed, 1920–1960* (New Haven: Yale University Press, 2010); Traci Parker, *Department Stores and the Black Freedom Movement: Workers, Consumers, and Civil Rights from the 1930s to the 1980s* (Chapel Hill: University of North Carolina Press, 2019); and Jan Whitaker, *Service and Style: How the American Department Store Fashioned the Middle Class* (New York: St. Martin's Press, 2006).

78 **It was the anchor:** "Janssen, McClurg, & Co.," *Chicago Daily Tribune*, October 9, 1872.

78 **The rare-book section:** "Story of the Saints and Sinners' Corner," *American Book-Lore*, April 1899, 86–91.

78 **"Let Col. McClurg":** Robert W. Twyman, *History of Marshall Field & Co., 1852–1906* (Philadelphia: University of Pennsylvania Press, 1954), 109; Wendt, *Give the Lady What She Wants!*, 303; "The Department Store," *WSJ*, April 4, 1904. For more on the early history of Marshall Field and Marshall Field & Company, see Twyman, *History of Marshall Field & Co.*; John Tebbel, *The Marshall Fields: A Study in Wealth* (New York: Dutton, 1947); Gayle Soucek, *Marshall Field's: The Store That Helped Build Chicago* (Charleston: History Press, 2010).

78 the US Supreme Court: Whitaker, *Service and Style*, 208–9; and R. H. Macy & Co. v. American Publishers' Association et al., 231 U.S. 222 (1913).

79 Her first task: Wendt, *Give the Lady What She Wants!*, 303; "Marcella Burns Hahner," Obituary Notes, *PW*, September 13, 1941, 925; and Arietta Wimer Towne, "Have You a Little Library in Your Home?," Folder 38, Box 2, MFCHS.

79 Part of Hahner's job: Harry Hansen, *Midwest Portraits: A Book of Memories and Friendships* (New York: Harcourt, Brace and Company, 1923), 198.

79 the retail square footage: *The Store Book: Views and Facts of the Retail Store of Marshall Field & Company* (Chicago: Marshall Field & Co., 1933); Wendt, *Give the Lady What She Wants!*, 268–72; Leach, *Land of Desire*, 30–31; and Goddard, *Remembering Marshall Field's*, 41.

80 And when they did: Robert S. Lynd and Helen Merrell Lynd, *Middletown: A Study in American Culture* (New York: Harcourt, Brace and Company, 1929), 230.

80 Even with smaller margins: Laura J. Miller, *Reluctant Capitalists: Bookselling and the Culture of Consumption* (Chicago: University of Chicago Press, 2006), 36; Orion Howard Cheney, *Economic Survey of the Book Industry, 1930–1931* (New York: R. R. Bowker Co., 1949), 296; and Jenison, *Sunwise Turn*, 6–7.

80 Field's had ladies-only: Emily Remus, *A Shopper's Paradise: How the Ladies of Chicago Claimed Power and Pleasure in the New Downtown* (Cambridge: Harvard University Press, 2019), 3, 121–25.

80 *The Defender* alleged: "Marshall Field's Drawing Color Line," *Chicago Defender*, June 10, 1916.

80 Those workers who: Parker, *Department Stores and the Black Freedom Movement*, 139.

81 The "bunch of loafers": Wendt, *Give the Lady What She Wants!*, 303.

81 "Books are not just": Towne, "Have You a Little Library in Your Home?"

81 She wanted to encourage: "Bookshop Housekeeping," n.d., Folder 7, Box 9, MFCHS.

81 Hahner loved violets: Book Section Training Division Instructions, 1 August 1938, Folder 38, Box 2, MFCHS.

81 "Every man and woman": "Marcella Burns Hahner," 926; and "Marcella Hahner Has a March Sale," *PW*, April 6, 1935, 1417–19.

82 They needed to be: Kimbrough, *Through Charley's Door*, 190.

83 The books were sent over: Kimbrough, *Through Charley's Door*, 184–88, 199–200.

83 In 1915, its first full year: Jenison, *Sunwise Turn*, 8; and Wendt, *Give the Lady What She Wants!*, 362–63.

83 In a 1915 endorsement: John Lane Company Advertisement, *PW*, June 5, 1915, 1695.

83 sellers skewed female: Whitaker, *Service and Style*, 210. By 1920, about half of all department store book buyers were women.

83 She called bookselling: Towne, "Have You a Little Library in Your Home?"

Notes

83 **The speaker professed:** "The Sixteenth Annual Convention of the American Booksellers' Association," *PW*, May 27, 1916, 1703–66.

83 **When Marcella Burns married:** Personal Notes, *PW*, February 28, 1920, 640.

83 **The wounded soldiers:** "Doughnuts Plus a Real Personality," *Evening Herald* (Shenandoah, PA), February 4, 1919.

83 **What struck her most:** Towne, "Have You a Little Library in Your Home?"

84 **They quickly realized the value:** "The Marshall Field Book Fair," *PW*, October 25, 1919, 1059; "Confetti from the Chicago Book Carnival," *PW*, November 13, 1920, 1571; "How Louisa Alcott Wrote," *Kansas City Times*, October 11, 1919; and "New Book-Trade Co-operation," *PW*, January 31, 1920.

84 **By the time the fair:** "Marshall Field Book Fair," 1059.

84 **There was also a "model":** "The Book Fair at Chicago," *Bookman*, December 1920, 326–30; and "The Book Fair Idea as Developed in Germany," *PW*, September 25, 1920, 825.

84 **Similar fairs sprung up:** "The Minneapolis Book Fair," *PW*, March 6, 1920, 685; "Editorial: The Book Fair Season," *PW*, October 19, 1940; and "Harrod's Book Fair," *PW*, February 19, 1921, 524.

85 **And the constant shuffling:** "Bookshop Housekeeping," MFCHS.

85 **Taxidermy bird mounts:** "The Spirit of Spring in Books," *PW*, April 15, 1922, 1105–6.

85 **A friend of Hahner's:** Sinclair Lewis to Marcella Burns, 1 January (1920?), Folder 1, Box 11, MFCHS; and Sinclair Lewis, "Bronze Bars," *SEP*, December 13, 1919.

85 **December book sales:** Cheney, *Economic Survey of the Book Industry*, 304.

85 **Carl Sandburg signed:** Advertisement, *PW*, May 15, 1926.

85 **There were so many people:** "Marcella Burns Hahner," 925; and Cerf, "Trade Winds," 4–6.

86 **Hahner procured liquor:** Kimbrough, *Through Charley's Door*, 201–4, 257–58.

86 **The store president joked:** Cerf, "Trade Winds," 4–6.

86 **"The department is like":** Kimbrough, *Through Charley's Door*, 197–98.

86 **each section had its own:** Benson, *Counter Cultures*, 16.

86 **"Just as many kinds":** "Bookshop Housekeeping," MFCHS.

87 **these customers were sent:** *Books: On the Third Floor* (Chicago: Marshall Field & Company, 1929).

87 **Everyone was supposed:** *New Books for the Holidays* (Chicago: Marshall Field & Company, n.d.); and *Books for Children* (Chicago: Marshall Field & Company, n.d.).

87 **Field's also employed:** Leach, *Land of Desire*, 68–70; and "Marcella Burns Hahner," 925.

87 **A typical issue featured:** "Significant Hats for North and South," *Fashions of the Hour*, January 1927, 10; Little Things Noticed on a Walk through the Store, column, *Fashions of the Hour*, January 1927, 32; John T. McCutcheon, "The Hoosier Salon—1927," *Fashions of the Hour*, January 1927, 23; and "The American

Notes

Express Service at Our Travel Bureau Will Make Arrangements for Your Trip,"
Fashions of the Hour, January 1927, 30.

87 **Because of Hahner's connections:** Christopher Morley, "The Stupid Magician,"
Fashions of the Hour, June 1926, 6.

87 **Hahner blurbed one:** Doubleday, Page & Co. Advertisement, *PW*, November 5,
1927, 1701.

87 **A 1921 ad:** Gold Shod advertisement, *NYT*, October 9, 1921.

88 **Writers desperate for:** Howard to Marcella Hahner, n.d., Folder 7, Box 9,
MFCHS.

88 **He did recognize:** H. Bedford-Jones to Mrs. M. B. Hahner, n.d., Folder 7, Box 9,
MFCHS.

88 **She convinced one friend:** Kimbrough, *Through Charley's Door*, 192; K. H. and
M. B. H., *100 Riddles and 101 Things to Do* (New York: Grosset & Dunlap, 1928);
and K. H. and M. B. H., *100 Points in Etiquette and 101 Don'ts* (New York: Grosset
& Dunlap, 1929).

88 **Morley urged readers:** Christopher Morley, *A Letter to Leonora* (Chicago: Book
Section of Marshall Field & Company, 1928).

88 **For his work:** Christopher Morley to Marcella Hahner, 9 July 1928, Folder 3, Box
10, MFCHS.

89 **A purchase from:** "Richard Leo Simon," Obituary Notes, *PW*, August 8, 1960,
40.

89 **"turned the department":** "Recollections of Some Booksellers," *PW*, May 19,
1975, 128.

89 **as *The Successful Bookshop*:** Frederic G. Melcher, George A. Hecht, and Harry J.
Feeley, *The Successful Bookshop: A Manual of Practical Information* (New York:
R. R. Bowker Co., 1949), 8.

89 **Owners of smaller:** Miller, *Reluctant Capitalists*, 24, 35.

89 **She was making one:** Kimbrough, *Through Charley's Door*, 191–92; Publishing
advertisements, Folder 23, Box 2, MFCHS.

89 **Attendees registered for:** "Convention of the American Booksellers'
Association," program, *PW*, May 2, 1925, 1498–99.

89 **The following year, the ABA:** "Marcella Burns Hahner," 925.

90 **It was about more:** Kimbrough, *Through Charley's Door*, 197–98.

90 **In Chicago alone:** "Department Store Buyers of Books," *PW*, February 12, 1921,
461–67.

90 **categorized department stores:** Cheney, *Economic Survey of the Book Industry*,
233–237.

90 **Department stores more:** Cheney, *Economic Survey of the Book Industry*, 250, 264.

90 **Another estimate suggested:** Miller, *Reluctant Capitalists*, 35.

91 **At the bottom were:** Cheney, *Economic Survey of the Book Industry*, 239, 238, 245;
and Kenneth C. Davis, *Two-Bit Culture: The Paperbacking of America* (Boston:
Houghton Mifflin, 1984), 16.

Notes

91 **Hawthorne's** *The Scarlet*: *Sears, Roebuck and Co.*, catalog no. 144 (Chicago: Sears, Roebuck and Co., 1922), 432–35.

91 **Getting books in:** For more on the history of the Book-of-the-Month Club, see Joan Shelley Rubin, "Self, Culture, and Self-Culture in Modern America: The Early History of the Book-of-the-Month Club," *Journal of American History* 71, no. 4 (March 1985): 782–806; and Janice A. Radway, *A Feeling for Books: The Book-of-the-Month Club, Literary Taste, and Middle-Class Desire* (Chapel Hill: University of North Carolina Press, 1997).

91 **its "hand-me-down opinions":** As quoted in Radway, *Feeling for Books*, 226–27.

91 **The effort flopped:** *ABA Almanac, 1950* (New York: American Booksellers Association, 1950), 31–32.

92 **When Hahner believed:** "In the Bookmarket," *PW*, August 23, 1930, 687; and Bobbs-Merrill Company Advertisement, *PW*, August 16, 1930, 571.

92 **she transformed the department:** Groff Conklin, "Marcella Hahner Has a March Sale," *PW*, April 6, 1935, 1417–19.

92 **Throughout the 1930s:** "Field's Installs G. & D. Display," *PW*, December 10, 1938, 2050; and "Grosset Offers Gift Feature as Part of Fall Promotion," *PW*, September 16, 1939, 1062–63.

92 **sponsor a giant book:** Bernadine Clark, *Fanfare for Words: Bookfairs and Book Festivals in North America* (Washington, DC: Library of Congress, 1991), 18–19; "Young Customers," *PW*, October 23, 1937, 1659; and "Currents in the Trade," *PW*, October 16, 1937, 1559.

92 **Visitors left with:** Christopher Morley, *Ex Libris* (New York: Christopher Morley, 1936).

92 **The department sold 33,425:** John Scheele to Robert DeGraff, 11 January 1940, in *PW*, January 20, 1940, 201.

93 **Letters of congratulations:** Benjamin H. Ticknor to Rose Oller Harbaugh, 21 February 1941, Folder 4, Box 10, MFCHS.

93 **"I hope I'll never":** Dorothy Parker to "Ollie," 28 February 1941, Folder 9, Box 9, MFCHS.

93 **Harbaugh kept most:** Rose Oller Harbaugh, "Bookshop Housekeeping in the Large Store," *PW*, May 24, 1941, 2080–83.

93 **While she was careful:** "Bookshop Notes," *PW*, September 20, 1941, 1132.

93 **as the war strangled:** Shop Talk, column, *PW*, November 13, 1948, 2080.

93 **But when the party:** Shop Talk, column, *PW*, December 2, 1944, 2162–63.

94 **Judy was not invited:** Rose Oller Harbaugh, *Eddie Elephant Has a Party* (Chicago: Rand McNally, 1947).

94 **The emcee was:** Bennett A. Cerf to Rose Oller Harbaugh, 27 September 1946, Folder 37, Box 2, MFCHS.

94 **"The hell with dough":** "Book Trade Flocks to Chicago to Honor Rose Oller Harbaugh," *PW*, February 9, 1952, 796–97; Fanny Butcher, Literary Spotlight, column, *Chicago Sunday Tribune Magazine of Books*, February 3, 1952; and Frederic

Notes

Babcock, Among the Authors, column, *Chicago Sunday Tribune Magazine of Books*, January 27, 1952.

95 **paperback section was "self-service":** "Give the Customer the Book He Wants," *PW*, September 19, 1960, 44–45.

95 **Even Bloomingdale's discounted:** Whitaker, *Service and Style*, 211. On the decline of department stores, see Vicki Howard, *From Main Street to Mall: The Rise and Fall of the American Department Store* (Philadelphia: University of Pennsylvania Press, 2015), chaps. 7–8.

95 **in and around Chicago:** "Around the Retail Bookstore," *PW*, May 16, 1980, 143.

The Architect

96 **The shop's own opening:** "Chicago's New Bookstore," *Dial*, November 16, 1907, 327. For an excellent overview of Browne's Bookstore, see Adam Morgan, "When Frank Lloyd Wright Designed a Bookstore," *Paris Review*, March 22, 2018, https://www.theparisreview.org/blog/2018/03/22/when-frank-lloyd-wright-designed-a-bookstore/. See also Frank Lloyd Wright, *Frank Lloyd Wright: Early Visions: The Great Achievements of the Oak Park Years*, Brigitte Goldstein, trans. (New York: Gramercy Books, 1995).

96 **At the far end:** Frank Lloyd Wright, Plans and Elevations, 0802.014, "Browne's Bookstore," Avery Architectural and Fine Arts Library, Columbia University.

97 *Publishers Weekly* **credited:** "A Unique Bookstore," *PW*, August 15, 1908, 352–53; and "A Notable Bookstore," Folder 256, Box 7, Francis Fisher Browne Papers, Newberry Library, Chicago.

97 **Trade publications warned:** Melcher, Hecht, and Feeley, *Successful Bookshop*, 28, 38, 40.

97 **Since it required a:** Javier Ramirez, interview by the author, May 2022.

Chapter 5: The Gotham Book Mart

100 **According to the editors:** Frances Steloff, "In Touch with Genius," *Journal of Modern Literature* 4, no. 4 (April 1975): 737.

100 **Even as the shop:** List of Quotes, n.d., Folder 11, Box 15, GBMPENN.

100 **was an unsuccessful peddler:** "Steloff Sued by City," *Saratogian*, August 18, 1915.

100 **A wealthy couple from Boston:** "Frances Steloff Dies at 101," *Sunday Saratogian*, April 16, 1989.

100 **At the first family:** W. G. Rogers, *Wise Men Fish Here: The Story of Frances Steloff and the Gotham Book Mart* (New York: Harcourt, Brace & World, 1964), 36.

101 **tired of doing chores:** "Frances Steloff, Devotee of Books, Writers, Dies at 101," *LAT*, April 16, 1989.

101 **"From then on":** Frances Steloff deposition, Supreme Court of the State of New York County of New York, 5 October 1987, Folder 14, Box 2, GBMPENN; and Rogers, *Wise Men Fish Here*, 46–48.

Notes

101 **she continued her education:** S. Kann, Sons & Co. to Frances Steloff, 8 and 22 October 1912, GBMNYPL; and Rogers, *Wise Men Fish Here*, 49–58.

101 **She couldn't help but:** Steloff, "In Touch with Genius," 839.

102 **A horse carried:** Steloff, "In Touch with Genius," 738, 749–50.

102 **A half block from Broadway:** Steloff, "In Touch with Genius," 750–51. For more on what Gotham sold in this era, see Gotham Book Mart, *Art Catalog*, catalog no. 14 (New York: Gotham Book Mart, 1930); Lynn Gilbert and Gaylen Moore, *Particular Passions: Talks with Women Who Have Shaped Our Times* (New York: Clarkson Potter, 1981), 4.

102 **Steloff decided to:** Steloff, "In Touch with Genius," 750, 755–60.

103 **"I was about to":** Frances Steloff to Carl Van Vechten, 13 December 1948, GBMNYPL; and Steloff deposition, GBMPENN.

103 **Steloff understood that:** Christine Stansell, *American Moderns: Bohemian New York and the Creation of a New Century* (New York: Metropolitan Books, 2000), 1–2.

103 **It featured a foreword:** American Book Bindery to Gotham Book Mart, 14 November 1928, GBMNYPL; and Benjamin De Casseres, *Anathema!: Litanies of Negation* (New York: Gotham Book Mart, 1928), x.

103 **Knowing that her customers:** Steloff, "In Touch with Genius," 782–83; Christopher Morley to Frances Steloff, 31 March 1955, HRUT.

104 **Though Steloff later admitted:** Rogers, *Wise Men Fish Here*, 93.

104 **A lifelong friendship:** Steloff, "In Touch with Genius," 759–60. For more on Shakespeare and Company, see Sylvia Beach, *Shakespeare and Company* (New York: Harcourt, Brace and Company, 1956). See also Sylvia Beach to Frances Steloff, 24 November 1936, Folder 22, Box 33, SBPU; Sylvia Beach to Frances Steloff, 26 July 1934, Folder 22, Box 33, SBPU; and Gotham Book Mart receipt, 20 February 1959, SBPU. When Beach came to the US, she, too, made a dash to Gotham, in her mind the "best modern bookshop." Beach and Steloff often traded back and forth. In 1934, Beach sent Steloff first-edition copies of Gertrude Stein's *The Making of Americans*, while Steloff shipped her copies of *Experimental Cinema* and selected works of E. E. Cummings. Both women encouraged their customers to check out their competitor across the ocean.

104 **"The real book-hunting":** As quoted in Carolyn Anspacher, "Wise Men 'Fish' With Her," *San Francisco Chronicle*, August 21, 1935.

104 **"Oh Bibliophile":** Christopher Morley to Frances Steloff, n.d., HRUT; and Oakley, *Three Hours for Lunch*, 249–50.

104 **The festivities began:** Steloff, "In Touch with Genius," 744, 786, 800.

105 **Whether to the backyard:** For an example of the "modern" titles offered by Gotham in the 1930s, see Gotham Book Mart, *Modern First Editions*, catalog no. 16 (New York: Gotham Book Mart, 1931); and Gotham Book Mart, *Along the Modernist Front*, catalog no. 31 (New York: Gotham Book Mart, 1934).

105 **when the dancer wanted:** Martha Graham, *Blood Memory* (New York: Doubleday, 1991), 108, 110.

Notes

105 **Steloff was miserable:** Gilbert and Moore, *Particular Passions*, 1.

106 **While women read more:** Orion Howard Cheney, *Economic Survey of the Book Industry, 1930–1931* (New York: R. R. Bowker Co., 1949), 35–38.

106 **Steloff went out:** Steloff, "In Touch with Genius," 827–28.

106 **Whether men or women:** *American Book Trade Manual* (New York: R. R. Bowker Co., 1922); and Megan Benton, "'Too Many Books': Book Ownership and Cultural Identity in the 1920s," *American Quarterly* 49, no. 2 (June 1997): 273.

106 **Days went by without:** Karen Burke LeFevre, "Gotham Bookseller: Frances Steloff and the Gotham Book Mart," book proposal, n.d., Folder 2, Box 1, GBMPENN.

106 **The fund was short lived:** Frances Steloff, statement of purpose of Writers' Emergency Fund, n.d., GBMNYPL.

106 **One recipient was Henry:** Miller donated the money back to the fund to help even more desperate types.

106 **He once asked her:** Henry Miller to Frances Steloff, n.d., GBMNYPL.

106 **"don't leave this":** Henry Miller to Frances Steloff, 20 January 1943, GBMNYPL.

106 **And when Miller asked:** As quoted in Rogers, *Wise Men Fish Here*, 124; and Alice Quinn, "Notes and Comment, Talk of the Town," *NYR*, January 25, 1988, 26.

106 **Miller was so appreciative:** As quoted in Rogers, *Wise Men Fish Here*, 148.

107 **Steloff managed to:** Gotham Book Mart to Archibald MacLeish, 20 October 1939, GBMNYPL; and Steloff, "In Touch with Genius," 808.

107 **Steloff took a copy:** "The Old Smut Peddler," *Life*, August 29, 1969, 51.

107 **They paid the $250:** "More Books Seized by Sumner in Raid," *NYT*, June 27, 1928; Rogers, *Wise Men Fish Here*, 100. For more on censorship, see Paul S. Boyer, *Purity in Print: Book Censorship in America from the Gilded Age to the Computer Age* (Madison: University of Wisconsin Press, 2002).

108 **She then set:** Steloff, "In Touch with Genius," 766–67; Christopher Morley, "Questio Quid Juris," Bowling Green, column, *Saturday Review of Literature*, January 4, 1936, 13; and Rogers, *Wise Men Fish Here*, 151.

108 **The following year's:** Gotham Book Mart, *Real Bargains in Real Books*, catalog no. 19 (New York: Gotham Book Mart, 1931).

108 **Though the book contained:** People of the State of New York v. Gotham Mart Inc., 158 Misc. 240, 285 N.Y.S. 563 (1936); Steloff, "In Touch with Genius," 768–71; "The New York Law Controlling the Dissemination of Obscene Materials to Minors," *Fordham Law Review* 32, no. 4 (1966): 692–710; and Morley, "Questio Quid Juris," 13.

108 **covered the breast:** Steloff, "In Touch with Genius," 768–71; Maya Deren, photograph, n.d., Folder 15, Box 32, Alexina and Marcel Duchamp Papers, Philadelphia Museum of Art Archives. For more on censorship and modernist bookshops, see Andrew Thacker, "The Pure and the Dirty: Censorship, Obscenity, and the Modern Bookshop," *Modernism/modernity* 29, no. 3 (September 2022): 519–41.

109 **She thought writers:** Deborah Dickson, dir., *Frances Steloff: Memoirs of a Bookseller* (Los Angeles: Direct Cinema Ltd., 1987), VHS.

Notes

109 **When Richard L. Simon of:** See, for example, Margaret Anderson to Frances Steloff, 1 March 1949, and Frances Steloff to Margaret Anderson, 4 March 1949, GBMNYPL.

110 **"I never could":** Arthur Davison Ficke to Frances Steloff, 3 October 1938, GBMNYPL; and Frances Steloff to Bennett Cerf, n.d., GBMNYPL.

110 **When Conrad Aiken:** Conrad Aiken to Frances Steloff, 6 April 1963, GBMNYPL.

110 **E. E. Cummings ordered:** E. E. Cummings to Frances Steloff, 28 October 1952, GBMNYPL.

110 **H. L. Mencken bought:** H. L. Mencken to Gotham Book Mart, 24 June 1941, GBMNYPL.

110 **Mencken visited in person:** Steloff, "In Touch with Genius," 780; and Andreas Brown, "My Forty Years as a Book Collector," lecture at San Diego State University, CA, January 20, 1990. For more on the Dreiser/Mencken incident, see Jude Davies, "'Either a Joke or a Miracle': Literary Reverence and Literary Commerce after Dreiser and Mencken Signed Bibles at the Gotham Book Mart," "Modernism - Materiality - Meaning: Session I," streamed on May 22, 2019, YouTube video, 1:17:24, https://www.youtube.com/watch?v=Y7QwpODMRfw.

110 **"The book has been":** Steloff, "In Touch with Genius," 827–28; and Edmund Wilson, Books, *NYR*, April 1, 1944, 78, 81–82. Wilson would continue to review and publicize Nin's work. See, for example, Edmund Wilson, Books, *NYR*, November 10, 1945, 97–102.

111 **Many were hard:** Press release for *Vertical*, n.d., GBMNYPL; and Rogers, *Wise Men Fish Here*, 114–16. For more on the "little magazines," see Frederick J. Hoffman, Charles Allen, and Carolyn F. Ulrich, *The Little Magazine: A History and a Bibliography* (Princeton, NJ: Princeton University Press, 1946).

111 **Most didn't survive long:** Gotham Book Mart, *We Moderns: Gotham Book Mart, 1920–1940*, catalog no. 42 (New York: Schoen Printing Company, 1940), 85–88.

111 **"You are invited":** Invitation to Finnegans Wake, n.d., GBMNYPL.

111 **The working title was:** Steloff, "In Touch with Genius," 745.

111 **John Dos Passos introduced:** Gotham Book Mart, *We Moderns*, 3, 24–25, 29, 54, 63.

112 **Cummings agreed only:** Steloff, "In Touch with Genius," 820.

112 **Morley addressed his:** Christopher Morley to Frances Steloff, 1944, HRUT.

112 **"I find myself":** Frances Steloff to Henry Miller, 13 June 1944, GBMNYPL.

112 **Over the course of just:** Frances Steloff, personal diary, 6 July, 8 July, 18 July, 4 October, and 19 October 1949, Folder 23, Box 1, GBMPENN.

112 **She didn't like any:** Rogers, *Wise Men Fish Here*, 189–90.

112 **Some called her a:** Dickson, *Frances Steloff*.

112 **One staff member even:** Norman Rush, "Labors," Work for Hire, *NYR*, October 14, 2013, 87.

113 **apparently didn't know:** Carl Van Vechten to Alice Toklas, 18 February 1935,

Notes

and Alice Toklas to Carl Van Vechten, 21 February 1935, in *The Letters of Gertrude Stein and Carl Van Vechten, 1913–1946*, ed. Edward Burns (New York: Columbia University Press, 2013), 392–93.

113 **When he showed up:** Herbert Mitgang, "Frances Steloff Is Dead at 101; Founded the Gotham Book Mart," *NYT*, April 16, 1989.

113 **"I have found it":** Parker Tyler to Frances Steloff, 14 April 1941, GBMNYPL; and Frances Steloff to Parker Tyler, 14 May 1942, GBMNYPL.

113 **Customers often asked:** Frances Steloff to Margaret Anderson, n.d., GBMNYPL; and Brown, "My Forty Years as a Book Collector."

113 **chatted with the literary kitties:** Susan Sheehan, "Bookstore Cat," *NYR*, May 13, 2002, 37.

113 **"everything converges to":** *The Diary of Anaïs Nin*, ed. Gunther Stuhlmann, vol. 3, 1939–1944 (New York: Harcourt Brace Jovanovich, 1969), 11, 179.

114 **When reading had become:** Joan Shelley Rubin, *The Making of Middlebrow Culture* (Chapel Hill: University of North Carolina Press, 1992), chaps. 3–4.

114 **"I can't bear to see":** Gilbert and Moore, *Particular Passions*, 9; and Andreas Brown, interview by Susan Resnik with Jayne Meyers, May 3, 2017, SDSUOH.

114 **In appreciation for Gotham's:** Steloff, "In Touch with Genius," 839.

115 **"starved for books":** Dickson, *Frances Steloff*.

115 **When Yale University wanted:** Norman Pearson to Frances Steloff, 7 and 15 April 1941, GBMNYPŁ.

115 **Books sat on shelves:** Quinn, "Notes and Comment," 25.

115 **Whether in the 1930s:** Cheney, *Economic Survey of the Book Industry*, 293; and Jeff Deutsch, *In Praise of Good Bookstores* (Princeton, NJ: Princeton University Press, 2022), 96.

116 **In the fall of 1948:** "The Sitwells," *Life*, December 6, 1948, 164–72.

116 **who called Gotham and Steloff:** As quoted in Matthew Tannenbaum, *My Years at the Gotham Book Mart with Frances Steloff, Proprietor* (Malden-on-Hudson, NY: Worthy Shorts, 2009), 21.

116 **It was "like a party":** Elizabeth Bishop to Carley Dawson, 10 November 1948, in *Elizabeth Bishop: One Art*, ed. Robert Giroux (New York: Farrar, Straus and Giroux, 1994), 174.

116 **Vidal evidently disagreed:** As quoted in Erwin R. Tiongson, "The Most Famous Photograph of Poets Ever Taken," *Slate*, December 11, 2019, https://slate.com /culture/2019/12/photo-elizabeth-bishop-marianne-moore-auden-tennessee -williams.html.

116 **As Bishop recalled:** Elizabeth Bishop, *Prose* (New York: Farrar, Straus and Giroux, 1984), 363.

117 **Unlike most of the others:** James Joyce Society articles of association, n.d., Folder 4, Box 140, James Joyce Society, 1956, SBPU; James Joyce Society application for membership, n.d., Folder 4, Box 140, James Joyce Society, 1956, SBPU; and Lillian Ross and John McCarten, "Far From the Liffey," Talk of the Town, *NYR*, February 14, 1959, 26–27.

Notes

117 **On her worst:** Frances Steloff to Henry Miller, 13 June 1944, GBMNYPL.

118 **maybe after a newsreel:** Frances Steloff, personal diary, 1949, Folder 23, Box 1, GBMPENN; Frances Steloff to Anaïs Nin, 24 November 1943, GBMNYPL; Frances Steloff to Harry Moore, 14 September 1948, GBMNYPL; and journal entries, Folder 13, Box 36, FSC.

118 **While she was preparing:** Frances Steloff to Maria Jolas, 26 March 1948, GBMNYPL.

118 **Steloff broke her:** Frances Steloff to Georgia O'Keeffe, 9 January 1954, GBMNYPL; and Rogers, *Wise Men Fish Here*, 174–75.

119 **And when Ferlinghetti:** Lawrence Ferlinghetti to Frances Steloff, 14 October 1963, 1 November 1963, and 16 April 1971, GBMNYPL.

119 **Screenwriter and filmmaker:** Eileen Shanahan to Gotham Book Mart, 26 February 1963, 4 March 1963, 28 August 1963, and 22 April 1964, GBMNYPL.

119 **Steloff sent a clerk:** Langston Hughes to Gotham Book Mart, 1966, GBMNYPL; and Brown, "My Forty Years as a Book Collector."

119 **The answer was "bookshop":** Crossword puzzle, *Chicago Daily News*, October 25, 1965.

119 **She wrote to Djuna:** Frances Steloff to Djuna Barnes, 26 October 1965 and 5 November 1965, GBMNYPL.

120 **A woman from Ohio:** As quoted in Rogers, *Wise Men Fish Here*, 171.

120 **"As long as the Gotham":** James Dickey to Frances Steloff, 20 March 1965, GBMNYPL.

121 **He was also neater:** For more on Andreas Brown, see Brown, interview by Susan Resnik.

121 **Steloff cried:** Dickson, *Frances Steloff.*

121 **"But Andy is":** Sandy Campbel and Anthony Hiss, "Frances Steloff, L.H.D.," Talk of the Town, *NYR*, August 16, 1969, 24.

121 **"The more I straightened":** Brown, interview by Susan Resnik; and Mel Gussow, "Where Wise Men Fish? It's Moved Down a Block," *NYT*, August 4, 2004.

122 **Smith was lodged:** Camille Davis, "Gotham Book Mart as Publisher," and "The Seventies," in *Wise Men Fished Here: A Centennial Exhibition in Honor of the Gotham Book Mart, 1920–2020*, cur. David McKnight (Philadelphia: University of Pennsylvania Libraries, 2019), 76, 115; and Brown, interview by Susan Resnik. For more on Smith, see Patti Smith, *Just Kids* (New York: Ecco, 2010).

122 **Brown introduced other:** For more on this era, see Kim Phillips-Fein's excellent book *Fear City: New York's Fiscal Crisis and the Rise of Austerity Politics* (New York: Metropolitan Books, 2017).

123 **he spoke of Frances:** Katherine Aid, "The Enigmatic Edward Gorey," in Davis, *Wise Men Fished Here*, 133–45.

123 **President Reagan sent:** Ronald Reagan to Frances Steloff, 5 January 1988, Folder 9, Box 1, GBMPENN.

123 **Forever seeking new:** *Books from the Library of Truman Capote with Important Additions* (New York: Gotham Book Mart, 1984); and *Tennessee Williams: A Catalogue* (New York: Gotham Book Mart, ca. 1983).

123 **He needed the money:** Brown, "My Forty Years as a Book Collector"; and Brown, interview by Susan Resnik.

124 **But the internet boom:** Brown also had to contend with a costly legal battle of his own, eventually settling with Joanne Carson (Johnny Carson's ex-wife) over a large investment.

124 **"If you aspire":** R. McGregor and Geoffrey T. Hellman, "Poet's Party," Talk of the Town, *NYR*, September 27, 1958, 33.

The Cat

126 **WonTon "became the mayor":** "Eff Yeah, Bookstores!: Chop Suey Books," *Annalemma* (blog), accessed November 23, 2022, http://annalemma.net/blog/eff -yeah-bookstores-chop-suey-books.html.

Chapter 6: The Strand

129 **there was also a book:** New York has been home to many other "rows" and districts, including Newspaper Row, Publishers' Row, Radio Row, Millionaire's Row, Striver's Row, Restaurant Row, Automobile Row, and Steamship Row. For more on the derivation of *row* and its use in New York and elsewhere, see David L. Gold, "Notes: *Row* in Some English Placenames," *Names* 32, no. 3 (1984): 347–52; and David L. Gold, "Notes: More on *Row* in English Placenames," *Names* 34, no. 1 (1986): 101–2. The terms *book row, booksellers' row*, and the like have been applied in other cities, most notably in reference to Charing Cross Road in London, and occasionally to stretches in Delhi, Baghdad, and elsewhere. See, for example, "Booksellers' Row," *Times of India*, February 6, 1958; Ben Reuven, "Westwood Blvd.'s New Booksellers' Row," *LAT*, February 29, 1976; "20 Miles of Shelves," *NYT*, October 13, 1912; and Edward Wong and Wissam A. Habeeb, "Baghdad Car Bomb Kills 20 on Booksellers' Row," *NYT*, March 6, 2007. For an overview of Book Row, see Marvin Mondlin and Roy Meador, *Book Row: An Anecdotal and Pictorial History of the Antiquarian Book Trade* (New York: Carroll & Graf, 2003).

130 **Just three were:** *The Trow Business Directory of New York City* (New York: Trow Directory, Printing and Bookbinding Co., 1897).

130 **"Scriptures in every":** "'Booksellers' Row,' New York," *PW*, April 28, 1917, 1350. For more on the history of the American Bible House, see Peter J. Wosh, *Spreading the Word: The Bible Business in Nineteenth-Century America* (Ithaca: Cornell University Press, 1994).

131 **None of the other:** Manuel B. Tarshish, "The 'Fourth Avenue' Book Trade—I," *PW*, October 20, 1969, 52; and Manuel B. Tarshish, "Peter Stammer: Bookseller," *Journal of Library History* 5, no. 3 (July 1970): 271–74.

Notes

131 **"Book shops are gregarious":** Guido Bruno, *Adventures in American Bookshops, Antique Stores and Auction Rooms* (Detroit: Douglas Book Shop, 1922), 39.

131 **After opening a small:** "Theodore Schulte, a Book Dealer, 83," *NYT*, May 4, 1950; and Herbert Hoover to Mr. Schulte, 26 June 1920, Folder 1, Box 1, SBSR.

131 **Browsers wending their way:** "'Booksellers' Row' Taking New Lease on Life," *PW*, October 6, 1917, 1145; *Dictionary of American Antiquarian Bookdealers*, ed. Donald C. Dickinson (Westport, CT: Greenwood Press, 1998), s.v. "Pesky, Wilfred P.," 164; and McCandlish Phillips, *City Notebook: A Reporter's Portrait of a Vanishing New York* (New York: Liveright, 1974).

131 **"If you were coming":** "New York City Bookshops in the 1930s and 1940s: The Recollections of Walter Goldwater," interview in *Dictionary of Literary Biography, Yearbook: 1993*, ed. James W. Hipp (Detroit: Gale, 1994), 152.

132 **In Christopher Morley's sequel:** Christopher Morley, *The Haunted Bookshop* (New York: Grosset & Dunlap, 1919); and Christopher Morley, "Thoughtmarks," Bowling Green, column, *Saturday Review of Literature*, July 4, 1925, 875.

132 **In October of 1917:** "Schulte's Bargains," advertisement, *NYT*, November 18, 1917; "Booksellers' Row," advertisement, *NYT Book Review*, October 7, 1917; "'Booksellers' Row' Taking New Lease on Life," 1145; "'Booksellers' Row,' New York," 1350; *A Catalogue of Quakeriana and Anti-Quaker Literature* (New York: Schulte's Book Store, 1917); and "Theodore E. Schulte," Obituary Notes, *PW*, May 13, 1950, 2068–69.

132 **He arrived at Ellis:** "New York Passenger Arrival Lists (Ellis Island), 1892–1924," roll 1059, vol. 2329–30, 11 Dec 1907, FamilySearch.

132 **He headed to New:** Entry for Benjamin Bass, 1919, "New York, U.S. District and Circuit Court Naturalization Records, 1824-1991," FamilySearch, https://www .familysearch.org/ark:/61903/1:1:QPTM-Z1WW; and Robert McG. Thomas Jr., "Benjamin Bass, 77, Was Founder of the Strand Used-Book Store," *NYT*, August 2, 1978.

132 **with $300 of his:** Donald Newlove, "The Beast in the Strand Book Store," *New York*, August 1, 1977, 45–47.

133 **The five-foot-five:** "Oral History Interview: Fred Bass," by Sarah Dziedzic, Greenwich Village Society for Historic Preservation Oral History Project, June 7, 2017; and William Grimes, "Fred Bass, Who Made the Strand Bookstore a Mecca, Dies at 89," *NYT*, January 3, 2018.

133 **As H. P. Lovecraft:** H. P. Lovecraft to Mrs. F. C. Clark, 20 May 1925, in H. P. Lovecraft, *Selected Letters II: 1925–1929* (Sauk City, WI: Arkham House, 1968), 7–8.

133 **When someone asked Stammer:** Jacob L. Chernofsky, "Biblo and Tannen: A Fourth Avenue Landmark," *AB*, April 14, 1986, 1666.

133 **Crowds continued to:** "Hey Day of Book Row," *AB*, July 16, 1949, 111.

133 **Judging by surviving:** John Wilcock, "Book Row," *VV*, February 16, 1961; and Harry Gold, *The Dolphin's Path: A Bookman's Sequel to the Odyssey of Homer* (Chapel Hill: Aberdeen Book Company, 1979), 15.

134 **Schulte found it:** William Krauss and Russell Maloney, "Review Copies," Talk of the Town, *NYR*, January 30, 1937, 12.

Notes

134 **It was their best:** Clinton P. Anderson to Schulte's Book Store, 5 April 1941, Folder 1, Box 1, SBSR; Schulte's Book Store to Mr. Sinclair Lewis, 15 October 1934, Folder 1, Box 1, SBSR; Frances Perkins to Sirs, 1 December 1949, Folder 1, Box 1, SBSR. For a take on the art of book collecting in the 1920s, see A. Edward Newton, *The Amenities of Book-Collecting and Kindred Affections* (Boston: Atlantic Monthly Press, 1922). For an account of an early twentieth-century book collector, see A. S. W. Rosenbach, *Books and Bidders: The Adventures of a Bibliophile* (Boston: Little, Brown and Company, 1927).

134 **They also knew the ins:** Phillips, *City Notebook*, 61–84.

134 **"There is such":** Bruno, *Adventures in American Bookshops, Antique Stores and Auction Rooms*, 82.

135 **"If I am short":** Phillips, *City Notebook*, 74.

135 **they'd head out:** Gold, *Dolphin's Path*, 14–15.

135 **He'd walk over:** Stanley Edgar Hyman, "Book Scout," Profiles, *NYR*, November 8, 1952, 39–84.

135 **"Now the book's":** As quoted in David A. Randall, *Dukedom Large Enough* (New York: Random House, 1969), 17.

136 **He was charged:** "Dealer Is Indicted as Rare Book Thief," *NYT*, November 26, 1931; "Indicted as 'Fences' for Rare Book Loot," *NYT*, December 5, 1931; "Romm Sent to Jail in Rare Book Thefts," *NYT*, January 6, 1932; and Travis McDade, *Thieves of Book Row: New York's Most Notorious Rare Book Ring and the Man Who Stopped It* (New York: Oxford University Press, 2013), chap. 7. Some Book Row dealers also traded in autographs, which were subject to forgery. See, for example, John Kobler, "Yrs. Truly, A. Lincoln," Profiles, *NYR*, February 25, 1956, 38–89.

136 **After serving his:** "Rare Book 'Fence' Gets Prison Term," *NYT*, June 7, 1933; and McDade, *Thieves of Book Row*, 13–16, 139–59, 178–80.

136 **Benjamin Bass was arrested:** "Buys Law Books; Law Holds Him," *NYDN*, March 20, 1939.

136 **"You were just":** "New York City Bookshops in the 1930s and 1940s," 151.

136 **and like the Los Angeles:** Raymond Chandler, *The Big Sleep* (New York: Vintage Crime/Black Lizard, 2022), 12.

136 **"a broad spectrum":** Jay A. Gertzman, *Bookleggers and Smuthounds: The Trade in Erotica, 1920–1940* (Philadelphia: University of Pennsylvania Press, 1999), 92.

137 **"Where is the pornography?":** Chernofsky, "Biblo and Tannen," 1668; "Oral History Interview: Fred Bass."

137 **They eventually got:** Chernofsky, "Biblo and Tannen," 1669.

137 **Soon they sold "pornographic":** Gertzman, *Bookleggers and Smuthounds*, 15; and An Act for the Suppression of Trade in, and Circulation of, Obscene Literature and Articles of Immoral Use, 42 Cong., Ch. 258, 17 Stat. 598 (1873).

137 **Down the Row:** Gertzman, *Bookleggers and Smuthounds*, 330n142.

137 **For Biblo and Tannen:** Robert McG. Thomas Jr., "Jack Biblo, Used Bookseller for Half a Century, Dies at 91," *NYT*, June 18, 1998.

137 **A 1930 study:** International Labour Office, *An International Enquiry into Costs of Living: A Comparative Study of Workers' Living Costs in Detroit (U.S.A.) and Fourteen European Cities* (London: P. S. King & Son, 1931); and Orion Howard Cheney, *Economic Survey of the Book Industry, 1930–1931* (New York: R. R. Bowker Co., 1949), 58.

137 **"If I wanted to":** Don Samson, "Book Row," *SEP*, December 30, 1944, 26–27.

137 **"You wander into":** Mel Heimer, "My New York," *Journal News* (White Plains), June 11, 1947.

137 **As the scholar:** Laura J. Miller, *Reluctant Capitalists: Bookselling and the Culture of Consumption* (Chicago: University of Chicago Press, 2006), 28.

138 **"I run a clinic":** "Peter Stammer, Book Shop Owner," *NYT*, June 15, 1946.

138 **"It's up to us":** Bruno, *Adventures in American Bookshops, Antique Stores and Auction Rooms*, 67.

138 **That's why they:** Heimer, "My New York."

138 **"We were all":** John Nielsen, "Old Bookstores: A Chapter Ends," *NYT*, May 31, 1981.

138 **One antiquarian buyer:** Larry McMurtry, *Books: A Memoir* (New York: Simon & Schuster, 2008), 138.

138 **Bathtubs turned into:** Samson, "Book Row," 26–27.

139 **"In a town like London":** As quoted in Gordon Bowker, "Orwell's Library," Orwell Foundation, accessed December 7, 2023, https://www.orwellfoundation.com/the-orwell-foundation/orwell/articles/gordon-bowker-orwells-library/.

139 **many of the dealers:** Theodore Wilentz, "American Bookselling in the 1960s," in *The American Reading Public: What It Reads, Why It Reads*, ed. Roger H. Smith (New York: R. R. Bowker Co., 1963), 151–66. Famous bookseller Ted Wilentz said something similar about booksellers in general: "A good number of them are not 'bookish,' and surprisingly, only a few are 'intellectuals.'"

139 **Although the stalls:** "Oral History Interview: Fred Bass."

139 **They sent Schulte:** Tarshish, "'Fourth Avenue' Book Trade," 54.

139 **Members held regular:** "Trade News," *AB*, December 3, 1949, 1277.

139 **cheered in *The New York*:** "Book Exchange," advertisement, *NYT*, December 26, 1948.

141 **Patterson was on:** Meyer Berger, "About New York," *NYT*, February 1, 1956.

141 **They politely declined:** Tarshish, "'Fourth Avenue' Book Trade," 54.

141 **The Book Row booksellers:** Grimes, "Fred Bass, Who Made the Strand Bookstore a Mecca, Dies at 89."

141 **Although the Strand:** Mondlin and Meador, *Book Row*, 289.

142 **"I simply *must*":** Newlove, "Beast in the Strand Book Store," 45.

142 **By the mid-1960s:** Mondlin and Meador, *Book Row*, 290.

142 **"When our generation":** McCandlish Phillips, "Dealers on Book Row Fear Rent Rises Will End an Era," *NYT*, September 30, 1969; and "The Last Bookshop," Topics of the Times, *NYT*, August 1, 1994.

Notes

142 **One of those next-generation:** Grimes, "Fred Bass, Who Made the Strand Bookstore a Mecca, Dies at 89."

142 **In the late 1960s:** Phillips, *City Notebook*, 78–84.

142 **Others switched exclusively:** Tarshish, "'Fourth Avenue' Book Trade," 52.

142 **Writing from East:** Helene Hanff, *84, Charing Cross Road* (New York: Penguin, 1990), 34.

142 **the barely breathing:** Tarshish, "'Fourth Avenue' Book Trade," 54.

143 **"You'll have a telephone":** Phillips, "Dealers on Book Row Fear Rent Rises Will End an Era."

143 **By the middle:** "The Book Row of America," advertisement, *NYT*, November 26, 1978; and Calvin Trillin, "Three Strand-Hounds," *NYR*, February 10, 1975, 76–81.

143 **"Absolutely nothing has":** Janet Malcolm, "About the House," On and Off the Avenue, *NYR*, May 6, 1972, 69.

144 **And manage the:** Michael Cordts, "Nothing Rivals Fred Bass and His Strand Book Store," *RDC*, August 5, 1979; Newlove, "Beast in the Strand Book Store," 45–47; and Mitch Broder, "Dealing in Volumes," *Journal News* (White Plains), January 22, 1989.

144 **"They don't feel":** Phillips, "Dealers on Book Row Fear Rent Rises Will End an Era."

144 **Benjamin was Mr. Bass:** Nancy Bass Wyden, interview by the author, August 2021.

144 **But there was a trick:** Annie Correal, "Want to Work in 18 Miles of Books? First, the Quiz," *NYT*, July 15, 2016.

144 **"At least in fiction":** James Barron, "Burt Britton, a Book Lover if Ever There Was One, Dies at 84," *NYT*, August 9, 2018; and Trillin, "Three Strand-Hounds," 79.

145 **He walked into:** Hendrik Hertzberg, "Literary Gathering," Talk of the Town, *NYR*, December 6, 1970, 40.

145 **Some twelve hundred volumes:** Michael Cordts, "Library Association Shocks Publishers," *RDC*, August 5, 1979.

145 **Watching him work:** Lynne Tillman, *Bookstore: The Life and Times of Jeannette Watson and Books & Co.* (New York: Harcourt Brace, 1999), 17.

146 **FSG had published:** Barron, "Burt Britton, a Book Lover if Ever There Was One, Dies at 84"; and Morris Lurie, *About Burt Britton, John Cheever, Gordon Lish, William Saroyan, Isaac B. Singer, Kurt Vonnegut and Other Matters* (New York: Horizon Press, 1977), 45–64.

146 **Britton got fussy:** Jerome Klinkowitz, *Keeping Literary Company: Working with Writers since the Sixties* (Albany: State University of New York Press, 1998), 179–80.

146 **When fashionable Korby:** Ellen Stern, "Baby Grand," Best Bets, column, *New York*, May 26, 1979, 80.

147 **Britton said he could:** Lurie, *About Burt Britton*, 45–64; Hertzberg, "Literary Gathering," 40; Bass Wyden, interview.

147 **He couldn't stand:** Burt Britton, *Self-Portrait: Book People Picture Themselves* (New York: Random House, 1976), 22, 37, 133, 135.

Notes

147 There were also a few: Britton, *Self-Portrait*, 261–62.

147 "some fifteen hundred literary eggs": Hertzberg, "Literary Gathering," 40; Trillin, "Three Strand-Hounds," 76–81; Lurie, *About Burt Britton*, 45–64.

148 Britton puts Hemingway: Martin Ritt, dir., *The Front* (Culver City: Columbia Pictures, 1976).

148 Britton left his "fiefdom": Bass Wyden, interview.

148 She again invited: Tillman, *Bookstore*, 16–17; and Whitney Balliett, "Books & Co.," Talk of the Town, *NYR*, November 13, 1978, 42.

148 One Three Lives founder: Jenny Feder, interview by the author, November 2022.

148 Both Britton and Watson: Tillman, *Bookstore*, 16–17; Balliett, "Books & Co.," 42–43.

148 He also had to promise: Agreement between Jeannette Watson and Burt Britton, 25 January 1980, Folder 30, Box 1, BCR; and Barron, "Burt Britton, a Book Lover if Ever There Was One, Dies at 84."

149 he managed a hamburger: Barron, "Burt Britton, a Book Lover if Ever There Was One, Dies at 84."

149 he had used the money: Michael Cordts, "Scandal Embarrasses Newspapers: 'Free' Books Sold by Editors," *RDC*, August 5, 1979.

149 they sold a whopping: Cordts, "Library Association Shocks Publishers."

149 The store first: "Strand Bookstore Tour," April 25, 1996, C-Span video, 38:19, https://www.c-span.org/video/?71579-1/strand-bookstore-tour; and Bill Hance, "Advice from Buyer: 'Don't Make Waves,'" *RDC*, August 5, 1979.

149 Even before then: Krauss and Maloney, "Review Copies," 12.

149 when Irita Van Doren: See, for example, Lorenzo U. Bergeron to Irita Van Doren, 11 June 1948, Folder 2, Box 1, SBSR; and Oscar Berger to Irita Van Doren, 9 April 1952, Folder 2, Box 1, SBSR.

149 there were only a handful: International League of Antiquarian Booksellers, *International Directory of Antiquarian Booksellers* (London: Antiquarian Bookseller's Association, 1977); "The Last Bookshop"; Thomas, "Jack Biblo, Used Bookseller for Half a Century, Dies at 91"; and Richard F. Shepard, "Survivors of Book Row," *NYT*, April 27, 1984.

150 Bass claimed he: Mitchell Duneier, *Sidewalk* (New York: Farrar, Straus and Giroux, 1999), 218, 224.

150 "We've been a superstore": Connie McCabe, "The Grand Strand," *NYDN*, December 11, 1994.

151 "When I make it": "It May Be Bookish, but This Store Also Has a Tough Streak," *WSJ*, August 21, 1986.

151 Strand II was different: Mitch Broder, "Second Edition: Manhattan's Strand Book Store Opens New Chapter," *Journal News* (White Plains), February 5, 1997.

151 "The Strand will": Alfred Gingold and Helen Rogan, "Guides: Cappuccino-Free Bookstores, Cafes with Big Ears," New York Bookshelf, *NYT*, October 1, 2000.

Notes

151 **The Strand even:** Julie Satow, "Club Monaco Will Offer Books and Coffee Alongside Fashion," *NYT*, October 15, 2013, https://www.nytimes.com/2013/10/16/realestate/commercial/clothier-club-monaco-will-offer-books-and-coffee-alongside-fashion.html.

151 **Her Fifth Avenue apartment:** Robin Finn, "Those Books Look Good? Imagine Reading Them," Public Lives, *NYT*, November 4, 2003.

152 **"Nobody any more talks":** Thomas L. Masson, "Domestic Bookaflage," *Independent* 110, no. 3840 (April 1923): 256.

152 **"Books by the foot" buyers:** Christopher Bonanos, "The Strand's Stand: How It Keeps Going in the Age of Amazon," *Vulture*, November 23, 2014; and Paul Harrison, "Book News," New York, column, *Poughkeepsie Eagle*, September 21, 1934.

152 **The Strand rented:** Jim Jerome, "Book Smarts," *People* 58, no. 15 (October 7, 2002): 141; Finn, "Those Books Look Good? Imagine Reading Them"; "Strand Bookstore Tour"; and "Strand Bookstore Co-owner Nancy Bass on Store's History," September 5, 2004, C-Span video, 11:36, https://www.c-span.org/video/?c4673135/strand-bookstore-owner-nancy-bass-stores-history.

152 **Its customers continued to run:** "Strand Bookstore Tour."

152 **Only 5.4 percent:** "At the Strand Bookstore, a Retail Labor Struggle in the Age of Amazon and Occupy," *Thirteen*, March 16, 2012, https://www.thirteen.org/metrofocus/2012/03/at-the-strand-bookstore-a-retail-labor-struggle-in-the-age-of-amazon-and-occupy/; and Greg Farrell, *On the Books: A Graphic Tale of Working Woes at NYC's Strand Bookstore* (Portland: Microcosm Publishing, 2014).

153 **"I did everything":** "Pay Cut Starts City's 1st Strike in a Book Store," *New York Herald Tribune*, April 1, 1933.

153 **there was a picket:** Cordts, "Nothing Rivals Fred Bass and His Strand Book Store"; and Rebecca McCarthy, "The State of the Bookstore Union," *Longreads*, October 25, 2018, https://longreads.com/2018/10/25/the-state-of-the-bookstore-union/.

153 **On May Day:** "Picket Line at the Strand and Evolving Labor Tactics," *Thirteen*, May 3, 2012, https://www.thirteen.org/metrofocus/2012/05/picket-line-at-the-strand-and-evolving-labor-tactics/.

153 **"Being a penniless":** Farrell, *On the Books*.

153 **the union accepted:** Farrell, *On the Books*.

154 **He left his heirs:** Grimes, "Fred Bass, Who Made the Strand Bookstore a Mecca, Dies at 89"; and Julia Marsh, "Late Owner of Strand Book Store Left $25M to Heirs," *New York Post*, March 4, 2018.

154 **The city was going:** Nancy Bass Wyden, "Breaking the Back of a Bookstore: How the City Landmarking Process Will Strangle the Strand," *NYDN*, June 14, 2019; Margaret Herman, *Designation Report: 826 Broadway Building*, ed. Katie Lemos McHale (New York: Landmarks Preservation Commission: 2019); and Zachary Small, "Strand Bookstore Fights to Keep Its Building Off New York City's Registry of Preserved Landmarks," *Hyperallergic*, December 4, 2018, https://

hyperallergic.com/474260/strand-bookstore-fights-to-keep-its-building-off
-new-york-citys-registry-of-preserved-landmarks/.

155 **Critics reminded the press:** Jacob Bogage, "When New York's Strand Bookstores
Asked for Help, 25,000 Online Orders Flooded In," *WP*, October 26, 2020.

The Kids

156 **She already knew:** Robert D. Hale, Allan Marshall, and Jerry N. Showalter, eds.,
A Manual on Bookselling: How to Open and Run Your Own Bookstore (New York:
Harmony Books, 1980), 1.

156 **"takes years to learn":** Nigel Beale, "Sarah McNally & Jeff Deutsch with All You
Need to Know about Bookselling," streamed on February 3, 2020, YouTube video,
59:38, https://www.youtube.com/watch?v=mdjtgzOh3Vo.

157 **The eldest don't:** Janet Malcom, "The Book Refuge," *NYR*, June 16, 2014,
62–73.

157 **She's deservedly proud:** Detroit Is Different, "Source Booksellers: 30 Yrs. Is
Non-Fiction," streamed on April 10, 2019, YouTube video, 1:12:39, https://www
.youtube.com/watch?v=ulMUvgBix6Y.

158 **"a little nicer":** Dwight Garner, "The Legend of Moe's Books," *NYT*, July 3,
2019. See also Doris Jo Moskowitz, *Radical Bookselling: A Life of Moe Moskowitz,
Founder of Moe's Books* (Moe's Books: Berkeley, 2016).

Chapter 7: The Aryan Book Store

159 **He was placed under:** Placard, n.d., Folder Anti-Semitic Material, Box 1, RG131,
NA; and R. B. Hood to FBI Director, 16 June 1944, FBI File 97-HQ-108.

160 **to recruit Californians:** Laura Rosenzweig, *Hollywood's Spies: The Undercover
Surveillance of Nazis in Los Angeles* (New York: NYU Press, 2017), 19, 32; and
Steven J. Ross, *Hitler in Los Angeles: How Jews Foiled Nazi Plots against Hollywood
and America* (New York: Bloomsbury, 2017), 21.

161 **As the Depression unfolded:** Rosenzweig, *Hollywood's Spies*, 33.

161 **One woman remarked:** Reports Originals, 29 August 1933, Folder 18, Box 7,
CRC1; and Reports, August–September 1933, Folder 18, Box 7, CRC1.

161 **We know these details:** Nazi Activities, 9 October 1933, Folder 8, Box 14, CRC1.
For more on the spy ring, see the excellent accounts in Ross, *Hitler in Los Angeles*,
and Rosenzweig, *Hollywood's Spies*.

161 **If they appeared receptive:** Reports Originals, August–September 1933, CRC1;
and Ross, *Hitler in Los Angeles*, 24–25, 39.

161 **He typed the letters:** Paul Themlitz to Fisch Department Store, 25 July 1933,
Folder 18, Box 12, CRC1.

161 **Themlitz often worked:** Carl Anton Sokoll, "The German-American Bund as a
Model for American Fascism, 1924–1946" (EdD diss., Columbia University,
1974), 116.

162 **Ideal employees were:** Reports, 7 September 1933, Folder 18, Box 7, CRC1.

Notes

162 **Themlitz gloated (and probably):** Reports Originals, August–September 1933, CRC1; and Rosenzweig, *Hollywood's Spies*, 31. In reality, shipments were sometimes intercepted at customs on both coasts.

162 **One tune was:** *Investigation of Nazi Propaganda Activities and Investigation of Certain Other Propaganda Activities*, Hearings No. 73-NY-7 (Washington, DC: Government Printing Office, 1934), 155–74; *Investigation of Nazi Propaganda Activities and Investigation of Certain Other Propaganda Activities*, Hearings No. 73-DC-4 (Washington, DC: Government Printing Office, 1934), 464–82.

162 **There were other Nazi:** Sokoll, "German-American Bund as a Model for American Fascism," 213.

162 **Above the generous:** Martin Ostrow, dir., *America and the Holocaust* (1994; San Francisco: Kanopy Streaming, 2018).

163 **Hitler's speeches played:** Hand-drawn floor plan of Aryan Book Store, September 1933, Folder 20, Box 7, CRC1; and Reports, 6 September 1933, Folder 18, Box 7, CRC1.

163 **A hallway led:** Aryan Book Store Notice, n.d., Folder 9, Box 544, HRC.

163 **President Roosevelt was Jewish:** Rosenzweig, *Hollywood's Spies*, 31; Report of 17, 13 October 1933, Folder 8, Box 14, CRC1.

163 **Off the reading:** Hand-drawn floorplan of Aryan Book Store, CRC1.

163 **Themlitz blamed the Communists:** "Vandals Smash Windows Again in Bookstore," *LAT*, October 8, 1934; "Blame Silver Shirt Foes for Vandalism," *Post-Record* (Los Angeles), April 23, 1934; and "Vandals Smash Store Windows," *Illustrated Daily News* (Los Angeles), April 23, 1934.

164 **"the truth about Germany":** *Investigation of Nazi Propaganda Activities and Investigation of Certain Other Propaganda Activities*, Hearings No. 73-DC-4, 541.

164 **"If you would go":** *Investigation of Nazi Propaganda Activities and Investigation of Certain Other Propaganda Activities*, Hearings No. 73-DC-4, 548.

164 **Dickstein also grilled:** *Investigation of Nazi Propaganda Activities and Investigation of Certain Other Propaganda Activities*, Hearings No. 73-NY-7, 155–74; and *Investigation of Nazi Propaganda Activities and Investigation of Certain Other Propaganda Activities*, Hearings No. 73-DC-4, 464–82.

164 **"Have you Shakespeare in there?":** *Investigation of Nazi Propaganda Activities and Investigation of Certain Other Propaganda Activities*, Hearings No. 73-DC-4, 474.

164 **"We are just":** *Investigation of Nazi Propaganda Activities and Investigation of Certain Other Propaganda Activities*, Hearings No. 73-DC-4, 549. For more on the McCormack-Dickstein Committee, see Rosenzweig, *Hollywood's Spies*, chap. 3.

165 **there were probably close:** Murray Blyne, "Socialist Workers Invited to Visit Workers Book Shop," *DW*, July 3, 1934; and *Investigation of Un-American Propaganda Activities in the United States*, vol. 7 (Washington, DC: Government Printing Office, 1940), 4869, 4917. Counting the number of Communist bookstores is imprecise. In his testimony before the HUAC in 1939, Alexander Trachtenberg, who had good reason to estimate on the low end, said that there were between forty and fifty official Communist Party bookshops. At a different point in the same testimony, he suggested that no more than 10 percent of his seven hundred accounts

were Communist bookstores. Aside from the outlets that had official ties to the Communist Party, there were many other shops that were considered Communist bookshops. See also Joshua Clark Davis, "The Forgotten World of Communist Bookstores," *Jacobin*, August 11, 2017, https://www.jacobin.com/2017/08/communist-party-cpusa-bookstore-fbi.

165 **The organization maintained:** A. Gusakoff, "Importance of Literature Task in Party," *DW* (New York edition), March 8, 1928.

165 **In New York in the:** Blyne, "Socialist Workers Invited to Visit Workers Book Shop"; and "Open Bronx Bookshop," *DW*, November 11, 1932.

165 **Originally opened in 1927:** R. Mason, "'Best Sellers' of Vital Import to the People," *DW*, December 31, 1939; and Lee Stanley, "Bookshop That Sets New Style for Readers and Writers," *DW*, April 3, 1940.

166 **more than five thousand:** *The Case of the Rand School* (New York: Rand School of Social Science, 1919), 11.

166 **Over the 1918–1919:** Madge Jenison, *Sunwise Turn: A Human Comedy of Bookselling* (New York: E. P. Dutton & Company), 121–22; and *Case of the Rand School*, 11.

167 **Fifty officers marching:** "Raid Rand School, 'Left Wing,' and I.W.W. Offices," *NYT*, June 22, 1919.

167 ***The New York Times* cheered:** "The Rand School," *NYT*, June 24, 1919.

167 **New York's attorney general:** "Moves to Close the Rand School," *NYT*, June 28, 1919.

167 **"character you condemn":** *Case of the Rand School*, 6.

167 **He charged the state:** *Case of the Rand School*, 9; and "Present-Day Socialism," advertisement, *Oklahoma Leader*, October 13, 1920.

167 **The store was bleeding:** Rand Bookstore Income and Expenses, October 1934 to December 1935, Folder 2, Box 47, RS.

168 **It hosted reading groups:** Oakley Johnson, "Fascinating Marxist Exhibit on View in Workers Bookshop," *DW*, February 7, 1935; and Blyne, "Socialist Workers Invited to Visit Workers Book Shop."

168 **Show your support:** "Seat of Communism in U.S.," *MST*, October 23, 1938.

168 **The shop offered periodic:** "Emma Goldman," advertisement, *NYDN*, February 9, 1934; and "Spain Speaks," advertisement, *NYDN*, December 21, 1936.

168 **Among them was *The Brown*:** World Committee for the Victims of German Fascism, *The Brown Book of the Hitler Terror and the Burning of the Reichstag* (New York: Knopf, 1933).

168 **The Roosevelt administration:** National Recovery Administration, *Codes of Fair Competition Nos. 374–416*, vol. 9 (Washington, DC: Government Printing Office, 1934), 833–41; and "Booksellers' Code Submitted to N.R.A.," *PW*, October 21, 1933, 1420–26.

168 **The new Booksellers' Code:** "Department Stores Agree to Abide by Code; Booksellers Lay Plans to Consolidate Gains," News of the Week, *PW*, April 21, 1934, 1518.

Notes

169 **the Supreme Court struck:** Sender Garlin, Change the World!, column, *DW*, March 8, 1934.

169 **There was a large auditorium:** "Don't Be a Fool," n.d., Folder Aryan Book Store, Box 1, RG131, NA; Report on the Activities of the Friends of New Germany, October 1935, Folder 13, Box 14, CRC1; and Rosenzweig, *Hollywood's Spies*, 107.

169 **He pledged that:** "Bund Plot for Coup D'Etat Is Revealed," *Index-Journal* (Greenwood, SC), June 27, 1944; News Research Service Typescript: Summary Report on Activities of Nazi Groups and Their Allies in Southern California, 1936–1938, Box 1, HRC; Rosenzweig, *Hollywood's Spies*, 103; and Ross, *Hitler in Los Angeles*, 244.

169 **On the bookcase:** Report on Hans Diebel re: Registration Act, 22 January 1941, FBI File 97-HQ-108.

169 **Goods came from:** "Bund Plot for Coup D'Etat is Revealed"; News Research Service Typescript, HRC; Rosenzweig, *Hollywood's Spies*, 103; and Ross, *Hitler in Los Angeles*, 244.

170 **In the entryway:** American Jewish Congress, ed., *Benjamin Franklin Vindicated: An Exposure of the Franklin "Prophecy" by American Scholars* (New York: American Jewish Congress, 1938), 3; "Report on activities at German House, 1939," 8 March 1939, *In Our Own Backyard: Resisting Nazi Propaganda in Southern California, 1933–1945* (online exhibit), CRC2, https://digital-collections.csun.edu/digital /collection/InOurOwnBackyard/id/104; Librarian of the Franklin Institute to J. B. Jenkins, 29 June 1939, Folder Franklin, Box 2, RG131, NA.

171 **Dressed in a storm:** "Bund Push Jewish Boycott," *Daily Times* (Chicago), September 16, 1937; What the Other Fellow Says, column, *Petaluma Argus-Courier*, June 27, 1938; and Rosenzweig, *Hollywood's Spies*, 111.

172 **"Do not permit":** "Confidential Political Information," n.d., Folder Anti-Semitic Material, Box 1, RG131, NA.

172 **They also entertained offbeat:** Report, 28 April 1936, Folder 25, Box 6, CRC1.

172 **One strategy Diebel:** "Report on activities at German House, 1939," CRC2; Rosenzweig, *Hollywood's Spies*, 113, 118.

172 **he preferred Perry's Cow:** Report on Hans Diebel re: Registration Act, 18 June 1941, FBI File 97-HQ-108; R-3 Contacts Diebel, 10 November 1938, Folder 26, Box 57, CRC2.

172 **"Ever since I":** Report on Hans Diebel re: Registration Act, 18 June 1941, FBI File 97-HQ-108.

172 **The gig came:** U.S. Department of Justice, Immigration and Naturalization Service, In the Matter of the Petition of Hans Diebel, 12 December 1940, FBI File 97-HQ-108; "S-2-'Blitzkrieg im Westen' and UFA News Reel Shown at German House," 3 May 1941, Folder 1, Box 33, CRC2.

172 **As was the case:** Report on Hans Diebel re: Registration Act, 26 December 1940, FBI File 97-HQ-108; and Reports, 7 September 1933, CRC1.

172 **Motivated by mission:** Report on Hans Diebel re: Sedition, 30 July 1943, FBI File 97-HQ-108.

Notes

173 **The World Service obliged:** Report on Hans Diebel re: Sedition, FBI File 97-HQ-108.

173 **In April of 1941:** Hans Diebel to Mr. Herrstrom, 29 April 1941, Folder Aryan Book Store, Box 1, RG131, NA.

173 **Customers sometimes asked:** Thomas Assenmacher to Hans Diebel, 28 September 1940, Folder Aryan Book Store, Box 1, RG131, NA.

173 **People wrote to Diebel:** Walter Rishelle to Aryan Book Store, 9 July 1937, Folder Corresp. 1938–41, Box 2, RG131, NA.

173 **Students writing term:** Jack R. Sutherland to Aryan Book Store, 14 March 1937, Folder Aryan Book Store, Box 1, RG131, NA.

173 **Yet they boasted:** Stanley, "Bookshop That Sets New Style for Readers and Writers."

173 **They also did better:** Blyne, "Socialist Workers Invited to Visit Workers Book Shop"; and Reports, 7 September 1933, CRC1.

173 **In 1940, the top:** Mason, "'Best Sellers' of Vital Import to the People"; and Stanley, "Bookshop That Sets New Style for Readers and Writers."

174 **The Chicago Workers':** Hammersmark to "Friends," 6 December 1926, Folder Bookstores, Box 558, HRC.

174 **Before fighting the ideological:** "Garland, Walter Benjamin," Abraham Lincoln Brigade Archives, accessed September 20, 2021, https://alba-valb.org/volunteers/walter-benjamin-garland/; Stanley, "Bookshop That Sets New Style for Readers and Writers."

174 **In early 1940:** Stanley, "Bookshop That Sets New Style for Readers and Writers."

174 **The holiday catalog of:** Catalog, Workers Bookshop, 1954, Folder Workers Bookshop, Box 25, JRC.

175 **The arsonists did:** "Communist Literature in Minneapolis Burned," *Winona Republican-Herald*, October 16, 1934.

175 **wrote a song about:** Shirley A. Wiegand and Wayne A. Wiegand, *Books on Trial: Red Scare in the Heartland* (Norman, OK: University of Oklahoma Press, 2007), 3–6, 30, 40–41, 58–59, 84–85; and "Publishers Protest against Censorship in Oklahoma," *PW*, September 13, 1941.

175 **Glass shrapnel sprayed:** John Martin and George Dixon, "Bomb Nazi Consulate, Red Party Office Here; 9 Hurt," *NYDN*, June 21, 1940.

176 **One testified that:** "Hitler Salutes Described," *LAT*, January 11, 1941.

176 **He denied being:** "Anti-American Cartoons and Publications Form Basis for U.S. Government's Attempt to Bar German Alien from Citizenship," *Corpus Christi Times*, January 10, 1941.

176 **Diebel's petition was:** "Denied U.S. Citizenship," *St. Joseph News-Press*, March 6, 1941.

176 **Key witnesses included:** "Un-American Investigation Opens Here," *LAT*, October 15, 1941.

176 **"I have nothing":** "Robert Noble for Germany, Hitler," *Daily News* (Los Angeles), October 18, 1941.

Notes

176 **Agents shadowed Diebel:** FBI File no. 97-31, 19 November 1941, Folder 146-6-146, Box 27, RG60, NA.

177 **The indicted included:** United States v. McWilliams, 54 F. Supp. 791 (D.D.C. 1944).

177 **The original presiding judge:** "29 Bund Leaders Indicted by U.S.," *Daily News* (Los Angeles), July 8, 1942; "Bund Member Enters Plea of Not Guilty in Alien Registration Case," *Sacramento Bee*, August 11, 1942; and Paul W. Ward, "One Missing at Sedition Case Trial," *Baltimore Sun*, April 18, 1944.

177 **the charge of violating:** Alien Registration (Smith) Act, Pub. L. No. 76-670, 54 Stat. 670 (1940) (codified as amended at 18 U.S.C. § 2385 (2018). For more on the trial, see Richard W. Steele, *Free Speech in the Good War* (New York: St. Martin's Press, 1999), chap. 14.

177 **Diebel pleaded to:** Hans Diebel, Sworn Statement, 15 May 1945, Folder 146-13–2-12-19, Box 160, RG60, NA; Attorney General Order in the Matter of Hans Diebel, FBI File 97-HQ-108; and "Report of Alien Enemy, Hans Carl Diebel," July 1948, Folder 146-13–2-12-19, Box 160, RG60, NA.

177 **A fortune teller:** "Survey Reading for Hans Diebel," n.d., Folder Hans Deibel, Box 2, RG131, NA.

178 **Having been to the shop:** David Caute, *The Great Fear: The Anti-Communist Purge under Truman and Eisenhower* (New York: Simon & Schuster, 1978), 392–93.

178 **Any federal employee:** Robert Justin Goldstein, "Watching the Books: The Federal Government's Suppression of the Washington Cooperative Bookshop 1939–1950," *American Communist History* 12, no. 3 (2013): 237–65; and Christopher Saunders, "How We Got Here: Ruth Schmidt Browses the Washington Bookshop," *Avocado*, August 24, 2019, https://the-avocado.org/2019/08/24/how-we-got-here-ruth-a-m-schmidt-and-the-washington-bookshop/.

178 **The Ranuzzis eventually:** Michelle M. Nickerson, *Mothers of Conservatism: Women and the Postwar Right* (Princeton, NJ: Princeton University Press, 2012), xix, 51, 60, 62, 142–44, 175–79 (app.). There was a concurrent, women-led evangelical bookstore boom. See Daniel Vaca, *Evangelicals Incorporated: Books and the Business of Religion in America* (Cambridge, MA: Harvard University Press, 2019), chap. 4. For more on recent radical bookstores generally, see Kimberley Kinder, *The Radical Bookstore: Counterspace for Social Movements* (Minneapolis: University of Minnesota Press, 2021).

179 **It sold "Black Lives Matter":** Left Bank Books (website), accessed December 8, 2023, https://www.left-bank.com/black-lives-matter-yard-sign.

179 **Like many of the newer:** Janet Filips, "Portland's Reed Bookstore Ends an Era of Radicalism," *Seattle Times*, April 12, 1992.

179 **it's more welcoming:** "About Red Emma's," Red Emma's (website), accessed November 19, 2022, https://redemmas.org/about/.

179 **Others attacked it:** Liz Button, "Revolution Books Stands Up to the Alt-Right," American Booksellers Association (website), October 25, 2017, https://www.bookweb.org/news/revolution-books-stands-alt-right-102162; and "Revolution Books Threatened Again by Proud Boy," press release, Revolution Books

Notes

Berkeley (website), October 20, 2020, https://www.revolutionbooks.org/Rev
-Books-Threatened-Again-by-Proud-Boy.

180 **During an author:** Alex Green, "White Supremacists Take Over D.C. Bookstore
Reading," *PW*, April 29, 2019, https://www.publishersweekly.com/pw/by-topic
/industry-news/bookselling/article/79907-white-supremacists-take-over-d-c
-bookstore-reading.html.

180 **It called for greater:** Josh Cook, *The Least We Can Do: White Supremacy, Free
Speech, and Independent Bookstores* (Windsor, ON: Biblioasis, 2021).

180 **The company says:** "Content Guidelines for Books," Amazon, accessed July 3, 2021,
https://www.amazon.com/gp/help/customer/display.html?ie=UTF8&
nodeId=15015801. For more on the ways in which white supremacist literature
finds its way to Amazon, see Ava Kofman, Moira Weigel, and Francis Tseng,
"White Supremacy's Gateway to the American Mind," *Atlantic*, April 7, 2020,
https://www.theatlantic.com/technology/archive/2020/04/white-supremacys
-gateway-to-the-american-mind/609595/.

The Grandmother

181 **"Books can change":** Roxanne J. Coady and Joy Johannessen, eds., *The Book
That Changed My Life: 71 Remarkable Writers Celebrate the Books That Matter Most
to Them* (New York: Gotham Books, 2006), xiv, xvi.

181 **Billy Collins recalls:** Coady and Johannessen, *Book That Changed My Life*, 51–
52, 99–100.

Chapter 8: Oscar Wilde

183 **There was a small:** Oscar Wilde Memorial Bookshop, press release, n.d.,
Folder Oscar Wilde Memorial Bookshop, Box 6, CRNYPL; Lionel Cuffie,
"Oscar Wilde Memorial Bookshop: Nine Years of Successful Service to the
Community," *GCN*, December 18, 1976; Oscar Wilde Memorial Bookshop, Mail
Order Catalog, Spring 1968, Folder 2, Box 106, FK; and Oscar Wilde Memorial
Bookshop, Mail Order Catalog, 1968, Folder Oscar Wilde Memorial Bookshop,
Box 6, CRNYPL.

184 **for the whole enterprise:** Frederic A. Sargeant to Friends, Spring 1970, Folder 2, Box
106, FK; Oscar Wilde Memorial Bookshop, Mail Order Listing, Winter 1972, Folder
2, Box 106, FK; Oscar Wilde Memorial Bookshop, Mail Order Catalog, 1968,
CRNYPL; Tony Guild, "Unique Homophile Bookshop!," *National Insider*, May 5,
1968; and Brad Mulroy, "New York City Journal," *Alive*, November 14, 1981.

184 **If they stood:** Craig Rodwell to Ray Gast, November 1983, Folder 1983, Box 3,
CRNYPL.

184 **lasted a lifetime:** Craig Rodwell to the Officers & Members of Daughters of
Bilitis, New York Chapter, 8 June 1970, Folder Professional and Political
Correspondence, 1963–1970, Box 1, CRNYPL; Oscar Wilde Memorial Bookshop,
"Grand Opening Weekend of the Oscar Wilde Memorial Bookshop," November

Notes

1967, Folder Oscar Wilde Memorial Bookshop, Box 6, CRNYPL; and Craig Rodwell, interview by Martin Duberman, 1990–91, transcript of Martin Duberman's interview with Rodwell for *Stonewall*, Box 12, CRNYPL. For more on activist-oriented businesses, bookshops included, see Joshua Clark Davis, *From Head Shops to Whole Foods: The Rise and Fall of Activist Entrepreneurs* (New York: Columbia University Press, 2017).

185 **belonged to the Village:** For more on Greenwich Village history, see John Strausbaugh, *The Village: 400 Years of Beats and Bohemians, Radicals and Rogues, a History of Greenwich Village* (New York: Ecco, 2013); Ross Wetzsteon, *Republic of Dreams: Greenwich Village: The American Bohemia, 1910–1960* (New York: Simon & Schuster, 2003); and Stephen Petrus and Ronald D. Cohen, *Folk City: New York and the American Folk Music Revival* (New York: Oxford University Press, 2015).

185 **The Village had become:** For more on the history of gay life in New York City generally, see George Chauncey, *Gay New York: Gender, Urban Culture, and the Making of the Gay Male World, 1890–1940* (New York: Basic Books, 1994); Hugh Ryan, *When Brooklyn Was Queer* (New York: St. Martin's Press, 2019); and Charles Kaiser, *The Gay Metropolis: The Landmark History of Gay Life in America* (New York: Grove Press, 2007).

185 **Novels and plays:** For more on these mail-order businesses and the origins of selling gay literature, see David K. Johnson, *Buying Gay: How Physique Entrepreneurs Sparked a Movement* (New York: Columbia University Press, 2019), chap. 2.

185 **In the late 1950s:** "Village Theater Center Bookshop," advertisement, *One: The Homosexual Viewpoint* 5, no. 8 (1957): 15.

185 **But Rodwell's was the first:** Johnson, *Buying Gay*, chap. 2. The Book Cellar might have been the first brick-and-mortar gay bookshop when it opened in Midtown Manhattan in 1953. There was also another store opened in San Francisco in 1967, the same year that Oscar Wilde appeared on the scene.

186 **He spent the next seven:** Birth Announcement, 1940, Family Snapshot Album, Box 14, CRNYPL; and *The Chicago Junior School Times*, 1954, Box 13, CRNYPL.

186 **"I thought the whole":** *Chicago Junior School Times*, CRNYPL; and Rodwell, interview by Duberman.

186 **he failed English:** Student's Progress Report, 1954–57, Folder 1954, Box 13, CRNYPL.

187 **One of these landed:** Rodwell, interview by Duberman. For more on gay culture in Chicago, see Timothy Stewart-Winter, *Queer Clout: Chicago and the Rise of Gay Politics* (Philadelphia: University of Pennsylvania Press, 2016).

187 **In city after city:** Stewart-Winter, *Queer Clout*, 20.

187 **He printed out flyers:** Rodwell, interview by Duberman.

187 **worked as a "salad boy":** Craig Rodwell to Gay Brothers & Gay Sisters, February 1972, Folder 1972, Box 2, CRNYPL; and Rodwell, interview by Duberman. See also Martin Duberman, *Stonewall* (New York: Dutton, 1993).

Notes

188 **He pushed (some):** Rodwell, interview by Duberman.

188 **a plainclothes officer:** Rodwell, interview by Duberman.

188 **he taught impromptu:** Rodwell, interview by Duberman.

189 **And at the time:** Rodwell, interview by Duberman; and Randy Shilts, *The Mayor of Castro Street: The Life and Times of Harvey Milk* (New York: St. Martin's Press, 1982), 24–28. For more on Milk, see Rob Epstein, dir., *The Times of Harvey Milk* (New York: Cinecom, 1984), film.

189 **He didn't want to go:** Rodwell, interview by Duberman.

189 **His roommate found:** Rodwell, interview by Duberman.

189 **The government had labeled:** Rodwell, interview by Duberman; Transfer for Armed Forces Physical Examination or Induction, 15 May 1963, and Mae Karper to Craig Rodwell, 19 September 1963, Folder CR's Selective Service Notice, Box 13, CRNYPL. For more on the military and homosexuality, see Margot Canaday, *The Straight State: Sexuality and Citizenship in Twentieth-Century America* (Princeton, NJ: Princeton University Press, 2009).

190 **Although Julius's was:** Thomas A. Johnson, "3 Deviates Invite Exclusion by Bars," *NYT*, April 22, 1966; Jim Farber, "Before the Stonewall Uprising, There Was the 'Sip-In,'" *NYT*, April 21, 2016; Rodwell, interview by Duberman; Lucy Komisar, "Three Homosexuals in Search of a Drink," *VV*, May 5, 1966; and Fred W. McDarrah, photograph, April 21, 1966, https://www.nyclgbtsites.org/site/julius/.

190 **Despite knowing "nothing":** Rodwell, interview by Duberman; and Craig Rodwell to Gay Brothers & Gay Sisters, CRNYPL. Rodwell officially joined the Mattachine Society when he turned twenty-one.

190 **But its eponymous name:** "Oscar Wilde Memorial Bookshop," advertisement, *VV*, November 23, 1967; Oscar Wilde Memorial Bookshop, press release, CRNYPL; and Craig Rodwell to Gay Brothers & Gay Sisters, CRNYPL.

191 **He didn't want his wife:** R. Bruce Bray to Craig Rodwell, 11 December 1967, Folder Oscar Wilde Memorial Bookshop: Business Correspondence, Box 6, CRNYPL.

191 **It didn't shy:** Craig Rodwell, "Mafia on the Spot," *NYH* 1, no. 1 (February 1968): 1–2; Carl Lee, "It's What's Happening," *NYH* 1, no. 1 (February 1968): 3; Rod Chase, "Gaystrology," *NYH* 1, no. 1 (February 1968): 4; Hettie Greene, "Bulls 'N Bears," *NYH* 1, no. 4 (May 1968): 6; "How to Meet Mr. Right," advertisement, *NYH* 1 no. 6 (August–September 1968): 3; Editorial, *NYH* 1, no. 3 (April 1968): 2; and "McCarthy Wins Poll," *NYH* 1, no. 4 (May 1968): 1, 3.

191 **Chartered buses (five dollars):** Annual Reminder Pamphlet, 1969, Folder Fifth Annual Reminder, Box 7, CRNYPL.

192 **Because participants were:** Rodwell, interview by Duberman.

192 **The self-described "gay militant":** Craig Rodwell to Gay Brothers & Gay Sisters, CRNYPL.

192 **This was the summer:** Frederic A. Sargeant to Franklin Kameny, 27 September 1968, Folder Eastern Regional Conference of Homophile Organizations, Box 5, CRNYPL. For more on Frank Kameny, see Eric Cervini, *The Deviant's War: The*

Notes

Homosexual vs. the United States of America (New York: Farrar, Straus and Giroux, 2020); and Peter Bonds, "Stonewall on the Potomac: Gay Political Activism in Washington, DC, 1961–1973" (master's thesis, James Madison University, 2016).

192 **Over the subsequent days:** Homophile Youth Movement, "Get the Mafia and the Cops Out of Gay Bars," 1969, Folder Homophile Youth Movement, 1969, Box 5, CRNYPL.

193 **Rodwell encouraged "legitimate":** Homophile Youth Movement, "Get the Mafia and the Cops Out of Gay Bars," CRNYPL.

193 **fathered Gay Pride:** Craig Rodwell, "Gay and Free," *Queens Quarterly*, June 1971; Oscar Wilde Memorial Bookshop, "Gay Pride Week," flyer, 1970, Folder 1983, Box 3, CRNYPL; and City of New York Police Department, Parade Permit, 24 June 1971, Folder Christopher Street Liberation Day Committee, 1971, Box 4, CRNYPL.

193 **The shop did about:** Oscar Wilde Memorial Bookshop, Mail Order Catalog, 1968, CRNYPL; and Craig Rodwell to Barb Harper, 23 May 1977, Folder 1977, Box 2, CRNYPL.

194 **Not wanting to feel:** Ed Kajkowski to Craig Rodwell, 29 August 1969, Folder 1969, Box 2, CRNYPL; Craig Rodwell to Anna Holser and Cheryl Greaney, 15 April 1984, Folder 1984, Box 2, CRNYPL; Craig Rodwell to Murray Corbett, 13 August 1979, Folder 1979, Box 3, CRNYPL; and Edward Brown to Craig Rodwell, 14 July 1969, Folder 1969, Box 2, CRNYPL.

194 **He wished to "help":** Collin Schwoyer to Craig Rodwell, 19 June 1969, Folder 1969, Box 2, CRNYPL.

194 **it would look out:** Oscar Wilde Memorial Bookshop, "Signs of the Times," May 1973, Folder 2, Box 106, FK. Initially, Rodwell kept both shops open, but he soon closed the Mercer Street location. Rodwell also planned to open another outlet in California but never did.

195 **Gay's the Word:** Sewell Chan, "Venerable Bookstore to Close in Village," *NYT*, February 3, 2009, https://www.nytimes.com/2009/02/04/nyregion/04book store.html; Marc Santora, "Plot Twist for a Gay Bookstore: The Last Chapter Actually Isn't," *NYT*, February 4, 2003; and Ernest Hole, "The Birth of Gay's the Word," *Polari*, January 17, 2012, http://www.polarimagazine.com/features/birth -gays-word/.

196 **from a Kentucky monastery:** Craig Rodwell to Ray Gast, 5 December 1983, Folder 1983, Box 3, CRNYPL; and Matthew Kelty to Craig Rodwell, 18 February 1983, Folder 1983, Box 3, CRNYPL.

196 **Others sought recommendations:** Louis Compton to Craig Rodwell, 13 November 1969, Folder 1969, Box 2, CRNYPL.

196 **Stonewall was not a household:** David D. Smith to Oscar Wilde Memorial Bookstore, 1977 August 30, Folder 1977, Box 2, CRNYPL.

196 **"As a matter of fact":** Oscar Wilde Memorial Bookshop, Mail Order Catalog, 1968, CRNYPL; Craig Rodwell to Michael Denneny, 20 November 1980, Folder 1980, Box 3, CRNYPL; Gene Janowski to Oscar Wilde Memorial Bookshop, 12 May 1977, Folder 1977, Box 2, CRNYPL; Craig Rodwell to Gene Janowski, 23

Notes

May 1977, Folder 1977, Box 2, CRNYPL; and Guild, "Unique Homophile Bookshop!" In 1970, Rodwell boasted that his was the "only Gay bookshop which does not handle primarily or exclusively the exploitative item." See Craig Rodwell to the Officers & Members of Daughters of Bilitis, CRNYPL. In addition, historian Jim Downs wrote that Rodwell "refused to sell erotica or any magazine that included pornography." See Jim Downs, *Stand By Me: The Forgotten History of Gay Liberation* (New York: Basic Books, 2016), 8. But in the early 1970s, Rodwell allowed that he'd carried some erotic books out of necessity. See Kay Tobin and Randy Wicker, *The Gay Crusaders* (New York: Arno Press, 1975), 71. And in 1977, Rodwell reported to a journalist that "I got out of the skin market as soon as I could, because I felt this obsession with the furtive, lurid aspects of sex presented homosexuality in a bad light." See Thom Willenbecher, "The Maturing Craig Rodwell," *Esplanade*, September 9, 1977, 8. But the historian Martin Duberman, who extensively interviewed Rodwell for his book *Stonewall*, said in a 2009 piece that while Rodwell initially balked at selling pornography, "he eventually relented, though I can't tell you how long it took, but I'm sure that helped him move from a marginal life to at least a semiprosperous one." See Chan, "Venerable Bookstore to Close in Village." For more on the Times Square pornography shops, see Samuel R. Delany, *Times Square Red, Times Square Blue* (New York: NYU Press, 1999).

197 **"The police might find":** Anonymous letters, July–August 1970, Folder Anonymous Threatening Letters to "Jack" of the Oscar Wilde Memorial Bookshop, Box 1, CRNYPL. For an analysis of the letters, see Downs, *Stand By Me*, 81–82.

197 **He also asked one:** Craig Rodwell et al. to Captain Rosenthal, 2 August 1977, Folder 1977, Box 2, CRNYPL.

197 **In a 1969:** Harriet Van Horne, "Enough of All This," *New York Post*, April 9, 1969.

198 **A woman who had started:** Craig Rodwell to the Officers & Members of Daughters of Bilitis, CRNYPL; Duberman, *Stonewall*, 165–66. For more on the Daughters of Bilitis, see Marcia M. Gallo, *Different Daughters: A History of the Daughters of Bilitis and the Rise of the Lesbian Rights Movement* (New York: Carroll & Graf, 2006).

198 **Within a month:** Willenbecher, "Maturing Craig Rodwell," 8; Rita Mae Brown, *Rubyfruit Jungle* (New York: Bantam Books, 1973); Jonathan Katz, *Gay American History: Lesbians and Gay Men in the U.S.A.* (New York: Avon Books, 1976); and "Jonathan Katz Discusses His Book Gay American History," interview by Studs Terkel, Studs Terkel Radio Archive, February 4, 1977, https://studsterkel.wfmt .com/programs/jonathan-katz-discusses-his-book-gay-american-history.

198 **And in the early '80s:** Photographs, n.d., Folder Rodwell Photographs, Box 14, CRNYPL. For more on the evolution of gay literature, see Christopher Bram, *Eminent Outlaws: The Gay Writers Who Changed America* (New York: Twelve, 2012); and Felice Picano, *Art and Sex in Greenwich Village: Gay Literary Life After Stonewall* (New York: Carroll & Graf, 2007).

198 **Anyone who brought:** Oscar Wilde Memorial Bookshop, "Heterosexism Can Be cured!," n.d., CRNYPL; Oscar Wilde Memorial Bookshop, "Gay History Series

#3," postcard, n.d., Folder 1979, Box 3, CRNYPL; and Oscar Wilde Memorial Bookshop, "June Is . . . 'Come Out to Your Parents' Month," 1978, Folder 1978, Box 2, CRNYPL.

199 **Mayor Ed Koch:** Craig Rodwell to Mayor Ed Koch, 24 July 1979, Folder 1979, Box 3, CRNYPL.

199 **He donated money:** Irving Cooperberg to Oscar Wilde Memorial Bookshop, 23 January 1984, Folder 1984, Box 3, CRNYPL; and Robert Epstein and Richard Schmiechen to Craig Rodwell, May 1984, Folder 1984, Box 3, CRNYPL.

199 **When a Dear Abby:** Dear Abby, "Wife Has Less-than-Loving Attitude Toward His Needs," *New York Post*, May 6, 1987; and Craig Rodwell to Dear Abby, 12 May 1987, Folder 1987, Box 3, CRNYPL.

199 **When they stereotyped:** Craig Rodwell to the San Francisco Gay Men's Chorus Tours America, 6 February 1981, Folder 1981, Box 3, CRNYPL.

199 **"Any books or T-shirts":** Craig Rodwell to George Whitmore, 6 May 1982, Folder 1982, Box 3, CRNYPL.

199 **One quipped that:** Boyd McDonald, "These Are a Few of My Favorite Frauds," *Connection*, June 11, 1985, 33.

199 **One remembered Rodwell:** Picano, *Art and Sex in Greenwich Village*, 93

200 **"I learned the":** "Helms for Senate," 2 August 1983, Folder 1983, Box 3, CRNYPL; and Jerry Falwell to "Friend," 9 August 1984, Folder Jerry Falwell, Box 5, CRNYPL.

200 **Just keep them:** Jerry Falwell to "Friend," CRNYPL.

200 **"For us to turn":** Twentieth Anniversary Sticker, Folder 1987, Box 3, CRNYPL; Craig Rodwell, "Our Objections to the Segal 'Gay Liberation' Statue," 5 September 1980, Folder Christopher Park Statues Controversy, Box 4, CRNYPL; and James M. Saslow, "A Sculpture without a Country," *Christopher Street*, February 1981, 23–32. For more on Rodwell's interest in broader civil rights campaigns, see Downs, *Stand By Me*, 70–73. The statue was ultimately installed in 1992. Although some of the controversy had died down, certain activists continued to highlight the piece's lack of inclusivity. In 2015, anonymous protesters painted two of the four figures brown and fitted them with wigs to memorialize the transgendered and the "Black and Brown people who led the movement [and] deserve credit for their courage and strength." See Adrian, "Anonymous Activists Just Painted the Stonewall Statues Brown for Miss Major," *Autostraddle*, August 18, 2015, https://www.autostraddle.com/anonymous-activists-just-painted-the-stonewall-statues-brown-for-miss-major-303357/.

201 **was the headline:** Craig Rodwell to *Newsday*, 12 May 1987, Folder 1987, Box 3, CRNYPL; and S. Ladd, "Village Retail Life: Another AIDS Victim," *Newsday*, May 11, 1987.

201 **when Doubleday sent:** Craig Rodwell to Loretta A. Barrett, 28 October 1985, Folder 1985, Box 3, CRNYPL.

201 **The books were proof:** Alexander Chee, *How to Write an Autobiographical Novel* (Boston: Mariner Books, 2018), 99–103.

201 **"I would never":** Jason Villemez, "Authors and Activism: A History of LGBT Bookstores," *Philadelphia Gay News*, October 10, 2019, https://epgn.com/2019/10/10/authors-and-activism-a-history-of-lgbt-bookstores/.

201 **But in the early twentieth:** Jayson Blair, "Bookstore on Gay Life Is a Victim of Tolerance," *NYT*, March 19, 2001. For more on the rise and fall of lesbian and gay bookshops, see Stephanie Nisbet, "LGBTQ+ Bookstores: Past, Present, and Future" (master's thesis, Emerson College, 2018).

202 **Countless friends of:** "Craig L. Rodwell, 52, Pioneer for Gay Rights," *NYT*, June 20, 1993; and "Craig L. Rodwell; Gay Rights Activist," *LAT*, June 24, 1993.

202 **Brinster closed the shop:** Chan, "Venerable Bookstore to Close in Village"; and Santora, "Plot Twist for a Gay Bookstore."

202 **"It's all Starbucks":** Marc Santora, "Hard Words for a Bookshop: The End," *NYT*, January 7, 2003.

202 **So did Three Lives:** Jenny Feder, interview by the author, November 2022.

202 **The bookstore had helped:** Blair, "Bookstore on Gay Life Is a Victim of Tolerance." For more on the demise of Oscar Wilde, as told by one its employees, see Christopher Adam Mitchell, "The Transformation of Gay Life from the Closet to Liberation, 1948–1980: New York City's Gay Markets as a Study in Late Capitalism" (PhD diss., Rutgers, 2015).

203 **As one writer:** Mulroy, "New York City Journal."

The Convener

204 **"suffered from an inferiority":** Mitchell Kaplan, interview by the author, May 2022.

204 **While he wasn't consciously:** Kaplan, interview.

205 **Kaplan understood:** Kaplan, interview.

205 **Kaplan called it:** Kaplan, interview.

205 **What our history shows:** Kaplan, interview.

Chapter 9: Drum & Spear

207 **That's how booksellers:** Kenneth Turan and Laton McCartney, "You Are What You Read: Sketches of Six Special Bookstores," *WP*, November 12, 1972.

207 **Up front was:** Joe Elam, "Drum and Spear: When the Smoke Cleared on 14th St., a Bookstore Came," *Washington Afro-American*, February 15, 1969.

208 **as the founders called:** Charlie Cobb, interview by Joshua Clark Davis, October 16, 2015, Civil Rights Movement Archive, transcript, https://www.crmvet.org/nars/cobb2015.pdf.

208 **That past February:** National Advisory Commission on Civil Disorders, *Report of the National Advisory Commission on Civil Disorders: Summary of Report* (Washington, DC: Government Printing Office, 1968).

208 **"Arising from the ashes":** J. Samuel Walker, *Most of 14th Street Is Gone: The Washington, DC, Riots of 1968* (New York: Oxford University Press, 2018); and "Black Culture Shop Opens Here Today," *WP*, May 31, 1968.

Notes

208 **When Judy Richardson:** Judy Richardson, interview by Joshua Clark Davis, October 11, 2012; and Adrienne Manns, "Ghetto Book Shop Finds Untapped Literary Mart," *WP*, August 27, 1968.

209 **in the Latin Quarter:** Cobb, interview.

209 **The booksellers wanted:** Afro-American Resources, "Social Resources and Institutional Development Projects in the Black Community" (undated proposal, pp. 3–5), Box 1, CCDU.

209 **As Courtland Cox:** Courtland Cox, interview by the author, March 17, 2021.

209 **When Cobb told:** Elam, "Drum and Spear."

209 **Now they would sell:** Cox, interview. In 1972, the bookstore changed its status to a for-profit incorporation. The reason is unclear.

210 **The drum symbolized:** "Drum and Spear Books Founded," SNCC Digital Gateway, accessed July 21, 2021, https://snccdigital.org/events/drum-and-spear -books-founded/.

210 **Richardson grabbed as much:** American Folklife Center, "Since 1968: The Drum & Spear Bookstore," September 24, 2018, video, 1:28:28, https://www.loc .gov/item/webcast-8548/.

210 **He was looking for Lewis:** American Folklife Center, "Since 1968: The Drum & Spear Bookstore."

210 **The Professor was always:** C. Gerald Fraser, "Lewis Michaux, 92, Dies; Ran Bookstore in Harlem," *NYT*, August 27, 1976.

210 **So were the picketers:** Vaunda Micheaux Nelson, *No Crystal Stair: A Documentary Novel of the Life and Work of Lewis Michaux, Harlem Bookseller* (Minneapolis: Carolrhoda Lab, 2013), 78–79; and Patrick Parr, "The First Assassination Attempt on Martin Luther King Jr.," HistoryNet, September 27, 2018, https://www .historynet.com/martin-luther-king-jr-s-first-assassination-attempt.htm.

211 **And never overstock:** Charlayne Hunter, "The Professor," *NYR*, September 3, 1966, 28–29; and American Folklife Center, "Since 1968: The Drum & Spear Bookstore."

211 **The Professor provided:** "National Memorial Book Store," *New York Amsterdam News*, May 4, 1976; Michele Wallace, interview of Dr. Lewis Michaux by Michele Wallace (New York: Hatch Billops Collection, 1997); The Civil Rights Documentation Project: Transcript of a Tape-Recorded Interview with Louis Michaux by Robert Wright, July 31, 1970.

211 **an arsonist burned:** Kristen Doyle Highland, "In the Bookstore: The House of Appleton and Book Cultures in Antebellum New York City," *Book History* 19 (2016): 221. For an early history of African American bookselling, see Alisha R. Knight, "'To Have the Benefit of Some Special Machinery': African American Book Publishing and Bookselling, 1900–1920," in *The Oxford History of Popular Print Culture*, vol. 6, *US Popular Print Culture, 1860–1920*, ed. Christine Bold (New York: Oxford University Press, 2012), 437–56.

211 **Books and bookstores continued:** For example, the novel *The Clansman: A Historical Romance of the Ku Klux Klan* debuted in 1905 and was later made into the film *The Birth of a Nation*.

Notes

212 **Drum & Spear opened in 1968:** Joshua Clark Davis, *From Head Shops to Whole Foods: The Rise and Fall of Activist Entrepreneurs* (New York: Columbia University Press, 2017), 38–39. Davis estimates that around seventy-five new Black bookstores opened in this period, extending through the 1970s.

212 **recordings of Malcolm:** Colin Anthony Beckles, "PanAfrican Sites of Resistance: Black Bookstores and the Struggle to Re-present Black Identity" (PhD diss., UCLA, 1995), 203–7.

212 **almost all of whom:** Turan and McCartney, "You Are What You Read."

212 **Asterisks were reserved:** Drum & Spear Bookstore, *Catalog I* (Washington, DC: Drum & Spear, 1968).

212 **The two others were:** FBI Director to SAC, WFO, 13 June 1968, FBI File 157-HQ-9594; J. Edgar Hoover, "The FBI Sets Goals for COINTELPRO," SHEC: Resources for Teachers, accessed October 19, 2021, https://shec.ashp.cuny.edu /items/show/814.

212 *The Washington Post* **ran:** "Black Culture Shop Opens Here Today."

213 **Be on the lookout:** FBI Director to SAC, Albany, 9 October 1968, FBI File 157-WFO-368.

213 **The initial FBI:** SAC, WFO to FBI Director, 22 July 1968, FBI File 157-HQ-9594.

213 **The FBI sent in:** WFO 157-1724, 14 January 1970, FBI File 157-HQ-9594.

213 **Someone also called:** SAC, New York to FBI Director, 30 January 1969, FBI File 157-HQ-9594; and SAC, WFO to FBI Director, 15 November 1968, FBI File 157-HQ-9594.

213 **When one of them:** "To the Bureau," *WP*, March 12, 1972.

213 **Despite a lack:** SAC, WFO to FBI Director, 18 August 1969, FBI File 157-HQ-9594.

214 **There were exhibitions:** Frederick Douglass Birth Celebration Invitation, 1974, Box 8, JRDU.

214 **the** *Washington Afro-American***:** Elam, "Drum and Spear."

214 **The usual mix:** Anthony Gittens and Jennifer Lawson, interview by the author, March 2021.

214 **Although that space:** Judy Richardson to Elinor Sinnette, 8 October 1968, Box 8, JRDU.

214 **In its regular:** "Children's Books, Black & Positive," *Latiko: The Drum & Spear Bookstore Newsletter*, October 1972, 3.

214 **Richardson returned one:** Judy Richardson to Marilyn Schwartz, 15 September 1970, Box 8, JRDU; Adrienne Manns, "Writing a New Chapter in Black Children's Books," *WP*, December 18, 1973. For more on the evolution of Black children's literature, see Judy Richardson's own article, "Black Children's Books: An Overview," *Journal of Negro Education* 43, no. 3 (Summer 1974): 380–400.

214 **School groups arrived:** "Statement from Board of Directors, Drum & Spear Bookstore," memo, n.d., Box 8, JRDU.

214 **Richardson hosted a:** Judy Richardson, interview by the author, March 22, 2021.

215 **Drum & Spear's expertise:** Judy Richardson, interview by Joshua Clark Davis, October 11, 2012.

215 **Like teary-eyed teachers:** Richardson, interview by Davis.

215 **As one Howard:** "Pan-Africanism, Part 2," SNCC Digital Gateway, accessed August 22, 2021, https://snccdigital.org/our-voices/internationalism/part-2/.

215 **"We were really":** Gittens and Lawson, interview.

215 **And when management:** Afro-American Resources Board Meeting Minutes, 28 February 1969, Box 1, CCDU; and Afro-American Resources Board Meeting Minutes, 18 March 1970, Box 1, CCDU.

216 **It propelled her:** Daphne Muse, interview by the author, March 16, 2021.

216 **Reissued as *A History*:** Cobb, interview; C. L. R. James, *A History of Pan-African Revolt* (Washington, DC: Drum & Spear Press, 1969).

216 **Heat was expensive:** "Drum and Spear: How a Local Bookstore Educated Washington about Black Power in the '60s and '70s," *Kojo Nnamdi Show*, aired May 15, 2018, on WAMU; and American Folklife Center, "Since 1968: The Drum & Spear Bookstore."

216 **The press's mission:** "Drum and Spear Press," *PW*, March 15, 1971, 46–47.

216 **The book quickly:** Carolyn L. Carter to Advisory Board Member, 12 April 1971, Folder 11, Box 8, Hoyt William Fuller Collection, Atlanta University Center Robert W. Woodruff Library.

216 **a teenage Lawson:** Gittens and Lawson, interview; and Michael Swindle, *Slouching Towards Birmingham* (Berkeley, CA: Frog Press, 2005), 168.

217 **The ambitiousness of:** They also planned, but never opened, bookstore branches in Tanzania, Atlanta, and Springfield, Massachusetts.

217 **The press also:** *We Are an African People: 1970 Calendar* (Washington, DC: Drum & Spear Press, 1969); *Watoto wa Afrika* (Dar es Salaam: Drum & Spear Press, 1971); Bernard K. Muganda, *Speaking Swahili: A Grammar and Reader* (Washington, DC: Drum & Spear Press, 1970); Eloise Greenfield and Eric Marlow, *Bubbles* (Washington, DC: Drum & Spear Press, 1972); and "Drum and Spear Press," 46–47.

217 **One hospital in:** Lenore Jenkins, "Kweli . . . Nandi . . . Kipchoge . . . Dinner's Ready!," *New York Sunday News*, October 29, 1972; and "African Names Gain Popularity," *Atlanta Daily World*, August 2, 1973.

217 **Black Studies programs at:** Richardson, interview by Davis.

217 **It wasn't clear which:** Richardson, interview by the author; and Drum and Spear Bookstore Accounts, FBI File 157-HQ-9594.

219 **The fire department found:** "Bookstore Records, Books Hit by Fire," *Washington Afro-American*, April 12, 1968; and "Drum and Spear Bookstore," memo, 29 April 1969, FBI File 157-HQ-9594.

219 **books were stolen:** Afro-American Resources Board Meeting Minutes, 14 September 1970, Box 1, CCDU.

219 **Daphne Muse asked:** Daphne Muse, interview by the author; Afro-American Resources Board Meeting Minutes, 21 September 1969, Box 1, CCDU.

219 **He and Feather:** Daphne Muse, interview by the author.

219 **Others argued that:** Russell Rickford, *We Are an African People: Independent Education, Black Power, and the Radical Imagination* (New York: Oxford University Press, 2016), 221; Peter Levy, "Who Killed Ralph Featherstone?," History News Network, March 8, 2020, https://historynewsnetwork.org/article/174474; and Kelly Gilbert, "Many Questions Still Posed in Bel Air Deaths," *Evening Sun* (Baltimore), March 17, 1970.

219 **Drum & Spear covered:** Afro-American Resources Board Meeting Minutes, 18 March 1970, CCDU; and Richardson, interview by the author.

220 **On the day of his:** Daphne Muse, interview by Joshua Clark Davis, n.d.

220 **The caption read:** Turan and McCartney, "You Are What You Read."

220 **the insurance company:** Afro-American Resources Board Meeting Minutes, 18 March 1970, CCDU; and Lawrence Feinberg, "Bomb Scare Here Empties All Schools," *WP*, March 14, 1970.

220 **"The white folks":** Drum & Spear Bookstore memo, 17 September 1970, FBI File 157-HQ-9594; Courtland Cox to Charlie Cobb, 17 November 1970, Folder Cox to Charles Cobb, Box 1, CCDU; and William L. Claiborne and B. D. Colen, "Police Find New Bomb at Embassy," *WP*, August 31, 1970.

220 **As if managing one:** Afro-American Resource Board Meeting Minutes, 12 April 1969, Box 1, CCDU. Drum & Spear had already been stocking a concession at the Anacostia Community Museum, an innovative space designed to bring the Smithsonian to an African American neighborhood.

220 **Secretary Elliot Richardson:** "Washington," *Black Business Digest*, October 1972, 46; "Will Richardson Bring Drum and Spear to Pentagon?," *Human Events*, December 9, 1972, 4.

220 **Critics said he:** Gary Allen, "Second Term: The New Nixon and Agnew Circus," *American Opinion*, March 1973, 75.

220 **Richardson wanted an:** Turan and McCartney, "You are What You Read"; "Washington," *Black Business Digest*, October 1972, 46; Richardson, interview by Joshua Clark Davis. Richardson remembers asking a colleague for the Swahili word for "books" and came up with Maelezo. Contemporary news articles reported that the name meant "information" or "to cause someone to understand."

221 **"Politics got in":** Richardson, interview by Joshua Clark Davis.

221 **When Richardson returned:** Richardson, interview by the author.

221 **"I was more":** Cox, interview.

221 **The press shut:** Seth M. Markle, *A Motorcycle on Hell Run: Tanzania, Black Power, and the Uncertain Future of Pan-Africanism, 1964–1974* (East Lansing: Michigan State University Press, 2017), 105–38; "General Press Report and Recommendations," n.d., Box 8, JRDU; and Press Board Meeting Minutes, 14 April 1972, Box 1, CCDU.

222 **And the store's buyer:** "Financial Situation and Outlook," n.d., Box 8, JRDU; Gerard Burke, "Hard Times for Drum and Spear," *Washington Afro-American*, March 23, 1974; and Bookstore Weekly Report, n.d., Box 1, CCDU.

222 **more than half of:** Martha Biondi, *The Black Revolution on Campus* (Berkeley, CA: University of California Press, 2012), 208.

222 **Everyone at the store:** "Statement from Board of Directors," n.d., Box 8, JRDU.

222 **there were eighty:** Carol Eron, "All Booked Up," *WP*, January 27, 1974; and Adrienne Manns, "Writing a New Chapter in Black Children's Books," *WP*, December 18, 1973.

222 **"There's a lot":** Judy Richardson to Drum & Spear Bookstore Board, 8 January 1974, Box 8, JRDU.

222 **But by their own:** "Statement from Board of Directors," n.d., Box 8, JRDU.

222 **A 1977 report:** "ABA Membership Profile, 1977," *American Bookseller*, January–February, 1978, 22–39.

223 **By the early 1980s:** Davis, *From Head Shops to Whole Foods*, 71; and Markle, *A Motorcycle on Hell Run*, 204n10.

223 **A group of Black booksellers:** Beckles, "PanAfrican Sites of Resistance," 310.

223 **Like independents of all:** Davis, *From Head Shops to Whole Foods*, 79–82.

223 **Friends donated tens:** Jessica Guynn, "Inside Historic Black Bookstores' Fight for Survival against the COVID-19 Pandemic," *USA Today*, May 11, 2020.

223 **Those Black-owned bookstores:** See, for example, "7 Anti-Racist Books Recommended by Educators and Activists," *New York*, June 5, 2020, https://nymag.com/strategist/article/anti-racist-reading-list.html; and McKenzie Jean-Philippe, "125 Black-Owned Bookstores in America That Amplify the Best in Literature," *Oprah Daily*, August 27, 2020, https://www.oprahdaily.com/entertainment/books/a33497812/black-owned-bookstores/.

223 **Droves of customers from:** Noelle Bellow, "Oakland's 'Marcus Books' Reports Increase in Book Sales Regarding History of Race in America," KRON4, June 12, 2020, https://www.kron4.com/news/bay-area/oaklands-marcus-books-reports-increase-in-book-sales-regarding-history-of-race-in-america/.

224 **The ABA launched an:** Ed Nawotka, "ABA's Priority Is 'Keeping Bookstores Open,'" *PW*, June 12, 2020, https://www.publishersweekly.com/pw/by-topic/industry-news/bookselling/article/83573-aba-s-priority-is-keeping-bookstores-open.html.

224 **They developed new:** Greenlight Bookstore (@GreenlightBklyn), "Greenlight Bookstore Public Apology and Statement of Purpose Regarding Anti-Racism," Instagram post, July 9, 2020, https://www.instagram.com/p/CCb_dguBTgY/.

224 **Because Spearman is:** Claire Kirch, "Denver's Tattered Cover Bookstore Sold to Two Entrepreneurs," *PW*, December 9, 2020, https://www.publishersweekly.com/pw/by-topic/industry-news/bookselling/article/85096-denver-s-tattered-cover-bookstore-is-sold-to-two-entrepreneurs.html.

224 **As the manager of Uncle:** Associated Press, "Colorado's Tattered Cover Bookstore to Become Country's Largest Black-Led Bookseller," *USA Today*,

Notes

December 10, 2020, https://www.usatoday.com/story/entertainment/books /2020/12/10/colorados-tattered-cover-become-largest-black-led-bookseller /3876719001/; and Alex Green and Claire Kirch, "Black Booksellers Denounce Tattered Cover Announcement," *PW*, December 11, 2020, https://www .publishersweekly.com/pw/by-topic/industry-news/bookselling/article /85106-black-booksellers-denounce-tattered-cover-announcement.html.

224 **But "it was more":** Muse, interview by the author.

The Guy Who Never Buys Anything

225 **When rumors around:** Marlene and Tom England, interview by the author, May 2022.

226 **the best-tasting water:** Marlene and Tom England, interview.

226 **She said there's value:** Marlene and Tom England, interview.

Chapter 10: Barnes & Noble

228 **Design is everything:** Len Riggio, interview by the author, November 2021.

229 **Brentano's moved into:** Edwin D. Hoffman, "The Bookshops of New York City, 1743–1948," *New York History* 30, no. 1 (January 1949): 60; and Hellmut Lehmann-Haupt, *The Book in America: A History of the Making and Selling of Books in the United States* (New York: R. R. Bowker Company, 1951), 244–45.

229 **A series of fires:** "Brentanos in Their New Store," *New England Stationer and Printer*, October 1901, 52

229 **To the contrary:** Hoffman, "Bookshops of New York City," 60.

229 **Inside opulent quarters:** David A. Randall, *Dukedom Large Enough* (New York: Random House, 1969), 26–31.

229 **In *This Side*:** F. Scott Fitzgerald, *This Side of Paradise* (New York: Charles Scribner's Sons, 1920), 51.

229 **Americans were familiar:** Marc Levinson, *The Great A&P and the Struggle for Small Business in America* (New York: Hill & Wang, 2011), 109.

230 **They accounted for 31.6:** "Government Census of Retailing," *PW*, January 23, 1932, 375; and Laura J. Miller, *Reluctant Capitalists: Bookselling and the Culture of Consumption* (Chicago: University of Chicago Press, 2006), 42.

230 **there were fifty:** "Government Census of Retailing," 375; and Miller, *Reluctant Capitalists*, 42.

231 **Public libraries loaned:** Maureen J. O'Brien, "Charting the Course for Waldenbooks," *PW*, March 2, 1990, 52–55.

231 **The most distinguishing:** "Driving Time to Northway Mall," *Pittsburgh Post-Gazette*, September 2, 1963. For more on the history of malls, see Alexandra Lange, *Meet Me by the Fountain: An Inside History of the Mall* (New York: Bloomsbury, 2022).

231 **As the company president:** "Dayton Turns Its Talent to Books," *Business Week*, September 7, 1968, 68–70.

Notes

232 **Nearly a quarter of all:** Miller, *Reluctant Capitalists*, 42.

232 **After a couple:** "Barnes & Noble to Move," *Bookseller and Stationer*, January 1, 1922, 13; "Barnes & Noble, Educational Bookstore, Celebrates 75 Years of Service," *PW*, February 12, 1949, 901–3.

232 **The warehouse doubled:** "Sixty-Five Years of Bookselling," *College Store Journal*, April 1939, 11.

234 **just before and after:** "Barnes & Noble Remodels Its Quarters for Efficiency," *PW*, December 6, 1941, 2090–93.

234 **The regular programming:** "Barnes & Noble Remodels Its Quarters for Efficiency," 2092.

234 **Barnes & Noble had two:** "Barnes & Noble, Educational Bookstore, Celebrates 75 Years of Service," 901–3.

234 **Customers walked around:** Arthur Hale, "The Mass Market," *PW*, February 1955, 1195–1202.

235 **he said to himself:** Riggio, interview.

235 **The biggest asset:** Riggio, interview.

236 **"Of course! Of course!":** Peter Farago, "Barnes & Noble, Of Course, Of Course! TV Commercials Circa 1976," streamed on February 26, 2009, YouTube video, 0:00:22, https://youtu.be/oFgHGi-HnOA?si=UuAUwu0nVUHudUcq.

236 **With its casual:** Ted Striphas, *The Late Age of Print: Everyday Book Culture from Consumerism to Control* (New York: Columbia University Press, 2009), 66–69.

236 **By the late 1970s:** "Specialties: How They Stack Up," *American Bookseller*, September 1979, 24–27.

236 **With just seventy:** Striphas, *Late Age of Print*, 70.

237 **Generous oak tables:** Barnes & Noble, "Barnes & Noble History," May 9, 2008, Internet Archive Wayback Machine, https://web.archive.org/web/20080509130810/http://www.barnesandnobleinc.com/our_company/history/bn_history.html.

237 **Barnes & Noble wasn't:** George Monaghan and Susie Hopper, "Bookstore Is Largest in State," *MST*, September 6, 1990; and Dan Wascoe Jr., "Here's a Little Bookstore Mystery," *MST*, August 23, 1990.

238 **If the bookseller didn't:** Emma Parry, interview by the author, November 2021.

238 **It was a major:** John B. Thompson, *Book Wars: The Digital Revolution in Publishing* (Cambridge, UK: Polity, 2021), 176–78; and Miller, *Reluctant Capitalists*, 100.

239 **"I don't give":** Riggio, interview.

239 **and coffee encouraged:** Riggio, interview.

239 **These were institutions:** Victor Navasky, "Buying Books: Theory vs. Practice," *NYT*, June 20, 1996.

239 **Within five years:** Karen Kawaguchi, "Feminist Feast and Famine," *PW*, July 24, 2000, 24–26. Determining the exact number of stores is near impossible. These figures represent the number of stores owned by members of the American Booksellers Association, an organization to which most independent bookstore owners belonged. Some owners operated multiple locations.

240 **shop was impervious:** Financial: Operations Statements, 1984, 1989, 1990, 1991–97, Folders 6–9, Box 9, BCR; and Books & Co. Advisory Board, n.d., Folder 1, Box 8, BCR. Books & Co. had faced financial difficulties for many years.

240 **"There was no way":** David Rohde, "As Barnes & Noble Looms, Two Bookstores Consolidate," *NYT*, June 22, 1997.

240 **it launched *American*:** Robert D. Hale, "Let the Dialogue Begin," *American Bookseller*, September 1977, 5.

240 **Booksellers pushed the:** Miller, *Reluctant Capitalists*, 170.

240 **the ABA launched Book Sense:** Penny Singer, "Independent Bookstores Harvest Their Zeal," *NYT*, January 17, 1999.

240 **the ABA sued:** Miller, *Reluctant Capitalists*, 168, 178; and John Mutter, "ABA Members Fighting for 'Level Playing Field,'" *PW*, June 7, 1993, 7–12.

240 **accounted for 43.3 percent:** Miller, *Reluctant Capitalists*, 52.

241 **Like Victor Navasky:** Nora Ephron, dir., *You've Got Mail* (Burbank, CA: Warner Home Video, 1999), DVD.

241 **Participants walked into:** Miller, *Reluctant Capitalists*, 52; and Wascoe, "Here's a Little Bookstore Mystery."

242 **Riggio described it:** Riggio, interview; and Robert Weber, cartoon, *NYR*, June 23, 1997.

242 **Customers would have easy:** Barnes & Noble, BarnesandNoble.com homepage, December 2, 1998, Internet Archive Wayback Machine, https://web.archive.org/web/19981202183957/http://barnesandnoble.com/.

242 **it had forty thousand:** Barnes & Noble, *2003 Annual Report* (New York: Barnes & Noble, Inc., 2003); and Barnes & Noble, *2007 Annual Report* (New York: Barnes & Noble, Inc., 2007).

242 **The average American home:** Kelly Hill, *Reading at Risk: A Survey of Literary Reading in America* (Washington, DC: National Endowment for the Arts, 2004), vii-xii.

243 **The TV was no longer:** Office of Research & Analysis, *To Read or Not to Read: A Question of National Consequence* (Washington, DC: National Endowment for the Arts, 2007), 7–8.

243 **But the expectation:** Barnes & Noble, *2007 Annual Report*.

243 **At rival Borders:** Booksellers Notebook, 1997, in the private collection of Carrie Cogan.

243 **They didn't want to steer:** Riggio, interview.

243 **Despite all the iterations:** Barnes & Noble, *2012 Annual Report* (New York: Barnes & Noble, Inc., 2012); and Barnes & Noble, *2015 Annual Report* (New York: Barnes & Noble, Inc., 2015).

244 **"We weren't a":** Riggio, interview.

244 **traditional book sales slowed:** "Book Store Sales in the United States from 1992 to 2022," chart, Statista, February 2023, accessed December 9, 2023, https://www.statista.com/statistics/197710/annual-book-store-sales-in-the-us-since-1992/.

244 **By measure of:** Barnes & Noble, *2013 Annual Report* (New York: Barnes & Noble, Inc., 2013).

244 **Between 2012 and 2019:** Barnes & Noble, *2012 Annual Report*; and Barnes & Noble, *2019 Annual Report* (New York: Barnes & Noble, Inc., 2019).

244 **It even sold 10.5 million:** "Quick Facts," Barnes & Noble, https://www .barnesandnobleinc.com/about-bn/quick-facts/, accessed September 4, 2020.

244 **rallied to save "my":** Riggio, interview.

244 **"It's just a part":** Ian Munro, "Barnes & Noble to Remain Open," *Daily News-Record* (Harrisonburg), November 15, 2019.

245 **He had built his:** Thomas Buckley and Scott Deveau, "Barnes & Noble's New Plan Is to Act Like an Indie Bookseller," *Bloomberg Businessweek*, March 4, 2020, https://www.bloomberg.com/news/features/2020-03-04/barnes-noble-wants -to-be-more-like-an-indie-bookseller.

245 **When in-person bookselling:** Elizabeth A. Harris, "With Stores Closed, Barnes & Noble Does Some Redecorating," *NYT*, July 9, 2020, https://www.nytimes .com/2020/07/09/books/barnes-noble-redecorating-virus.html.

245 **Yet he never sees:** James Daunt, interview by the author, October 2021.

245 **His turnaround plan:** Buckley and Deveau, "Barnes & Noble's New Plan Is to Act Like an Indie Bookseller."

246 **"We used to be":** Daunt, interview.

246 **And shouldn't that same:** Daunt, interview.

246 **Some of the more:** Daunt, interview; David Segal, "The Bookstore Wizard," *NYT*, August 11, 2019; and "Barnes and Noble Plots Renewal," *WSJ*, December 5, 2020.

246 **"We were playing":** Ann Patchett, interview by the author, January 2022.

247 **he'd prefer that they:** Daunt, interview.

247 **"If something happened":** Allison Hill, interview by the author, September 2021.

247 **Daunt grinned:** Daunt, interview.

The Weirdo

248 **The bookstore ran out:** Michael Hoinski, "With Words on Paper, Independent Defies Trend," *NYT*, November 21, 2010.

248 **The report found:** Civic Economics, *Economic Impact Analysis: A Case Study* (Austin: Civic Economics, 2002).

248 **The murderer was:** "BookPeople Celebrates Distinction as PW's Bookseller of the Year," American Booksellers Association, May 4, 2005, https://www .bookweb.org/news/bookpeople-celebrates-distinction-pws-bookseller-year.

Chapter 11: The Sidewalk

249 **Zach was from:** Jason Rosette, dir., *BookWars* (2000; New York: Camerado, 2003), DVD.

251 **"How may one":** Elaine Sciolino, *The Seine: The River That Made Paris* (New York: Norton, 2020), 201–5; and Honoré de Balzac, *A Street of Paris and Its Inhabitant* (New York: Meyer Brothers and Co., 1900), 14–15.

Notes

251 **"ready-to-wear spectacles"**: Irving Howe, *World of Our Fathers: The Journey of the East European Jews to America and the Life They Found and Made* (Newburyport: Open Road Integrated Media, 2017), 249.

251 **Nor was it a safe**: F. A. Austin, "Thinning Ranks of Sidewalk Vendors," *New York Times Book Review and Magazine*, August 19, 1923, 8.

252 **a first-of-its-kind paperback**: "And Now a Book Machine," *NYT*, December 20, 1946.

252 **In Jack Kerouac's seminal**: Dorothea Lawrance Mann, "A Bookstall in the Old South Meeting House Churchyard," *PW*, April 29, 1933, 1405–6; and Jack Kerouac, *On the Road* (New York: Penguin, 2003), 103.

252 **And yet thousands**: Eagle v. Koch, 471 F. Supp. 175 (S.D.N.Y. 1979); and Peter Kihss, "Street Peddling Now a Booming Business in New York," *NYT*, August 27, 1982.

253 **the law allowed**: Administrative Code of the City of New York § 20– 473 as amended by Local Law No. 33 (1982); and Mitchell Duneier, *Sidewalk* (New York: Farrar, Straus and Giroux, 1999), 132–36.

253 **And so it was**: Robert Egan, *The Book-Store Book: A Guide to Manhattan Booksellers* (New York: Avon, 1979).

253 **He was an Afghan immigrant**: John Blades, "New York's Fifth Avenue Merchants Annoyed by Sidewalk Book Peddlers," *Albuquerque Journal*, December 30, 1988.

254 **He settled uptown**: Joseph Berger, "Book Peddlers Setting Up Shop on New York Sidewalks," *NYT*, December 26, 1984.

254 **He kept a separate**: Berger, "Book Peddlers Setting Up Shop on New York Sidewalks."

254 **He became a fixture**: Corey Kilgannon, "The Sidewalk, the Final Frontier," *NYT*, September 21, 1997.

254 **Foss was willing**: Richard F. Shepard, "Vestige of Book Row: Ex-Owner on Sidewalk," *NYT*, May 9, 1989.

254 **So did "bad religion"**: Rosette, *BookWars*.

255 **The sidewalks were**: Rosette, *BookWars*.

255 **Sidewalk bookselling usually**: Berger, "Book Peddlers Setting Up Shop on New York Sidewalks."

255 **"Books are going"**: Rosette, *BookWars*.

255 **Good days meant**: Rosette, *BookWars*. Average sales figures varied widely. See also Calvin Reid, "N.Y. State Probes Book Peddlers; Retailers Call for Crackdown," *PW*, November 4, 1988, 12; and Scott Ladd, "Bookseller Boom on City Streets," *New York Newsday*, November 7, 1988.

256 **The driver rolled**: Rosette, *BookWars*.

256 **The Sixth Avenue stock**: Rosette, *BookWars*.

256 **the selection was broad**: *Sidewalk*, directed by Barry Alexander Brown, written by Mitchell Duneier (Princeton, NJ: Princeton University, 2010), DVD.

Notes

257 **Some of them slept:** Duneier, *Sidewalk*, 98. Duneier's book offers an excellent and in-depth account of the Sixth Avenue sidewalk booksellers.

257 **He assigned books:** Duneier, *Sidewalk*, 24–27.

257 **"In the bookstore," he said:** Duneier, *Sidewalk*, 31–32.

257 **While Hasan had:** Hakim Hasan, "Off the Books," Lives, *NYT*, November 7, 1999.

257 **By 10:00 p.m., he called:** Rosette, *BookWars*.

257 **His competitors taught:** Brown and Duneier, *Sidewalk*; and Rosette, *BookWars*.

258 **The Sixth Avenue dealers:** Duneier, *Sidewalk*, 86, 88, 92.

258 **Among the sellers was:** Seth Kugel, "For an Enterprising Bookseller, It's Sidewalk, to Store, and Back," *NYT*, June 5, 2005; and Robert Polner, "Putting a Spanish Accent on the Selling of Books," *New York Newsday*, July 28, 2003.

258 **"as if these books bore":** Anatole Broyard, "That Old Book Magic," *NYT*, February 21, 1982.

259 **"Just a few feet away":** Reid, "N.Y. State Probes Book Peddlers," 12.

259 **Sometimes the accusation:** Blades, "New York's Fifth Avenue Merchants Annoyed by Sidewalk Book Peddlers."

259 **The Association of American:** Terry Pristin, "Behind the Sidewalk Book Bargains: A Manhattan Mystery," *NYT*, March 15, 1998.

259 **Hasan walked over:** Duneier, *Sidewalk*, 217–18.

259 **She went for Modern:** Larry McMurtry, *Books: A Memoir* (New York: Simon & Schuster, 2008), 20; and Benjamin Moser, *Sontag: Her Life and Work* (New York: Ecco, 2020), 72, 101.

259 **Three Lives and eleven:** "Don't Buy Books from Thieves," flyer, n.d., Folder 16, Box 8, RK.

259 **it was Sontag:** Barbara Livingston, "New York's Three Lives & Company," *American Bookseller*, December 1980, 29.

259 **Its targets were:** Reid, "N.Y. State Probes Book Peddlers," 12.

259 **That didn't stop:** Blades, "New York's Fifth Avenue Merchants Annoyed by Sidewalk Book Peddlers."

260 **One of the only booksellers:** Reid, "N.Y. State Probes Book Peddlers," 12.

260 **An ABA executive complained:** Blades, "New York's Fifth Avenue Merchants Annoyed by Sidewalk Book Peddlers."

260 **Bike messengers and:** Ladd, "Bookseller Boom on City Streets"; and Evan Friss, *On Bicycles: A 200-Year History of Cycling in New York City* (New York: Columbia University Press, 2019), 131–32.

260 **A few residents maintained:** Ladd, "Bookseller Boom on City Streets."

260 **a fifty-one-year-old:** David Bahr, "2 Peddlers, New Tension," *NYT*, October 13, 1996.

260 **"People like me are":** Jane Jacobs, *The Death and Life of Great American Cities* (New York: Vintage, 1963), 35, 68–71; and Duneier, *Sidewalk*, 6, 17–18.

261 **It was how:** Brown and Duneier, *Sidewalk*.

Notes

261 **One of the attorneys:** Duneier, *Sidewalk*, 234–39.

261 **But they still:** Local Law No. 33 (1982); and Local Law No. 45 (1993).

261 **Any vendor within:** Marvine Howe, "Disappearing in the East Village: Sidewalk Peddlers," *NYT*, July 10, 1994.

262 **As the Washington:** "NYU: Sidewalk Booksellers Want to Be Left Alone," *New York Newsday*, October 23, 1994.

262 **Having never actually:** "NYU: Sidewalk Booksellers Want to Be Left Alone."

262 **"We're all for booksellers":** "Book Vendors Asking N.Y.U. to Redraw Planter Plans," *Villager*, September 29, 1993, 10.

262 **The Sixth Avenue guys:** Rosette, *BookWars*.

262 **And although the summons:** "Sixth Ave. Vendors Summonsed but No Goods Are Confiscated," *Villager*, December 8, 1993, 6.

262 **On another occasion, the police:** Duneier, *Sidewalk*, 278.

262 **Then they came for Mudrick:** Rosette, *BookWars*.

262 **Find more books:** Bahr, "2 Peddlers, New Tension."

263 **Fights broke out:** "Peddlers Irk Stores in Harlem," *NYT*, September 24, 1990; Jonathan P. Hicks, "Police Move Street Vendors in Harlem," *NYT*, October 18, 1994; and Paul Stoller, "Spaces, Places, and Fields: The Politics of West African Trading in New York City's Informal Economy," *American Anthropologist* 98, no. 4 (December 1996): 776–88.

263 **"the idea of buying":** Kugel, "For an Enterprising Bookseller, It's Sidewalk, to Store, and Back"; Polner, "Putting a Spanish Accent on the Selling of Books"; and John High, "Taking It to the Streets," *PW*, July 3, 2000, 18–19.

264 **Others spent their:** Corey Kilgannon, "A Sidewalk Vendor Amasses Books, Lawsuits and Nearly 200 Summonses," *NYT*, August 11, 2016.

264 **"This could very well":** Jennifer Medina, "In Bookstore's End, No Joy for Sidewalk Seller," *NYT*, September 14, 2010, https://www.nytimes.com/2010/09/15/nyregion/15about.html; and Corey Kilgannon, "Sidewalk Bookseller Returns to Find Shop Gone," *NYT*, May 10, 2012, https://cityroom.blogs.nytimes.com/2012/05/10/sidewalk-bookseller-returns-to-find-shop-empty/.

264 **Mysak had long:** Kerry Burke and John Marzulli, "Book Busters," *NYDN*, July 4, 2012.

264 **As two Sixth Avenue:** Sociology Subculture, "Sidewalk 8/8," streamed on February 1, 2013, YouTube video, 9:45, https://youtu.be/YaUC63pYF1w?si=Ip2Tdjb-Yc568Z-q.

265 **"retail sucks":** "Bookseller Braves Cold Streets, Lukewarm Market," Spirit (New York), February 17, 2015, https://www.westsidespirit.com/news/bookseller-braves-cold-streets-lukewarm-market-BVNP1320131126311269999.

265 **When anyone gave:** Jen Fisher, interview by the author, February 2022.

265 **"I won't sell Auster":** Fisher, interview.

265 **A book that spends:** Fisher, interview.

266 **She wishes there were:** Fisher, interview; and Jen Fisher, "Interview with a Bookseller," by Ben Fama, *Newest York*, http://www.newestyork.co/jen-fisher.

266 **She does worry:** Fisher, interview.

266 **also "really magical":** Fisher, interview.

Chapter 12: Amazon Books

271 **When Julia Morse:** Marg Zack, "Amazon Bookstore Run for Women's Liberation," *MST*, August 19, 1970.

272 **Activists like Gloria:** "Amazon Before Amazon," Wearing Gay History (website), accessed January 14, 2021, https://www.wearinggayhistory.com/exhibits/show /lakesoflavender/amazon.

272 **"the first bookstore planned":** Ted Bishop, "The Sunwise Turn and the Social Space of the Bookshop," in *The Rise of the Modernist Bookshop: Books and the Commerce of Culture in the Twentieth Century*, ed. Huw Osborne (London: Routledge, 2015), 44n50.

273 **They functioned as:** Kristen Hogan, *The Feminist Bookstore Movement: Lesbian Antiracism and Feminist Accountability* (Durham: Duke University Press, 2016), chap. 1; and Junko Onosaka, *Feminist Revolution in Literacy: Women's Bookstores in the United States* (New York: Routledge, 2006).

273 **By the early 1990s:** Hogan, *Feminist Bookstore*, 195n4.

273 **The staff couldn't:** David Phelps, "Minneapolis Bookstore Sues Amazon.com Over Name," *MST*, April 15, 1999.

273 **The outraged board:** "Bookstore Fights Amazon.com's Sexual Orientation Argument in Suit," *St. Cloud Times*, October 21, 1999.

273 **the little feminist:** Stewart Van Cleve, *Land of 10,000 Loves: A History of Queer Minnesota* (Minneapolis: University of Minnesota Press, 2012), 203–5; and Laurie Hertzel, "True Colors Bookstore Puts Out a Plea for Help," *MST* (blog), https:// www.startribune.com/true-colors-bookstore-puts-out-a-plea-for-help/1359 41753/. The settlement stipulated that Minneapolis Amazon would have to change its name if and when its corporate structure changed, which occurred in 2008 when it was bought and renamed True Colors.

274 **As his preschool:** Brad Stone, *The Everything Store: Jeff Bezos and the Age of Amazon* (New York: Little, Brown and Company, 2013), 46.

274 **He wanted to be the gorilla:** G. Bruce Knecht, "Reading the Market: How Wall Street Whiz Found a Niche Selling Books on the Internet," *WSJ*, May 16, 1996.

274 **They met at the local:** Knecht, "Reading the Market."

275 **"If I saw him":** Jerry Mitchell, "Bezos Learned Customer Service from Miss. Bookseller," *Clarion Ledger*, August 5, 2014, https://www.clarionledger.com/story /journeytojustice/2014/08/06/jeff-bezos-square-books/13657367/.

275 **As Riggio now:** Len Riggio, interview by the author, November 2021.

276 **Publishers and authors worried:** Jeff Bezos, "Amazon.com Books," speech at Lake Forest College, IL, February 26, 1998, C-Span video, 1:13:48, https:// www.c-span.org/video/?101493-1/amazoncom-books.

276 **Between 1995 and 2000:** Ryan L. Raffaelli, "Reinventing Retail: The Novel Resurgence of Independent Bookstores" (Working Paper No. 20-068, Harvard

Notes

Business School, Cambridge, MA, January 2020), 6, https://www.hbs.edu/ris /Publication%20Files/20-068_c19963e7-506c-479a-beb4-bb339cd293ee.pdf.

276 **The Kindle sold:** Erick Schonfeld, "Liveblogging the Amazon Kindle E-Reader Show with Jeff Bezos," TechCrunch, November 19, 2007, https://techcrunch .com/2007/11/19/liveblogging-the-amazon-kindle-e-reader-show-with-jeff -bezos/.

277 **"Proceed as if":** Brad Stone, *Amazon Unbound: Jeff Bezos and the Invention of a Global Empire* (New York: Simon & Schuster, 2021), 9.

277 **"You can be inspired":** Schonfeld, "Liveblogging the Amazon Kindle E-Reader Show with Jeff Bezos."

277 **They seemed to want:** Jennifer Cast, "Foster the Product: Working Backwards from the Customer," December 3, 2020, Foster School of Business, University of Washington, video, 40:13, https://blog.foster.uw.edu/foster-product-working -backward-customer/.

277 **The process was repeated:** Cast, "Foster the Product."

277 **"We realized that":** Jay Greene, "Amazon Opening Its First Real Bookstore—at U-Village," *ST*, November 2, 2015, https://www.seattletimes.com/business/amazon /amazon-opens-first-bricks-and-mortar-bookstore-at-u-village/.

277 **decided its stock:** Cast, "Foster the Product."

278 **Even though the executives:** Stone, *Everything Store*, 44.

278 **The staff-favorites section:** Stone, *Amazon Unbound*, 64; and Jim Milliot, "Amazon VP on Amazon's New Bookstore: 'We Have No Idea What's Going to Happen,'" *PW*, November 6, 2015, https://www.publishersweekly.com/pw/by -topic/industry-news/bookselling/article/68617-amazon-vp-on-amazon-s -new-bookstore-we-have-no-idea-what-s-going-to-happen.html.

278 **"hero of the store":** Taylor Soper, "Inside Amazon's First Bookstore: How the Online Giant Is Combining Digital with Physical Retail," GeekWire, November 2, 2015, https://www.geekwire.com/2015/inside-amazons-first-bookstore-how -the-online-giant-is-combining-digital-with-physical-retail/.

278 **By the end of 2017:** Alexander Kunst, "Print Book Purchasing from Store /Online by U.S. Consumers 2017," Statista, December 20, 2019, https://www .statista.com/statistics/706121/print-book-purchasing-online-in-stores/.

279 **A *New Republic*:** Alex Shephard, "The Amazon Bookstore Isn't Evil. It's Just Dumb," *New Republic*, May 30, 2017, https://newrepublic.com/article/142935 /amazon-bookstore-isnt-evil-its-just-dumb.

279 **For *The New Yorker*, Jia:** Jia Tolentino, "Amazon's Brick-And-Mortar Bookstores Are Not Built for People Who Actually Read," *NYR*, May 30, 2017, https://www .newyorker.com/culture/cultural-comment/amazons-brick-and-mortar -bookstores-are-not-built-for-people-who-actually-read.

279 **"What we do":** Jake Swearingen, "Why Is Amazon Building Brick-and-Mortar Bookstores?," *New York*, June 1, 2017, https://nymag.com/intelligencer/2017/06 /why-is-amazon-building-bookstores.html.

279 **As soon as the first:** James Daunt, interview by the author, October 2021.

279 **"That's all you got?":** Allison Hill, interview by the author, September 2021.

279 **they were also "soulless":** Nancy Bass Wyden, interview by the author, August 2021.

279 **At the outset:** Rachel Lerman, "U Village Rumors Fly That Amazon Bookstore Is Coming," *ST*, October 8, 2015, https://www.seattletimes.com/business/technology /u-village-rumors-fly-that-amazon-bookstore-is-coming/.

279 **Paige had worked:** "Meet the Book Curators," Amazon, accessed August 18, 2021, https://www.amazon.com/b/ref=s9_acss_bw_cg_ABNAV_2c1_cta_w ?node=20017650011&pf_rd_m=ATVPDKIKX0DER&pf_rd_s=merchandised -search- 3&pf_rd_r=1T5KC0TM9166CGKJG6HF&pf_rd_t=101&pf_rd_p=cab9 fc77-02ec-47ac-9ae7-eb4269fccf29&pf_rd_i=13270229011.

279 **When journalists asked:** Greene, "Amazon Opening its First Real Bookstore— at U-Village."

280 **Although Amazon Books:** "Amazon Books," Amazon, accessed August 12, 2021, https://www.amazon.com/amazon-books/b?ie=UTF8&node=13270229011.

280 **His company sold:** Jeffrey A. Trachtenberg, "'They Own the System': Amazon Rewrites Book Industry by Marching into Publishing," *WSJ*, January 16, 2019; and Benedict Evans, "What's Amazon's Market Share?," Benedict Evans (website), December 19, 2019, https://www.ben-evans.com/benedictevans/2019/12/amazons -market-share19.

280 **"The future is":** Stone, *Everything Store*, 11.

280 **"It was hard to give":** Annie Palmer, "Iconic Portland Bookstore Powell's Says It Won't Sell Directly on Amazon Anymore: 'We Must Take a Stand,'" CNBC, August 27, 2020, https://www.cnbc.com/2020/08/27/portland-bookstore-powells -wont-sell-on-amazon-we-must-take-a-stand.html.

281 **Legislation or a Federal:** Hill, interview.

281 **the French government:** Booksellers could discount up to 5 percent.

283 **The preferred qualification:** Amazon Jobs (website), accessed August 18, 2021, https://www.amazon.jobs/en/jobs/OL900/amazon-books-retail-associate -bethesda-row-flex-time.

283 **Bradley Graham of Politics:** Bradley Graham, "Here's the Difference Between Jeff Bezos and Me," *WP*, March 6, 2002, https://www.washingtonpost.com /opinions/2022/03/06/amazon-politics-and-prose-jeff-bezos-versus -independent-bookstores/.

The Teacher

284 **And there's an optional:** "Onsite Bookstore Operations," Bookstore Training Group, accessed June 6, 2022, https://openingabookstore.com/onsite-bookstore -operations/.

285 **They respond cheerfully:** "FAQs," Bookstore Training Group, accessed June 6, 2022, https://openingabookstore.com/faqs/.

Notes

Chapter 13: Parnassus

288 **As an eight-year-old:** Ann Patchett, "How to Practice," *NYR*, March 8, 2021, 16–22; "Ann Patchett: By the Book," *NYT*, October 31, 2013, https://www.nytimes.com/2013/11/03/books/review/ann-patchett-by-the-book.html.

288 **When not playing:** Ann Patchett, "The Guns of My Girlhood," op-ed, *NYT*, July 16, 2016, https://www.nytimes.com/2016/07/17/opinion/sunday/the-guns-of-my-girlhood.html.

288 **"Books, puppies, french fries":** Ann Patchett, interview by the author, January 2022.

289 **Her columns offered:** Ann Patchett, "The News of My Suicide," *Seventeen* 47, no. 2 (February 1998): 104–5, 116–17; Ann Patchett, "The Joy Luck Club," review, *Seventeen* 48, no. 8 (August 1989): 125–26; Ann Patchett, "Buy the Book," *Seventeen* 53, no. 10 (October 1994): 132; Ann Patchett, "Surviving a Breakup," *Seventeen* 51, no. 6 (June 1992): 36, 41, 44; Ann Patchett, "Making the First Move," *Seventeen* 52, no. 10 (October 1993): 130–31; and Ann Patchett, "Virginity," *Seventeen* 53, no. 6 (June 1994): 116–19.

289 **It had been a full:** Ann Patchett, "Nonfiction, an Introduction" and "The Getaway Car: A Practical Memoir about Writing and Life," in Ann Patchett, *This Is the Story of a Happy Marriage* (New York: Harper, 2013), 1–10, 19–60.

289 **Davis-Kidd was a beloved:** Ann Patchett, "The Bookstore Strikes Back," in Patchett, *This is the Story of a Happy Marriage*, 226.

289 **One had worked:** Patchett, interview.

290 **She would later run:** Patchett, interview.

290 **At least not what:** There were, in fact, some used bookstores, at least one children's bookstore, and a Christian bookstore.

291 **"I was miserable":** Karen Hayes, interview by the author, October 2021.

291 **Patchett thought to herself:** Hayes, interview.

291 **"There's no way":** Patchett, interview.

291 **Patchett didn't like:** Patchett, "Bookstore Strikes Back," 229.

292 **The shop did ultimately:** "About Us," Parnasuss Books, accessed December 9, 2023, https://www.parnassusbooks.net/about-us.

292 **She also thought back:** Patchett, "Bookstore Strikes Back," 228.

292 **"Maybe it's just":** Margaret Renkl, "'It's a Gift I Want to Give the City I Love,'" *Chapter 16*, June 13, 2011, https://chapter16.org/its-a-gift-i-want-to-give-the-city-i-love/; and Ann Patchett, "Ann Patchett's Guide for Bookstore Lovers," *NYT*, December 6, 2016, https://www.nytimes.com/2016/12/06/travel/an-international-bookstore-guide.html.

292 **Tuck the children's:** Julie Bosman, "Novelist Fights the Tide by Opening a Bookstore," *NYT*, November 16, 2011.

292 **As opening day:** Bosman, "Novelist Fights the Tide by Opening a Bookstore."

292 **"I'm not in this":** Andy Humbles, "Parnassus Brings Books Back to Green Hills," *Tennessean*, November 17, 2011.

292 **"the way bookstores used":** "Author Ann Patchett Opens Own Indie Bookstore,"

Notes

All Things Considered, aired November 16, 2011, on NPR, https://www.npr.org /2011/11/16/142413792/ann-patchett-opens-parnassus-books-in-nashville.

294 **Here were real:** Parnassus Books Archive, "Ann Patchett's Spontaneous Speech," streamed on November 21, 2011, YouTube video, 1:30, https://youtu.be/cBMu 7jTBqqA?si=QyIVOt3l7xJiv6Da.

294 **"This is nothing":** Ann Patchett, "Owning a Bookstore Means You Always Get to Tell People What to Read," *WP*, April 22, 2015.

294 **Talking books in:** Laurie Hertzel, "Ann Patchett Hits Close to Home," *MST*, October 16, 2016.

294 *The New York Times* **ran:** Bosman, "Novelist Fights the Tide by Opening a Bookstore."

294 **Patchett appeared on:** Cover, *PW*, November 7, 2011.

294 **Even Patchett likened:** "Novelist Ann Patchett on How Independent Bookstores Build Community," *PBS News Hour*, September 13, 2016, https://www.pbs.org /newshour/show/novelist-ann-patchett-independent-bookstores-build -community.

295 **"You may have heard":** Patchett, "Bookstore Strikes Back," 226.

295 **The cycle lasted:** Ann Patchett, "Of Bugs and Books," op-ed, *NYT*, August 27, 2011.

295 **One of the world's greatest:** Patchett, "Bookstore Strikes Back," 233–34.

295 **She said it again:** Judith Rosen and Claire Kirch, "A Winning Winter Institute," *PW*, January 30, 2012, 22.

295 **She appeared on:** *The Colbert Report*, season 8 episode 58, "Ann Patchett," aired February 20, 2012, on Comedy Central, https://www.cc.com/video/tqad40/the -colbert-report-ann-patchett.

295 **"Can one determined":** Elizabeth Gilbert, "Ann Patchett," Time 100: The List, *Time*, April 18, 2012, http://content.time.com/time/specials/packages/article /0,28804,2111975_2111976_2112138,00.html.

296 **vantage point of the 2020s:** Mitchell Kaplan, interview by the author, May 2022.

296 **back in the 1950s:** John B. Thompson, *Merchants of Culture: The Publishing Business in the Twenty-First Century* (New York: Plume, 2012), 31–32.

296 **Major newspapers started:** Ruth Leigh, "Bookselling and Chain Store Methods," *PW*, May 17, 1930, 2514–16.

296 **Purpose-built for the area:** "About," Word Up Books (website), accessed November 20, 2021, https://www.wordupbooks.com/about.

297 **"really odd shit":** Veronica Liu, interview by the author, November 2021.

297 **serving the community:** Liu, interview.

297 **a onetime book scout:** For more on McMurtry's experience in the book trade, see Larry McMurtry, *Books: A Memoir* (New York: Simon & Schuster, 2008); and Calvin Trillin, "Scouting Sleepers," *NYR*, June 14, 1976, 86–92.

298 **As bookishness trended:** For more on the rise of bookishness, see Jessica Pressman, *Bookishness: Loving Books in a Digital Age* (New York: Columbia University Press, 2020).

298 **Parnassus was among:** Sydney Jarrard, "James Patterson Begins Distributing $1 Million to Indie Bookstore," American Booksellers Association, February 20, 2014, https://www.bookweb.org/news/james-patterson-begins-distributing-1-million -indie-bookstores.

298 **Patterson gave to:** US Census Bureau, "County Business Patterns: 2019," dataset, US Census Bureau (website), April 22, 2021, updated February 28, 2023, https:// www.census.gov/data/datasets/2019/econ/cbp/2019-cbp.html.

298 **Its mission was:** For more on the Seminary Co-op, see Jeff Deutsch's wonderful meditation on bookstores, *In Praise of Good Bookstores* (Princeton, NJ: Princeton University Press, 2022).

298 **The benefit was:** Jeff Deutsch, "The Seminary Co-op: A Not-for-Profit Bookstore," Seminary Co-op (website), accessed February 12, 2023, https://www .semcoop.com/seminary-co-op-not-profit-bookstore.

299 **It was part charity:** Ezra Marcus, "The Independent Bookstore, as Imagined by a Corporate Lobbyist," *NYT*, August 11, 2022, https://www.nytimes.com/2022 /08/11/style/new-independent-bookstore.html.

299 **Hayes would run:** Hayes, interview.

299 **Parnassus also added:** Bosman, "Novelist Fights the Tide by Opening a Bookstore."

300 **Patchett was dead certain:** Ann Patchett, "A Talk to the Association of Graduate School Deans in the Humanities," in Ann Patchett, *These Precious Days* (New York: Harper, 2021), 203–4.

300 **She vowed to stop:** Travis Loller, "Novelist Ann Patchett Has Nashville Bookstore Customers Swooning," FOX17 Nashville, June 26, 2020, https://fox17 .com/news/local/novelist-ann-patchett-has-nashville-bookstore-customers -swooning.

300 **Patchett's own dog:** Brian Wilson, "At Parnassus, Patchett's Dog Weds Playful Pal," *Tennessean*, August 4, 2014.

300 **They posted holiday:** Parnassus Books, *Shop Dog Diaries*, column, *Musing* (blog), accessed July 21, 2021, https://parnassusmusing.net/category/shop-dog-diaries/.

300 **When Lesley Stahl:** CBS Sunday Morning, "Author Ann Patchett's Bookstore," streamed on September 24, 2017, YouTube video, 7:36, https://www.youtube.com /watch?v=yC4e3ngcX50&t=51s.

301 **Parnassus's success was:** Patchett, interview.

301 **Roughly 85 percent of bookstore:** US Census Bureau, *Annual Business Survey: Statistics for Employer Firms by Industry, Sex, Ethnicity, Race, and Veteran Status for the U.S., States, Metro Areas, Counties, and Places*, 2017, https://data.census.gov /table/ABSCB2017.AB1700CSCB02.

301 **It was started by Hannah:** Stephanie Williams, "A D.C. Dream Day with Loyalty Bookstore's Hannah Oliver Depp," *WP*, February 3, 2020.

302 **The 2019 bestseller:** Claire Kirch, "PLA 2020: Indie Booksellers Keep Nashville Humming," *PW*, February 7, 2020, https://www.publishersweekly.com/pw /by-topic/industry-news/bookselling/article/82346-pla-2020-indie-booksellers -keep-nashville-humming.html.

Notes

302 **One of her essay:** Advertisement for *These Precious Days*, *NYR*, December 6, 2021.

302 **In early 2020, a:** Ryan L. Raffaelli, "Reinventing Retail: The Novel Resurgence of Independent Bookstores" (Working Paper No. 20-068, Harvard Business School, Cambridge, MA, January 2020), https://www.hbs.edu/ris/Publication%20Files/20-068_c19963e7-506c-479a-beb4-bb339cd293ee.pdf; and "Reinventing the Store: Achieving Growth in the Face of New Business Risks," American Booksellers Association (website), https://www.bookweb.org/reinventing-store-achieving-growth-face-new-business-risks.

302 **In the five years:** "Number of Independent Bookstores in the United States from 2009 to 2023," chart, Statista, May 2023, accessed December 9, 2023, https://www.statista.com/statistics/282808/number-of-independent-bookstores-in-the-us/.

303 **Between 1998 and 2021:** US Census Bureau, *County Business Patterns 1998* (Washington, DC: Government Printing Office, 2000), https://www2.census.gov/programs-surveys/cbp/tables/1998/cbp98-01.pdf; US Census Bureau, "County Business Patterns: 2012," dataset, US Census Bureau (website), May 29, 2014, updated February 28, 2023, https://www.census.gov/data/datasets/2012/econ/cbp/2012-cbp.html; US Census Bureau, "County Business Patterns: 2020," dataset, US Census Bureau (website), April 28, 2022, updated August 31, 2023, https://www.census.gov/data/datasets/2020/econ/cbp/2020-cbp.html; US Census Bureau, "County Business Patterns: 2021," dataset, US Census Bureau (website), April 27, 2023, updated May 25, 2023, https://www.census.gov/data/datasets/2021/econ/cbp/2021-cbp.html; and "Book Store Sales in the United States from 1992 to 2022," chart, Statista, February 2023, accessed December 9, 2023, https://www.statista.com/statistics/197710/annual-book-store-sales-in-the-us-since-1992/. These numbers do not include non-employing bookstores, of which there are many, though they account for a small percentage of sales. Nearly 30 percent of them generated less than $5,000 in annual sales. See Andrew W. Hait, "Despite Our Love of All Things Electronic, Bookstores Still Relevant This Holiday Season," US Census Bureau Resource Library, December 15, 2021, https://www.census.gov/library/stories/2021/12/do-not-turn-the-page-on-bookstores.html.

303 **When Parnassus opened:** Karen Kawaguchi, "Feminist Feast and Famine," *PW*, July 24, 2000, 24–26; and Penny Singer, "Independent Bookstores Harvest Their Zeal," *NYT*, January 17, 1999.

303 **The average American consumer:** "Mean Annual Expenditure on Books per Consumer Unit in the United States from 2007 to 2022, by Type," chart, Statista, September 2023, accessed December 9, 2023, https://www.statista.com/statistics/191043/us-consumer-spending-on-books-since-2002/.

303 **30.4 percent of Americans:** Office of Research & Analysis, *How Do We Read? Let's Count the Ways: Comparing Digital, Audio, and Print-Only Readers* (Washington, DC: National Endowment for the Arts, 2020), 12, https://www.arts.gov/sites/default/files/How%20Do%20We%20Read%20report%202020.pdf.

303 **He doesn't buy:** Patchett, interview.

304 **"We were dancing"**: Allison Hill, interview by the author, September 2021.

304 **sales of actual books**: Hait, "Despite Our Love of All Things Electronic, Bookstores Still Relevant This Holiday Season."

304 **In her inaugural**: Allison Hill, "A Letter from ABA CEO Allison Hill," American Booksellers Association (website), March 10, 2020, https://www.bookweb .org/news/letter-aba-ceo-allison-hill-576717.

304 **While they were at**: Elizabeth A. Harris, "How to Sell Books in 2020: Put Them Near the Toilet Paper," *NYT*, July 22, 2020, https://www.nytimes.com/2020/07 /22/books/books-coronavirus-retail-walmart-target-costco.html.

304 **As the owner**: Ellen Driscoll and Ryan Mavity, "Dewey, Rehoboth, Lewes Cautious [as] Phase 1 Reopening Begins," *Cape Gazette*, June 2, 2020; and Alex George, "Bookstores Are 'Essential Businesses.' Let Us Stay Open—Safely," *WP*, April 2, 2020.

305 **They just wanted**: Ann Patchett, "Ann Patchett on Running a Bookshop in Lockdown: 'We're a Part of Our Community as Never Before,'" *Guardian*, April 10, 2020; and Patchett, interview.

305 **By the summer of 2021**: Ed Nawotka, "Bookshop.org Continues to See Strong Sales," *PW*, July 8, 2021, https://www.publishersweekly.com/pw/by-topic /industry-news/bookselling/article/86828-bookshop-org-continues-to-see -strong-sales.html; Alexandra Alter, "Bookstores Are Struggling. Is a New E-Commerce Site the Answer?," *NYT*, June 16, 2020, https://www.nytimes.com /2020/06/16/books/bookshop-bookstores-coronavirus.html.

305 **The things that booksellers**: Deutsch, *In Praise of Good Bookstores*, 166. For more on the feeling of being "book-wrapt," see Reid Byers, *The Private Library: The History of the Architecture and Furnishing of the Domestic Bookroom* (New Castle, DE: Oak Knoll Press, 2021).

306 **Compared with 2019**: "Unit Sales of Printed Books in the United States from 2004 to 2022," chart, Statista, January 2023, accessed December 9, 2023, https:// www.statista.com/statistics/422595/print-book-sales-usa/; "Bookstore Sales Fell 28.3% in 2020," *PW*, February 17, 2021.

306 **Roughly 70 percent**: Amy Watson, "Online Purchasing Locations for E-Books Worldwide 2020," Statista, December 3, 2021, https://www.statista.com/statistics /1265702/ebook-purchasing-locations-worldwide/.

306 **Over the first six**: Elizabeth A. Harris, "Your Local Bookstore Wants You to Know That It's Struggling," *NYT*, October 15, 2020.

306 **Hill described the**: Hillel Italie, "Indie Bookstores Avoid the Worst—So Far— from Pandemic," AP, May 27, 2021, https://apnews.com/article/amazoncom -inc-health-coronavirus-pandemic-business-arts-and-entertainment-ede 783f276dae54ad4eb4f2c8a7d1138.

306 **The pandemic only**: James Daunt, interview by the author, October 2021.

307 **Most (nineteen out of twenty-four)**: Claire Kirch, "Will Indie Bookstores Sell a Trump Title?," *PW*, November 13, 2020, https://www.publishersweekly.com/pw /by-topic/industry-news/bookselling/article/84902-will-indie-bookstores-sell -a-trump-title.html.

307 **The two remain friends:** Patchett, interview.

307 **It's important to be:** Alex Mutter, "2020 Census Part of Mission for NYC's Word Up," *Shelf Awareness*, February 11, 2020, https://shelf-awareness.com/issue.html ?issue=3673#m47416.

308 **Books with "Trump":** Liu, interview.

309 **"really sort of weird":** Nobel, interview by the author, November 2021.

309 **They have to go cold:** Hill, interview.

310 **the not-terribly-large Books:** Books Are Magic (@BooksAreMagicBK), "2021 in Numbers," Instagram post, December 22, 2021, https://www.instagram.com /p/CXzCvg_vaV_/?utm_source=ig_web_button_share_sheet.

310 **These were stories:** Alexandra Alter and Elizabeth A. Harris, "Some Surprising Good News: Bookstores Are Booming and Becoming More Diverse," *NYT*, July 10, 2022, https://www.nytimes.com/2022/07/10/books/bookstores-diversity -pandemic.html.

310 **the number of ABA member:** American Booksellers Association, *ABA 2022 Annual Report* (White Plains, NY: American Booksellers Association, 2022), https://www.bookweb.org/aba-2022-annual-report.

The Bookstore Book

311 **Fans over at:** "Books about Bookstores," Goodreads, accessed November 23, 2022, https://www.goodreads.com/list/show/7027.Books_About_Bookstores.

311 **Penguin Random House has:** "Our Favorite Romances Set in Bookstores," ReadDown, Penguin Random House, accessed November 23, 2022, https://www .penguinrandomhouse.com/the-read-down/bookstore-romances/.

IMAGE CREDITS

p. 29: American Broadsides and Ephemera, 1789.

p. 42: *Annals of American Bookselling.*

p. 49: "Interior view of Appleton's Book Store, 346 & 348 Broadway, New York," New York Public Library Digital Collections.

p. 68: Christopher Morley Collection, Harry Ransom Center, University of Texas at Austin.

p. 70: James D. Phelan Photograph Albums, Bancroft Library, University of California, Berkeley.

p. 82: Target Corporation's Records of Marshall Field & Company, Chicago Historical Society.

p. 94: Courtesy of Leslie Goddard.

p. 105: Henry W. and Albert A. Berg Collection of English and American Literature, The New York Public Library, Astor, Lenox and Tilden Foundations.

p. 109: Alexina and Marcel Duchamp Papers, Philadelphia Museum of Art Archives; © 2023 Artists Rights Society (ARS), New York / ADAGP, Paris; © Association Marcel Duchamp / ADAGP, Paris / Artists Rights Society (ARS), New York 2023.

p. 117: *Life*, December 6, 1948.

p. 120: Gotham Book Mart Collection, University of Pennsylvania.

p. 134: Alexander Alland, Jr., Getty Images.

Image Credits

p. 140: Mahlon Blaine, *Antiquarian Bookman*, July 15, 1950.

p. 143: Courtesy of the Strand.

p. 146: Courtesy of Charles Wiesehahn.

p. 163: Jewish Federation Council of Greater Los Angeles, Community Relations Committee Collection, Special Collections and Archives, University Library, California State University, Northridge.

p. 170: Jewish Federation Council of Greater Los Angeles, Community Relations Committee Collection, Special Collections and Archives, University Library, California State University, Northridge.

p. 171: Jewish Federation Council of Greater Los Angeles, Community Relations Committee Collection, Special Collections and Archives, University Library, California State University, Northridge.

p. 174: Library of Congress Prints and Photographs Division [LC-DIG-fsa-8d08139].

p. 195: Photo by Kay Tobin ©Manuscripts and Archives Division, The New York Public Library.

p. 211: Jack Garofalo, Getty Images.

p. 218 (top): Courtesy of Willard Taylor.

p. 218 (bottom): Courtesy of Willard Taylor.

p. 230: Archives of Charles Scribner's Sons, Special Collections, Princeton University Library.

p. 233 (top): Courtesy of *Publishers Weekly*.

p. 233 (bottom): Courtesy of *Publishers Weekly*.

p. 266: Lucia Buricelli.

p. 271: Photo by the author, 2021.

p. 272: Tretter Collection in GLBT Studies. University of Minnesota Libraries/Wearing Gay History.

p. 282: Courtesy of the American Booksellers Association.

p. 293: Photo by the author, 2022.

p. 308: Franck Bohbot, 2017.

INDEX

Note: Italicized page numbers indicate material in tables or illustrations.

Index

Index

Index

Index

Index

Index

Parker, Dorothy, 93
Parks, William, 27–28
Parnassus Books, 287–310
  and Amazon Books, 288, 294–95, 299–300
  atmosphere of, 293
  and celebrity of Patchett, 287–88
  cofounders of (see Hayes, Karen; Patchett, Ann)
  dog weddings at, 300
  location of, 292–93
  name of, 291–92
  online book sales, 305
  opening of, 288, 292, 294
  origins of, 289–91
  and political activism, 307
  staff of, 294
  stock of, 299
  success of, 299, 300–301, 302, 310
Parnassus on Wheels (Mendelsohn's traveling bookstore), 70
Parnassus on Wheels (Morley), 61–63, 64, 65, 66, 69, 71, 72, 101, 311
Parnassus on Wheels (Shay's traveling bookshop), 68–69
Patchett, Ann
  background of, 288–89
  on Barnes & Noble, 246
  cofounding of Parnassus, 287, 290, 291–92
  as defender of indie bookshops, 287, 295, 300, 310
  and e-commerce platform, 305
  as media sensation, 287–88
  opening of Parnassus, 294–95
  and political activism, 307
  promotions for Parnassus, 300–301, 302
  and *Time*'s "100 Most Influential People," 295
  writing career of, 288–90
  See also Parnassus Books
Patterson, James, 298
Patterson, Richard C., 141
peddler's licenses, 69, 252, 253, 259–60
Pelican Book Shop, 132
Pelley, William Dudley, 170
Penguin paperbacks, 34
Penguin Random House, 40, 308, 311
The Pennsylvania Gazette, 22, 29
People's House, 166
Pickwick Book Shop, 259
Pine's bookstore, 131
Pitney, Elizabeth H., 69
Pocket Books, 92, 234

poetry, 45, 239
political books, 308–9
Politics and Prose bookstore, 179, 270, 283, 301, 304
Pollan, Michael, 300
Poor Richard's Book Shop, 178
pornography, 137, 234–35, 250, 256
Porter Square Books, 180
Post, Emily, 87
Pound, Ezra, 111–12
Powell, Emily, 156, 280
Powell's bookstore, 35, 130, 280, 292
power of books and bookshops, 5–7, 160, 181, 205, 226
Printed Matter, 310
printers, 15–16, 17, 32, 38
profitability of bookstores, 7, 39, 137–38, 222
Progressive Book Store, 175
public spaces, bookstores as, 7, 38
publishers and publishing
  arrests of communists protested by, 175
  books promoted by, 58
  and chain bookstores, 229, 238
  clustered in the northeast, 38
  department stores as, 88
  and discounting practices of stores, 78, 168
  and Drum & Spear, 219
  gay/lesbian themes embraced by, 198
  Hahner's influence with, 88
  and marketing in Great Depression, 92
  and Marshall Field's book department, 76–77
  and Nazism in America, 162
  number of American books published, 40–41
  overlap in book-related businesses, 38
  and quality of book binding, 47
  retail combined with, 44–45, 46, 47–49
  review copies of, 149
  and Rodwell's influence, 199
  Shay's work in, 67
  Steloff's influence on, 109–10
Publishers Weekly, 64, 84, 97, 259, 294, 296, 306
punk scene, 122

Quimby's, 310

Radcliffe Rambler traveling bookstore, 70
radical bookstores, 159–80
  Amazon as, 180
  Communist bookstores, 164–65, 168–69, 173–75, 177–79
  importance of physical space, 180

399

Index

Index

Index

A NOTE ON THE TYPE

The body text of this book was set in Fournier MT Pro. It is clean, light, and uses greater contrast and vertical emphasis than old-style types. In 1924, Monotype created this font based on the work of Pierre-Simon Fournier (1712–1768), who was a French engraver and typefounder. In 1736, he opened his own typefoundry in Paris and produced many of the earliest known transitional types of the eighteenth century, combining old-style and modern serif elements of typography. He also crafted many decorative typographic ornaments, which were strong examples of the rococo style of the time.